AF352712

LOOKING FORWARD BY LOOKING BACK

Looking Forward by Looking Back

75 Years of Modern Legal Education at the University of Toronto

EDITED BY JUTTA BRUNNÉE
AND CHRISTOPHER ESSERT

UNIVERSITY OF TORONTO PRESS
Toronto Buffalo London

ISBN 978-1-0498-0513-9 (cloth)   ISBN 978-1-0498-0515-3 (EPUB)
                                 ISBN 978-1-0498-0514-6 (PDF)

Publication cataloguing information is available from Library and Archives Canada.

Cover design: Tamara Hawkins
Cover image: Alice Xue Photography

We wish to acknowledge the land on which the University of Toronto Press operates. This land is the traditional territory of the Wendat, the Anishnaabeg, the Haudenosaunee, the Métis, and the Mississaugas of the Credit First Nation.

University of Toronto Press acknowledges the financial support of the Government of Canada, the Canada Council for the Arts, and the Ontario Arts Council, an agency of the Government of Ontario, for its publishing activities.

Funded by the   Financé par le
Government   gouvernement
of Canada   du Canada | Canadä

Contents

LOOKING FORWARD BY LOOKING BACK

1 Seventy-Five Years of Legal Education and Scholarship at the 'Modern' Faculty of Law

JUTTA BRUNNÉE AND CHRISTOPHER ESSERT

I. Introduction

During the 2024–5 academic year, the Faculty of Law celebrated the seventy-fifth anniversary of the 'modern' law school at the University of Toronto, culminating in the second 'Law in a Changing World' conference in March 2025.[1] The conference presented an excellent opportunity to take stock of, and to celebrate, the wealth of scholarship that the faculty's members have produced over its history. In planning this milestone, we decided to structure our consideration of that scholarship around the theme of 'Looking Forward by Looking Back.' By doing this, we wanted to emphasize the range of ways in which leading lights of the faculty have consistently set out approaches to legal and social problems that were not only powerful and novel when they were first published but that continue to be insightful and generative in today's changing world.

Listening to our colleagues at the conference and then reading their contributions to this collection, it struck us that a celebration of the faculty's history also serves to affirm the vision of legal education upon which the modern Faculty of Law was founded. This is not the place for another retelling of our creation story.[2] The basic contours are known well enough, at least to anyone likely to be reading this volume. Cecil

---

1 The first 'Law in a Changing World' conference took place in 2023 and focused on the implication of the climate crisis for law. The papers presented at that conference are published in Jutta Brunnée et al, eds, *Law in a Changing World: The Climate Crisis* (Toronto: University of Toronto Press, 2025).

2 The story is best told in C Ian Kyer & Jerome Bickenbach, *The Fiercest Debate: Cecil A. Wright, The Benchers and Legal Education in Ontario, 1923–1957* (Toronto: University of Toronto Press, 1987) [Kyer & Bickenbach, *Fiercest Debate*].

"Caesar" Augustus Wright, the founding dean of the Faculty of Law, along with his colleagues Stanley Edwards, Bora Laskin, and John Willis, resigned from their positions as faculty of Osgoode Hall Law School, which was operated at the time by the Law Society of Upper Canada. These colleagues rejected the Law Society's continued insistence upon an apprenticeship-based model of legal education. According to Wright, that model failed to 'qualify, not merely practitioners as we have known them in the past, but lawyers capable of acting in their respective communities as informed leaders of opinion in public affairs.'[3]

What might Wright have had in mind in writing these words? The obvious thought – that the university was a more academically serious environment – is not quite the right one. Serious intellectual study of the law was already very much at home at the University of Toronto under the guiding hand of WPM Kennedy.[4] But faculty and students at Kennedy's school studied law as a part of the study of social sciences and humanities, and Kennedy himself never seemed to have had the ambition 'to create a professional law school that would produce practicing lawyers.'[5] Moreover, Wright himself denied this framing of the issue: 'The problem is not one of "academic" as against "practical", nor is it a matter of the internal management of a corporation. The question is essentially one of whether a sound and liberal professional education in law is to be a possibility in Ontario.'[6] Wright's reconceptualization of legal education, firmly grounded in faculty members' scholarship and alert to the role of lawyers in society, has proven to be an enduring key to the faculty's success. The articles that follow, we think, demonstrate the value of legal education as Wright conceived it, both by reminding us of the enduring insights to be gained from some of the most

---

3 Cecil A Wright, 'The Legal Education Controversy in Ontario: The Academic View' (1949) 44 Brief 177 at 183 [Wright, 'Legal Education Controversy'].

4 William Kennedy's contributions to legal education at the University of Toronto are described and defended in RCB Risk, 'The Many Minds of W.P.M. Kennedy' (1998) 48 UTLJ 33. For a broader review of Kennedy's life and work, see Martin L Friedland, *Searching for W.P.M. Kennedy: The Biography of an Enigma* (Toronto: University of Toronto Press, 2020).

5 Kyer & Bickenbach, *Fiercest Debate*, supra note 2 at 115. As our colleague Jim Phillips points out in his contribution to this collection, it seemed that Kennedy's school taught law in a traditional way and taught a range of social science and humanities subjects, but failed to connect the two sets of materials in the way that modern law schools tend to do.

6 Wright, 'Legal Education Controversy,' supra note 3 at 182.

prominent works produced by some of the most prominent members of the faculty over its history and, in their own terms, by illustrating the lessons that current faculty have drawn from the works of their predecessors.

Before turning to an overview of the articles to come, we want to take a brief look at Wright's vision for the school, to bring out the power of that vision and its enduring value in our changing world.

II. Wright's 'qualities of mind'

The idea of a 'liberal professional education' articulated in the passage quoted above allows us to triangulate an abstract idea of what Wright was thinking and what, we believe, is still the animating aim of the Faculty of Law. On the one hand, Wright thought that the 'strictly vocational training' that the Law Society wanted to offer was inadequate. Surely, though, the education that was available at Osgoode Hall before the founding of the modern Faculty of Law counted as professional education if anything ever did. But, on the other hand, Wright denied that the solution was in a kind of education that was 'academic' rather than 'practical.' And, again, the education that was on offer at the University of Toronto under Kennedy surely counted as academic and, indeed, as a form of a liberal education. So Wright might have been suggesting that a third path was needed: a liberal professional education would be one that was not merely vocational but, at the same time, not merely academic. What could that mean?

We draw on a pair of articles published a dozen years apart in the *Canadian Bar Review*, in which Wright tried to answer that question – to formulate 'a clear understanding of the objectives and aims of a university law school.'[7] Wright's overarching thought was that, if part of the role of a university law school is the training of future lawyers, we need a clear understanding of what lawyers do (so we can understand what they need to be trained to do). But even by the middle of the twentieth century, answering that question was not simple:

Today we find fewer and fewer of the profession engaged in litigation [or criminal law]. Conveyancing and property work is still important

---

7 The articles we draw on are Cecil A Wright, 'Law and the Law Schools' (1938) 16 Can Bar Rev 579 [Wright, 'Law and the Law Schools']; Cecil A Wright, 'The University Law Schools' (1950) 28 Can Bar Rev 140 [Wright, 'University Law Schools'] (from which the quoted passage above is drawn, at 141).

> but ... the profession is performing a myriad of jobs seemingly quite
> unlike: appearing before municipal boards on questions of municipal
> financing; advising a labour union on the methods of bargaining; appe-
> aring on and before arbitration boards; advising business on policy and
> finances; and so forth.[8]

It seems that this range of things that lawyers were doing – a range that
surely has only widened in the intervening seventy-five years – was,
for Wright, among the central reasons that the sort of vocational training offered by the Law Society was inadequate.[9] Wright's solution, and
really his central insight, was to abstract from these particulars: 'The
only other solution is to *educate* persons who will come to these tasks
with the *qualities of mind* and general discipline which should characterize the group to whom a monopoly on social control through law has
been given. The university law school must find and train in that common denominator if it is to fulfil its task.'[10] In contemporary parlance,
Wright was saying that the point of a university law school is to teach
its students how to think like a lawyer. But what does that mean, and
how is it done?

Wright started to answer by insisting on the importance of a theory
of the legal profession itself. And to think about law as a profession,
for Wright, meant to think about it as an essentially practical enterprise, one dedicated to the solution of a particular problem. As we have
already seen, though, Wright thought that the breadth of the activities
of practising lawyers meant that a certain abstraction was required in
articulating an enterprise common to all members of the legal profession as such: 'Law should be concerned with the problems of human
relations and society with the ultimate object of enabling men to live
in peace with their neighbours, groups with groups and nations with
nations.'[11] In other words, without denying law's status as a worthy
object of purely academic study in any number of departments of
the university (historical, sociological, economic, and so on), Wright
seemed to be insisting on a distinctive practical role of law and the legal
profession in contemporary society. That is, law has a social purpose
in ordering human relations, and the legal profession is supposed to
work with law to do something for society. And so, he thought, the

---

8 Ibid at 142.
9 'It would seem to me impossible to train lawyers for all these myriad specialized
    tasks even if we wanted to.' Ibid.
10 Ibid [emphasis in original]. We will return to Wright's point about monopoly below.
11 Ibid at 143.

point of professional legal education was to give students the capacity to participate in the profession, the capacity to do the work of lawyers, conceived at the appropriate level of abstraction.

But the diversity of the work of lawyers that leads to the need for abstraction was paired with a recognition of the increasing complexity of society and, thus, of the increasing complexity of the tasks to which lawyers were and would be drawn. Hence, Wright saw that the vocational model of education was inadequate because, in its focus on something like rote repetition of existing forms, it did not provide students with the tools they needed to solve the problems of the modern world. So we can see why Wright thought there was a need for a liberal professional legal education. It needed to be a liberal *professional* education so as to equip students with the means to participate in the project of the law, but it also needed to be a *liberal* professional education because of the increasing complexity, touching on issues best considered from a range of theoretical perspectives, of the problems to which law was a solution. Wright put all this together into a framework: 'I would suggest that the three big objectives of a university law school are (i) education in the *qualities* that should be found in a legal practitioner; (ii) education that will train a man not merely in the work of solving problems of individual clients but of the society in which he lives; and (iii) to act as a centre of research, criticism and contribution to the better understanding of the laws by which societies are held together.'[12]

We turn to the third of these three objectives below when we introduce the faculty's scholarship assembled in this collection. As for the other two objectives, Wright viewed the first as inextricably linked with the second: knowing what it is to think like a lawyer, thought Wright, requires knowing the role that lawyers (and law) play in society at large. Much of Wright's essays is taken up, in various ways and from various directions, with the task of trying to explicate just what it means to think like a lawyer (and so with what it means to teach someone to think like a lawyer). This is not a simple task, especially if it is meant to be done in the abstract: at one point, Wright even describes it as 'mysterious.'[13] Wright leans on anecdotes[14] and answers given by

---

12 Ibid at 143–4 [emphasis in original].

13 Wright, 'Law and the Law Schools,' supra note 7 at 580.

14 Not that that's a problem with the anecdotes are as good as this: 'I think the story of Patterson of Columbia expresses well the general feeling of law teachers on this point. Patterson relates how a father of one of his recent graduates came back in a highly irritable mood and complained bitterly that his son, on reaching his office, had not

others.[15] Wright seems more comfortable speaking in his own voice when he connects the work of lawyers across all areas of practice to the second of his objectives – namely, the idea that the law exists to solve a set of human problems. And not just any problems: at one point, Wright goes so far as to say that 'participation in lawyer's work is in its highest sense the building of a civilization.'[16]

And it is this essential role of lawyers in society that, Wright suggests, ought to structure their thinking (and, in turn, to structure the requirements of legal education). He put this point so clearly that we can do no better than simply replicating Wright's own words, with some of our own commentary interspersed:

> In a sense finding the law is the whole concern of a lawyer and consequently of the law schools. The difficulty is that there is often a tendency to regard the law as a set of detailed rules or concepts, rigid and unwavering, waiting merely to be found so that on a set of given facts a solution automatically results. This 'slot-machine' conception of the legal process is one that has had, and still does have, a tremendous influence in both our legal thinking and teaching. It is characterized by the search for a case 'on all

---

known how to draw a replevin bond. Patterson expressed his sorrow and inquired what the father had done. The father admitted that he had been compelled to show the boy how to do it. He was asked by Patterson how long this process took. The answer was, roughly, five minutes. To which, I am pleased to say, Patterson is reported to have replied "I thought so. You see, we are teaching our students things which you couldn't teach him in a life time."' Wright, 'University Law Schools,' supra note 7 at 147.

15 In Wright, 'Law and Law Schools,' supra note 7 at 146, Wright reproduces the following numbered list of 'the qualities which law school training should provide' from Barton Leach, 'Property Law Taught in Two Packages' (1948) 1 J Leg Educ 28 at 30–1: '1. *Fact consciousness.* An insistence upon getting the facts, checking their accuracy, and sloughing off the element of conclusion and opinion; 2. *A sense of relevance.* The capacity to recognize what is relevant to the issue at hand and to cut away irrelevant facts, opinions, and emotions which can cloud the issue; 3. *Comprehensiveness.* The capacity to see all sides of a problem, all factors that bear upon it, and all possible ways of approaching it; 4. *Foresight.* The capacity to take the long view, to anticipate remote and collateral consequences, to look several moves ahead in the particular chess game that is being played; 5. *Lingual sophistication.* An immunity to being fooled by words and catch-phrases; a refusal to accept verbal solutions which merely conceal the problem; 6. *Precision and persuasiveness of speech.* That mastery of the language which involves (a) the ability to state exactly what one means, no more, no less, and (b) the ability to reach other men with one's own thought, to create in their minds the picture that is in one's own; 7. And finally, and pervading all the rest, and possibly the only one that is really basic: *self-discipline in habits of thoroughness,* an abhorrence of superficiality and approximation.'
16 Wright, 'Law and the Law Schools,' supra note 7 at 585.

fours', and leads to the belief that all the creative work in the common law has been performed somewhere in the dark recesses of history.[17]

For better or worse, the misconception that Wright is concerned to clear up in this passage is a stubborn one. But it is that stubbornness that makes room for one of the most satisfying elements of teaching law students. This is the opening of their eyes to the radical divergence between legal education and their earlier educational experiences that lies in the difference between learning sets of facts and learning a way to think about the world displayed in the recorded reasoning of the greatest practitioners of this way of thinking:

> A strict adherence to teaching law as static, as something awaiting only to be found, ill prepares a student for the actual work in which he is to take part. It may teach him to 'make a noise like a lawyer' but it gives no training in what lawyers do. In short, while a student must be trained in the principles and concepts developed from past judgments and in the policies of modern legislation, it seems to me impossible to ignore in our conception either of law or law teaching the creative or the 'ought' element – what, in light of the past we ought to do now.[18]

Here, Wright introduces a more positive characterization of the qualities of mind with which he was concerned, one that aligns with the theme of this volume. In other words, the core of legal education (and the core of legal reasoning more generally) might be said to consist, in a certain way, in looking forward by looking back: by reading and reflecting upon past judgments and modern legislation, one learns to discern from them the principles and concepts appropriate to some set of circumstances and then – and this, for Wright, is the crucial move – to apply those concepts and principles to new circumstances and to develop new concepts and new principles to apply in turn to their own circumstances. It is this process that allows students to begin to develop a feel for the distinctive patterns of reasoning and argumentation that make up so much of the law and to understand the relationship between those patterns and ideas of judgment, the relevance and irrelevance of particular facts, and so on.

Wright's characterization is as apposite today as it was in his day, illustrating the power of clear thinking about the legal profession and

---

17 Ibid at 582–3.
18 Ibid at 584.

legal education. For example, it is fascinating in its application to the rise of artificial intelligence (AI) technologies in the legal services sector. The proliferation of AI is surely as serious a challenge to lawyers' monopoly over the provision of legal services as anything has ever been. Thinking about the role of lawyers in a world of generative AI, then, requires a conception of what lawyers do. We find Wright's invocation of 'making noise like a lawyer' to be a striking characterization of the outputs of AI legal technologies. As Wright says, though, lawyers do not merely make noise: they think about how we ought to proceed in the face of novel problems, interactions, and disputes. Some of these are narrow and some are broad, some simpler and some more complex. But they all require, we believe, the distinctive expertise of someone trained in the collective human project that Wright described as 'the building of a civilization.'[19]

This rather grand notion connects us directly to the third of the objectives of Wright's framework of liberal professional education. And it is here that we turn to a summary of this collection, as the articles to come, along with the work they discuss, demonstrate as clearly as one could hope the ways in which the University of Toronto Faculty of Law has contributed and continues to contribute to the 'better understanding of the laws by which societies are held together.' What is more, it is precisely this 'better understanding' of law in an ever evolving societal context, grounded in rigorous academic inquiry, that enables the liberal professional education that Wright had in mind. As we will see, over the decades, members of the University of Toronto Faculty of Law have engaged in precisely this sort of inquiry, in a multitude of substantive areas and from a variety of theoretical and methodological vantage points, in law and beyond.

In order to capture a range of these privotal contributions to our understanding of the law, we invited current colleagues to select a former faculty member and an aspect of their work to engage in their article. Practicalities of various sorts meant that our collection could not be comprehensive, and, thus, many members of the faculty are not celebrated here with the articles that their work surely merited. Indeed, we are confident that another collection could have been put together with an entirely different set of contributions that would make the same point – namely, that the history of the faculty has more than vindicated Wright's ambition to create an institution dedicated to rigorous

---

19 Ibid at 585.

'research, criticism and contribution to the better understanding of the laws by which societies are held together.'[20]

We introduce these articles chronologically, reflecting the first year of the affiliation with the faculty of the scholar whose work is being discussed.[21]

III. Faculty scholarship across the decades

As we noted already, Wright was joined in his exodus from Osgoode Hall by Stanley Edwards, Bora Laskin, and John Willis. Of these three, the latter two left a more lasting academic legacy.[22] And so it is fitting that the first essay, by Mariana Mota Prado, looks back to John Willis's influential 1935 *University of Toronto Law Journal* (*UTLJ*) article on 'Three Approaches to Administrative Law: The Judicial, the Conceptual, and the Functional,' to shed new light on Willis's frequently noted 'strong opposition' to judicial review of administrative decisions. She does so by reading Willis's approach to administrative law through a pragmatist lens, illuminating the contextual, reflexive, and continuously evolving role of law and legal institutions. Willis famously argued for a 'functionalist' approach to capture the emergence of the administrative state, acknowledging that the different elements of the evolving constitutional structure serve different functions. Willis, suggests Prado, may well have approved of the modern version of judicial review. After all, today's courts 'are neither imposing their judicial views … nor abstaining from controlling administrative action.'[23] Instead, she argues, they engage in what might be described as an effort to strike a balance between functions – a 'search for the public interest that is balanced against individual rights as a requirement of the rule of law.'[24]

When RCB Risk joined the faculty in 1962, it marked a major step into interdisciplinary work, given Risk's core interest in legal history. As Jim Phillips notes in his contribution, Risk's scholarship focused both on

---

20 Wright, 'University Law Schools,' supra note 7 at 143–4.

21 Brief biographies of the scholars whose works are the subjects of the Chapters in this volume can be found starting on page 297.

22 For Willis, see 'Special Issue: Administrative Law Today: Culture, Ideas, Institutions, Processes, Values' (2005) 55:3 UTLJ 313. For Laskin, see 'Chief Justice Bora Laskin: A Tribute' (1985) 35:4 UTLJ 321.

23 See Mariana Prado, 'A Pragmatist Approach to the Administrative State: A New Interpretation of John Willis's "Three Approaches to Administrative Law,"' in this volume, at [38].

24 Ibid at [35].

Canadian legal history broadly construed and, more precisely, on the history of the Faculty of Law. On the first, Phillips shows that Risk was instrumental in transforming the inquiry into Canadian legal history into an academic discipline as well as producing a body of scholarship on late nineteenth-century and mid-twentieth-century legal history that continues to illuminate the development of Canadian law – notably, with respect to the role of courts and the common law. With respect to the second, Phillips reminds us that, as we celebrate the seventy-fifth anniversary of the modern law school, the study of law at the University of Toronto has a considerably longer history. Risk illuminated that history through his writing about Kennedy. As we noted at the beginning of this introduction, Kennedy led the law school as a department of the Faculty of Arts and Sciences (between 1927 and 1949). As Phillips observes, he was a pioneer of the interdisciplinary study of law that is one of the hallmarks of the faculty's approach to legal education today.

The Faculty of Law's attention to interdisciplinarity took massive strides forward during the deanship of Marty Friedland. This is one of two themes pursued by Kent Roach in his *tour d'horizon* of Friedland's voluminous and wide-ranging scholarship, much of which has been concerned with the administration of justice. First, Roach identifies in Friedland's scholarship a preoccupation not with abstract theories of justice but, rather, with injustice and its concrete, real-life manifestations and consequences. Roach canvasses decade-spanning scholarship, often grounded in specific, 'true crime,' situations on matters such as pre-trial detention or wrongful convictions and other miscarriages of justice. Second, Roach highlights Friedland's longstanding commitment to multidisciplinary approaches. Perhaps because of his focus on the administration of justice and attendant injustices, as well as his engagement with law reform efforts and numerous public inquiries, Friedland was acutely aware of the need for lawyers to draw on the expertise of other disciplines, such as medicine, social work, psychology, forensic science, policing, or engineering. For Roach, Friedland's 'injustice-based research agenda' remains as vital as ever, and he urges that the legal academy emulate his 'wide-ranging and pluralistic approach to multidisciplinary study of the law' to build 'critical linkages between the practice of law and other professions.'[25]

The 1960s were marked by debates about the reform of the regulation of sexual offences, including, notably, the decriminalization of homosexuality and attendant debates about morality and law. Alan

---

25 Kent Roach, 'Multidisciplinary Marty Friedland, Miscarriages of Justice and the Modern Law School,' in this volume, at [75].

Mewett's work on these issues displays yet again the importance of understanding law as a central social institution, as Brenda Cossman's article shows, illuminating Mewett's trail-blazing proposals for the reform of sexual offences in the Canadian Criminal Code.[26] As Cossman demonstrates, Mewett's recommendations were revolutionary at the time, challenging entrenched religious and traditional conventions to argue forcefully that moral disapproval ought not to justify criminalization. He insisted that sexual offences instead should be defined with a view to the prevention of social harm – violence, corruption of youth, exploitation, and the violation of the rights of others. While Mewett did not use this frame, Cossman suggests, these proposals could be seen as foreshadowing the contemporary focus on consent and capacity to consent. Mewett's conceptualization of sexual offences was well ahead of his time, Cossman shows, and his warnings against potential over-reach of the criminal law and insistence on interrogating underlying assumptions remain acutely relevant.

· The late 1960s and early 1970s mark the appointment to the Faculty of Law of some of its most prominent members. The first of those is Stephen Waddams, who joined in 1968. Peter Benson's essay on Waddams's work in contract theory sheds light on Wright's crucial insights about legal education from a different direction. Waddams's work is determined in its careful and measured focus on legal doctrine, especially (but not only) in the area of contract law. As Benson shows, a crucial element of legal scholarship is that it is *legal* scholarship; Waddams's body of work on ideas of equity and fairness in contract law is distinctive and illuminating in the way in which it focuses on 'the inclusive unities of ideas and principles which [Waddams] saw animating contract law itself at its most fundamental level.' Benson aptly describes Waddams's work as 'transformative,' noting that, as much as Waddams would have described it as doctrinal, it nevertheless counts as a significant contribution to contract theory.

The value of attention to legal doctrine for legal theory is also a central theme in the work of Ernest Weinrib, who joined the Faculty of Law in 1972. Some thirty years after its publication, Weinrib's *The Idea of Private Law* is 'as compelling and illuminating and important as ever.'[27] Arthur Ripstein attributes the book's enduring force to its 'relentless development of a single simple yet powerful idea,' the proposition that 'the key to understanding private law is to focus on the relation between

---

26 *Criminal Code*, RSC 1985, c C-46.
27 Arthur Ripstein, 'The Law's Own Terms,' in this volume, at [119].

the plaintiff and the defendant.'[28] Ripstein's article outlines the central features of this relationship and reflects on the internal conception of private law that it entails. He examines Weinrib's claim that the relation between plaintiff and defendant in private law litigation is bilateral and correlative, focused upon the corrective justice necessitated by the private wrong done by one party to the other. These features give rise to a distinctive notion of coherence, demanding justifications and remedies consistent with the structure of the plaintiff-defendant relationship. They also explain why social policy goals or distributive justice considerations, however sound on their own terms, are inconsistent with the structure of private law. Ultimately, Ripstein suggests, 'Weinrib's distinctive contribution to both legal philosophy and the study of private law is the idea of form.'[29]

Michael Trebilcock also joined the Faculty of Law in 1972; that year could be said to have been an *annus mirabilis* for faculty hiring. Edward Iacobucci engages three broad themes in Trebilcock's wide-ranging body of work. First, Trebilcock has carved a distinctive path within law and economics, a field he helped establish. While demonstrating the analytical power of careful economic thinking, he also challenges the assumption that the field's efficiency and welfare considerations can answer all legal questions – questions that typically engage other normative considerations as well. Thus, second, just as Trebilcock directs our attention to the trade-offs inevitably involved in legal questions, he also underscores the importance of distinguishing different types of trade-offs. In turn, the need for careful distinction entails a third theme – the importance of institutions. For example, whereas competition law should focus on efficiency, other important normative goals, such as distributive fairness, are better addressed through other areas of law, such that politically unaccountable competition tribunals ought to leave the necessary balancing to legislatures. At the core of much of Trebilcock's work, Iacobucci shows, is the insight that, '[w]hile in principle there is a correct ... answer to an economic analysis, there is no correct answer in a contest between normative frameworks,' which is why institutional choices matter.[30]

Robert Sharpe joined the Faculty of Law in 1976, which was also the year that his first book, *The Law of Habeas Corpus*, was published. Hamish Stewart's discussion of the book presents another illustration

---

28 Ibid.
29 Ibid at [136].
30 Edward Iacobucci, 'Trebilcock and Trade-Offs,' in this volume, at [156–7].

of the benefits of careful legal thinking, showing how doctrinal work can have important theoretical and societal implications. As Stewart notes, Sharpe, whose scholarship encompasses 'doctrinal' works, works of legal history, and reflections on judicial decision-making, evidently considered *Habeas Corpus* to be doctrinal, but concluded in his recent memoir that it may have contained 'more legal theory' than he thought.[31] Following some reflections on the nature of legal theory, Stewart's article shows why a book that is concerned with tracing the development of the state of the law around the writ of *habeas corpus* and with describing a series of *habeas corpus* cases is doctrinal and theoretical at once. For Stewart, Sharpe's *Habeas Corpus*, in its effort to make sense of the case law, has a normative orientation. As Stewart concludes, *Habeas Corpus* was not only the first book-length treatment of its topic but also a project about the role of the *habeas corpus* writ, and, therefore, judges, 'in a system of law ... oriented towards human freedom.'[32]

The later 1970s and early 1980s were a time during which the Faculty of Law's female complement increased significantly. Katherine Swinton arrived in 1979 when she began teaching and writing about Canadian constitutional law and, in particular, the law of federalism. As Jean-Christophe Bédard-Rubin shows in his chapter, Swinton's writing on federalism was, to an important degree, bucking a contemporaneous trend. During the 1980s and 1990s, a group of critics argued that federal-provincial jurisdictional boundaries were more plausibly viewed as a matter of political bargaining and intergovernmental relations. As Bédard-Rubin shows, *The Supreme Court and Canadian Federalism: The Laskin-Dickson Years*, Swinton's distinctive and essential contribution to the field of constitutional law, made a compelling case for the centrality of law and legal reasoning to the understanding of federalism. Swinton's perspective not only illuminates the case law that she discussed; it also provides valuable insights into debates about issues that have arisen since the time she wrote. Bédard-Rubin focuses in particular on the law of constitutional amendment and Aboriginal law. The lessons he draws there from Swinton's work speak to the power of her legally oriented analysis and, more generally, to the importance of legal thought in an area often viewed as merely a matter of politics.

Denise Réaume was, in 1982, another relatively early arrival among female faculty members. Réaume's 2006 article on '*Law v. Canada*

---

31 Hamish Stewart, '"More Legal Theory Than I Thought": Robert Sharpe and Legal Scholarship,' in this volume, at [170].
32 Ibid at [164].

(Minister of Employment and Immigration),' rewriting a decision of the Supreme Court of Canada from a feminist perspective on gender discrimination, turned out to be instrumental in launching a wave of feminist rewrites of judicial decisions that has since swept around the globe. Angela Fernandez introduces the Supreme Court of Canada's decision in *Law*, Réaume's rewrite, and the 'Women's Court of Canada' project that Réaume helped found.[33] She surveys the many applications of the rewrite approach that the Canadian initiative inspired, including, notably, her own effort to rewrite the prominent property law case of *Pierson v Post* from an animal rights vantage point and, more specifically, the vantage point of the fox that was at the heart of the case.[34] Fernandez acknowledges the challenges inherent in the approach. But, as she shows, the rewrite project, which has aimed to demonstrate both the importance of judicial vantage point and the scope for plausible alternate decisions, has emerged as a significant methodology for a range of critical legal work, within the feminist frame that Réaume had used and considerably beyond.

Carol Rogerson joined the Faculty of Law in 1983, and, over her decades teaching family law, she had a front-row seat to the evolution of Canadian divorce law from its common law roots into a modern system of no-fault divorce, captured in the 1985 Divorce Act.[35] Throughout this evolution, a series of intricate questions about the role and objectives of spousal support remained unresolved. Notwithstanding judicial efforts to streamline the approach to determining appropriate support, clear guidance remained elusive. Martha Shaffer's article traces these developments, providing the context in which to appreciate Rogerson's remarkable contribution in shaping Canadian law and policy on a fraught matter of profound importance to Canadians experiencing marriage breakdown. A leading scholar of family law and expert on spousal support, Rogerson was asked by the Department of Justice to co-lead a process to develop spousal support guidelines. The product of this multi-year process, involving extensive research and consultations with judges, lawyers, and mediators from across the country, were the Spousal Support Advisory Guidelines, adopted in final form in 2009. Shaffer's article illuminates the significance of Rogerson's contribution, showing why, notwithstanding their advisory nature, the guidelines have been taken up by courts and lawyers to a

---

33 *Law v Canada (Minister of Employment and Immigration)*, [1999] 1 SCR 497 at para 38.
34 *Pierson v Post*, (1805) 3 Cai Rep 175.
35 *Divorce Act*, RSC 1985, c 3 (2nd Supp).

degree that, *de facto*, they have become an 'obligatory starting point' for any effort to determine spousal support.[36]

Alan Brudner's arrival at the Faculty of Law in 1984 added to its cohorts of legal theorists and criminal law scholars a highly original thinker steeped in Hegelian political theory and legal philosophy. In developing a distinctive, Hegelian account of criminal law, Malcolm Thorburn's essay shows that Brudner's work set itself apart from 'the received wisdom in Anglo-American criminal law theory.'[37] Whereas the dominant Anglo-American approaches, observes Thorburn, view criminal justice as a tool for pursuing certain 'pre-legal' goods,[38] Brudner argues that criminal law must be understood in the context of the wider legal order. Specifically, for Brudner, the purpose of criminal law is 'to secure the authority of law and the state's exclusive right to rule.'[39] What is more, his Hegelian account 'treats legal subjects in a way that is consistent with their status as free persons,'[40] something Brudner considers that the standard accounts fail to do. As Thorburn demonstrates in his article, Brudner's account develops Hegel's legal and political theory in a unique, liberal way. Brudner's work, Thorburn concludes, ranks among the most illuminating contributions to Anglo-American criminal law scholarship over the last fifty years, opening up new ways of thinking about the field.

For close to four decades, since she arrived at the Faculty of Law in 1987, Rebecca Cook's scholarship has pursued the advancement of women's rights, gender equality, and women's health through international human rights law and, in so doing, has been uniquely attentive to the concerns and voices from different parts of the world. Anna Su explores the continuing relevance of Cook's pioneering scholarship on gender equality in the context of what she terms a 'new frontier' – the fast-growing realm of AI.[41] Over the decades, Cook's early scholarship has challenged the invisibility of women in the international legal and political order by drawing on international human rights law to articulate women's rights

---

36 Martha Shaffer, 'Transforming Spousal Support from the Ground Up: Carol Rogerson and the Development of the Spousal Support Advisory Guidelines,' in this volume, at [229].

37 Malcolm Thorburn, 'Individual Freedom and the Supremacy of Law: Alan Brudner on Criminal Justice,' in this volume, at [233].

38 Ibid at [234].

39 Ibid.

40 Ibid.

41 Anna Su, 'Gender Equality, AI, and the Future of Human Rights,' in this volume, at [253].

as human rights and has sought to harness human rights law to address gender equality. It is in this latter strand that Su sees potential for informing the turn to human rights-based strategies and for challenging the propensity of AI to amplify gender inequalities and gender stereotypes. She concludes that Cook's work helps illuminate the need to innovate the doctrines, strengthen the institutions, and grapple with the limits of human rights law in an emerging algorithmic society.

Lorraine Weinrib joined the Faculty of Law in 1988, after an outstanding career as a constitutional litigator at the Ontario Ministry of the Attorney-General. Weinrib's integration of her practical experience in this area into her scholarship illustrates in yet another way the value of Wright's vision for legal scholarship. Richard Stacey's article engages Weinrib's writing about section 33 of the Constitution Act, 1982, the 'notwithstanding clause,' which enables legislatures to override certain rights enshrined in the Canadian Charter of Rights and Freedoms.[42] As Stacey illustrates, Weinrib ascribes to section 33 a 'distinctively Canadian' version of rights protection, bringing constitutional values and democracy together through public discourse and deliberative dialogue. Governments and legislatures invoking section 33 must be transparent and take seriously their obligation to justify and explain recourse to it to override rights, requirements that Stacey points out are central to the rule of law. Through the lens of Weinrib's work, Stacey's article traces the evolving uses of, and attitudes toward, section 33. Whereas the dialogic and justificatory dynamics highlighted by Weinrib are in evidence in the earlier invocations of the notwithstanding clause, more recent instances mark a turn to majoritarian and populist justifications for, and invocations of, the notwithstanding clause. As Stacey shows, the enduring vitality of Weinrib's scholarship in grappling with these developments and their implications for the rule of law in Canada is evident.

IV. Conclusion

To close, let us return to Wright's framework of liberal professional education. The specific form of professional education that Wright contemplated, we have seen, was one that is tethered to rigorous 'research, criticism and contribution to the better understanding of the laws by which societies are held together' and that self-consciously

---

42 *Canadian Charter of Rights and Freedoms,* Part I of the *Constitution Act 1982,* being Schedule B to the *Canada Act 1982* (UK), 1982, c 11.

embraces the fact of, and elaborates the implications of, the distinctive modes of legal reasoning. That is, it might be possible to figure out how to 'make a noise like a lawyer' without really knowing, in some deeper sense, what one is doing, and this might have been the paradigmatic learning of the form of legal education that existed in Ontario before Wright and his colleagues took their famous walk up University Avenue. Yet 'law is something bigger than the mere handling of legal tools, and that participation in lawyer's work is in its highest sense the building of a civilization. In this aim the unsolved problems of today are of equal importance as the solved problems of yesterday.'[43]

Wright's picture of legal education and the role of lawyers in society remains current and highly relevant to the unsolved problems of our day. Wright's framework gives us a way to think about these new challenges that is just as valuable now as it was seventy-five years ago. The unsolved problems of today seem dire. They range from technological challenges, such as the assertions that generative AI can discharge legal functions to which we already referred, to environmental challenges such as climatic change, to rising polarization within societies and in geopolitics, and to the profound challenges to the role of law in society, such as the mounting pressures on the rule of law at the national and international levels. It is worth noting, though, that the two articles we have been considering were written by Wright on either side of the greatest human conflict ever known. And, yet, even the horrors of World War II did not shake Wright's faith in the essential role of law and legal education or of the need for those engaged in the building of civilization. Our own world can only reaffirm that need.

---

43 Wright, 'Law and the Law Schools,' supra note 7 at 582–4.

2 A Pragmatist Approach to the Administrative State: A New Interpretation of John Willis's 'Three Approaches to Administrative Law'

MARIANA MOTA PRADO

John Willis was one of the most influential jurists in Canadian history.[1] Born in England, Willis studied at Oxford and Harvard before starting his academic career at Dalhousie University in 1933, later moving to the University of Toronto Faculty of Law.[2] One of his most significant pieces, 'Three Approaches to Administrative Law: The Judicial, the Conceptual, and the Functional,' published in the *University of Toronto Law Journal* in 1935, argued that '[t]he delegation of legislative power to a government department, a practice of very respectable antiquity, is now universally recognized by responsible persons as a practical necessity if the work of government is to be carried at all.'[3] For him, the existence of administrative tribunals performing adjudicative functions and of administrative agencies performing regulatory functions was directly connected with the economic conditions of the time.

While celebrated as one of the founding fathers of Canadian administrative law, Willis has also been heavily criticized for his strong opposition to judicial review of administrative action. According to him, the expansion of public services and of economic activity in general made it unfeasible for courts to handle all disputes using the standard common law approach of the time. This position was reinforced in later publications[4] but was originally and most forcefully articulated in 'Three Approaches.' Critics have argued that Willis 'fundamentally

---

1 RCB Risk, 'John Willis: A Tribute' (1985) 9:3 Dal LJ 521 [Risk, 'Tribute'].

2 RCB Risk, 'In Memoriam: John Willis' (1997) 47:3 UTLJ 301.

3 John Willis, 'Three Approaches to Administrative Law: The Judicial, the Conceptual, and the Functional' (1935) 1:1 UTLJ 55 [Willis, 'Three Approaches'].

4 John Willis, 'Administrative Law and the British North America Act' (1939) 53:2 Harv L Rev at 251; John Willis, 'Canadian Administrative Law in Retrospect' (1974) 24:3 UTLJ 229 [Willis, 'Canadian Administrative Law'].

viewed administrative law as a project of politics' and believed that 'courts should butt out, in service of the expertise, efficiency and progressive orientation of administrative decision-makers.'[5] David Dyzenhaus describes Willis's argument as a 'cult of the expertise located in government.'[6] However, he also highlights Willis's nuanced position on judicial review: while keen to limit the involvement of generalist judges, Willis believed that it was necessary to review administrative action not only on the basis of *vires* but also on substantive issues. Yet Dyzenhaus sees this nuanced position as being grounded in an empty conception of law, which 'is simply an instrument of the social policy of the powerful.'[7]

In this article, I offer an alternative interpretation of 'Three Approaches.' More specifically, I argue that there is significant alignment between the American pragmatist tradition and Willis's proposal of a functionalist approach to administrative law and his resistance to judicial review.[8] I hope to show that, if we interpret Willis's contribution according to philosophical pragmatism's assumptions,[9] many (if not most) of the accusations against him fade away, and what emerges is an interesting set of concepts and tools to help us navigate administrative law today. The scope of this exercise is not historical in nature. I have no ambition of challenging, correcting, or replacing the extensive literature on John Willis's contributions to Canadian legal academia

---

5 Mark Mancini, 'On John Willis and the Pesky Politics of Administrative Law,' *Double Aspect* (14 September 2020), online: <doubleaspect.blog/2020/09/14/on-john-willis-and-the-pesky-politics-of-administrative-law> [Mancini, 'On John Willis'].

6 David Dyzenhaus, 'The Logic of the Rule of Law: Lessons from Willis' (2005) 55:3 UTLJ 691 at 704 [Dyzenhaus, 'Logic of the Rule of Law'].

7 Ibid at 692.

8 Martin Loughlin discusses American pragmatism as one among a variety of influences on the functionalist 'style' (which is too amorphous to be considered a school of thought). However, Loughlin only discusses the effect of the pragmatist influence on one functionalist, RH Tawney, and even then only briefly. See Martin Loughlin, 'The Functionalist Style in Public Law' (2005) 55:3 UTLJ 361 [Loughlin, 'Functionalist Style'].

9 It is important to distinguish between pragmatism as used in ordinary language ('a concern for political or practical expediency rather than principle') and pragmatism as a school of thought (which is not anti-theoretical). Susan Haack, 'The Pragmatist Tradition: Lessons for Legal Theorists' (2018) 95 Wash UL Rev 1049 at 1049–50 [Haack, 'Pragmatist Tradition']. The school of thought, which I call philosophical pragmatism, 'is difficult to define with a great deal of precision' as the term refers to a variety of authors with different assumptions and conceptions. Loughlin, 'Functionalist Style,' supra note 8 at 388. For an overview of American pragmatism, see Cheryl J Misak, *The American Pragmatists* (Oxford: Oxford University Press, 2013).

and Canadian administrative law. There are careful and detailed historical analyses showing how Willis was influenced by American legal realism[10] and how 'Three Approaches' is an exemplar of this influence.[11] Challenging these narratives would require grounded historical work. Instead, I am engaging in a purely academic exploration of the implications of reading his work under a different set of assumptions. Yet the exercise is not totally asynchronous: pragmatism was already active in the United States and was embraced by some legal scholars (for example, Oliver Wendell Holmes Jr) around the time that Willis was exposed to their scholarship. It is, therefore, possible to hypothesize that these ideas may have informed his work.

After looking back at Willis's functionalist approach and reading it as a pragmatist proposal, I look forward by suggesting that pragmatism offers a useful framework for Canadian administrative law today as it articulates alternative solutions to disputes between legal realists and formalists that have marked Canadian administrative law throughout its history.

I. Willis's functionalist approach to administrative law

In the 1930s, there were fierce debates about the constitutional status of administrative agencies and the administrative state in Canada and in England.[12] In 1933, Willis had responded to English critics of the administrative state, arguing that the English government should delegate administrative powers to government departments and analyse which parliamentary procedures could be used for this purpose.[13] In 'Three Approaches,' Willis turns to Canadian law to ask 'how to fit into our constitutional structure these new institutions whose growth seems inevitable.'[14] The answer to this question, he claims, depends on the approach that one adopts to administrative law. In Canada, challenges to the constitutional validity of the administrative state were and are either based on a judicial or a conceptual approach to administrative law. After criticizing the assumptions embedded

---

10 RCB Risk, 'Lawyers, Courts and the Rise of the Regulatory State' (1984) 9:1 Dal LJ 31; Risk, 'Tribute,' supra note 1.

11 R Blake Brown, 'The Canadian Legal Realists and Administrative Law Scholarship' (2000) 9:2 Dal LJ 36.

12 Ibid at 38–44.

13 John Willis, *The Parliamentary Powers of English Government Departments* (Cambridge, MA: Harvard University Press, 1933).

14 Willis, 'Three Approaches,' supra note 3 at 59.

in these two approaches, Willis articulates the functional approach, which seeks to avoid the abstract, conceptual foundations of the prior approaches. The judicial approach aims at preserving the internal coherence of the common law's protection of individual rights, creating a response that is 'frankly hostile' to the administrative state.[15] The conceptual approach resorts to abstract categories like the rule of law, presuming that only courts can review administrative action. In contrast, Willis's functional approach articulates the need to consider what works by looking at the functions performed by governmental bodies and which are the best fitted to perform them both in the exercise of government functions and in their review. And 'if there is no such body, a new one is created *ad hoc*.'[16]

What body should perform which function? Willis provides three scenarios. First, applying the functional approach in the context of regulations, Willis suggests that one should not ask the question '"is the legislature delegating legislative power?" but rather "[i]s the department or the legislature itself better fitted to make a decision of this kind?"'[17] For instance, there seems to be a strong claim that a department specialized in the regulation of conditions for issuing license plates for motor vehicles would be better equipped than parliament to perform this function. Second, he engages in the same exercise about adjudicative functions by claiming that courts are equipped to adjudicate common law disputes and may not be trained to adjudicate interests that are based on 'a philosophy that conflicts with the philosophy of the common law,' as is the case with 'workmen's compensations.'[18] Finally, turning to licenses, Willis argues that this is a privilege that requires both an assessment of policy goals and questions of fact. Parliament is equipped to do the former but not the latter, while courts are equipped to do the latter but not the former. Existing government departments may not have the expertise or accountability structure suitable for this function. The solution would be to create a new type of body, 'called a commission, a government in miniature,' which would be 'free from political pressure' and would frame its own procedures.[19]

What body should review the exercise of discretion of the bodies described above? Willis disputes the assumption that all questions of law

---

15 Ibid.
16 Ibid at 75.
17 Ibid at 76.
18 Ibid at 77.
19 Ibid at 78.

should be decided by judges, including in cases where what is at stake is the limits of the administrative body's own jurisdiction. He acknowledges that some form of control is necessary both for jurisdictional questions and for errors of law, but he is sceptical that courts would be equipped to do a decent job 'for they have no experience of administrative policy.'[20] In addition, an internal control mechanism would also be unsatisfactory as the government is 'an interested party.' Therefore, the preferred solution would be 'an independent body, composed of persons trained in the practice of the whole law pertaining to administration.'[21] This summary provides a glimpse of the reasons why there has been resistance to Willis's position. Willis prioritizes policy (or 'the social purpose' of a statute) over 'rights protection'[22] and sees judges as old school formalists who are incapable of adopting a different approach to law and to legal disputes and are systemically biased against the progressive aims of the administrative state.[23] As stated at the outset, I will neither investigate whether or not such accusations are accurate, nor try to uncover what Willis was looking to articulate in 'Three Approaches.' Rather, the remainder of this article provides an alternative interpretation of Willis's claims, using philosophical pragmatism. While this alternative interpretation may not be true to Willis's actual intentions or informed by his intellectual influences at the time, it does provide an argument to dispel the criticisms to which he has been subjected by suggesting that perhaps his resistance to judicial review was more circumstantial and circumscribed than critics have acknowledged.

II. Rejecting the judicial approach based on epistemological pragmatism

Pragmatism is a philosophical school of thought that assumes that any scientific assertion about the world is based on beliefs.[24] Born in the

---

20 Ibid at 80.

21 Ibid.

22 In David Dyzenhaus's terms, Willis follows an 'uncompromising utilitarianism,' in which persons 'do not count as individuals ... any more than individual petrol tanks do in the analysis of the national consumption of petroleum.' See Dyzenhaus, 'Logic of the Rule of Law,' supra note 6 at 704.

23 Specifically, Willis identifies three 'judicial prejudices': a preference for the common law as against statute law, a bias toward law which prioritizes individual rights over public welfare, and a hostility to the exercise of discretion by the executive. See Willis, 'Three Approaches,' supra note 3 at 61.

24 There are competing theories of truth among pragmatists, making it hard to coherently describe this school of thought. See Richard J Bernstein, *The Pragmatic Turn* (Cambridge, UK: Polity Books, 2010), ch 5. See also the sources cited at note 9 above.

United States in the nineteenth century, pragmatists do believe that there is an objective world out there that is independent of us and our beliefs, but they resist the idea of metaphysical, universal truths. Rather, we hold beliefs that can be revised based on our experiences.[25] As Charles Peirce put the point, '[i]nquiry is not standing upon the bedrock of fact. It is walking upon a bog, and can only say, this ground seems to hold for the present. Here I will stay till it begins to give way.'[26] The lack of certainty about our beliefs, however, does not prevent them from guiding human action, as I will discuss in Part III.

In arguing that a functionalist approach to administrative law is superior to what he calls the judicial approach, Willis seems to be challenging the way in which the judicial discourse at the time was ignoring changes that were happening in the administrative state and civil society broadly. To put this in pragmatist terms, the judicial approach to administrative law was holding on to beliefs that no longer fit with experience. More specifically, Willis pointed out that the judicial approach to administrative law was hostile because it refused to accept the three basic premises that informed the administrative state: (a) its legislative origin (in contrast with the common law); (b) its objective of enhancing social welfare, which should prevail over individual rights; and (c) the allocation of discretionary power to bodies that are neither legislative nor judicial.[27] In making this point, Willis seems aligned with pragmatic thinking: by refusing to accept these premises, the judicial approach was not aligned with experience and, as a consequence, became unable to guide action.

Willis's claims have been read as emphasizing the policy dimensions of administrative law to the complete detriment of the legal or juridical dimension.[28] It is entirely possible that Willis was rejecting legal formalism and emphasizing the political realities that informed legal disputes, as legal realists do. There is, however, an alternative interpretation of his claims. In proposing that an independent body conduct judicial review, Willis states that 'existing conditions ... call

---

25 William James, *Pragmatism and the Meaning of Truth* (Cambridge, MA: Harvard University Press, 1975) at 29 [James, *Pragmatism*] ('[t]rue ideas are those that we can assimilate, validate, corroborate and verify. False ideas are those that we cannot').

26 Charles Sanders Peirce, *Collected Papers of Charles Sanders Peirce*, vols 1–6, edited by Charles Hartshorne and Paul Weiss; vols 7–8, edited by Arthur Burks (Cambridge, MA: Belknap Press, 1931–58) at 5.589. See also James, *Pragmatism*, supra note 25 at 32 ('[t]heories thus become instruments, not answer to enigmas, in which we can rest').

27 Willis, 'Three Approaches,' supra note 3 at 59–69.

28 See Mancini, 'On John Willis,' supra note 5; Dyzenhaus, 'Logic of the Rule of Law,' supra note 6.

for the constitution of a special court.'[29] The reference to 'existing conditions' may suggest that the claim is circumstantial. The judiciary, as it was functioning at the time of his writing, was 'not trained' to perform judicial review functions.[30] But, according to pragmatism, this assumption could be revised based on experience; if courts proved able to engage with the issues beyond the common law, it is possible that his scepticism of their ability to adjudicate on administrative matters would lessen.

The pragmatic undertones of his argument are illustrated by Willis's resistance to analogies between the administrative state in the 1930s and the royal prerogative as used by King Henry VIII and the Stuarts. His claim is partially based on a rejection of the historical versions that focus on the abstract and ahistorical legal concepts formulated at the time rather than the opposing economic interests of the 'aristocrat royalists' and 'middle-class parliamentarians.'[31] While the reference to historical conflict of interests clearly resonates with legal realism, his argument does not veer into an account of the opposing economic interests affected by the administrative state of the 1930s. Rather, he uses the historical analogy to argue that the royal prerogative created a 'legacy of popular distrust of discretionary power' that was 'derived from the political facts of 1688' and was based on a time when 'the simplicity of social conditions made resort to discretionary power unusual.'[32] In 1930, he argues, the political and social conditions are entirely distinct from those of the seventeenth century, and such distrust needs to be abandoned or at least justified on novel grounds.

It stands to reason that his distrust of the courts was driven by historical conditions in the 1930s and could also be abandoned if experience showed that judges and legal doctrines evolved to embrace more than the common law. Dyzenhaus, analysing a broader arc of Willis's work that includes his writing from the 1930s to the 1970s, seems sceptical of this interpretation:

Willis thought that the way to avoid being 'global and theological' was to be 'specific and practical,' to focus on reality, which he always claimed

---

29 Willis, 'Three Approaches,' supra note 3 at 81.

30 Ibid at 76–7 ('the legal mind is not trained to interpret legislation on subjects of which its possessor is entirely ignorant. When the legislature passes an act creating a new interest of a type which is based on a philosophy that conflicts with the philosophy of the common law, the courts find themselves asked to do something for which they are not trained').

31 Ibid at 54.

32 Ibid at 54–5.

was his method. But he did not trust judges to adopt this focus, since they would inevitably be attracted to abstract theological questions about fundamental constitutional values. And their answers to these questions would involve their imposing 'individualist values whose sole claim to validity is that they are lawyer's values based, as lawyer's values always are, on a long-dead eighteenth-century past.'[33]

I am not disputing Dyzenhaus's interpretation of Willis's work or suggesting that my analysis is uncovering a hidden meaning in his claims. Instead, I am proposing an alternative interpretation of this 1935 piece according to a pragmatic framework that could potentially strengthen Willis's claim and mitigate these criticisms. Willis seems fully cognizant that the lack of supervision of the discretion delegated to the public administration can lead to abuse.[34] His question is which body is best equipped to exercise control over this discretion. Based on his experience at the time, the judiciary was ill equipped to perform this function. But, under a pragmatist framework, there is nothing inevitable about this belief regarding the capacity of the judiciary to perform this function.

According to the alternative interpretation proposed here, there are two important pragmatist assumptions of an epistemological nature embedded in Willis's claim. The first assumption is the rejection of an abstract, essentialist view of the judiciary – that is, determining what courts should or should not do based on abstract concepts or pure ideas,[35] like the concepts of adjudicative and administrative action. Willis was not challenging the role that courts perform in the common law and their importance in protecting individual rights. Rather, he was pushing for recognition of the fact that the role that the state played in the lives of individuals had changed while the courts had not. In the 1930s, the administrative state was expanding to a multitude of corners (health, education, welfare, and so on), becoming increasingly present in the daily lives of individuals – a time that Willis himself

---

33 Dyzenhaus, 'Logic of Rule of Law,' supra note 6 at 692.
34 Willis, 'Three Approaches,' supra note 3 at 71 ('[e]veryone would agree with the statement confirmed as it is by history that, when the power to make and the power to interpret the laws is vested in one and the same person or body of persons, both powers are likely to be abused').
35 James, *Pragmatism,* supra note 25 at 31 ('[a pragmatist] turns away from abstractions and insufficiency, from verbal solutions, from bad *a priori* reasons, from fixed principles, closed systems, and pretended absolutes and origins. He turns towards concreteness and adequacy, towards facts, towards action, and towards power').

labeled as 'when the world turned upside down.'[36] The dominant judicial approach directed courts to adjudicate based only on the rights-centred logic of the common law. To him, this view ignored the social welfare philosophy that motivated and shaped the changing nature of the state and its relationship with individuals. Saying that courts could not adequately perform judicial review functions under the conditions that existed at the time of writing is very different from saying that courts could never perform such a function.

The second epistemological premise of this alternative interpretation of Willis is that law is neither a comprehensive nor an internally coherent system. Rejecting the judicial approach was also a rejection of the view that the entire legal system and the operation of the judiciary should follow a single logic. As Holmes had articulated, '[t]he distinctions of the law are founded on experience, not on logic.'[37] By identifying that the common law is focused on protecting individual rights, while the administrative state aims at enhancing social welfare, Willis calls attention to the fact that these are portions of the legal system designed to perform different functions and respond to different needs. Allowing courts to intervene in the administrative state based on an entirely different mindset (that is, rights protection) would ultimately threaten the function that the administrative state was trying to perform, undermining its overall purpose. Therefore, Willis calls for recognition that administrative law operates according to a different mindset and answers to an entirely distinct set of human needs and that the clash of the two systems is not constructive to either.

Recognizing this second assumption, however, is very different from reducing administrative law to a non-legal logic (for example, politics). Willis's account leaves intact not only a complex role that law needs to play within the administrative state but also the need for legally trained professionals to be involved in the review of administrative action. His functional approach calls for '[a]n independent body, composed of persons trained in the practice of the whole law pertaining to administration, [that] would have sufficient special knowledge of the legislation which is to be put into force ... a court of review whose members are

---

36 RCB Risk, 'Canadian Law Teachers in the 1930s: When the World Was Turned Upside Down' (2004) 27:1 Dal LJ 1, n 1 (reporting a phone call with Willis).

37 Oliver Wendell Holmes Jr, *The Common Law*, edited by Stuart E Thiel and David Widger (2000) at 312, online: *Project Gutemberg* <www.gutenberg.org/cache/epub/2449/pg2449-images.html> [Holmes, *Common Law*].

trained in a field wider than that of pure law.'[38] It is important to note that he does not dismiss legal knowledge and analysis. These sentences may be referring to a different kind of legal knowledge and analysis than the one displayed by lawyers and judges at the time.

For a pragmatist, it is less important to determine the abstract essence of a particular action (for example, asking if something is law or politics). Instead, a pragmatist would be more interested in analysing which function a certain legal arrangement is performing. Willis's functionalism, according to the interpretation proposed here, allows law to perform an array of different functions, including both rights protection and the promotion of social welfare.[39] The instruments and institutional arrangements required for each of these functions will naturally vary, based on the human necessities they are trying to address. And for each of the different functions that law may perform, an assumption about whether a particular arrangement is adequate or not should be entirely based on experience rather than on abstract legal concepts or *a priori* beliefs.

III. Rejecting the conceptual approach based on action pragmatism

In addition to its epistemological claims, pragmatism also has a philosophy of action. The beliefs that pragmatists emphasize serve not only to conceptualize how we understand the world but also as a basis for action. Religious, ethical, and legal rules that guide action are grounded in these beliefs, which are in turn informed by experience (see Part II). It is important to clarify that, for pragmatists, rules are not fully determined or given by experience but, rather, are influenced by it. It is our needs that dictate these rules. In this context, law is conceived as a social phenomenon – that is, a program of action to be tested by experience.[40] According to Holmes, whose work offers a bridge between pragmatism and legal thinking, law is a growing and evolving enterprise that

---

38 Willis, 'Three Approaches,' supra note 3 at 80.

39 For an interpretation of Willis that also tries to reconcile these two dimensions, see Lorne Sossin, 'From Neutrality to Compassion: The Place of Civil Service Values and Legal Norms in the Exercise of Administrative Discretion' (2005) 55:3 UTLJ 427. For an interpretation of pragmatism in line with what is proposed here, see Haack, 'Pragmatist Tradition,' supra note 9 at 1071–5.

40 John Dewey, *The Quest for Certainty* (New York: Capricorn Books, 1960) at 211–12. See also Brian Z Tamanaha, 'Pragmatic Reconstruction in Jurisprudence: Features of a Realistic Legal Theory' (2021) 34:1 Can JL & Jur 171 at 185–6.

responds to the 'felt necessities of the time, the prevalent moral and political theories, intuitions of public policy, avowed or unconscious, even the prejudices which judges share with their fellow-men.'[41] Along similar lines, the prominent pragmatist John Dewey argued that the valuation of the law cannot be found in 'a source higher and more fixed than that of experience.'[42]

Willis's criticism of the conceptual approach to administrative law is deeply grounded in experience, bearing similarities with pragmatist thinking. While acknowledging that the conceptual approach was widespread in legal thinking,[43] he argues that 'no concept can safely be accepted as a guide to future action unless (i) it has an accurate meaning, and (ii) the theory upon which it is based, if it ever was valid, still retains its validity.'[44] He uses bureaucracy as an example of a concept that can lack accurate meaning as it has at least three different meanings: 'irresponsibility, government by experts not amateurs, [or] action in accordance with a professional tradition other than that of the profession of law.'[45] This conceptual ambiguity can be resolved by testing the validity of the theories upon which each of these three meanings is based. Irresponsibility is based upon a continental tradition in which the 'civil service owed a duty to the monarch alone, and could not be held responsible by any popularly elected body,'[46] which clearly was no longer the case at the time of writing. Willis then proceeds to associate government by experts to 'the theory that the affairs of the country can be administered in accordance with the fund of experience possessed by an ordinary educated man.'[47] This theory was valid under the system where justices of the peace comprised the administration in the eighteenth century. But it is no longer valid in the twentieth century when 'the state provides medical and educational services and such like, and regulates utilities.'[48]

---

41 Holmes, *Common Law*, supra note 37 at 1.

42 Cited in Cheryl Misak, 'Dewey on the Authority and Legitimacy of Law' in Stephen Fesmire, ed, *The Oxford Handbook on Dewey* (Oxford: Oxford University Press, 2019) at 200 [Misak, 'Dewey'].

43 Willis, 'Three Approaches,' supra note 3 at 70 ('[a] large number of men in public life are lawyers. In their legal practice they know what they are doing; their fitting of facts into a concept is deliberate').

44 Ibid at 72.

45 Ibid.

46 Ibid.

47 Ibid.

48 Ibid.

The structure of Willis's argument seems to closely track the episte-mological assumptions described earlier and also to embrace a prag-matist system of validation of rules that serve as guidance for future action. Dewey argued that what gives law authority is experience and that searching for an immutable source of validation of the law is a fruitless and dangerous mission.[49] Pragmatists reject the assumption that, if law is not predetermined, it is entirely arbitrary; humans are trying to get things right, but what is right is determined by human needs, both our most basic needs as well as the more complex require-ments of social cooperation. In challenging the conceptual approach to administrative law, Willis seems to be also resisting the assumption that law's validation can proceed on a purely intellectual basis. His dis-cussion of the rule of law bears a very close resemblance to pragma-tist thinking on guidance for action. He resists the abstract formulation of the rule of law according to which 'all questions of law should be decided by the judges,'[50] while agreeing with the general premise that lack of control over power is likely to lead to abuse.[51] He then proceeds to challenge the separation of powers principle by claiming that either 'there is no essential distinction between the three supposedly distinct types of power' or 'even if there is … the necessities of the particular case require deviation from the rule.'[52] Therefore, to determine what is valid law, it is necessary to inquire into the functions that are being performed, and 'the ultimate deciding factor is always what the public interest requires.'[53]

Willis's argumentative moves are very similar to the process that Dewey uses to determine the validity of the law: a problematic situation suggests that our existing beliefs may no longer be valid, prompting an inquiry into our current body of beliefs and practices. If inquiry reveals that our previous beliefs are no longer valid, we proceed with a search for a new settled belief, which will lead to a new rule to guide future action.[54] Willis's inquiry into the conceptual approach reveals that existing beliefs are no longer valid. A key element in this inquiry is his view that the separation of power principle cannot provide guidance for future action. In fact, Willis seems to conceive of the administrative state as entirely separate from any of the three branches of government.

---

49 See Misak, 'Dewey,' supra note 42.
50 Willis, 'Three Approaches,' supra note 3 at 79.
51 Ibid at 71.
52 Ibid.
53 Ibid at 72.
54 John Dewey, *Human Nature and Conduct* (New York: Henry Holt & Company, 1922).

He describes it as 'government in miniature' since all three functions may be performed by one single body. He also indicates that the concept of 'administrative' was used by American courts to describe acts that contravened the separation of powers doctrine.[55] In summary, if read through the lens of pragmatism, the functionalist approach invites us to embrace the novelty of the administrative state as it was designed to respond to the needs of modern society. Instead of getting bogged down in abstract conceptual analysis, we should focus on analysing which functions the administrative state performs and assess whether these functions are in the public interest.

Pragmatism may also allow us to articulate an alternative interpretation of Willis's position regarding judicial review in 1935. Dyzenhaus nicely summarizes his thought on the topic:

> In 1935, [Willis] advocated getting rid of judicial review of administrative decisions altogether. He saw the need for an independent check on public officials because government could not be expected to guard itself, so he recommended establishing a specialized administrative court with general review authority over administrative decisions. Indeed, ... he wanted this body to have a much more extensive review authority than that which the courts of that time claimed. For this essay was written in the days when judges denied themselves review authority in certain matters: for example, they would not review decisions they categorized as 'administrative,' but only those they considered 'judicial' or 'quasi-judicial.' Willis regarded such categories as the product of a bad conceptualism. But while he considered conceptualism bad mainly because judges used it as a smokescreen to cover their expansion of their jurisdiction, he also saw that conceptualism could, and did, go in the other direction – that of wrongly protecting administrative decisions from independent review.[56]

Similarly to Dyzenhaus, other authors focus on Willis's 1935 proposal of taking the judiciary out of the picture entirely.[57] The pragmatist framework may offer a different focus: the proposal to create a new body to control administrative action that did not exist at the time of Willis's writing and that did not fit within the separation of powers

---

55 Willis, 'Three Approaches,' supra note 3 at 71.
56 Dyzenhaus, 'Logic of the Rule of Law,' supra note 6 at 692–3.
57 See e.g. Mancini, 'On John Willis,' supra note 5.

system.[58] As stated earlier, Willis argued that, if the administrative state has to be controlled, the proposed body to exercise this control had to be independent of it to be effective. Therefore, this body should not be administrative in nature. His proposal could suggest a fourth branch of government staffed with people trained both in law and administrative policy.[59] In other words, according to the pragmatist interpretation of Willis's work advanced here, our institutional imagination could fly a bit higher than simply creating another administrative tribunal.[60]

This alternative interpretation would perhaps mitigate concerns that Willis was subscribing to a 'culture of government' to the detriment of courts.[61] It does so by suggesting not only that Willis would reject the usefulness of categories such as judiciary and executive but also that he could be embracing institutional arrangements that did not exist at the time and that did not have to conform to the strict conceptual categories imposed by the separations of powers principle, let alone the questionable distinctions between questions of law, fact, and policy. Under this assumption, it does not make sense to assume that he was favouring the executive branch to the detriment of courts, as he was not thinking within these categories. He was concerned about creating a review body that would avoid undermining what the administrative state was trying to accomplish. According to the interpretation proposed here, he was denying neither the importance of people with legal training in this review body nor the need to protect individual rights; instead, he was acknowledging that there should also be people trained to address welfare concerns in this review process.[62]

---

58 For a later articulation of this idea, see Bruce Ackerman, 'Good-bye Montesquieu' in Peter L Lindseth & Susan Rose-Ackerman, eds, *Comparative Administrative Law* (Cheltenham, UK: Edward Elgar, 2010) 128.

59 For contemporary examples of this thinking, see e.g. Mark Tushnet, *The New Fourth Branch: Institutions for Protecting Constitutional Democracy* (Cambridge, UK: Cambridge University Press, 2021); Rosalind Dixon & Mark Tushnet, 'Democratic Constitutions, Poverty and Economic Inequality: Redress through the Fourth Branch Institutions?' (2023) 51:3 Fed L Rev 285.

60 John Dewey, *The Public and Its Problems* (New York: Henry Holt & Company, 1927).

61 Dyzenhaus, 'Logic of the Rule of Law,' supra note 6 at 702, 706.

62 This point is more explicitly stated in one of his later writings. See Willis, 'Canadian Administrative Law,' supra note 4 at 229 ('[i]s somebody being actually hurt by some actual defect in the machinery of government and, if so, what is that defect and how can it be remedied: these are the questions I should like to see asked').

IV. The functionalist approach in Canada today

This section turns to an inquiry about what Willis's functionalist approach, if interpreted according to a pragmatist framework, would say about Canadian administrative law today. In general, I would argue that the assessment would be positive overall. First, Canadian courts currently interact with the administrative state in very different terms than they did in the 1930s, perhaps reducing the need for an independent review body. Second, the Canadian jurisprudence on procedural review of administrative action seems to have addressed most of the concerns articulated by Willis, including by abandoning judicial review based entirely on formalist categories (for example, judicial, quasi-judicial, and administrative decisions). Third, the substantive review of administrative action now has embedded within it an acknowledgement of expertise and rejects questions of jurisdiction, which could be – according to Willis – used by courts to intervene in substantive matters.

A. *Judicial review in Canada today*

If he accepted the pragmatist interpretation of his 1935 piece proposed here, I believe Willis would be delighted with the fact that judicial review of administrative action is now concentrated in relatively specialized courts (for example, the Divisional Court in Ontario or the Federal Court). Moreover, Canadian courts now conceive of judicial review as a dialogic exercise between the state and the individual affected by administrative decisions.[63] As Geneviève Cartier articulates, 'while Willis objected to lawyers and courts invoking values designed in abstract to rule the administrative state, he should welcome [the dialogic] approach that is grounded in actual practice and in which actual practice shapes the way fundamental values are articulated and applied.'[64] Similarly, Joanne Murray argues that judicial review today does not mimic bilateral, adversarial adjudication but, rather, is structured around a process of quasi-administrative jurisdiction in which courts do engage with administrative (that is,

---

63 Geneviève Cartier, 'Administrative Discretion as Dialogue: A Response to John
    Willis (or: From Theology to Secularization)' (2005) 55:3 UTLJ 629 [Cartier,
    'Administrative Discretion'].
64 Ibid at 650.

polycentric) questions with a view to advancing the public interest.[65] According to Murray's account, judicial review today is not based on a logic that is antithetical to the one deployed by the administrative state. Rather than social welfare versus individual rights, there is a search for the public interest that is balanced against individual rights as a requirement of the rule of law. This all may be in line with a pragmatic interpretation of Willis's demands for review of administrative action.

B. *Procedural fairness in Canada today*

Procedural fairness in Canada was originally structured around the formalist distinction between judicial, quasi-judicial, and administrative functions. On the one hand, judicial and quasi-judicial functions were based on the law; on the other hand, administrative functions were discretionary. The former were subject to judicial review, while the latter were not. Until *Nicholson,* natural justice was confined to the realm of judicial and quasi-judicial functions, whereas administrative functions were not subject to procedural guarantees and protections.[66] Willis would probably be delighted to learn that this distinction was progressively abandoned in *Nicholson* in 1979, *Martineau* in 1980, and *Cardinal* in 1985.[67] Yet it is unclear how Willis would assess the current jurisprudence on procedural fairness. While arguing for a move away from formalism (especially in the judicial approach), in 'Three Approaches,' he never articulates what a functionalist review of administrative action would look like. Considering his description of the function that review of administrative action should perform, I argue in this part that procedural review in Canada could potentially perform such a function.

Willis was not the only scholar concerned with formalism in Canada. In a 1975 article, David Mullan set out a series of reasons for Canadian courts to abandon the use of formal categories (administrative, judicial, and quasi-judicial decisions) when determining the requirements

---

65 Joanne Murray, 'Judicial Review as a Quasi-Administrative Jurisdiction' (2024) 74:4 UTLJ 355.

66 *Nicholson v Haldimand-Norfolk Regional Police Commissioners,* [1979] 1 SCR 311 [*Nicholson*].

67 Ibid; *Martineau v Matsqui Institution,* [1980] 1 SCR 602; *Cardinal v Director of Kent Institution,* [1985] 2 SCR 643.

of procedural fairness.[68] He argued – very similar to Willis – that the state was then (as it still is) performing a range of functions that were neither clearly judicial nor quasi-judicial nor clearly administrative and that rigid classifications missed these nuances.[69] In 1979 in *Nicholson*, the Supreme Court of Canada abandoned the categorical distinction that only judicial and quasi-judicial decisions were subject to procedural fairness, citing Mullan in its reasoning.[70]

Baker has governed procedural fairness in Canada since 1999.[71] It maintains a certain degree of formalism by prescribing a fixed list of factors:

1. the nature of the decision being appealed: administrative/ discretionary decisions get less fairness than adjudicative decisions;
2. the nature of the statutory framework: whether it includes an internal appeal mechanism, or any other stipulated procedural requirements;
3. the impact of the decision on the individual affected;
4. the affected person's legitimate expectations;
5. the 'terms of the statute pursuant to which the body operates,' and 'the choices of procedure made by the agency itself.'[72]

While a list of factors is a type of formalism, only two of the *Baker* factors – the nature of the decision and the statutory framework – may be considered formalistic. Nevertheless, Canadian jurisprudence has asserted that they exist on a spectrum rather than being rigid categories. Moreover, they are informed by the actual function that the decision is performing rather than its form as asserted by the dissenting opinion in *Homex Realty* in 1980.[73] In this case, a municipal by-law was considered to be an adjudicative decision in nature. The municipality was involved in a dispute with the use of land by a developer, and the by-law was a mechanism to deal with such a dispute. The dissenting opinion, which later became prevailing law in Canada, considered the by-law's function rather than its form (which would be legislative).

---

68 David J Mullan, 'Fairness: The New Natural Justice' (1975) 25 UTLJ 281.
69 Ibid at 300.
70 *Nicholson*, supra note 66 at 325.
71 *Baker v Canada (Minister of Citizenship and Immigration)*, [1999] 2 SCR 817.
72 Ibid at para 34.
73 *Homex Realty & Development Co v Wyoming (Village)*, [1980] 2 SCR 1011, Dickson and Ritchie JJ dissenting.

This solution may address some of Willis's concerns with the use of abstract concepts.

Most importantly, the non-formalistic factors, such as the impact of the decision on the individual affected and legitimate expectations, does not raise some of the concerns that a consequentialist reasoning would have raised. Rather than considering the purpose of a certain statute or policy, and what kind of procedural protection could guarantee a certain outcome, the impact of the decision on an individual and their legitimate expectations only modulates the intensity of the protection offered. This modulation potentially eliminates concerns that, in a non-formalist system, courts would need to be operating on a case-by-case basis, tailoring procedures to the goals of a particular administrative system.[74]

Martin Loughlin's analysis in 1978 provides a typology of strategies that courts may adopt *vis-à-vis* formalism:

1. '[a]ctivist formalist strategy' (adjudicative values are imposed over all administrative procedures, even those that involve policy considerations);
2. '[a]ctivist informalist strategy' (courts abandon the adjudicative role but exercise a flexible supervisory role over all administrative procedures, which can reduce distortions in policy-making activities, but does require courts to act outside their traditional roles);
3. '[i]nactivist formalist strategy' (only administrative decisions that resemble adjudication are required to comply with adjudicative procedures, which leaves 'a range of decision-making processes free from judicial review ... suggesting that such processes are subject to legislative scrutiny).[75]

In 1935, Willis was concerned with the third of the above strategies – inactivist formalism (that is, the fact that, by reviewing only adjudicative decisions, courts were leaving other spheres of administrative action outside of judicial scrutiny). He also seemed concerned with the first strategy – activist formalim (that is, the fact that courts could end up meddling with administrative decisions under the guise of reviewing questions of law). Yet he did not believe that it would be advisable

---

74 Martin Loughlin, 'Procedural Fairness: A Study of the Crisis in Administrative Law Theory' (1978) 28 UTLJ 215 at 235 [Loughlin, 'Procedural Fairness'].
75 Ibid at 221.

for courts to engage in the second strategy – activist informalism – since they did not have the expertise to engage with or evaluate administrative decisions. His solution was to propose a new body to conduct such review. Yet, according to Cartier, through dialogue, Canadians courts have found a way to engage in activist informalism to reduce distortions in policy-making and curtail abuse while remaining deferential to the expertise of administrative decision makers.[76] Therefore, Canadian courts are neither imposing their judicial views nor attempting to become administrators or abstaining from controlling administrative action.

Within a pragmatist framework, the question would be whether courts are equipped to perform review of administrative action. The procedural review doctrines developed in recent decades in Canada may have equipped the courts to perform the same functions ascribed to the new body envisioned by Willis in 1935.

C. *Substantive review in Canada today*

In 1935, Willis specified that substantive review of administrative action required a review of questions of both law and jurisdiction as well as questions of fact (evidence) to determine if the administrative policy was adequately applied in a concrete case. He resisted granting judicial review powers to courts because 'the judges of the ordinary courts … know nothing of the problems of administration and are debarred by the rules of interpretation from discovering the purposes which the statute is designed to effect.'[77] While the courts at the time were ill-equipped to perform these functions, the same may not be said about today's judiciary. The question, then, is whether substantive review in Canada today would address Willis's concerns. In this section, I argue that the 2019 Supreme Court of Canada decision in *Canada (Minister of Citizenship and Immigration) v Vavilov*, which governs substantive review in Canada today, embraces a culture of justification.[78] Such a culture has significant overlaps with what Dewey, a prominent pragmatist, considered necessary for the legitimate exercise of power. Therefore, within a pragmatist framework, it seems possible that the current system of judicial review in Canada would

---

76 Cartier, 'Administrative Discretion,' supra note 63.
77 Willis, 'Three Approaches,' supra note 3 at 80.
78 *Canada (Minister of Citizenship and Immigration) v Vavilov*, 2019 SCC 65 at paras 131, 133 [*Vavilov*].

satisfy a pragmatist conception of the legitimate exercise of power. If we interpret Willis's concerns as pragmatist, it could potentially satisfy his as well.

The majority in *Vavilov* articulates the need for courts to look primarily at the administrative decision maker's reasons and states that this analysis can be supplemented by the record, which 'may explain an aspect of the decision maker's reasoning process that is not apparent from the reasons themselves, or may reveal that an apparent shortcoming in the reasons is not, in fact, a failure of justification, intelligibility or transparency.'[79] The majority also makes reference to the context in which the decision is made, pointing to the institutional setting, internal precedents, as well as publicly available policies and guidelines that may have informed the decision.[80] This Vavilovian emphasis on the information available in reasons, record, or context is aligned with a culture of justification and the idea of deference as respect.[81] *Vavilov* also indicates that internal records or any other documents (for example, guidelines or policies) that were not available to the affected party cannot provide justification for the exercise of public power.[82] This means that a culture of justification is focused on creating a record that reveals the reasoning process of the administrative decision maker to the reviewing court. Such a culture of justification 'adopts the assumption that what justifies all public power is the ability of its incumbents to offer adequate reason for the decisions which affect those subject to them.'[83] This is intrinsic to the very idea of a review court's respecting, rather than blindly submitting to, the administrative decision.

Vavilov structures judicial review of administrative decisions in a way that closely maps onto the pragmatist view of the law, especially the one articulated by Dewey. In general, pragmatists who confront the

---

79 Ibid at para 94.

80 Ibid at paras 94, 137.

81 Dyzenhaus's concept of deference as respect 'requires not submission but a respectful attention to the reasons offered or which could be offered in support of the decision, whether that decision be the statutory decision of the legislature, a judgment of another court, or the decision of an administrative agency.' David Dyzenhaus, 'The Politics of Deference: Judicial Review and Democracy' in Michael Taggart, ed, *The Province of Administrative Law* (Oxford: Hart Publishing, 1997) 279 at 286 [Dyzenhaus, 'Politics of Deference'] ('even if the reasons in fact given do not seem wholly adequate to support the decision, the court must first seek to supplement them before it seeks to subvert them').

82 *Vavilov*, supra note 78 at para 95.

83 Dyzenhaus, 'Politics of Deference,' supra note 81 at 305.

issue of normative beliefs resist the idea that moral and legal obligations can be defined *a priori* (by God, reason, or nature). As explored in Part II, for pragmatists, inquiry is the process through which descriptive/ scientific beliefs are settled. For Dewey and others, inquiry also plays a central role in the formation of normative beliefs, such as morality and law. Besides being experimental in nature, the legal inquiry aims at fixing a problem, 'reaching decisions that subsequent experience will show to have been the best, under the circumstances.'[84] Dewey considers 'a legal trial to be a paradigmatic instance of a problematic situation to be resolved by inquiry.'[85] The legitimacy of these decisions comes from the fact that they offer a space to 'convince and be convinced by reason.'[86] Dewey promotes a culture of justification through reason, giving two concepts that significantly overlap with the way in which courts conduct judicial review of administrative decisions according to *Vavilov*. This could potentially address Willis's concerns about courts' knowledge about the issues handled by the administration and the judges ability to understand the purpose of the statutes that empower administrative decision makers.

V. Conclusion

In this article, I have offered an alternative interpretation of Willis's 1935 article 'Three Approaches'; his proposal for a functionalist approach to administrative law can be reinterpreted as being aligned with the American pragmatist tradition. According to this reinterpretation, I have looked back to argue that the philosophical assumptions of this school of thought can shed new light on Willis's resistance to judicial review at the time of his writing. And I have looked forward to claim that, if we reinterpret Willis's proposal according to philosophical pragmatism's assumptions, a functionalist approach to administrative law seems very much in line with Canadian administrative law today.

---

84 Misak, 'Dewey,' supra note 42 at 200.
85 Ibid at 199.
86 Ibid at 198.

3 Richard Charles Bosworth (Dick) Risk: Maker of Canadian Legal History

JIM PHILLIPS

It is a profound pleasure and honour to write a few words about my friend and mentor RCB Risk, who everybody knows as Dick but who always published as RCB Risk. It is appropriate for me do this, in part, because we taught Canadian legal history together many times. But mostly because, apart from members of his family, I am perhaps the only person who knows what the 'B' stands for in RCB. It is obvious what the R stands for, and while it is not obvious that the C stands for Charles, that is not unusual or interesting. But when people asked about the 'B,' he would always coyly tell them to work it out – red and white rose, York and Lancaster, and, for the slower ones, he would add the 'end of the Plantagenets' and/or Henry Tudor. Dick knew his English history, but he left his indelible mark on Canadian legal history.

This brief article covers three topics. I will begin by highlighting Dick's contribution to the field of Canadian legal history in general. I follow this by examining two particular papers that he published. Here, I adopt the suggestion of the editors of this volume that we not try to cover everything our subjects wrote about but concentrate on pieces that illustrate large themes in his scholarship. Specifically, I have chosen his study of the emergence of workmen's compensation, as it was called at the time, in Ontario and his analysis of the career and legal thought of William Paul McLure Kennedy. The former exemplifies both his interest in the growth of the regulatory state and his adept use of empirical evidence. The latter combines his interests in legal thought and legal education and the delight he took in unearthing unusual and little-known features of our legal past.

When Dick began working in the area in the 1970s, the field of Canadian legal history was very much in its infancy, and that may be putting it too generously. Dick himself acknowledged this in an article published in the *Dalhousie Law Journal* in 1974, entitled 'A Prospectus for

Canadian Legal History.' Canadian legal history, he told us, had been greatly neglected by professional historians and academic lawyers. In his pithy way, he added that '[w]e have not even accumulated and organized most of the major facts, let alone thought about them.'[1] A colleague and I were recently asked to write about 'Fifty Years of Canadian Legal History' for the fiftieth anniversary issue of the same *Dalhousie Law Journal*, and we emphatically agreed with what Dick had said then, calling the scholarship on Canadian legal history in the common law provinces before the 1970s, almost all of it written by judges, 'in equal measure antiquarian, descriptive and hagiographic.'[2]

In the 1970s, Dick, a teacher of real estate law and prominent in the developments that led to the passage of Ontario's first Condominium Act in 1967,[3] took on the Herculean task of changing that and amply succeeded. As Hamar Foster, one of the leading legal historians of British Columbia observed in a *festschrift* in his honour published some twenty-five years ago, Dick 'deserves a goodly share of the credit' for transforming Canadian legal history 'from professional pastime to academic discipline.'[4] His initial explorations were published before and just after that 1974 'Prospectus' article. By the mid-to-late 1970s, a few others had joined him, including, as cheerleader and facilitator, the late Roy McMurtry, who had played on the same University of Toronto football team as Dick in the 1950s and who as attorney-general of Ontario founded the Osgoode Society for Canadian Legal History in 1979 to encourage research in the area. The fruits of Dick's first ventures into the field were three deeply researched articles on law and

---

1 RCB Risk, 'A Prospectus for Canadian Legal History' (1973–4) 1 Dal LJ 227.

2 Jim Phillips & Philip Girard, 'Fifty Years of Canadian Legal History' (2023) 46 Dal LJ 403 at 404.

3 *An Act to Facilitate the Division of Properties into Parts That Are to Be Owned Individually and Parts That Are to Be Owned in Common, and to Provide for the Use and Management of Such Properties*, SO 1967, c 12. See also RCB Risk, 'Condominiums and Canada' (1968) 18 UTLJ 1; RCB Risk, 'The Legal Concept of the Condominium and the Legislative Response, with Particular Reference to Ontario' in Hudson Janisch, ed, *The Law and Condominium Development* (Halifax: Dalhousie University, 1973). For his other work on real estate law, see RCB Risk, 'The Records of Title to Land: A Plea for Reform' (1971) 21 UTLJ 465; RCB Risk & Barry Reiter, *Real Estate Law* (Toronto: Emond Montgomery, 1979).

4 Hamar Foster, 'A Romance of the Lost: The Role of Tom MacInnes in the History of the British Columbia Indian Land Question' in G Blaine Baker & Jim Phillips, eds, *Essays in the History of Canadian Law*, vol 8: *In Honour of R.C.B. Risk* (Toronto: Osgoode Society for Canadian Legal History and University of Toronto Press, 1999) 171 [Baker & Phillips, *Essays in the History of Canadian Law*].

economy published between 1973 and 1977.[5] It is telling that, when the Osgoode Society brought out its first volume of *Essays in the History of Canadian Law* in 1981, most of the authors published their first serious essays in the field in that volume. But Dick's contribution was different. He was asked to write a chapter summarizing the work that he had already done on the relationship between law and the economy in Canada West.[6]

Dick's subsequent work was all about post-Confederation Canada, and it progressed through three distinct subfields of Canadian legal history: the emergence of the administrative state, distinctively Canadian approaches to Canadian legal thought, and Canadian constitutional history, although a number of his articles combined elements of at least two of these subfields. Hence, when the late G Blaine Baker and I edited and introduced a collection of his essays published in 2006 following Dick's retirement, we referred to his work as a broad-ranging contribution to Canadian intellectual history – specifically, as a 'unique body of scholarship on the late-nineteenth and mid-twentieth century Canadian legal mind.'[7] His work was well known outside of Canada as well. His retirement *festschrift* featured as its lead chapter a tribute to him by leading UK and US legal historians David Sugarman and Robert Gordon, which stated simply that he was 'the most respected academic authority on Canadian legal history.'[8]

When I was asked to contribute an article on Dick to this symposium, I thought of the 'Prospectus' article from 1974 because, in it, he suggested eight themes around which the then new project of making historical inquiries into Canadian law could be organized. Three

---

5   RCB Risk, 'The Nineteenth-Century Foundations of the Business Corporation in Ontario' (1973) 23 UTLJ 270; RCB Risk, 'The Golden Age: The Law About the Market in Nineteenth-Century Ontario' (1976) 26 UTLJ 307; RCB Risk, 'The Last Golden Age: Property and the Allocation of Losses in Ontario in the Nineteenth Century' (1977) 27 UTLJ 199.

6   RCB Risk, 'The Law and the Economy in Mid-Nineteenth Century Ontario: A Perspective' in David Flaherty, ed, *Essays in the History of Canadian Law*, vol 1 (Toronto: Osgoode Society and University of Toronto Press, 1981) [Flaherty, *Essays in the History of Canadian Law*]. As some people will know, between 1841 and 1867, Canada West was the official name of what is now Ontario. It was one half of the colony of the Province of Canada, with Canada East (Quebec) being the other half.

7   G Blaine Baker & Jim Phillips, eds, *A History of Canadian Legal Thought: Collected Essays of R.C.B. Risk* (Toronto: Osgoode Society for Canadian Legal History and University of Toronto Press, 2006) at 3 [Baker & Phillips, *History of Canadian Legal Thought*].

8   Robert W Gordon & David Sugarman, 'Richard C.B. Risk: A Tribute' in Baker & Phillips, *Essays in the History of Canadian Law*, supra note 4, vol 8, 3.

of those themes – the contribution of the law to Canadian identity, the involvement of the law in community or distributive initiatives, and the relationship of agencies of government to the courts and the common law tradition – are all present in one of the two works by Dick that I will discuss in this article, his exemplary account of the introduction of workers' compensation in Ontario.[9] It was the first of four essays in which he laid out the parameters of Canada's crucial transition from the common law and the courts reigning supreme to their sharing the legal spotlight with administrative agencies.[10] It bears noting that, as he made this transition in his legal history scholarship, he also moved to teaching administrative law, a change in orientation which also involved co-authoring the principal Canadian casebook in that area.[11] This was a move that was typical of Dick. When he later moved to the history of Canadian constitutional thought, he made a similar change to teaching constitutional law and was similarly one of the co-authors of a leading casebook in that area.[12]

Many common law jurisdictions introduced workers' compensation schemes in the later nineteenth and early twentieth centuries, and while he acknowledged that the Ontario experience was not unique, he also insisted that it was distinctive – most notably, in the use of one of the province's first administrative agencies and in the fact that this fundamental turn away from the common law to a form of socialized justice was brought about by a commission headed by one of the pillars of the Ontario legal establishment. Dick's account begins with the common law rules on compensation for workplace injuries, which as many people will know were transformed in the Anglo-American world of the early to mid-nineteenth century by the introduction of doctrines designed to shield employers from liability for injuries caused by the machinery of the industrial revolution. Most notable was the fellow-servant rule, which held that an injured worker could not sustain an

---

9 RCB Risk, '"This Nuisance of Litigation": The Origins of Workers' Compensation in Ontario' in Flaherty, *Essays in the History of Canadian Law,* supra note 6, vol. 2, 418 [Risk, 'This Nuisance of Litigation'].

10 RCB Risk, 'The Beginnings of Regulation' in EG Baldwin, ed, *The Cambridge Lectures* (Toronto: Butterworths, 1983) 252; RCB Risk, 'Sir William Meredith, C.J.O.: The Search for Authority' (1983) 7 Dal LJ 713 [Risk, 'Sir William Meredith']; RCB Risk, 'Lawyers, Courts and the Rise of the Regulatory State' (1984) 9 Dal LJ 31.

11 JM Evans et al, *Administrative Law: Cases, Text and Materials* (Toronto: Emond Montgomery, 1980).

12 Constitutional Law Group, *Canadian Constitutional Law* (Toronto: Emond Montgomery, 1998). Now in its seventh edition from 2022, although Dick no longer appears as one of the authors.

action against the employer if the injury was caused by the carelessness or negligence of another employee. That other employee was liable but, most of the time to all intents and purposes, impecunious. The rule, and other doctrines such as voluntary assumption of risk and contributory negligence, had the effect of severely curtailing employer liability and has been labelled by some historians as a subsidy on infant industry. Dick did not deny that such was the effect, but he was careful to situate particular legal doctrines in the common law *mentalité* of the time:

> General beliefs about the substance and form of the common law shaped [such doctrines]. At the centre was a belief that the law should establish and encourage individual autonomy. ... Each person should be responsible for his or her own fate. This responsibility depended upon individual will, and fault was both a moral failing and a condition of liability. ... Individuals could choose to work or not to work, and ... [l]iability and fault were a product of personal failing which a person could, by taking care, have avoided.[13]

Dick was not expressing his own political-legal beliefs. He was doing what all good historians should do – reconstructing a world far removed from his own.

This consensus was broken down in the late nineteenth century in part by ameliorating legislation which reduced the scope of the fellow-servant rule and, much more significantly, by the decisions of juries and the rulings of judges. The interaction between juries, trial judges, and appeal courts was complicated, much too complicated for me to explain here, not having the space that Dick had or his nimbleness of intellect. For our purposes, the point is that Dick showed that plaintiffs won much more often from the late 1880s than they had before, especially in cases involving serious injury or death which left workers' families without support. He came to this conclusion through a wide-ranging analysis of both reported cases and the case files of unreported cases in the archives, an impressive research exercise in the notoriously difficult-to-use court records.

Importantly, he attributed the workers' success in part to a subtle shift in judicial views and a lessening of judicial faith in 'individual responsibility and freedom.' This change was not overt because, as he subtly and perhaps cheekily explained, 'the form of [judicial] reasoning denied admission of change let alone an attempt to explain and

---

13 Risk, 'This Nuisance of Litigation,' supra note 9 at 421.

justify it.' He continued: 'Beliefs about the value of individual responsibility and freedom were declining in the late nineteenth century. ... As industrial capitalism matured and the power of employers increased, it became obvious that individual workers usually had no significant opportunity to choose the terms of their work.'[14] The rise of workers' organizations was important in this transformation, but so too were the changing attitudes of those who applied the common law. Courts began to believe that the limited legislative reforms 'encouraged and authorized them to make changes of the same nature.'[15] Leading judges noticed the movement in Europe and the United States toward providing compensation without fault and were increasingly receptive to a Canadian initiative along those lines.

At this point, enter Sir William Ralph Meredith, a successful London, Ontario, lawyer and, for sixteen years, leader of the opposition Conservatives in the Ontario legislature. In that capacity, he led the party through five consecutive election defeats to Oliver Mowat's Liberal party, partly the result of being a part-time leader who continued an active law practice and partly the result of being seen as something of a radical who took up various reform causes, especially those that favoured urban workers. In 1894, he was rewarded for many years of devoted service to the Conservative party by being appointed chief justice of common pleas in 1894. Sixteen years later, he was appointed by Conservative premier James P Whitney to head a royal commission into workers' compensation.[16] Dick's work always considered the role of personality in explaining the development of legal ideas, and he argued that Meredith was the right man for the job at the right time. He had long been torn between his politics and his faith in the judicial process, especially the importance of adherence to precedent. When during one of the commission hearings he was assailed by a union representative for being a member of a class that was antipathetic to workers, he made clear in response the crucial difference in his mind between changing the law and administering justice, using the third person when he was obviously referring to himself:

> I venture to say that as a whole the sympathies, as far as a judge is permitted to have sympathies, have been with the working man, and where

---

14 Ibid at 448.

15 Ibid at 449.

16 In addition to Risk's work, see e.g. Meredith Peter Dembski, 'Sir William Ralph Meredith,' *Dictionary of Canadian Biography*, online: <www.biographi.ca/en/bio /meredith_william_ralph_15E.htm>.

they have had to determine against him in hard cases it is because they have been compelled by the law to do so. ... [Y]ou think a court is entitled to do natural justice, but the court has no such power. The court is confined to administering justice according to law. ... The fault is not in the administration of justice; you must change the law. It is the law that is at fault.

Dick perceptively saw through what he called Meredith's 'mask of formalism.' He 'was clearly more sympathetic to workers than most of his colleagues.'[17]

The Workmen's Compensation Act that passed in 1914 was the first of its kind in Canada, and it created a system that is still in place today in its essentials.[18] There is no point in going into details here, although, of course, as the careful and exacting scholar that he was, Dick did so in a long article that others would have made a book out of. What mattered to Dick, in addition to writing a piece of labour history that is still the go-to source, was the link between what Meredith himself called 'social legislation,' with the employers being 'simply tax gatherers,' and a fundamental shift in dominant ways of thinking about the common law.[19] As he concluded, '[t]he courts and the doctrine of fault appeared more and more unsatisfactory ... after the late nineteenth century.'[20] Employers and workers alike condemned the court-based fault system for the conflict it encouraged and the delay, uncertainty, and inefficiency manifested in its operation. It was replaced by a state-run welfare scheme which sought to ensure compensation regardless of fault because, in most cases, injuries were not caused by fault but were endemic to industrial production. Hence, compensation was joined as a goal of the new order by prevention, the costs of which, like the costs of compensation, were shared by employers, consumers, and the state. Dick's analysis of how all this came about was detailed, sophisticated, and combined empirical research with a deep understanding of the revolution in ways of thinking that was required.

I have chosen as my second piece of Dick's work to highlight his analysis of Kennedy, in part because it reflects one of the themes in

---

17 Cited in Risk, 'This Nuisance of Litigation,' supra note 9 at 456. Dick's interest in Meredith's judicial philosophy was pursued in a 'spin-off' article. Risk, 'Sir William Meredith,' supra note 10.

18 *An Act to Provide for Compensation to Workmen for Injuries Sustained and Industrial Diseases Contracted in the Course of their Employment*, SO 1914, c 25.

19 Cited in Risk, 'This Nuisance of Litigation,' supra note 9 at 418.

20 Ibid at 459.

the above-mentioned 'Prospectus' article – the contribution of the law to Canadian identity – and in part because, like the workers' compensation study, it charts a transformation in thinking about law and legal institutions. But the principal reason for my choice is that it was a major original contribution to the history of this law school and, therefore, an ideal candidate for inclusion in a collection devoted to that history. It is true that it was about the history of the law school before 1949, emphasizing the fact that this law school did have a history before Caesar Wright and Bora Laskin left Osgoode Hall, but this simply makes it even more appropriate, for history never starts or stops in a particular place. Indeed, I am convinced that, had we held an event like this one when we celebrated 'Fifty Years of Modern Legal Education' in 1999, Dick would have presented this article as part of it. In fact, in the first paragraph of 'The Many Minds of W.P.M. Kennedy,' Dick said that his study of Kennedy and the pre-Wright law school would serve as 'a chastening reminder to contemporary law schools that they were not the first to embrace the interdisciplinary study of law.'[21]

Rightly described by Kennedy's biographer as 'brilliant,'[22] Dick's account of Kennedy has two large themes. There is Kennedy the scholar of Canadian constitutional history and Kennedy the dean of a law school. Both had an unlikely beginning because Kenndy was a serious and well-respected scholar of early modern English ecclesiastical history when he came to Canada in 1913 to teach at what was then St Francis Xavier College in Antigonish, Nova Scotia. He moved to Toronto as a history professor soon after and developed an interest in Canadian constitutional history while continuing his work on Tudor England. Thus, between 1914 and 1924, he published five books in this order: *Parish Life under Elizabeth*,[23] *Studies in Tudor History*,[24] *Documents of the Canadian Constitution*,[25] *The Constitution of Canada: An Introduction*

---

21 RCB Risk, 'Many Minds of Kennedy' (1998) 48 UTLJ 353, reprinted in Baker & Phillips, *History of Canadian Legal Thought*, supra note 7, 300 at 300 [Risk, 'Many Minds of Kennedy']. All subsequent page numbers in this chapter are to the latter version.

22 Martin L Friedland, *Searching for W.P.M. Kennedy: The Biography of an Enigma* (Toronto: University of Toronto Press, 2020) at x.

23 WPM Kennedy, *Parish Life under Elizabeth* (London: Manresa Press, 1914).

24 WPM Kennedy, *Studies in Tudor History* (London: Constable, 1916).

25 WPM Kennedy, *Documents of the Canadian Constitution* (Toronto: Oxford University Press, 1918).

to Its Development and Law,[26] and *Elizabethan Episcopal Administration*.[27] Kennedy was not the only Canadian law teacher to start in a field other than law and then switch, but he was surely the first, and one of the very few, who did this without any formal legal training. His major work on the Constitution was also distinct from those of legally trained scholars on the same subject, such as Augustus Henry Frazer Lefroy and Dennis O'Sullivan,[28] in not being very concerned with the division of powers under the British North America Act.[29] *The Constitution of Canada* began with four chapters on New France, continued with three more on Quebec and the conquest, and took another twelve to go from the 1791 Constitutional Act to the British North America Act. Only chapters 20–5 covered the years between 1867 and the book's publication in 1922, and, of these, only one – chapter 24 – dealt with 'The Distribution of Legislative Power' in a scant twelve pages.

The Constitution of Canada was thus not a book which today we would label a legal treatise or a case book. Its major themes were representative and responsible government, which necessarily have to precede the division of powers. Until you have political decisions being made by executives who are responsible to elected majorities, you cannot really argue about which areas the different elected majorities can legislate in. But to say that *The Constitution of Canada* was not a law book is to beg the question of what a law book is. Why should a book on our Constitution not include responsible government? Just as importantly, why should it not include, as Kennedy's did, an extensive discussion of the difficulties of operating the Constitution created by the Act of Union of 1840, given that it was those difficulties that led to Confederation? The Confederation pact was essentially a way to federalize the political unit known as the Province of Canada (now Ontario and Quebec), which by the 1860s was proving unworkable.

As noted above, Kennedy's history covered the half-century from 1867, including the Privy Council decisions of the late nineteenth

---

26 WPM Kennedy, *The Constitution of Canada: An Introduction to Its Development and Law* (London: Oxford University Press, 1922). A second edition of the book, updated, was published in 1938. A third edition was recently published in 2014 in a new edition with an introduction by Martin Friedland, but with no changes to the text.

27 WPM Kennedy, *Elizabethan Episcopal Administration* (London: AR Mowbray, 1924).

28 RCB Risk, 'Constitutional Scholarship in the Late Nineteenth Century: Making Federalism Work' (1996) 46 UTLJ 427; RCB Risk, 'A.H.F. Lefroy: Common Law Thought in Late-Nineteenth Century Canada: On Burying One's Grandfather' (1991) 41 UTLJ 196, both reprinted in Baker & Phillips, *History of Canadian Legal Thought*, supra note 7, 33 and 66.

29 *British North America Act* (UK), 30 & 31 Vict, c 3.

century, but, with those sections, Dick moved from admirer of the scope and approach of *The Constitution of Canada* to critical reviewer, albeit in his typically gentle way. Kennedy was not wrong or lacking in essential understanding; he 'went astray.' He said that Canada had been able to avoid divisive quarrels over the division of powers, a statement that 'ignored much of the politics of the late nineteenth century,' and that the Privy Council's insistence on treating the British North America Act as an ordinary statute was a 'benign' approach, a characterization which 'masked a tension (if not a deep gulf) between his [Kennedy's] account of Confederation and the rise of the provinces.' On this issue, Kennedy made two significant errors. He took the Privy Council at its own word when it had stated that it had interpreted the British North America Act in the same way that courts construed any British statute, finding the obvious 'right answer' embedded in the statute's words, only 'without considering evidence about the context and the making of a statute.' This had been the dominant understanding of interpretation in the later nineteenth century, but it expressed a myth in that, in Dick's words, 'it denied that the court made choices and exercised any creative function.'[30] They always made choices whether they said so or not, and the choices made by the Privy Council, especially from the mid-1880s, favoured an expansive view of provincial power even if that preference was concealed behind a formal 'plain-words' approach to interpretation.

Dick was not wholly critical of Kennedy as constitutional lawyer/historian. He praised him for undermining the traditional Austinian theory of sovereignty, which stressed that each state must have one sovereign only, 'exercising omnipotent and unlimited power.' In this formulation, there was no room for a divided sovereignty, yet Kennedy's was a long history of the evolutionary, not revolutionary, development of Canadian statehood. The key to achieving this was the distinction between local and imperial matters in the British North American colonies, without which responsible government could not have been achieved. Hence, Kennedy was implicitly correct to see the history of the Canadian Constitution and of Canadian constitutional law as one going back to the colonial founding and evolving from there. Kennedy's vision of the development of the Canadian Constitution as a challenge to Austinian notions of sovereignty grew increasingly explicit over time – most notably, in his 1932 published lectures *Some Aspects of the Theories and Workings of Constitutional Law*. Dick noted that these lectures 'rejoiced in the passing of the nineteenth-century world of laissez-faire,

---

30 Risk, 'Many Minds of Kennedy,' supra note 21 at 305–6.

autonomous individuals and their rights, and the jurisprudence of Austin, Holland and Salmond.' They also heralded an entirely new 'general approach to law and legal thought,' which is my next topic.[31]

Before I get to that topic, a brief and speculative thought about Dick. He did not say this, but I think his analysis of Kennedy was, at one and the same time, an assertion of the usefulness of a historian without legal training writing constitutional history and of the limits of that enterprise occasioned by that same lack of legal training. I say this in part to ensure that the reader recalls that I am writing about Dick and not about Kennedy. Dick's interest in Kennedy grew out of his interest in the long history of the law school, a history which extended back well beyond Wright, but he was not content merely to talk about Kennedy as a character. He wanted to place Kennedy among the other legal intellectual figures from Canada's past: Lefroy, Edward Blake, John Skirving Ewart, and Meredith.[32] He also used Kennedy's place among Canadian constitutional historians as a starting point to discuss two other notable and novel themes in 'Many Minds of Kennedy' – the Canadian legal realist movement and the uniqueness of the 'Kennedy Law School.'

These two themes were linked, both chronologically and substantively, and, thus, nothing compels separating them. I will deal first with Canadian legal realism only because in the 'Many Minds of W.P.M. Kennedy,' Dick also did so first. He pointed out that the question 'did Canada have a [legal] realist' movement similar to' that of the United States would usually be answered with a firm 'no' but that this answer would come from people who had not read any of the scholarship by Canadians who wrote about legal thought and the role of law in society in the 1930s. Dick, of course, had read it and written about it extensively. He listed the principals as Alex Corry of Queens, Jacob Finkelman and Bora Laskin of Toronto, Vincent Macdonald and John Willis of Dalhousie, Percy Corbett, Frank Scott, and Herbert Smith of McGill,

---

31 WPM Kennedy, *Some Aspects of the Theories and Workings of Constitutional Law* (New York: Macmillan, 1932). Quotations taken from Risk, 'Many Minds of Kennedy,' supra note 21 at 309, 310.

32 For Augustus Lefroy and Meredith, see notes 16 and 28 above. For Edward Blake, see RCB Risk & Rob Vipond, 'Rights Talk in Canada in the Late Nineteenth Century: The Good Sense and Right Feeling of the People' 14 (1996) Law and History Review 1; RCB Risk, 'Blake and Liberty' in Janet Ajzenstat, ed, *Canadian Constitutionalism, 1791–1991* (Ottawa: Canadian Study of Parliament Group, 1992) 189. For Ewart, see RCB Risk, 'John Skirving Ewart: The Legal Thought' (1987) 37 UTLJ 335. All three of these essays are reprinted in Baker & Phillips, *History of Canadian Legal Thought*, supra note 7 at 94, 130, and 152.

and Caesar Wright of Osgoode Hall as well as Kennedy.[33] (Some may be surprised to see Wright placed in this group, a point to which I will return.) Dick insisted that, of this group, Kennedy was 'not only one of the first to make a major and comprehensive manifesto,' proclaiming the advent of Canadian legal realism, but he was also 'the most prolific and wide ranging.'[34] By this last phrase, Dick meant in part 'Kennedy's small contribution to a major watershed in legal thought [the refutation of Austin].' He also meant something much larger: Kennedy's 'rejection of nineteenth-century thought, an embrace of modernity, and a new understanding of the state.'[35]

Dick located the origins of Kennedy's legal realism in his 1931 published lectures and in other work in which he denied and deprecated the idea that there was a sharp divide between the individual and the state. I quote from Dick's summary of Kennedy's credo, not from Kennedy:

> The individual could only be understood as a member of a community. ... Because the state was made by the will of the citizens, there was no antithesis between the individual and the state. [Thus] [t]hinking about rights as the centre of private law must give way to thinking about interests, without diminishing the centrality of the individual and the human personality. ... The standard for designing and assessing laws was essentially functional: had they achieved their social ends?[36]

Thus, and here I am quoting Kennedy from Dick's article, 'law making would in the future be more difficult than when laws were guided by the simple mantra of laissez-faire individualism.' It was necessary 'to create social machinery for making law if law is to serve social ends.' To achieve this, lawmakers would have to undertake 'a comprehensive survey of social values' and a 'carefully sifted examination of social facts.' Thus, lawyers would need to learn new skills and approaches drawn from the social sciences.[37]

---

33 For Dick on Willis, see RCB Risk, 'John Willis: A Tribute' (1984) 9 Dal LJ 521; RCB Risk, 'In Memoriam: John Willis' (1997) 47 UTLJ 301. For Corbett, Finkelman, Wright, Corry, Willis, and MacDonald, see RCB Risk, 'Volume One of the Journal: A Tribute and a Belated Review' (1987) 37 UTLJ 193. For Kennedy, Scott, and MacDonald, see RCB Risk, 'The Scholars and the Constitution: POGG and the Privy Council' (1996) 23 Manitoba LJ 496; RCB Risk, 'Canadian Law Teachers in the 1930s: "When the World Was Turned Upside Down"' (2004) 27 Dal LJ 1.

34 Risk, 'Many Minds of Kennedy,' supra note 21 at 313.

35 Ibid at 311.

36 Ibid at 310.

37 Quotations from various works by Kennedy cited in ibid at 310.

As I stated above, the identification of legal realism as part of Canadian legal thought in the 1930s was intimately linked by Dick to Kennedy's understanding of what a law school education should be. In 'The Many Minds of W.P.M. Kennedy,' Dick made the connection explicit (here, I quote seamlessly from both Kennedy and from what Dick said about Kennedy, although the sentiments expressed throughout are Kennedy's): '[L]egal education must be transformed to save us from the black-letter lawyer at a time when we are still so ill-fitted to mold law to social ends. Law must be taught, not in isolation, but together with the other social sciences.'[38] This was the vision that Kennedy operated with as the head of the University of Toronto Faculty of Law for over two decades, from 1927 to 1949. I have used the phrase 'head of the University of Toronto Faculty of Law' deliberately, eschewing the title dean, because 'head' captures the fact that, in 1924, a history professor at St Michael's College, he was given the task of establishing a law curriculum in the Faculty of Arts. He created two programs – the honour bachelor of arts in law and the master of law, the latter a graduate program for people who completed the honour bachelor of arts. Irrespective of his title – he was not a 'dean' until 1943 – Kennedy ran the department of law from 1927. He 'dominated the school, setting its general objectives, designing the curriculum, hiring the staff, admitting the students, and deciding their fates.'[39] Students with an honour bachelor of arts in law were not qualified to article and be called to the bar. For that, they had to go to the Law Society's school at old Osgoode Hall, which was still the case until 1957, long after the beginnings of 'modern' legal education in 1949 following the appointment of Wright as dean to replace Kennedy.[40]

Dick's account of the Kennedy law school relies principally on pieces on legal education penned by Kennedy and on school calendars and similar sources preserved in the university archives. Dick cited, in particular, an article in the *South African Law Journal* published in 1934:

[W]e have no professional ends to serve. We are concerned with legal education – to examine the law in relation to society, to probe into its social

---

38 Ibid.

39 Ibid at 314.

40 For the long struggle over university legal education as the path to practice in Ontario, see principally C Ian Kyer & Jerome E Bickenbach, *The Fiercest Debate: Cecil A Wright, the Benchers, and Legal Education in Ontario, 1923–1947* (Toronto: Osgoode Society, 1987).

functionings, to create a body of citizens endowed with an insight into law as the basic social science, and capable of making those examinations into its workings as will redeem it from being a mere trade and technique as to make it the finest of all instruments in the service of mankind.[41]

Three years later, Kennedy said much the same thing and emphasized that, as a result, law was legitimately a university subject – indeed, more a university subject than the focus of professional training: 'The great general principle behind our work is the conviction that law is one of the greatest of university subjects ... the fundamental social science on which every aspect of our civilization must inevitably rest. ... It must be taught amongst the intellectual clash of university activities as well as in relation to the other social sciences.'[42]

Dick devoted a couple of pages to detailing the essential features of the Kennedy law school of the 1930s, features which sharply differentiated it from other law schools at the time. He stressed two general differences. One was that the curriculum required students to take a mixture of law courses – contracts, torts, property, criminal, and the like – and Faculty of Arts courses – Roman history, philosophy, economics, and political science. Students had to take some of each kind every year for four years. The other large difference was that the law courses included courses not then taught anywhere else and, thus, 'remarkably modern.'[43] They included courses which are now part of the standard curriculum – notably, administrative law, labour law, and international law as well as courses that now exist but which are not generally considered more than a fringe interest for the few. Comparative law was one such course; legal history was another. I know from many conversations that we had that he was disappointed that legal history played such a small role in the modern law school, and I suspect that Dick's admiration for the Kennedy school resulted in part from the prominence that it had in the 1930s. Dick also singled out for mention Kennedy's creation of the *University of Toronto Law Journal* in 1935 – at that time, the only common law school-based law journal in Canada.[44]

---

41 WPM Kennedy, 'Law as a Social Science' (1934) 3 SALJ 100 at 100, cited in Risk, 'Many Minds of Kennedy,' supra note 21 at 314 [Kennedy, 'Law as a Social Science'].
42 WPM Kennedy, 'A Project of Legal Education' [1937] Scots Law Times 1 at 1, cited in Risk, 'Many Minds of Kennedy,' supra note 21 at 314.
43 Ibid at 315.
44 The *Osgoode Hall Law Journal* was established in 1958, shortly after the school became part of York University.

Dick clearly saw Kennedy as a man ahead of his time, someone whose ideas were consonant with his own, for Dick liked being part of what the law school had become by the 1970s. Yet he perceptively pointed out that there was a profound inconsistency in Kennedy's model of legal education and what he talked about within the university as the sources of his inspiration. In his published writing, he made vague general references to, in Kennedy's words, 'the sociological jurisprudence as expounded by modern French, German and American jurists.'[45] Yet, in his correspondence with university officials, he stressed the British models – Oxford and Cambridge – which, as Dick noted, 'were bastions of nineteenth-century legal thought during the 1920s and 1930s.'[46] Perhaps, Kennedy was a clever, if not necessarily honest, advocate for his program. He thought he could sell radical content by telling the uninformed that it was all the rage at Oxbridge.

Dick's enthusiasm for Kennedy was also tempered by his knowledge in hindsight of the Kennedy school for he knew that, in the 1940s, it had 'lost its vitality and drifted.'[47] In part, this was because scholars like Laskin had left and were replaced by others not of the same stature. But Dick, taking the long view, mused that a more fundamental cause was that Kennedy believed that a liberal education in law, separate from the pursuit of a professional qualification, 'was at odds with the dominant North American belief that a legal education could be both a liberal education that belonged in a University and at the same time a preparation for practice.' As Chris Essert and Jutta Brunée's introductory chapter in this volume makes clear, this was very much Wright's view, which he 'firmly established' at the University of Toronto, in the process 'erasing any memory of Kennedy.'[48] In fact, Kennedy's name does live on through the WPM Kennedy Silver Medal, awarded annually to the graduating student with the second highest cumulative average in three years of law school. But it is the silver medal, not the gold.

---

45 Kennedy, 'Law as a Social Science,' supra note 41 at 101, cited in Risk, 'Many Minds of Kennedy,' supra note 21 at 315.
46 Ibid at 315.
47 Ibid at 316.
48 Ibid at 316–17.

4 Multidisciplinary Marty Friedland, Miscarriages of Justice, and the Modern Law School[†]

KENT ROACH

Martin L Friedland, CC, FRSC, KC (or Marty, as he is affectionately known to most), is one of the most celebrated of the many celebrated members of the University of Toronto Faculty of Law. His deanship from 1972 to 1979 is rightly credited for setting the faculty on its modern path characterized by extensive and multidisciplinary scholarship. Marty hired me as one of his research assistants after my first year as a student at the faculty. We went on to become colleagues, co-authors, and friends. His influence on my scholarship has been significant, and my debt to him has been immense.

I wish to make two points in this article. The first is that Marty's research agenda throughout his long and continuing career was focused on injustice more than on what is required for justice. Marty's concerns about injustice or miscarriages of justice can be seen from his first book, *Detention before Trial*,[1] published in 1965, to his latest book, *Canadian Criminal Law in Ten Cases*,[2] published in 2024. The risk of injustice was a prominent theme in Marty's 'true crime' trilogy, especially *The Trials of Israel Lipski*.[3] To some, a focus on injustice rather than justice may seem too atheoretical. Nevertheless, I will argue that it remains an important

---

† I thank Marty Friedland and Robert J Sharpe for helpful comments on an earlier draft of this article. Any shortcomings of this article are my own responsibility.

1 Martin L Friedland, *Detention before Trial: A Study of Criminal Cases Tried in the Toronto Magistrates' Courts* (Toronto: University of Toronto Press, 1965) [Friedland, *Detention before Trial*].

2 Martin L Friedland, *Canadian Criminal Law in Ten Cases* (Toronto: University of Toronto Press, 2024) [Friedland, *Canadian Criminal Law*].

3 Martin L Friedland, *The Trials of Israel Lipski: A True Story of a Victorian Murder in the East End of London* (London: MacMillan, 1984) [Friedland, *Trials of Israel Lipski*].

research and teaching agenda for academic lawyers. We have a distinct ability and calling to call out injustice in the legal system.

My second point is that Marty's multidisciplinary approach to legal scholarship has been under-appreciated. Marty's colleague, the late John Edwards, is rightly credited as the founding director of a multidisciplinary centre of criminology at the University of Toronto in 1965. In the same year, however, Marty established his credentials as a criminologist by publishing what is still the leading empirical monograph on bail decisions in Canada. Marty's classmate and good friend Harry Arthurs is famous for being the driving force behind the 1983 *Law and Learning* report (henceforth the Arthurs report), which moved legal scholarship in a more multidisciplinary and scholarly direction.[4] Marty's approach was similar to the Arthurs report in demanding more sophisticated scholarship from law professors and engaging more with other disciplines. It differed, however, in two important respects. Marty saw that the entire university including other professional schools and not just the humanities and social sciences are relevant to the study of the law. Second, Marty appreciated that the legal profession relied upon and needed assistance from multiple disciplines.

I. A research agenda addressed at injustice and miscarriages of justice

A common link in Marty's large and impressive body of scholarship is a concern with injustice. This is more modest than his colleagues who developed theories of justice but no less important or worthy.

A. Detention before trial and the injustice of money bail

Marty's first book, *Detention before Trial*, detailed how most people arrested by the Toronto police were detained before trial.[5] Those who were granted bail were often required to post cash bonds. Many could not afford to and were detained as a result. In his memoirs, Marty revealed that, at one point during his three years of research on the project, he loaned a young man fifty dollars to make bail, adding: 'The police officers were greatly amused. I never saw the accused or the

---

4 HW Arthurs, *Law and Learning: Report to the Social Sciences and Humanities Research Council of Canada* (Ottawa: Social Sciences and Humanities Research Council of Canada, 1983).

5 Friedland, *Detention before Trial*, supra note 1.

money again.'[6] The incident reveals much about Marty's heart and feelings about the injustice of being imprisoned because one does not have money required for bail. Marty was not soured by the lost fifty dollars, which was a not insignificant sum at the time for a young professor with a young family. He concluded *Detention before Trial* by arguing that 'failure to raise a certain sum of money should never be the reason for the accused remaining in custody.'[7] Both Marty's money and mouth were devoted to avoiding the injustice caused by cash bail.

Many, including the Supreme Court of Canada,[8] have traced a direct line from Marty's path-breaking empirical research to the 1972 Bail Reform Act, which applied a presumption of release and made cash bail a last resort.[9] These developments show the connection between researching and documenting injustices and law reform. Good positive analysis of what exists is important and is connected to building a better sense of what ought to occur.

Marty has documented injustices caused by backsliding from the 1972 law.[10] Subsequent amendments have placed many reverse onuses on the accused in a bail hearing. In addition, there has been increased use of sureties by persons who often have to pledge money for an accused to receive bail as well as increasing populations of those subject to pre-trial detention. Bail and high-profile crimes committed by those released on bail are election issues. Amendments have tried to limit extra credit for time spent in pre-trial detention, something started by judges appalled at conditions at Toronto's Don Jail where many of the detainees that Marty studied had been imprisoned. Release is often subject to many conditions, and breach of the condition is a frequently prosecuted offence adding to the accused's criminal record and increasing the likelihood of being denied bail in the future. Bail remains critical to criminal justice.

Simple but catchy slogans such as 'catch and release' illustrate how criminal justice is shaped by both politics and law. Marty documented how wives of police officers were instrumental in creating the first reverse onuses that required the accused to establish that pre-trial

---

6 Martin L Friedland, *My Life in Crime and Other Academic Adventures* (Toronto: University of Toronto Press, 2007) at 94 [Friedland, *My Life in Crime*].

7 Friedland, *Detention before Trial*, supra note 1 at 191.

8 *R v Antic*, 2017 SCC 27 at paras 25–8, 58–9; *R v Zora*, 2020 SCC 14 at para 62; *R v Myers*, 2019 SCC 18 at para 22.

9 *Bail Reform Act*, SC 1970–71–72, c 37.

10 Martin L Friedland, 'The Bail Reform Act, 1972 Revisited' (2012) 16 Can Crim L Rev 315.

detention was not necessary.[11] Governments continue to expand the use of reverse onuses as a means to respond to public anxieties about bail. Marty knew that criminal justice cannot be understood without studying the role of politics, pressure groups, and the media. Detention before trial remains an extremely important topic. Today, scholars have related pre-trial detention to the risk of false guilty pleas.[12] A recent and excellent doctorate at the University of Toronto Faculty of Law assessed wrongful detention in the forms of people subject to prolonged pre-trial detention only to be acquitted or have their charges dropped.[13] Some countries, including Italy, Germany, and France, provide compensation to those who have been acquitted after being detained before trial. The International Criminal Court is struggling with this issue, and it is especially important in countries such as India in the global South where a significant majority of all prisoners are imprisoned awaiting trial.[14]

B. Miscarriages of justice and the Truscott case

Marty's innovative 1968 teaching materials included a detailed case study of the Stephen Truscott case, which concerned a fourteen year old who was convicted of murdering a classmate and sentenced to die. It forced students to grapple with the possibility of error, especially with respect to fact finding, something that the casebook, which is now in its twelfth edition, still does.[15] As will be discussed in the second part of this article, the Truscott case also demonstrated the need for criminal lawyers to use and understand disciplines outside of law.

---

11 Marty researched the role of interest groups long before many others. Martin L Friedland, 'Pressure Groups and the Development of the Criminal Law' in Peter Glazebrook, ed, *Reshaping the Criminal Law: Essays in Honour of Glanville Williams* (London: Stevens and Sons, 1978). See also David Cole, *Engines of Liberty* (New York: New Press, 2017).

12 Cheryl Marie Webster, 'Remanding Justice for the Innocent: Systemic Pressures in Pretrial Detention to Falsely Plead Guilty in Canada' (2022) 3:2 Wrongful Conviction Law Review 128; Kent Roach, 'Canada's False Guilty Pleas: Lessons from the Canadian Registry of Wrongful Convictions' (2023) 4:1 Wrongful Convictions Law Review 16.

13 Nathan Gorham, *Wrongful Remand: Miscarriages of Justice in the Canadian Bail System* (SJD thesis, University of Toronto Faculty of Law, 2022).

14 Kent Roach, 'International and Comparative Law on Compensation for Miscarriages of Justice' (2024) 62 Colum J Transnat'l L 721.

15 Martin L Friedland, *Cases and Materials on Criminal Law and Procedure* (Toronto: University of Toronto Press, 1968) [Friedland, *Cases and Materials*]. See also Kent Roach et al, *Cases and Materials on Criminal Law and Procedure*, 12th ed (Toronto: Emond Montgomery, 2020).

Marty returned to the Truscott case in his latest book. He recounted how the day after the Ontario Court of Appeal upheld Truscott's murder conviction in 1960, the Diefenbaker Cabinet commuted Truscott's death sentence to life imprisonment. The next year, it enacted legislation prohibiting the execution of those under eighteen years of age. It made a difference that the federal government was headed by a former defence lawyer opposed to capital punishment. Canada's Parliament was well ahead of the United States in this regard.[16] Although he was aware of American developments, Marty was never a 'branch plant' academic who wrote for American audiences.[17] In his teaching materials, Marty included excerpts from Isabel Lebourdais's 1966 best-selling book arguing that the Truscott case was a miscarriage of justice.[18] No Canadian publisher was at first willing to publish this book, and, when it was published in England, some lawyers and judges called for Lebourdais to be prosecuted for contempt of court. In a display of academic independence and freedom, Marty included excerpts from the controversial book in his innovative teaching materials.[19]

Marty moonlighted and researched evidentiary issue for GA Martin when he represented Truscott on a reference to the Supreme Court of Canada. Marty taught evidence and did not hesitate to include aspects of evidence and procedure in his first-year criminal law course. Over the sole dissent of Justice Emmett Hall, the Supreme Court upheld Truscott's conviction.[20] Marty's daughter, Jenny Friedland, had better luck. She was on the legal team that won Truscott's acquittal in 2007 on another discretionary reference of his 1959 murder conviction.[21] Marty was concerned about wrongful convictions long before Canada's seven commissions of inquiry confirmed their reality and long before the Supreme Court of Canada decided in 2001 that the risk of wrongful

---

16 Between 1976 and 2005, the United States executed twenty-two juveniles. Half of the executed were Black, and all were executed in former Confederate states. 'Executions of Juveniles in the US 1976–2005,' online: *Death Penalty Information Centre* <deathpenaltyinfo.org/policy-issues/juveniles/executions-of-juveniles-since-1976>. The US Supreme Court finally ruled that the execution of juveniles was unconstitutional in 2005. *Roper v Simmons*, 543 US 551 (2005).

17 And when he gave a lecture at Harvard, he stressed what was distinctive about Canada, including the influence of its parliamentary system on gun control. Friedland, *My Life in Crime*, supra note 6, ch 14.

18 Isabel LeBourdais, *The Trial of Steven Truscott* (Toronto: McClelland & Stewart, 1966). She skirted Canada's restrictive laws by interviewing the jurors in the case.

19 Friedland, *Cases and Materials*, supra note 15.

20 *Re Truscott*, [1969] SCR 309.

21 *Re Truscott*, 2007 ONCA 575.

convictions made it unconstitutional to extradite fugitives to face the death penalty.[22] Marty's experience shows how legal academics who document injustice can persuade legislatures and courts to address it.

C. *Miscarriages of justice and the true crime trilogy*

My favourite quote from Marty's vast oeuvre appears in the preface of his first true crime history, *The Trials of Israel Lipski*. It states:

> This story will place one trial in the context of the social, political and economic conditions of the time. A trial may in theory be an objective pursuit of truth, but in practice there are many subjective factors which influence the course of events. Justice may in theory be blind, but in practice she has altogether too human a perspective.[23]

Marty would later describe this book as being linked to his own family's roots. It 'involved emigration from Eastern Europe and anti-Semitism' and was 'a way of personally understanding the struggles of those seeking a better life in a new country and the fate of those who remained.'[24]

Israel Lipski, a twenty-two-year-old Jewish immigrant to England, was arrested and charged with murder after being found unconscious in a locked room with Miriam Angel who had been killed with nitric acid poured down her throat. After Judge James Fitzjames Stephen summed up the evidence in a manner unfavourable to Lipski, the London jury took only eight minutes to convict him, rejecting Lipski's claims to the police that two other men had killed the victim.[25] Lipski could not testify at the time, but he did not even enter an unsworn statement at his trial. One factor was that it would have had to be translated from Yiddish.[26]

Both the trial judge and the home secretary opposed the commutation of Lipski's death sentence. They assumed that Lipski's motive was sexual. Those who unsuccessfully campaigned for Lipski's reprieve argued, in the language of the Victorian times, that the 'lust' motive was unfair and inaccurate given 'no outrage had been committed on

---

22 *United States v Burns and Rafay*, 2001 SCC 3.
23 Friedland, *Trials of Israel Lipski*, supra note 3 at 11–12.
24 Friedland, *My Life in Crime*, supra note 6 at 18.
25 Friedland, *Trials of Israel Lipski*, supra note 3 at 99.
26 Ibid at 96.

the woman.'[27] The *Pall Mall Gazette* argued in a lengthy series of articles that Lipski was innocent and should not be hanged.[28] Scholars after Friedland would comment on the critical role that the media played with respect to miscarriages of justice. The eventual creation of the Court of Criminal Appeal in 1907 was a largely unsuccessful attempt to avoid re-trial by newspaper in controversial cases.[29]

Lipski's case may have delayed the creation of the Court of Appeal because of a last-minute confession he made after consulting with a rabbi. The confession explained that his motive was to steal money. Long before they became a growing field of study for both psychologists and lawyers, Marty speculated that Lipski's confession may have been false and made to place London's Jewish community in a better light. He also noted that Lipski may have preferred death to life imprisonment under harsh conditions. Lipski's confession and hanging did not stop growing anti-Semitism. The next year, some blamed the Jack the Ripper murders on Jews, even writing Lipski at the scenes of the crimes. The Lipski case was soon followed by restrictions on Jewish immigration to England. Marty's understanding of injustice and miscarriages of justice was broad. He did not follow the American focus on factual and proven innocence by arguing that Lipski was innocent.[30] He suggested that the truth will never be known. At the same time, he concluded that 'if the trial had been properly conducted, the jury might well have found a reasonable doubt about his guilt.'[31]

The next book in his true crime trilogy told the case of Valentine Shortis, an Irish immigrant to Canada who killed two men in a robbery. The trial judge did not change the trial's venue even after a crowd had tried to lynch Shortis. Another injustice was that the word 'and' had been wrongly inserted by Parliament between the two arms of Canada's codified insanity defence instead of an 'or.' This made it more difficult for Shortis and his expert psychiatrist witnesses to establish the

---

27 Ibid at 109.

28 Ibid at 140.

29 Richard Nobles & David Schiff, *Understanding Miscarriages of Justice* (Oxford: Oxford University Press, 2000) [Nobles & Schiff, *Understanding Miscarriages of Justice*].

30 For an exploration of the origins of the American focus on proven factual innocence and its relation to a moralistic approach to criminal justice, populism, and mass imprisonment, see Kent Roach, *Justice for Some: A Comparative Study of Miscarriages of Justice and Wrongful Convictions* (Cambridge, UK: Cambridge University Press, 2026) chs 2, 6 [Roach, *Justice for Some*].

31 Friedland, *Trials of Israel Lipski*, supra note 3 at 204.

insanity defence. A mixed jury of six francophones and six anglophones rejected the insanity defence, and Shortis was convicted of murder.

Shortis, unlike Lipski, had his death sentence commuted because his parents were wealthy and had political connections with the governor general's wife. It was not an entirely happy ending. Shortis was imprisoned for forty-two years. Part of this time was spent in appalling conditions in the Kingston Penitentiary. Shortis also served time in Guelph where he was free to roam the grounds and visit the town unattended. Despite his exemplary prison record and clean bills of mental health, Shortis was Canada's longest-serving prisoner when he was released a few years before his death after serving forty-two years or, as Marty notes, 15,071 days.[32] Injustice for Marty included harsh or unnecessary punishment.

Marty's third true crime book involved the 1902 New York City conviction of a lawyer, Albert Patrick, for killing his wealthy client, William Rice. He raised the issue that Rice's death may have been accidental.[33] Marty was ahead of his time as both the American and Canadian registries of wrongful convictions record that between 40 per cent and one-third of remedied wrongful convictions involve imagined crimes that never happened.[34] Patrick's trial featured an inflammatory appeal by the prosecutor to the jury that crime was rampant and that 'we are nearing the point of anarchy.'[35] It also featured testimony by incentivized witnesses and competing handwriting experts. In the end, Patrick lost his appeal in a four-to-three decision, even though one of the judges in the majority had a conflict of interest.[36]

The New York governor commuted Patrick's death sentence in large part because three judges had dissented so strongly.[37] As in the other two cases, the criminal process was closely related to the political process. Patrick opposed his commutation because he wanted a free and full pardon to vindicate his innocence. He eventually received one.[38] Alfred Dreyfus had also reluctantly accepted a pardon after his second

---

32 Martin L Friedland, *The Case of Valentine Shortis* (Toronto: University of Toronto Press, 1986).

33 Martin L Friedland, *The Death of Old Man Rice* (New York: New York University Press, 1994) at 182 [Friedland, *Death of Old Man Rice*].

34 Kent Roach, *Wrongfully Convicted: Guilty Pleas, Imagined Crime and What Canada Must Do to Safeguard Justice* (New York: Simon and Schuster, 2025) chs 4–6 [Roach, *Wrongfully Convicted*].

35 Friedland, *Death of Old Man Rice*, supra note 33 at 212.

36 *People v Patrick*, 74 NW 843 (1905).

37 Friedland, *Death of Old Man Rice*, supra note 33 at 323.

38 Ibid at 332, 342, 356.

wrongful conviction but, like Patrick, craved and eventually obtained a fuller exoneration. Innocence consciousness was a thing even before DNA exonerations. Marty started writing the book thinking Patrick was guilty but became convinced that given the frailties of the expert evidence in the case that Patrick 'was probably not guilty of murder,' though he may have been guilty of stealing money from Rice.[39] Marty's research agenda has consistently concerned itself with injustice broadly conceived. It is no coincidence that, in the cases Marty studied, Lipski, the immigrant Jew, was hanged while the more advantaged, Shortis and Patrick, were saved from the noose.

II. Comparative miscarriages of justice

Marty's true crime trilogy underlined the universal dangers of the death penalty and harsh imprisonment. They also revealed differences between England, Canada, and the United States and a Canadian advantage in comparative law. England's blurred separation of powers is revealed by how involved the trial judge was in the Home Secretary's decision to allow Lipski to be hanged. The press played an important role in Lipski, confirming what Richard Nobles and David Schiff have written about conflicts between an English legal system that values finality and the media that has its own particularistic discourse of innocence.[40] Today, there are similar conflicts. The fact that the English Court of Appeal refused leave to former nurse Lucy Letby to appeal her conviction for murdering babies in her care has not stopped the press and experts, including a retired University of Toronto neonatologist Dr Shoo Lee, from questioning her guilt. Her case is not over, but I expect that, as in Lipski's case and 'unlike a fictional mystery novel, there will be no "solution" to the case.'[41] Marty was aware that the truth in true crime was often illusive.

The New York book is the longest of the three books in part because Patrick was able to engage in multiple rounds of litigation seeking postconviction relief in state and federal courts. All of this litigation still failed Patrick. It was the executive that pardoned him. This confirmed the importance of Marty's broad approach to the criminal process that examined all branches of governments and the role of the media and interest groups. This approach is no longer fashionable, but it still serves legal academics well.[42]

---

39 Ibid at 377.
40 Nobles & Schiff, *Understanding Miscarriages of Justice,* supra note 29.
41 Friedland, *Trials of Israel Lipski,* supra note 3 at 205.
42 Kent Roach, 'What's New and Old About the Legal Process' (1997) 47 UTLJ 363.

Shortis's death sentence was only commuted by the governor general after a federal Cabinet concerned with French/English relations split on whether to commute the sentence. In his most recent book, Marty picks up on the role of politics and continues the story in relation to the hanging of Louis Riel after the Conservative government refused to commute his death sentence. The different treatment of Shortis and Riel contributed to the Conservative's defeat in the 1896 election.[43] It is also consistent with the message of Marty's true crime trilogy. The most disadvantaged are hanged, and the more advantaged, such as Shortis with his wealthy parents and connections to the Governor General, are not. Marty's understanding of miscarriages of justice included inequalities.

III. A multidisciplinary research agenda with humility and respect for the entire university and the legal profession

Although I was familiar with Marty's work, it was not until I started research for this article that I appreciated the breadth of Marty's multidisciplinary approach. *Detention before Trial* could have been written by a criminologist. It was a bold experiment in empirical research that paid off. Empirical research is both difficult and risky. As Marty admits in his autobiography, he is not that sure that untenured professors, as he was at the time of the research, should take such gambles today.[44]

Marty and I worked together on an empirical study and comparison of criminal justice in Niagara Falls, New York, and Niagara Falls, Ontario. I recall taking students to visit Kingston Penitentiary and Attica Prison with Marty and being in a lockdown in the latter. Marty stressed experiential learning before it was in vogue. Marty and I spent many weekends riding with the police on both sides of the border. Our most important finding was that there were many more police on the American side. This resulted in far more minor charges such as disorderly conduct. We expressed a preference for the Canadian approach where there were fewer police, and they reacted more to calls for assistance rather than generating their own business. We also concluded that the economics of policing and the law in action, more than the prospect of enforcing a bill of rights, influenced police behaviour.[45]

---

43 Friedland, *Canadian Criminal Law*, supra note 2, ch 2.

44 Friedland, *My Life in Crime*, supra note 6 at 60–1.

45 Kent Roach & Martin L Friedland, 'Borderline Justice: Policing in the Two Niagaras' (1995) 23 Am J Crim L 241. This inspired my subsequent research on policing. Kent Roach, *Canadian Policing: Why and How It Must Change* (Toronto: Delve Publishing, 2022). We also concluded that juries were much more widely used in New York than

A. *Where Marty and the Arthurs report differ on multidisciplinarity*

Long before the 1983 Arthurs report, Marty had followed its advice to 'turn to more fundamental studies using historical, theoretical, comparative and empirical approaches.'[46] Marty and Harry Arthurs were classmates and friends, and both did much to elevate Canadian legal scholarship. Despite these broad similarities, there are important differences between Marty's approach to the multidisciplinary study of law compared to that laid out in the influential Arthurs report. The Arthurs report had very little to say about the broader university other than pointing out that law professors' research was often not up to university-wide standards and that law professors did too much consulting. When it looked to the university, the Arthurs report looked exclusively to the social sciences and humanities. Marty's approach was broader. As befitting a person who was the long-serving chair of the University of Toronto Press's manuscript committee and wrote its history, Marty looked to the entire university. As a criminal lawyer, Marty appreciated the role that medical and other professional experts played in criminal trials.

B. *The legal profession needs the assistance of multiple disciplines*

From its first pages, the Arthurs report voiced its firm conviction that the legal profession appeared uninterested in legal scholarship. It also expressed scepticism of law reform work done in the law schools for governments. It argued that there 'inevitably will, and should' be a 'tension between the humane-intellectual goals of a law faculty and its professional-training activities.'[47] In contrast, throughout his career, Marty has engaged with the profession on a wide variety of law reform projects, including conditions in remand centres, legal aid, military and national security law reform, and discipline in the judiciary. He has frequently engaged in research for public inquiries such as the McDonald Commission on the Royal Canadian Mounted Police and the Somalia Commission of Inquiry.

Ontario and left more to their own devices. Martin L Friedland, 'Borderline Justice: Choosing Juries in the Two Niagaras' (1997) 31 Israel L Rev 120. For my subsequent research on juries, see Kent Roach, *Canadian Justice, Indigenous Injustice: The Gerald Stanley and Colten Boushie Case* (Montreal and Kingston: McGill-Queens University Press, 2019) ch 5.

46 Arthurs, *Law and Learning*, supra note 4 at 157.
47 Ibid at 49.

As noted above, Marty's 1968 innovative teaching materials on criminal law and procedure included a case study of the Steven Truscott case. In addition to exposing students to the possibility of injustice, this case study exposed them to the multidisciplinary reality of the practice of criminal law by featuring contested expert evidence in forensic medicine and other forensic sciences. Marty was also influenced by Lebourdais's 1966 book, which argued that Dr John Penistan's estimate of the victim's time of death was based on assumptions about digestion of stomach contents that were not supported by any 'textbook in use in our universities.' She supported this conclusion by surveying the leading treatises on forensic medicine.[48] She also interviewed one of the jurors who convicted Truscott who stated that Dr Penistan 'was tops' because he did not need notes to testify.[49] Marty understood that a good criminal lawyer often had to have multidisciplinary competence and assistance from those in different parts of the university.

When Marty asked me to join the casebook, I insisted that we replace Truscott with a case study of Donald Marshall Jr's wrongful conviction assisted by the then new and revolutionary report of the public inquiry that concluded that Marshall was wrongfully convicted in part because he was Indigenous. Marty indulged me, recognizing that for me the Marshall case stirred a similar passion as he had for the Truscott case. It was only later in 2007, when I served as the research director for the Goudge inquiry into forensic pathology, prompted by multiple wrongful convictions caused by Charles Smith's faulty forensic pathology evidence, that I finally appreciated the wisdom of Marty's multidisciplinary ways and how forensic medicine and science were critical parts of the criminal justice system. The current controversy over Lucy Letby's convictions in England and her application to the Criminal Cases Review Commission on the basis of new medical evidence underlines how criminal justice depends on proper understandings of multiple disciplines.[50]

---

48 Isabel Lebourdais, *The Trial of Stephen Truscott* (Toronto: McClelland & Stewart, 1966) at 68. Including excerpts from the book was potentially controversial given that there had been calls for Lebourdais to be cited for criminal contempt for writing the book and arguing that Truscott's conviction was a miscarriage of justice.

49 Ibid at 74. She also noted that 'the word "consistent" was frequently used during the trial … as though it had incriminating implications' when it did not. Ibid at 201. This ambiguous word was also used in the wrongful convictions caused by Charles Smith, the Guy Paul Morin case, and, most recently, that of Kathleen Folbigg in Australia.

50 *Letby v Rex*, [2024] EWCA Crim 748 at para 191 (denying the request to hear new evidence from Dr Shoo Lee). Statistical evidence should also be included. See Christian Yates, 'Experts Have Challenged the Medical Evidence against Lucy

It is a mistake to dismiss the profession as being all about law: the actual practice of law is deeply multidisciplinary. Rather than following the Arthurs report and dismissing the profession as uninterested in scholarship, the modern law school could assist lawyers to find and understand expert witnesses who are often featured in some of the most complex criminal, commercial, family law, and Charter litigation. The Goudge Commission recommended that the University of Toronto host a centre on forensic medicine and forensic science and reflected developments that stressed the need for more research into all the forensic sciences.[51] William PM Kennedy's law department had a psychiatrist teach students about the mental disorder defence.[52] Alas, there are no similar courses in today's law faculty. Today's faculty embraces Arthurs's vision that we should focus on excellence in the social sciences, especially economics, and the humanities, especially philosophy.

C. *It takes a university: Marty's broad and humble approach and his multidisciplinary collections*

I was first introduced to Marty's work as a politics and history undergraduate at the University of Toronto through his edited 1975 collection *Courts and Trials*.[53] It may have been the first book about law that I bought. It has stood the test of time, even if my disintegrating paperback copy has not. Marty's preface explained that the essays in the 1975 collection were taken from talks given at the Faculty of Law that were

---

Letby: What About Statistical Evidence?' *The Conversation* (7 February 2025). For my arguments that psychiatric evidence might also be helpful, as it was in the Folbigg case, in countering the impact of Letby's notes of self-blame, see Roach, *Justice for Some*, supra note 30 at 406–8.

51 Honourable Stephen Goudge, *Report on Pediatric Forensic Pathology*, vol 3 (Toronto: Queens Printer, 2007) at 298. On the scientific weaknesses of the forensic sciences, see National Academy of Science, *Strengthening Forensic Science in the United States: A Path Forward* (Washington, DC: National Academies Press, 2009). On the relevance of this report to Canada and the Goudge Commission, see Kent Roach, 'Forensic Science and Miscarriages of Justice' (2010) 50 Jurimetrics 67.

52 William Kennedy also 'hired' Kenneth Gray, a lawyer who was also a psychiatrist to teach for free a criminology course on the medical aspects of insanity. Martin L Friedland, *Searching for W.P.M. Kennedy* (Toronto: University of Toronto Press, 2020) at 199–200. Marty arguably one-upped Kennedy by bringing Northup Frye across Queens Park Circle. See Northup Frye, 'Crime and Sin the Bible' in Martin L Friedland, ed, *Rough Justice: Essays on Crime in Literature* (Toronto: University of Toronto Press, 1991) 3 [Friedland, *Rough Justice*].

53 Martin L Friedland, ed, *Courts and Trials* (Toronto: University of Toronto Press, 1975) at ix [Friedland, *Courts and Trials*].

designed 'to show that non-lawyers can make a significant contribution to the study of legal institutions.'[54] The collection included contributions from two philosophers (one writing from a psychoanalytic perspective on the Truscott case), two political scientists, a mathematician, an economist, a sociologist, and a historian. Marty conceded that 'there are obvious gaps' in the line-up that he assembled, noting that an anthropologist would have been an asset.[55] Still, this represented a diverse lot. Indeed, it is a more diverse lot than represented in most law faculties. Marty also demonstrated humility[56] in recognizing that the contributions were multidisciplinary as opposed to interdisciplinary because 'we are still a long way from an effective integration of the experience of different disciplines in the study of legal problems.'[57]

Marty would follow this recipe of inviting true outsiders to the law faculty to contribute to most of the subsequent multidisciplinary collections that he edited. I think this is still a good strategy both in making the law school more aware of what is out there in the larger university and demonstrating to those outsiders that the law faculty is genuinely interested in their work. If law faculties attempt to replicate the expertise found throughout the university, they will fail to do so. To be sure, the richer law schools may make room for a handful of philosophers, economists, and maybe even a historian or a political scientist. But this is short of the breadth of *Courts and Trials*. Also note that the focus of the 1975 collection was on courts and trials. In other words, Marty invited those from different disciplines to train their distinct disciplinary insights on a fundamental legal phenomenon. This also helped to ensure that the overall result would still be of interest to law professors, law students, and the legal profession.

In 1989, Marty edited *Sanctions and Rewards: A Multidisciplinary Approach*.[58] Only three of its ten chapters were written by law professors. Other chapters were contributed by professors of anthropology,

---

54 Ibid at ix.

55 Ibid at xi.

56 On the importance of humility as an ethical value, see John Borrows, *Law's Indigenous Ethics* (Toronto: University of Toronto Press, 2019) ch 4. I have argued that humility taken from the seven gifts of the Anishnaabe is an important safeguard against wrongful convictions. Roach, *Wrongfully Convicted*, supra note 34 at 350–1. For arguments about the importance of humility and its relation to multidisciplinarity, see C Thi Nguyen, 'Self-Trust and Epistemic Humility' in Jennifer Cole Wright, ed, *Humility* (Oxford: Oxford University Press, 2019) 325.

57 Friedland, *Courts and Trials*, supra note 53 at xi.

58 Martin L Friedland, ed, *Sanctions and Rewards: A Multidisciplinary Approach* (Toronto: University of Toronto Press, 1989).

business, history, psychology, sociology, and politics. Again, this is broader than the disciplines represented in most law schools. The collection was the first stage of a project on sanctions and rewards in the legal system. In his preface, Marty suggested that sociology, economics, psychology, anthropology, and political science could all contribute to our understanding of deterrence. He looked to business studies for inspiration about how the legal system with its reliance on sanctions could make better use of rewards. This was a thoroughly pluralistic approach.

The second collection to emerge from this project included more academic lawyers, perhaps reflecting the success of the Arthurs report. Nevertheless, it continued to draw from criminology, economics, and sociology.[59] Marty's chapter on traffic safety, written with Michael Trebilcock and myself, relied heavily on the insights of public health epidemiologists who, unlike lawyers, focused on the most practical way to prevent or mitigate harm (such as airbags and rumble strips) rather than deterring bad or drunk driving. We were influenced by Fraser Mustard, who was a founding member of the McMaster medical school, and William Haddon, another medical doctor who founded the National Traffic Safety Agency in the United States and who had advocated for air bags as a way to reduce harm from inevitable car crashes.[60] I subsequently used this public health approach and the Haddon matrix used in injury prevention and epidemiology in my own work on counter-terrorism, including the still under-appreciated example of how better evacuation routes after the 1993 bombing of the World Trade Centre saved thousands of lives on 9/11.[61] Lawyers can learn much from other professions.

Marty was interested in literature but, again, had the humility to defer to the specialists in the English department who wrote all the chapters in his 1991 collection *Rough Justice*.[62] The essays relate some literature to law reform, including laws against duelling. It also discussed Walter Scott's recognition in 1808 of the complexities of comparative law, including the differences between English and Scottish

---

59 Martin L Friedland, ed, *Sanctions and Rewards in the Legal System* (Toronto: University of Toronto Press, 1990) [Friedland, *Sanctions and Rewards*].

60 Martin L Friedland, Michael Trebilcock & Kent Roach, 'Regulating Traffic Safety' in Friedland, *Sanctions and Rewards*, supra note 59.

61 Kent Roach, *September 11: Consequences for Canada* (Montreal and Kingston: McGill-Queens University Press, 2003) ch 7.

62 Friedland, *Rough Justice*, supra note 52 at xvii.

legal systems and his still relevant argument that 'it is only in its natural soil ... that the tree may be expected to flourish.'[63]

The essays revealed the importance of studying the entire criminal process if only because, as in his three true crime novels, 'the quest for a commutation' was 'often a more dramatic process than the investigation and trial.'[64] Many of the chapters returned to the theme of miscarriages of justice, indicating that the criminal law was often a form of 'rough' justice, both in convicting the innocent and failing to convict the guilty. Truth in both true and fictional crime was illusive.

Marty's multidisciplinary approach drew on expertise and resources within the larger university, including insights from professional business and medical schools. Marty's edited collections of essays reveal much about his broad approach to multidisciplinary studies and his humility in relying on outside experts and not thinking that the modern law school can or should replicate the riches of the entire university.

D. Access to the law and artificial intelligence

Marty has taken well, indeed better than me, to the move to electronic databases. He tried to use early computer technology in his 1965 study of *Detention before Trial* but, in his autobiography, had admitted that the computer cards for six thousand cases never actually made it to the computer and were sorted by hand.[65] Again, a refreshing instance of humility. After he left the Law Reform Commission of Canada to take up the deanship, Marty continued to work on what is perhaps that commission's most innovative research. The topic that Marty took on was the challenging one of increasing the ability of non-lawyers to have access to, and understand, the law. Again, Marty took a broad multidisciplinary approach. He worked with those from library science, linguistics, the political scientist (the late) Peter Russell, and Tony Doob, a trained psychologist and former chair of the University of Toronto's Centre of Criminology.

In his 1975 book *Access to the Law*, Marty proposed that legal advice be made publicly available in libraries 'so citizens can determine their rights and obligations without necessarily first going to lawyers.'[66] He also contemplated that police officers, civil servants, and accountants be

---

63 Ibid at xvii.
64 Ibid at xxi.
65 Friedland, *My Life in Crime*, supra note 6 at 96.
66 Martin L Friedland, *Access to the Law* (Toronto: Carswell, 1975) at 183.

able to make use of this advice, as intermediaries. He tried to promote links rather than barriers between law and other professions, including non-elite professions such as policing and accountancy. Marty revived work on the project in 2002. He concluded that, while primary sources of law can be found on the Internet, 'the law is one of the last institutions to take significant advantages of the Internet to provide reliable information to the layperson.'[67] Unfortunately this project stalled because of lack of funding. The partners who Marty sought to work with included legal aid and the new Law Commission but not the Law Society, which might have been concerned with the unauthorized practice of law.

The access to the law project again demonstrated Marty's great intellectual curiosity about what other disciplines and technology can bring to the law. It also showed Marty as being concerned more with the public interest than the interests of the legal profession. Indeed, he argued that 'it is surely wrong in principle to preserve the law in a form that only lawyers can find and interpret. We should not require high priests to keep the law.'[68]

Access to the Law may seem old-fashioned in its reference to libraries, but it remains relevant to current work on artificial intelligence and the law. Marty wisely recognized that, while new technologies cannot be ignored, the root of the problem of access to the law is not technology but the law itself. He looked to linguistics in order to change the drafting of statutes to make them easier for laypeople to understand. The focus on the law as opposed to technology also engaged the interests of lawyers who might be uninterested and even a little scared by technology.

Marty's unfinished project on access to the law could today be taken up by those interested in the use of artificial intelligence. Investment in multidisciplinary clusters could possibly be a new route to implementing Marty's vision of a broad approach to multidisciplinary studies and engagement with different professions, including engineering and computer science. My colleagues Abdi Aidid and Benjamin Alarie devoted a chapter of their recent book to 'Towards Universal Legal Literacy.'[69] They examine the possibility of a 'legal singularity' in which legal answers are easily within reach. They focus more than Marty did on the challenges that more accessible law presents for the legal profession. Nevertheless, they share Marty's concern expressed half a

---

67   Ibid at 189.

68   Ibid at 6.

69   Abdi Aidid & Benjamin Alarie, *The Legal Singularity* (Toronto: University of Toronto Press, 2023) ch 7.

century ago that law remains unnecessarily complex, unaffordable, and unknowable.

As Marty wisely reminded us fifty years ago in *Access to the Law*, it will take more than technology, even artificial intelligence, to make the law more accessible. There is a danger that electronic databases and now artificial intelligence will become a way to manage, rather than reduce, the complexity of law. As Marty suggested, what is needed is more fundamental changes to the nature of law to make it more accessible to ordinary persons. The radical changes to law that are necessary are not without dangers. Hopefully, the insights of the entire university will be brought to bear on any project to simplify law.

More and more people today are self-represented and likely lost in the complexity of the law. This makes Marty's Access to Law project urgent. Law schools that ignore the combined crisis of unaffordable legal services and overly complex law strike me as being akin to the tuxedoed band that played on as the Titanic sunk. In an admirable display of academic independence, Marty stressed in 1975 that, while the interests of the legal profession are relevant, they should not be determinative. The legal academy should not ignore or disparage the legal profession, but it should also not cater to it.

E. *The Charter and legal complexity*

The law has become much more complex since 1975. Marty was perhaps the first of still only a few Canadian law professors who have questioned whether reliance on complex and voluminous Charter litigation has actually improved criminal justice. As a person who grew up with the Charter, I was originally sceptical of Marty's heretic view. As with other matters, I have come to appreciate the wisdom of his approach.[70]

Marty was not opposed in principle to the Charter, but his legal process approach recognized the limitations of relying on the judiciary as the dominant criminal justice regulator. Codified police powers like those found in England have the potential to give both the police and individuals a better understanding of what can and cannot be done. They can also require the collection of statistics which are necessary

---

70 Marty, who played a role in helping draft the *Charter* and wrote early article on the legal rights in the *Charter*, observed in 2007 that for 'the majority of law professors,' the *Charter* 'has taken the place that Holy Scripture once occupied.' Friedland, *My Life in Crime*, supra note 6 at 281; *Canadian Charter of Rights and Freedoms*, Part I of the *Constitution Act 1982*, being Schedule B to the *Canada Act 1982* (UK), 1982, c 11.

to determine the extent to which police powers are exercised in effective and discriminatory ways.[71] Michael Code's thesis written under our joint supervision made a strong case about the merits of legislative, rather than judicial, regulation of speedy trials.[72] Nevertheless, we continue to rely on Charter litigation as the main way to regulate both the police and the length of trials. In his most recent book, Marty concludes that the Charter has had a positive effect on criminal justice, but he laments that 'Parliament has backed away from filling in the details of criminal law, procedure, and the law of evidence.'[73]

IV. The future of Marty's injustice-based and multidisciplinary research agendas

There will never be another Marty, but it is important to explore the viability of his research agenda and multidisciplinary approach to scholarship in the future. Marty's injustice-based research agenda may survive. An important task for law schools is to illustrate what is wrong with our legal system. As a former dean, Marty has been acutely aware of the incentives provided to faculty. In my view, it would be a mistake to follow the Arthurs report and discourage consulting on issues of public concern, which are often triggered by well-publicized injustices and miscarriages of justice. I fear that modern law schools may be following the Arthurs report and devaluing engagement with the injustices and concerns of the day in what the Arthurs report condescendingly called *"recherches ponctuelles"* as opposed to *"recherche sublime."*[74]

Marty agreed with the Arthurs report that legal scholarship needed elevating and needed to learn from other disciplines. He did more than his share of such work. But he also exercised his freedom to move from topic to topic and to engage in the issues of his times, including through consulting work both with Stephen Truscott's defence and with many law reform efforts. His example demonstrated that such an approach is more than compatible with academic excellence. *Detention before Trial* showed that the Arthurs report was wrong to dichotomize fundamental research and law reform research. Marty documented injustice so that we could have a more just bail system, underlining the close relation between fundamental research and law reform.

---

71 *Police and Criminal Evidence Act 1984* (UK), c 60.
72 Michael Code, *Trial within a Reasonable Time* (Toronto: Carswell, 1992).
73 Friedland, *Canadian Criminal Law*, supra note 2 at 204.
74 Arthurs, *Law and Learning*, supra note 4 at 144–5.

I am less optimistic about the future of Marty's wide-ranging and pluralistic approach to the multidisciplinary study of the law. The Arthurs report has moved law schools closer to the social sciences and humanities. Given the limited resources that are available, it is perhaps not surprising that economics and philosophy have emerged as the dominant cognate disciplines. Many other disciplines and professions are under-represented. The gap between law schools and the professions has grown considerably since the Arthurs report. Marty's broad multidisciplinary approach includes, but goes beyond, the social sciences and the humanities. It includes disciplines such as medicine, nursing, social work, forensic science, business, policing, and engineering, which are left out of the Arthurs report's vision of humane professionalism. Marty's scholarship points to an approach to multidisciplinarity that could build more informed and critical linkages between the practice of law and other professions. It represents a path not yet taken, but one that could assist the modern law school in developing more respectful, humble, and rewarding intellectual relationships with both the entire university and the legal and other professions.

5 Professor Alan Mewett on Morality and the Criminal Law

BRENDA COSSMAN

Alan W Mewett was one of Canada's most distinguished legal scholars in the fields of criminal law and evidence. His iconic status extended beyond academia, influencing judicial reasoning, legal education, and public policy in Canada. He quite literally wrote the book on criminal law, co-authoring the first Canadian criminal law textbook and shaping the foundation for modern Canadian legal thought. Much could be written about Mewett's lasting contribution to Canadian criminal law, but, in this article, my focus will be on his view of the relationship between criminal law and morality. In his 1962 article 'Morality and the Criminal Law,' published in the *University of Toronto Law Journal* (*UTLJ*), he argued that 'the criminal code is not and should not be a moral code with criminal sanctions attached.'[1]

The 1960s were a heady time for debates about morality and law. The 1957 Wolfenden report had recommended the decriminalization of homosexuality in the United Kingdom as well as significant legal reforms to prostitution laws.[2] The report argued that the function of law was not to enforce private morality but, rather, to prevent harm. It laid the groundwork for the decriminalization of homosexuality in England and Wales through the Sexual Offences Act 1967.[3] It also sparked a major legal and philosophical debate about morality, law, and individual freedom. In what would become known as the Hart-Devlin debate, Lord Devlin, in his 1959 work *The Enforcement of Morals*,

---

1 Alan W Mewett, 'Morality and the Criminal Law' (1962) 14:2 UTLJ 213 [Mewett, 'Morality'].
2 Departmental Committee on Homosexual Offences and Prostitution, *Report of the Committee on Homosexuality and Prostitution*, by John Wolfenden (London: Her Majesty's Stationery Office, 1957) [*Wolfenden Report*].
3 *Sexual Offences Act 1967* (UK), c 60.

opposed the recommendations of the report, arguing that society had the right to enforce morality through law, even in private matters, because shared morality is essential for societal cohesion. In his view, immorality such as homosexuality and prostitution threatened the very moral fabric and cohesion of society. HLA Hart countered in 1963 in *Law, Liberty, and Morality* that law should not enforce private morality unless it caused harm to others.[4] In Hart's view, moral disapproval did not justify criminalization.

Enter Alan Mewett. While he did not directly engage with the Hart-Devlin debate, his writings were of a piece with the zeitgeist of the moment, aligning in spirit with the Wolfenden report and Hart's position on the relationship between morality and law. Even before the *UTLJ* article, Mewett had written not only on the appropriate scope of the criminal law but also, quite specifically, on how sexual offences in the Criminal Code should be reformed.[5] His recommendations for reform were nothing short of revolutionary for the time. His work would become a touchstone in the subsequent arguments for decriminalization, and he would later testify before the Standing Committee on Justice and Legal Affairs while Parliament was debating the omnibus bill of May 1969 to partially decriminalize homosexuality and abortion. In this article, I discuss Mewett's work arguing for removing private morality from the regulation of sexual offences. I suggest that the reforms and the principles he articulated continue to have purchase for the legal regulation of sex and sexuality today. My article joins the theme of looking forward by looking back in arguing that Mewett's ground-breaking scholarship from the late 1950s and early 1960s can continue to guide our thinking of the relationship between sexual morality and the law.

I. 'Sexual Offences in Canada'

In 1959, Mewett published 'Sexual Offences in Canada' in what was only the second volume of the *Criminal Law Quarterly*, a journal he would go on to edit for over thirty years.[6] He argued that the sections dealing with sexual offences in the Criminal Code, long influenced by religious and traditional morality, should be reformed to better reflect

---

4 HLA Hart, *Law, Liberty, and Morality* (Stanford, CA: Stanford University Press, 1963).

5 See also Alan W Mewett, 'The Proper Scope and Function of the Criminal Law' (1960–1) 3 Crim LQ 371; Alan W Mewett, 'Sexual Offences in Canada' (1959) 2 Crim LQ 21 [Mewett, 'Sexual Offences']; *Criminal Code*, RSC 1985, c C-46.

6 Mewett, 'Sexual Offences,' supra note 5.

a modern, rational approach. He began the article by observing that 'there really is not much in the way of sexual activity which a person can definitely do without at least the possibility of running counter to some section or other of the Criminal Code.'[7] He then provided a list of the relatively few ways that sex could legally take place between a man and a woman:

> (a) Both parties fully realize the nature of the act; (b) No force or fraud is used; (c) Both parties are of the requisite age; (d) The act takes place in private; (e) But not in an establishment devoted to such purposes; (f) No children are present; (g) The parties are not within the degrees of affinity; (h) No money changes hands; (i) The act takes the form of coitus per vaginam only.[8]

He noted that a tenth requirement that the parties be married did not make it into the Criminal Code, though it was not by lack of trying: 'As late as 1857, attempts were made in the Imperial Parliament to have adultery and fornication declared crimes, but the projected legislation was never passed.'[9] After reviewing these exceptions from sexual offences, Mewett concluded that virtually all other forms of sexual activity were criminalized:

> In broad classifications we can say that the following are sexual offences: (a) By males only: rape, intercourse with under-age females, intercourse with females under his control or who are mentally retarded, and any sexual assault. (b) By males and females: all anal intercourse, all grossly indecent acts, incest, and all offences relating to procuring, pimping, brothel-keeping, etc.[10]

Mewett then argued that three points underlay the current state of sexual offences in Canada. First, 'that the Code, even today, is based upon a 19th century supposition that a woman has no sexual impulses or desires.'[11] Sexual advances, and, thus, in turn, sexual offences, could only be initiated by men. Second, 'that we are – or rather that we were – preoccupied with the irrational horror of homosexuality, but

---

7 Ibid.
8 Ibid at 22.
9 Ibid.
10 Ibid at 26.
11 Ibid.

again only primarily as between males.'[12] Mewett saw in the Wolfenden report evidence that society was moving away from this preoccupation with 'superstition … giving way to rationality.'[13] Third, and, for him, the most significant, was 'the horror of anything which is not generally done – that is, which is not "normal" – even between females and males.'[14] Mewett argued that it was now time to sweep away these views – and laws – from another age. While criminal law would still need to regulate sexual activities, it should do so as little as possible. In his view, there were four grounds for intervention in the sexual activities of private individuals: '(a) Violence or fraud; (b) Corruption of youth; (c) Exploitation of the weak; and (d) Violation of the rights of others.'[15] He then elaborated on each of the grounds. First and most obviously, sex through violence or force was rape and appropriately criminalized. That said, he noted that it should be a gender-neutral offence: while men may be more likely to commit the offence, it should apply to men and women alike.

Second, he turned to sex with anyone 'too young … to know what he or she really wants' or to know what is right and wrong for them. Rather than basing this on the capacity to consent, Mewett spoke of preventing 'corruption' – the language of the day – youth would be corrupted by this sexual contact. And this focus on corruption led him to make a distinction between heterosexual and homosexual acts: 'Homosexuality is unquestionably undesirable, even although this does not mean that it should be legislated against.'[16] Reflecting the sentiment of the time, Mewett conceded that homosexuality was regarded as 'undesirable.' But, in his view, this should not lead to legislation against all of it but only that which may 'corrupt youth.' For him, that meant that any homosexual acts between a person over the age of twenty-one with a person under the age of twenty-one should be criminalized. But where both parties are over twenty-one, or both under twenty-one, the offence should be removed, making his recommendations differ slightly from the Wolfenden report.[17] It is noteworthy that Mewett slipped his recommendations for decriminalizing homosexuality into a discussion of preventing the corruption of youth. On the age of heterosexual sex, he argued for retaining the age rules that anyone under the age of fourteen

---

12 Ibid.
13 Ibid.
14 Ibid at 27.
15 Ibid at 28.
16 Ibid at 29.
17 Ibid.

is incapable of sexual intercourse. The law at the time prohibited sexual intercourse between a male over the age of eighteen and a female (not his spouse and of previously chaste character) between the age of fourteen and sixteen. He argued that should remain, but a similar provision should be adopted to prohibit sexual intercourse between a female over the age of twenty-one and a male (not her spouse and of previously chaste character) between the age of fourteen and sixteen.

The third ground for legal intervention was to prevent the exploitation of the weak. Mewett argued that the law should intervene when individuals are vulnerable to exploitation, particularly those who are 'mentally deficient' or in relationships where power imbalances exist, such as between parents and children or guardians and wards. He also discussed prostitution within this ground. While critiquing outdated notions about prostitution (the 'Victorian notion of the prostitute as a fallen woman, oppressed by some wicked procurer'), he suggested legal intervention is appropriate to prevent one person compelling a second person 'to indulge in sexual activities with a third person, and the offence may be increased in gravity if the offender receives any payment, directly or indirectly, for the services performed.'[18] Lastly, he argued that legal interference in sexual activities is justified when they infringe upon the rights of others, supporting restrictions on public sexual acts, nuisance establishments, and intrusive solicitation to prevent annoyance or harm. Based on the third and fourth principle – exploitation of the weak and violation of the rights of others – prostitution could be regulated based on compulsion or nuisance, but not morality.

Mewett then provided a draft of the revised Criminal Code provisions dealing with sexual offences. Most sexual offences would remain, though, in his view, they should be rationalized. While his desire appeared to be the removal of the sexual morality of the past, much of his revision remained steeped in the discourse of the past: from 'indecent assault' to sex with a young person 'of previous chaste character' to 'illicit sexual intercourse.' But his proposed revisions did contain significant changes. Women would no longer be immune from being charged with sexual offences, although the age at which women would be charged was higher than for men (twenty-one years versus eighteen years). The existing provision on buggery and gross indecency would be repealed, but so too would the age of consent for these sexual offences be different for same-sex and opposite-sex acts. He would also provide specific definitions of various sex acts, such as sexual intercourse and

---

18 Ibid at 30.

gross indecency 'since generalities in sexual matters are only meaningful in the context of the particular morality of the person having to interpret the generalities.'[19] The Criminal Code should eschew '[w]ords and phrases such as "indecent," "sexual immorality" or "vice"' as much as possible.'[20]

Notwithstanding the gender, age, and sexual orientation distinctions that remained, as well as the enduring morality-soaked language, to which I return below, it was a noble and, indeed, radical effort for the time. Perhaps most notably, and also notwithstanding the language of the 'unquestionable undesirability' of homosexuality, Mewett's proposed reforms would have decriminalized homosexual sexual acts between persons over the age of twenty-one. It was a theme to which he would continue to return. I would also suggest that his insistence that criminal intervention in the sexual lives of citizens rest on the four grounds he enumerated – violence, corruption, exploitation, and protection of the rights of others – foreshadowed a far more progressive transformation in the understanding of sexual offences. While Mewett did not articulate it as such, these grounds could be reframed to focus the criminal law of sexual offences on issues of consent and the capacity to consent. Indeed, much of his discussion and recommendations focused on the challenges of the capacity to consent: when were individuals either too young, too 'mentally feeble,' or too 'weak' to consent to sexual activity? I will return to these grounds as harbingers of changes that would come and changes that were still to come.

II. 'Morality and the Criminal Law'

Mewett began his 1962 article 'Morality and the Criminal': 'It is not yet axiomatic that the criminal law does not punish sin, or that the criminal law is not a regulator of morals.'[21] His article then argues that it should in fact become so. In this piece, Mewett made explicit what was implicit in his argument in 'Sexual Offences in Canada': that the Criminal Code should deal 'only with acts which are demonstrably socially harmful.'[22] Mewett focused on offences premised on moral corruption – that is, where the criminal law sought to prevent the moral corruption of others. These corruption of morals offences included a mix of

---

19 Ibid at 35.
20 Ibid.
21 Mewett, 'Morality,' supra note 1 at 213.
22 Ibid.

sexual and non-sexual offences, including gambling, alcohol, and drug use. 'Many sexual offences,' Mewett noted, were 'premised upon the assumption that the victim or accomplice may be corrupted by the act.' For the offences of sexual intercourse with a girl between the age of fourteen and sixteen, and the seduction of females between sixteen and eighteen, the female must be of 'previously chaste character.' The harm lay in her corruption since if she was not of previously chaste character there would be no offence: 'Similarly, the rationale of many homosexual offences is the fear of proselytization and perhaps this fear plays a large part in the retention of otherwise anomalous offences,' citing to his earlier article.[23]

Some offences were directed at the corruption of children;[24] others at the corruption of the public more generally such as obscenity. Noting the reforms to the obscenity provisions of the Criminal Code, Mewett observed that the test would 'still revolve around the syllogistic principle of *R. v. Hicklin* whether it is likely to deprave and corrupt those whom it is likely to deprave and corrupt.'[25] The prohibitions on obscenity and crime comics were both, in his view, based entirely on corrupting the minds of those into whose hands the materials would fall. Other offences seeking to prevent the corruption of others included the prohibitions on bawdy houses, gaming houses, lotteries, and various offences dealing with prostitution and gambling. But Mewett did not argue that all these activities should be decriminalized. Rather, he distinguished between those offences that only sought to prevent corruption from those offences that sought to protect the public from 'what is outrageously offensive or indecent.' In his view, 'things which are publicly offensive may be crimes, not because of their morally corrupting effect, but because of their general social offensiveness.' The 'essentially public nature' of gambling and bawdy houses, which were seen as public nuisances, should be understood then not as preventing corruption but, rather, as protecting the public from that which is 'outrageously offensive or indecent.'[26]

Mewett turned again to the Wolfenden report on the function of the criminal law, which was to 'preserve public order and decency, to protect

---

23 Ibid at 216.
24 For example, then section 157 of the *Criminal Code,* supra note 5: 'Everyone who, in the home of a child participates in adultery or sexual immorality ... and thereby endangers the morals of the child.'
25 Mewett, 'Morality,' supra note 1 at 218, citing the Minister of Justice and G Arthur Martin's views.
26 Ibid at 220.

the citizen from what is offensive or injurious, and to provide sufficient safe-guards against exploitation and corruption of others, particularly those who are especially vulnerable because they are young, weak in body or mind, inexperienced, or in a state of special physical, official or economic dependence.'[27] The challenges then arose in four areas: 'drinking, gambling, narcotics, and illicit sexual practices.'[28] He described these activities as 'indulgences' that are generally desired. Here, he argued, the law should not be seeking to prevent the indulgences per se because they are immoral but, rather, the undesirable consequences of engaging in them. Prohibiting acts simply because they are immoral would lead, in his view, to its own undesirable consequences, including the proliferation of underground criminality:

> To declare something illegal because it is immoral before considering whether it will flourish in spite of its illegality is to ascribe to the law a power it does not possess. Criminally to proscribe immoral acts because they are immoral but which will flourish in spite of – or perhaps because of – their immorality is necessarily to drive such acts underground with all the resultant consequences.[29]

Mewett argued that isolated acts that may be considered immoral but are not harmful to society should not be criminalized because they are immoral: 'Thus adultery and fornication are not crimes, nor drinking, nor prostitution, nor gambling, nor the actual taking of a proscribed drug.' But the law can and should concern itself with 'the socially detrimental excesses and socially detrimental side-products' of these activities. Here, he fully conceded that prostitution, drug addiction, and gambling were socially detrimental. While the act should not be prohibited, it could and should be subject to government regulation. He then specifically turned to the question of whether 'sexual indulgences' should be treated any differently. To address this question, he again considered the distinction between isolated acts which are not harmful and limiting their 'socially deleterious side-effects (the infringement of public decency or order or the opportunity for criminal rackets and so on).'[30] He observed the failure of previous attempts to 'proscribe adultery and fornication.'

---

27 *Wolfenden Report*, supra note 2.

28 Mewett, 'Morality,' supra note 1 at 224. He noted parenthetically that 'the word "illicit" rather begs the question but it is a convenient phrase to cover all forms of sex apart from socially acceptable matrimonial duties.'

29 Ibid at 224.

30 Ibid at 226.

Although a society premised on the family unit might ideally aspire to 'only sanction marital sexual intercourse,' morality should not be the point, and, practically, the law should focus on limiting excess:

> [S]odomy is no more and no less immoral than fornication, and fornication no more and no less immoral than lying or gambling. But the devices for control and limitation of illicit sexual intercourse depend upon the gravity of the harm likely to result to society from excessive indulgence. Adultery is adequately controlled by civil and moral sanctions. Experience has shown that fornication is not a grievous danger and is limited by moral ideals sufficiently.[31]

Homosexuality, he noted, might be different because of the lack of understanding about its potential social harm: 'I am not at all sure that one can talk blandly about homosexual activity between "consenting adult males" when so little is known about the psychological effect of consenting to the specific act but not perhaps realizing the consequences.'[32] On the other hand, he noted that the criminal law did not proscribe 'fornication because the consenting to an act of sexual intercourse by an adult female may have disastrous consequences for her and, ultimately, for society.' The same consideration should be extended to other 'deviations from normal sexual intercourses.' He concluded that, given that homosexual acts will continue regardless of their criminal status, and that they do not have morally harmful effects, 'the law should be more concerned with controlling and limiting the means for indulgence than with declaring the indulgence itself to be illegal.'[33] Mewett ended his essay as he began it: the criminal law should not concern itself with its citizens' moral corruption.

III. Reading Mewett reparatively

As a defence of so-called illicit sexual practices, Mewett's position might, by contemporary standards, leave much to be desired. From 'chaste character,' to 'offensive and indecent,' to the very category of 'illicit sexual practices' (which he admittedly recognized as problematic but deployed nonetheless), his language continued to have a considerable moral hue. So too did his language around homosexuality, in

---

31 Ibid at 227.
32 Ibid.
33 Ibid.

particular. Homosexuality was, in his writing, 'unquestionably undesirable' and a 'vexed problem'; even in relation to private acts between consenting adults, Mewett mused: 'I am not at all sure that one can talk blandly about homosexual activity between "consenting adult males" when so little is known about the psychological effect of consenting to the specific act but not perhaps realizing the consequences.'[34]

Mewett's texts could be read as deeply contradictory, promoting the very moralism he claimed to be against. For example, one mode of reading – a mode that has been dominant in critical theory including critical legal theory – would be to read the text according to a hermeneutics of suspicion – a reading of 'texts against the grain and between the lines, of cataloging their omissions and laying bare their contradictions, of rubbing in what they fail to know and cannot represent.'[35] A similarly critical or 'paranoid reading' could argue that the text reveals the structures and discourses of the homophobia of the day.[36] It could also be

---

34 Ibid.

35 Rita Felski, 'Suspicious Minds' (2011) 32:2 Poetry Today 215. The term 'hermeneutics of suspicion' was coined by the French philosopher Paul Ricoeur to describe what had become a dominant form of reading in political and social theory.

36 Eve Kosofsky Sedgwick, 'Paranoid Reading and Reparative Reading; or You're So Paranoid You Probably Think This Essay Is About You' in *Touching Feeling: Affect, Pedagogy, Performativity* (Durham, NC: Duke University Press, 2003) 123 [Sedgwick, 'Paranoid Reading'] (who developed the idea of paranoid reading, a critical reading practice based on Ricoeur's 'hermeneutics of suspicion,' which reveals and exposes what lies beneath a text, the truth that is hidden within it. Paranoid queer theory provided a set of analytic tools that helped to reveal the deep structures and discourses of homophobia. But it also led to a kind of reading that was negative and rigid; one that did not like surprises; one that relied on exposure sought to reveal deep truths that lay beneath texts. Sedgwick contrasts it with a more reparative reading: '[T]he desire of a reparative impulse … is additive and accretive.' Sedgwick did not provide a blueprint for reparative reading, but she gestured toward different ways of reading:

> To read from a reparative position is to surrender the knowing, anxious, paranoid determination that no horror, however apparently unthinkable, shall ever come to the reader as new; to a reparatively positioned reader, it can seem realistic and necessary to good ones. Hope, often a fracturing, even traumatic thing to experience, is among the energies by which the reparatively positioned reader tries to organize the fragments and part-objects she encounters.

Ibid at 146. As Heather Love has described, '[r]eparation in the essay is on the side of multiplicity, surprise, rich divergence, consolation, creativity, and love.' Heather Love, 'Truth and Consequences: On Paranoid Reading and Reparative Reading' (2010) 52 Criticism 235 at 237. I elaborate on my approach to reparative readings of law in Brenda Cossman, *The New Sex Wars: Sexual Harm in the #MeToo Era* (New York: New York University Press, 2021) [Cossman, *New Sex Wars*].

read as an anti-feminist text, concerned more with the failure to punish women than protecting them and/or protecting them only if they were previously chaste. But I would suggest that this is not how these texts should be read or, at least, not exclusively. I bring a different reading, one that more closely accords with Eve Kosofsky Sedgwick's reparative reading, a mode of reading that seeks to bring generosity, plenitude, and surprise in a text; reading what is in plain sight but often missed.[37] The texts did indeed reflect the discourses of the day – homophobic and otherwise – but, even within them, Mewett's writings were remarkable in both their radicality and foresightedness.

Mewett was undoubtedly deeply entrenched in the ambivalent and, at times, contradictory discourses of the day. While eschewing the role of morality in the criminal law, his views were shaped by the prevailing discourses and debates that continued to rely on deeply entrenched attitudes toward sexual morality. Lord Devlin observed that the Wolfenden report itself retained a role for criminal law in enforcing morality. As Nikola Lacey has argued, it assumed 'a role for criminal law in enforcing morality, as disclosed by its references to reframing the law so as to continue to prevent "the corruption of youth" and to proscribe living from "immoral earnings."'[38] Indeed, its very statement on the functions of the criminal law as preserving decency and protecting the public from offence demonstrated the extent to which the Wolfenden report did not itself reject the role of morality. Rather, the Wolfenden report drew the line between public and private morality and, in the specific context of homosexuality and prostitution, between the public and private commission of these activities.

Indeed, as many critics have since argued, while the Wolfenden report recommended the decriminalization of private acts of homosexuality between two consenting adults, the report was by no means an unproblematic statement of acceptance or liberation. Rather, it was a highly negative attitude toward homosexuality that animated the establishment of the committee, and this was ultimately reflected in the report.[39] The committee was appointed by Home Secretary Sir David Maxwell Fyfe, who was concerned primarily with removing prostitution

---

37 Sedgwick, 'Paranoid Reading,' supra note 36.

38 Nikola Lacey, 'Patrick Devlin's The Enforcement of Morals Revisited' in Chloe Kennedy & Lindsay Farmer, eds, *Leading Works in Criminal Law* (Milton Park, UK: Routlege, 2024) 82 at 85 [Lacey, 'Patrick Devlin'].

39 Derek McGhee, 'Wolfenden and the Fear of Homosexual Spread: Permeable Boundaries and Legal Defences' (2000) 21 Studies in Law, Politics, and Society 65 [McGhee, 'Wolfenden']; Patrick Higgins, *Heterosexual Dictatorship: Male*

from the streets as well as with the embarrassment of recent high-profile prosecutions of homosexual offences.[40] But this was a man who 'regarded homosexuals as "in general … exhibitionists and proselytisers and a danger to others, especially the young."'[41] Lacey describes this period as one that saw the 'beginnings of a shift in the mid-1950s from the vilification of homosexuality as evil or sinful towards a less retributive, though equally problematic, view of homosexuality as a form of illness or pathology,' a shift that 'underpinned both the establishment of the Wolfenden Committee and much of the evidence presented to it.'[42] Alongside the decriminalization of private acts of homosexuality, the Wolfenden report recommended further study into the 'etiology of homosexuality and the effects of various forms of treatment.'[43] The report also suggested preventive measures to 'diminish the incidence of homosexual offenses.'[44]

The Wolfenden report would come to represent a shift away from legal moralism in the criminal law and would become part of an emerging rallying cry for the decriminalization of homosexuality. But it was neither a wholesale rejection of moralism – sexual or otherwise – nor an unapologetic embrace of homosexual liberation. Rather, it sought to create a private space where a newly emergent category of 'good homosexuals' could exist, away from the public eye, and, therefore, away from the reach of the criminal law.[45] While the report

---

Homosexuality in Postwar Britain (London: Fourth Estate, 1996) [Higgins, *Heterosexual Dictatorship*].

40 See McGhee, 'Wolfenden,' supra note 39; Higgins, *Heterosexual Dictatorship*, supra note 39; Lacey, 'Patrick Devlin,' supra note 38. According to Kate Gleeson, Sir David Maxwell Fyfe 'was not interested in altering the laws that criminalised men's homosexual sex, but speculated that if an inquiry were held into prostitution there would be strong criticism if no comparable investigation was made into homosexual offences.' See Kate Gleeson, 'Discipline, Punishment and the Homosexual in Law' (2007) 28 Liverpool Law Review 327 at 331 [Gleeson, 'Discipline'].

41 Lacey, 'Patrick Devlin,' supra note 38 at 96. Fyfe also refused to sit at the Cabinet table when the recommendations of the committee were discussed.

42 Ibid.

43 *Wolfenden Report*, supra note 2 at 147, para 216.

44 Ibid at 147, para 217.

45 Gleeson, 'Discipline,' supra note 40 at 71 (who writes that the committee's promotion of 'the decriminalisation of well-behaved homosexuals and their private sexual activities, as well as the therapeutic manipulation of indiscreet and uncontrolled homosexuals, can be described in terms of what Anna Marie Smith refers to as the promotion of "the good homosexual subject".' She cites Anna Marie Smith, *New Right Discourse on Race and Sexuality: Britain 1968–1990* (Cambridge, UK: Cambridge University Press: 1994) at 207. See also Sebastion Buckle, *The Way Out: A History*

would be deployed, in the United Kingdom and Canada alike, by those advocating for decriminalization, and while it no doubt contributed to the changing public opinion over the decade following its publication, UK and Canadian society continued to experience rampant homophobia.[46]

This was the context in which Mewett wrote his two articles, in 1959 and 1962. His language of things 'outrageously offensive or indecent' and his endorsement of the continued role of the criminal law in regulating non-private conduct – from buggery and gross indecency to obscenity – very much reflected the 'progressive' tone of the day. And Mewett would go on to publicly support the decriminalization of private homosexuality in the Canadian debates. He would appear before the Standing Committee on Justice and Legal Affairs while Parliament was debating Bill C-150 in the spring of 1969. The bill proposed a defence to the criminal offences of buggery (section 147) and gross indecency (section 149): 'Section 149(a): (1) Sections 147 and 149 do not apply to any act committed in private between (a) a husband and his wife, or (b) any two persons, each of whom is twenty-one years or more of age, both of whom consent to the commission of the act.'[47] When asked his opinion of the proposed reforms, Mewett responded: 'There has not been a prosecution in Canada for buggery between consenting adults in private since the revisions in 1953. My view is that it is desirable that the Criminal Code conform with actual practice.'[48] Mewett did not argue for a broader decriminalization of buggery or gross indecency, nor for harmonizing the age of consent for these sexual

---

of Homosexuality in Modern Britain (London: IB Tauris, 2015) (on the distinction between respectable and unrespectable homosexuals embedded in the report, where respectable homosexuals were private and unrespectable homosexuals were 'characterised by their public character, disrespect of the law, and in some cases, paedophilia.' Ibid at 22.

46 See Lacey, 'Patrick Devlin,' supra note 38; Gleeson, 'Discipline,' supra note 40; McGhee, 'Wolfenden,' supra note 39; Higgins, *Heterosexual Dictatorship*, supra note 39. See also Jeffrey Weeks, *Coming Out: Homosexual Politics in Britain from the Nineteenth Century to the Present* (New York: Quartet Books, 1977). On the Canadian legislative debates, see Robert Leckey, 'Repugnant: Homosexuality and the Criminal Family Law' (2020) 70:3 UTLJ 225 at 226 (noting that the 'reform supporters wore their homophobia on their sleeves' and 'even those leading the reforms … laboriously affirm[ed] their disgust for [homosexuality]'); Gary Kinsman *The Regulation of Desire: Homo and Heterosexuality*, rev ed (Montreal: Blackrose Books, 1996).

47 *Criminal Law Amendment Act*, SC 1968–69, c 38.

48 Standing Committee on Justice and Legal Affairs, *Minutes of Proceedings* (13 March 1969) at 341. Most of Mewett's testimony before the Standing Committee addressed the proposed reforms to abortion.

activities with that for other sexual acts. He did not critique the distinction between public and private; indeed, Mewett would become an ardent defender of privacy.[49] He simply stated his support for the partial decriminalization of homosexual acts that occurred between two people in private. Despite the criticisms that have emerged since that time of the limited scope of the 1969 amendments by many that they did not go far enough, or led to the increased prosecution of gay men, or further entrenched the public/private divide,[50] this simple statement of support was a deeply radical act.

Mewett's positions on other sexual offences were also ahead of his time, although in some ways less obviously so. His argument against the reliance on morality in sexual offences was part of an emerging shift from legal moralism to a more liberal, harm-based utilitarian approach to the criminal law.[51] The four grounds that he articulated in 'Sexual Offences' for criminal intervention in private acts – (a) violence or fraud; (b) corruption of youth; (c) exploitation of the weak; and (d) violation of the rights of others[52] – were based in his conceptions of harm rather than morality. Again, Mewett's principles and recommendations for reform very much reflected the legal discourse of the day: corruption of youth, exploitation of the feeble minded, and protection of the previously chaste. But he was seeking to reframe these sexual offences through the lens of harm, admitted harm that remained shaped by the prevailing morality-infused discourses. The four grounds for intervention were his effort at articulating harm. Forcing sex upon another 'unwilling' person was a harm. Sex with a person who was 'too young ... to know what he or she really wanted' was a harm. Sex with a person who was weaker was a harm. This was potentially a broad harm, but the basis for what constituted 'weaker' was not clear: it included those with mental disabilities, it included a parent-child relationship. It also included exploitation by 'pimps and procurers' if the element of 'the exploitation of the weak is present.' Although not articulated

---

49 See Alan Mewett, 'Privacy and Permissiveness' (1971) 14:1 Crim LQ 1 [Mewett, 'Privacy'].

50 See Tom Hooper, 'Queering 1969: The Recriminalization of Homosexuality in Canada' (2019) 100:2 Canadian Historical Review 257 (for the queer critiques of Bill C-150). Contra, see Brenda Cossman 'The 1969 Criminal Amendments: Constituting the Terms of Queer Resistance' (2020) 70:3 UTLJ 245.

51 See Lacey, 'Patrick Devlin,' supra note 38 (on the shifts in criminal law from absolutist, legal moralism to a rationalist, utilitarian harm-based approach, following the Hart-Devlin debate).

52 Ibid at 28.

in those terms, it hinted at inequality. Finally, sex that interfered with the rights of others was a harm. Here, Mewett was referring to 'sexual acts committed in public or in private in the presence of others that may excite, embarrass or annoy.' From sex in public to an establishment where sex occurs or solicitation, this harm was one akin to nuisance, although he did not use that term. These harms – rather than a conservative, Victorian, sexual morality – should be the sole basis for criminal intervention. This articulation of sexual harm in 1959 was a valiant, if incomplete, effort to shift the lens of the criminal law from legal moralism to harm. It would take the Criminal Code a long time to catch up.

We can see in his texts an argument for the reform of criminal law not only through the lens of harm but also through what we would frame today as consent. Mewett did not say much about consent, but the idea of consent – or, rather, the absence thereof – underlies many of his grounds for intervention. Consent was part of the definition of rape in the Criminal Code of the day; rape was sexual intercourse without consent or with consent if that consent was obtained through illicit means.[53] Mewett's reformulation of the rape law, and sexual offences more generally, retained this basic structure. In his proposed revisions of the Criminal Code, he specifically referred to consent for the purpose of rape, and it was its absence that defined the offence.[54] But I would suggest that three of his four grounds for intervention – violence or fraud, corruption of youth, and exploitation of the weak – can be read through the lens of consent. Violence was all about the absence of consent; imposing sex on an unwilling partner. Fraud was

---

53 Section 135 of the *Criminal Code*, SC 1953–4, c 51 (which states: 'A male person commits rape when he has sexual intercourse with a female person who is not his wife, (a) without her consent, or (b) with her consent if the consent (i) is extorted by threats or fear of bodily harm (ii) is obtained by personating her husband, or (iii) is obtained by false and fraudulent representations as to the nature and quality of the act').

54 Mewett, 'Sexual Offences,' supra note 5 at 31 (who proposed rewriting the rape provisions to render them gender neutral, replacing '[a] male person commits rape when he has sexual intercourse with a female person who is not his wife' with any person. Rape was '[a]ny person who has sexual intercourse with another person who is not his or her spouse, (a) without that person's consent, or (b) with that person's consent if the consent (i) is extorted by threats or fear of bodily harm, (ii) is obtained by personating his or her spouse, or (iii) is obtained by false and fraudulent representations as to the nature and quality of the act, is guilty of rape'). Consent, in the Criminal Code at that time and in his proposed revision, was about sex without consent or consent that was inappropriately obtained such as to effectively negate it.

not elaborated; reproducing the extant Criminal Code provisions of the day, he wrote only of 'partners whom he has obtained by fraud.' This too hints at the absence of real consent; a partner who would not have agreed but for the fact that they were tricked into sex. The idea of 'compulsion' also appeared multiple times in his discussion. The corruption of youth and the exploitation of the weak raised concerns about the very capacity of individuals to consent, either because they are too young or too unequally positioned. Mewett's discussion of sex work – that is, 'pimps and procurers' and prostitutes – through the language of exploitation similarly evokes the idea of the absence of consent through compulsion. Although his grounds were not framed in the language of consent, it was its absence that informed three of the four of them.

But, let me be clear, Mewett was not a sexual radical by any means, at least not as that term has come to be understood in feminist and queer circles in the decades that followed.[55] He saw in sex and sexuality the potential for harm; it was simply that harm, not morality, needed to be the basis for criminal intervention. Public nuisances like sex or solicitation in public were the kind of harms against which persons should be protected. Although he was an ardent defender of privacy, Mewett would continue to be concerned with 'public permissiveness,' writing in 1971: 'Permissiveness in private is one thing. I do not care in the slightest what two adults (however they are defined) do in private, or what they read, or what they smoke. ... Permissiveness in public ... is not at all the same.'[56] In the late 1980s, he would wade into the pornography sex wars – ever so slightly – in commenting on the federal government's

---

55 Sex radical feminism and queer theory would develop in the 1980s and 1990s, articulating a positive vision of sex and sexuality. See e.g. Gayle Rubin, 'Thinking Sex: Notes for a Radical Theory of the Politics of Sexuality' in Carol Vance, ed, *Pleasure and Danger: Exploring Female Sexuality* (Boston: Routledge, 1984) 267; Carol Queen, 'Sex Radical Politics, Sex-Positive Feminist Thought, and Whore Stigma' in Jill Nagle, ed, *Whores and Other Feminists* (New York: Routledge, 1997) 125; Cossman, *New Sex Wars*, supra note 36.

56 Mewett, 'Privacy,' supra note 49. The editorial, in its defence of privacy, opaquely referred back to the laws of homosexuality and the need for further reform in this area and others: 'No one is an advocate of the necessity to protect privacy in its real sense more than I. Indeed, I think the law should seriously reconsider various substantive offences which now impinge on privacy, should rethink what is called the age of consent, should wonder what is so bad about three people doing what two can do with impunity, and so on. But the law is moving in the right direction.' Indeed, it was done in part in the language of consent.

proposed reforms to the criminal law of obscenity.[57] Bill C-54 would have prohibited a broad range of categories of sexually explicit material, including material that was non-violent, non-degrading, and did not involve children. In his editorial 'Pornography and Erotica,' Mewett would again express his concerns with privacy and morality balanced with his reservations about sexual permissiveness:

> Whether we are entering a new era of sexual morality or not, the frightening spectre of an uncontrolled and, up to now, incurable AIDS epidemic, has led all governments to embark upon a programme to discourage casual sexual encounters – not for reasons of morality but for reasons of survival. This has added a new dimension to the debate that cannot be answered by glib cliches about getting the State out of the bedrooms of the nation.[58]

The spectre of the sexual harm of the AIDS epidemic created reason for pause and reflection; harking back to the arguments of removing conservative sexual morality from the Criminal Code – and the state from the bedrooms of the nation – was not sufficient. But Mewett followed with his signature concerns about morality: 'No government of the 1980s – at least western government – wishes to be the guardian of private morals and none wishes to be seen in that role.'[59] On the question of regulating sexually explicit materials, he returned to the principles for criminal intervention that he had articulated decades earlier. The state, he argued, should legislate 'against the distribution of materials that encourage or promote activity that conflicts with the underpinnings of our society and while there may be disagreements over the wording, few could reasonably object to the criminalization of themes depicting violence, degradation or

---

57 Alan Mewett, 'Pornography and Erotica' (1987) 29:4 Crim LQ 401 [Mewett, 'Pornography']. Debates on pornography and obscenity raged in the 1980s and 1990s in Canada, with conservatives and some feminists arguing for stricter criminal regulation. Bill C-114 and Bill C-54, introduced by the federal government in 1986 and 1987 respectively, sought to amend the obscenity provisions. Bill C-54 would have introduced categories of prohibited pornography: pornography showing physical harm in a sexual context, sexually violent pornography, 'degrading' pornography, as well as non-violent, non-degrading sex acts. Both bills failed. For a discussion of these debates, see Brenda Cossman et al, *Bad Attitude/s on Trial: Feminism, Pornography and the Butler Decsion* (Toronto: University of Toronto Press, 1997) [Cossman et al, *Bad Attitude/s*]; Dany Lacombe, *Blue Politics: Pornography and the Law in the Age of Feminism* (Toronto: University of Toronto Press, 1994).

58 Mewett, 'Pornography,' supra note 57.

59 Ibid.

exploitation of the weak or young.' But Mewett further cautioned against removing materials that did not involve violence, degradation, or exploitation from the definition of pornography. Doing so, he argued, would allow

> not only depictions of acts acceptable as matters of personal choice and pleasure (and hence solely within the realm of private morality) but also depictions of acts that will unquestionably be seen to countenance, if not encourage, casual sexual encounters, which seems to me rather inconsistent with any programme discouraging casual sexual encounters. This has nothing to do with legislating private morality but everything to do with the pursuit of legitimate, and desirable, public policy.

For Mewett, then, prohibiting sexually explicit materials could be done not in the name of morality but of preventing harm.

This was a proposition that I would subsequently come to harshly critique in the decade that followed.[60] While Bill C-54 would be defeated, much of its spirit returned in the Supreme Court of Canada's decision in *R v Butler*, where the Court defined three categories of pornography – sex with violence, sex that was degrading and dehumanizing, and sex that was not violent, not degrading and dehumanizing, and did not involve children – and found that the first two categories would generally violate the obscenity provisions, while (breaking with Bill C-54) the third would not.[61] My critique was one that built on the spirit – if not the letter – of Mewett's earlier works. Like Mewett, I argued that conservative sexual morality did not belong in the criminal law. But I would take his argument further, arguing that the very categories of degrading and dehumanizing were themselves inherently informed by an underlying conservative sexual morality. I would argue that the Supreme Court's claim to be regulating in the name of harm was really just 'morality in drag.' I doubt very much that he would have agreed with me, and I now regret never having had this conversation with him. My views were informed by a kind of sex radical feminism and queer legal theory that I can only imagine he would not have entertained (although he may well have found it entertaining). But, as I reflect on the corpus of his work on the legal regulation of sexuality, I feel enormously indebted to the areas of inquiry that his work opened and to his refusal to adopt simplistic either/or approaches.

---

60 See Cossman et al, *Bad Attitude/s*, supra note 57.
61 *R v Butler*, [1992] 1 SCR 452.

IV. Conclusion

Alan Mewett was not only ahead of this time,[62] but his writings on criminal law should also continue to inspire our thinking today. His critique of sexual moralism, his foresightedness on issues of harm and consent, and his instrumentalist vision of the criminal law give Mewett's writings on sexual offences continued traction. Long since the Criminal Code was amended to decriminalize homosexuality, lessons can be gleaned about the role of criminal law in the regulation of sexuality. Mewett brought a scepticism to the role of the criminal law; as Kent Roach has written, '[f]or Mewett, the criminal law was a "very heavy-handed way" of protecting people from themselves.' He warned against using the criminal law to try to prohibit the kind of moral 'indulgences' that would continue regardless of their criminalization, serving only to drive these activities underground. Mewett saw potential harms with prostitution and drug use, for example, but not moral ones, and he expressed concern that seeking to prohibit them, not only in public but also in private, would create its own harms.

These words of warning are worth heeding today. Contemporary debates around the criminalization of sex and sexuality – from sex work, to the non-consensual distribution of intimate images, to the regulation of online adult content – would do well to heed Mewett's warnings about the potential for overreach of the criminal law and the need to interrogate the harms underlying sexual offences. There are many reasons to consider the regulation of sex, including those specifically considered by Mewett: violence, exploitation, and the violation of the rights of others. To this, we might add, in today's language, harms to dignity, autonomy, and self-determination. But his work reminds us not to take the criminalization of sexual offences at face value. We should, instead, continue to interrogate the assumptions underlying sexual offences – extant or proposed – to ensure that they are not simply based on morality and on a sense that certain kinds of non-normative sex and sexuality are deemed 'bad' just because they are non-normative.

---

62 Kent Roach in reviewing thirty years of Mewett's editorials in the *Criminal Law Quarterly* has written: 'My dominant impression when reading the editorials is how often they were well ahead of their time.' Kent Roach, 'Thirty Years of Alan Mewett's Editorials' (1998) 40 Crim LQ 257 at 258. Roach was speaking to all of Mewett's writings, on a broad range of criminal law topics, where his legacy has been extraordinary. But the same holds true for his writings on sexual offences, in particular.

I would add that, for me, the legacy of Alan Mewett's work also lies well beyond his interrogation of the proper scope and function of the criminal law *vis-à-vis* sexual offences. He wrote about difficult, controversial issues in Canadian criminal law, including the decriminalization of homosexuality, when no one else in the legal academy was doing so and in the face of widespread opposition. His work should continue to inspire us to be courageous, to push against the orthodoxies of the time, and to ask hard and uncomfortable questions. And to do it with grace and humour.

6 Some Leading Themes in the Contract Scholarship of Stephen Waddams

PETER BENSON

I. Introduction

Among the leading themes in Stephen Waddams's monumental contributions to the development and deeper understanding of modern contract law, there are two in particular that I wish to discuss in this short article. From the beginning to the end of his scholarly career, these themes preoccupied him, and with good reason. For they are truly fundamental. The first concerns the proper significance and roles of equity and common law after their integration in 1875 in a single court. Perhaps even more important for contract law, the second has to do with the meaning and place of principles of contractual fairness in the overall doctrinal framework of contract law, and, more particularly, in relation to the doctrines of contract formation and also the need for certainty and security in contractual transactions.

These sets of questions are of course intimately interconnected, and, with respect to both, Waddams argued, compellingly in my view, for a transformative approach that went against the tendencies of virtually all commentators and even many leading decisions that had dominated the thinking of Anglo-Commonwealth lawyers for at least several generations. Among modern writers on the law of contract, he was pre-eminent in the way in which he systematically challenged and changed our understanding of these matters. And even though Waddams did not present his work as an effort in contract theory, it was also that. Indeed, in my view, it made a lasting contribution, which any theory of contract law henceforth must either build on or risk failing to advance our understanding of the law. His work did this, not by applying to contract law pre-existing ideas and frameworks drawn from philosophical or other theoretical works, but rather, by bringing out more fully the inclusive unities of ideas and principles which he saw animating contract law itself at its most fundamental level.

Perhaps the most abstract, and, therefore, the most inclusive, unity of this kind was what he called the 'concept of contractual enforceability.' Waddams understood both sets of issues noted above as relating to, and, indeed, as specifying, this concept. In the following pages, I shall first present in some detail certain key aspects of his view and then briefly suggest a line of inquiry of my own that builds on his ideas and that may, I hope, further elaborate the concept of enforceability as he understood it.

II. Waddams's arguments

In his 1976 article 'Unconscionability in Contracts,' which the great legal historian David Ibbetson characterized as seminal, Waddams announced his challenge to the long dominant view of contract law with the following opening words:

> Several generations of common lawyers have been educated in the belief that the common law of contract admits no relief from contractual obligations on grounds of unfairness, or inequality of exchange. The rule might seem hard, it is said, in an individual case, but it is justified by the need for certainty and commercial stability, for 'the Chancery mends no man's bargain.' … My view is that the law of contract, when examined for what the judges do, as well as for what they say, shows that relief from contractual obligations is in fact widely and frequently given on the grounds of unfairness, and that general recognition of this ground of relief is an essential step in the development of the law.[1]

In this early piece, Waddams's aim was to bring out the fact that, in many instances – including the contractual enforceability of forfeitures, penalties, deposits, and exemption clauses, the interpretation of contracts and the incorporation of documents, the withholding of discretionary remedies, and the protection of weaker parties – courts have taken into account considerations of fairness between the parties and modified or struck down clauses and even whole agreements on the grounds that

---

1 Stephen Waddams, 'Unconscionability in Contracts' (1976) 39:4 Mod L Rev 369 at 369 [Waddams, 'Unconscionability in Contracts'] (citations omitted). For Ibbetson's assessment, see David J Ibbetson, *A Historical Introduction to the Law of Obligations* (Oxford: Oxford University Press, 1999) at 254, n 58.

the terms are unconscionable, oppressive, or grossly unequal. While this was predominantly the work of the Court of Chancery, it was not exclusively so. Waddams contended that these instances demonstrate conclusively that the fairness of provisions was, and should be fully recognized as, a criterion of their contractual enforceability and that a modern court, being a court of equity and common law, should ensure and further develop this criterion by recognizing a general power to give relief on this basis. In that early article, he chose the term 'unconscionability' as the most acceptable word for this general ground of relief.[2] By recognizing such a general power as an integral part of contract law, courts would not only be able to ensure fairness in transactions, even where the kind of transaction was not already specifically covered by a settled practice of equity or common law – for instance, remedial clauses payable on an event other than breach. By making clear the true rationale underlying these instances of non-enforcement, they would also avoid mechanically striking down clauses or agreements that were not unfair.

In this article, Waddams did not elaborate much on the content of this general principle of unconscionability, apart from noting that a large inequality of the values exchanged combined with inequality of bargaining power would, in his words, go far in suggesting a case for relief. Nor did he engage the still vexed question of the proper understanding of the meanings and roles of equity and common law since the Judicature Acts. As just indicated, his primary aims were to establish the historical and contemporary fact that the fairness of contractual terms – and not just the validity of the process of contract formation – has played an essential role in determining contractual enforceability itself and that, as with other doctrines of contract law, this should openly and fully be recognized as a general principle reflected in, but not exhausted by, past and present judicial practices.

In itself, this was already a signal contribution to our understanding of contract law. Following this early piece and in a series of comprehensive treatises, theoretically oriented books, and numerous important articles on the conceptual underpinnings of contract law, Waddams developed the scope of his basic contentions, giving further specificity to the content of this general principle across the full range of its actual and possible instances. As we will see, he also came to characterize the general power to set aside unfair transactions in a different way. For the purposes of this short article, I will mainly focus on his view as

---

2 Ibid.

presented in what was to be his last, but also, arguably, his most important, theoretical work, *Sanctity of Contracts in a Secular Age*.[3]

In this book, Waddams makes at least two fundamental claims. First, in the face of a still simmering debate a century and a half after the Judicature Acts as to whether there has been partial or complete 'fusion' between equity and law and over what their respective roles should be in a modern unified contract law – a debate that he deems unresolvable in its own terms – he proposes what he calls a 'common or integrated framework of thought' that enables us to transcend the historical and conceptual divide between law and equity in basic contract law. He suggests that this can be done by articulating 'a concept of enforceability as itself containing inherent limits.'[4]

Thus, in contrast to a conception in which the principles of contract formation are treated as the sole necessary and sufficient conditions of enforceability, subject to whatever external and exceptional limits equity and fairness may be deemed to supply, he argues for a unified view that also places considerations of fairness at its very centre in determining whether mutually assented-to terms are to be contractually enforced. According to him, this unified concept of enforceability rests on, and gives full expression to, a notion of justice between the parties in their voluntary transactions. While this unified concept naturally draws on historical equity and incorporates what Waddams terms an 'equitable perspective,' it need not establish or maintain normatively or historically distinct and separate equitable considerations. In fact, he emphasizes that it does and should also integrate understandings of contractual fairness and reasonableness gleaned from common law sources apart from historical equity.

Waddams's key point is that, in addition to the principles of formation, the proposed concept of contractual enforceability includes a further dimension that is best conceived in terms of a general and equally basic power of a court to set aside or modify unfair, oppressive, or highly unreasonable provisions. But how then should this further dimension and power be specified? What content should be given to such notions as highly unreasonable or unfair? And how might this content fit with, or at least not undermine, the requirements of stability and certainty of contracts flowing from the application of settled principles of contract formation? Waddams contends that current contract scholarship and contract theory have not provided a satisfactory

---

3 Stephen Waddams, *Sanctity of Contracts in a Secular Age: Equity, Fairness and Enrichment* (Cambridge, UK: Cambridge University Press, 2019) [Waddams, *Sanctity of Contracts*].
4 Ibid at 159–60.

answer to these questions: the fact that 'no agreed principle can be identified that describes or explains the power of the court to grant relief from unreasonable contracts … must be regarded as a deficiency.'[5] A modern legal system, he says, ought to be able 'to articulate a principle in general terms that reflects the law on this fundamental question, without resorting to perpetually controverted and insoluble historical questions.'[6] The answer he gives in *Sanctity of Contracts* refines and deepens his earlier view.

In striking contrast with his earlier characterization of the needed general principle of fairness, Waddams expressly rejects framing it in terms of unconscionability, with its twin necessary elements of inequality of values and inequality of bargaining power.[7] Nor, he contends, should it be assimilated to an organizing principle of good faith or abuse of rights.[8] While all these doctrines, he certainly thinks, illuminate and instantiate the needed general principle, they do so in different ways and, therefore, do not properly express its content and scope at the highest level of abstraction. In this last book, Waddams specifies the content of this general principle in terms of a general power to modify or set aside terms which, even though they may satisfy the minimally required elements for consideration, would confer, if enforced, a highly disproportionate gain on one party at the expense of the other that cannot be justified on the basis of the gaining party's legitimate contractual interests, the risks reasonably allocated by their agreement or assumed by the losing party, the price paid, and other such contractually relevant factors and considerations. He contends that, independently of paternalistic reasons or the facilitation of party autonomy and cooperation in the pursuit of individual and shared purposes, the law's treatment of such transactional disproportion is justified as a requirement of justice between the parties where, as will always be the case, a court is deciding whether to use its coercive powers to enforce ostensibly agreed terms via law-imposed remedies.[9]

---

5   Ibid at 4. See also Stephen Waddams, *Principle and Policy in Contract Law: Competing or Complementary Concepts?* (Cambridge, UK: Cambridge University Press, 2011) at 117 [Waddams, *Principle and Policy*].

6   Ibid.

7   Ibid at 118–21.

8   Ibid at 122–7. Compare with his earlier discussion of good faith in Stephen Waddams, 'Unfairness and Good Faith in Contract Law: A New Approach' (2017) 80 SCLR (2d) 309.

9   See ibid at 7 and elsewhere. See also Stephen Waddams, 'Autonomy and Paternalism from a Common Law Perspective: Setting Aside Disadvantageous Transactions' (2010) 3:2 Erasmus L Rev 121.

In my view, Waddams's final formulation of his argument for this general power is – and remains – correct and, indeed, compellingly so. To give the reader a better sense of what this idea of contractually unjust disproportionality involves, it will be helpful to present, even if very briefly, a few of the major instances and discussions with which he builds toward this conclusion.

A. *Forfeitures*

Beginning with what was perhaps historically the earliest and most notable instance where courts of equity commonly gave relief are the cases of relief against forfeitures, with the most clearly established case being that of a mortgage of land.[10] This was done even against the unambiguous and express language of their agreement and even where the document was worded, not as a mortgage but, rather, as an outright conveyance of the land, if the court was convinced that the substance of the transaction was in fact a mortgage. In this way, the right to redeem was fully protected as a matter of justice between the parties. The court would not allow the contract to convert a loan into a sale and required that the consequences of late repayment of the loan be commensurate with what the lender should reasonably expect by way of compensation for this delayed repayment and nothing more. Characteristically, Waddams draws on Joseph Story's seminal 1836 work *Commentaries on Equity Jurisprudence*, which says that equity would not allow the borrower to 'suffer an enormous loss, *wholly disproportionate to the injury*. ... Where a penalty or forfeiture is designed merely as security to enforce the principal obligation, it is as much against conscience to allow a party to pervert it to a different and oppressive purpose, as it would be to substitute it for the principal obligation.'[11]

Although the Chancery Court's formulation of the basis for relief was standardly expressed in terms of a want of conscience on the lender's part, this lack of conscience, Waddams emphasizes, was found by the court in the very fact of a lender insisting on the enforcement of terms which he now knows are grossly disproportionate, without

---

10 See his discussion in Waddams, *Sanctity of Contracts,* supra note 3 at 9–15 ff. From the start and in all his subsequent writings, Waddams highlighted this instance of relief against forfeitures. See, for example, Waddams, 'Unconscionability in Contracts,' supra note 1 at 370–3.

11 Waddams, *Sanctity of Contracts,* supra note 3 at 15, 26 ff. See also Joseph Story, *Commentaries on Equity Jurisprudence: As Administered in England and America,* vol 2 (Boston: Hillard, Gray & Company, 1836) at s 1316 [emphasis added].

needing to show any wrongful conduct on his part either leading up to or after contract formation. Nor, importantly, was it necessary to show that the terms resulted from an inequality or weakness of bargaining power suffered by the borrower. As for modern contract law, throughout *Sanctity of Contracts*, Waddams highlights the leading Privy Council case of *Cukurova Finance International v Alfa Telecom Turkey* as completely consistent with, and, indeed, as making fully explicit, the underlying rationale of this equitable perspective.[12] To establish the unjust disproportion, a modern court must assess the contractual provision against the ostensible purpose or substance of the transaction and ensure commensurability between the operation and effects of the provision and the legitimate interest in securing that transactional purpose. The contract should not be a way for the lender to derive 'random and disproportionate profits from trivial [and reasonably compensable] defaults.'[13]

B. Penalties

Waddams suggests that this same approach is evident in both early and modern decisions concerning the contractual enforcement of penalty clauses.[14] The court of equity gave relief from penal bonds, a common form being a covenant to pay a fixed sum of money unless some other act, which might itself involve payment of a sum of money, was performed by a given date. Where the court determined that the bond was, in substance, a means to secure repayment of the loan (even if without an immediate transfer of property to be forfeited), the legitimate interest of the lender was held to be only in the repayment of the principal (along with interest and costs) and no more.

This idea of proportionality, Waddams argues, was effectively made the foundation for relief by the recent UK Supreme Court decision in *Cavendish Square Holding BV v Makdessi*, a case which, more than any other, he discusses repeatedly throughout *Sanctity of Contracts* as demonstrating modern contract law's capacity to incorporate fully and dynamically an equitable perspective, without linking it to what, in his

---

12 *Cukurova Finance International Ltd v Alfa Telecom Turkey Ltd (Nos 3 to 5)*, [2013] UKPC 2, 20, 25. See also Waddams's discussion of the case in Waddams, *Sanctity of Contracts*, supra note 3 at 11–15 and elsewhere.

13 Waddams, *Sanctity of Contracts*, supra note 3 at 15. This same reasoning underpins Cardozo's seminal judgment in *Jacob and Youngs, Ltd v Kent*, [1921] 129 NE 889, 891 (NYCA).

14 Waddams, *Sanctity of Contracts*, supra note 3 at 16. See also the parallel earlier discussion in Waddams, 'Unconscionability in Contracts,' supra note 1 at 373–5.

view, must necessarily remain controverted and inconclusive determinations of equity's historically or normatively distinct meaning and role in contract law.[15] In determining the enforceability of the provision, the UK Supreme Court rejected the traditional tests that mechanically determine whether the clause is a genuine pre-estimate of loss or designed to have a deterrent effect in favour of a new approach that turns on whether the clause is 'extravagant,' 'disproportionate,' or 'unconscionable.' In this context, reasonable proportionality must obtain between, on the one side, the amount stipulated in the clause and, on the other side, the nature and extent of the legitimate contractual interest which, to the reasonable knowledge of both parties at formation, the party claiming under the clause has in the other's performance. In this way, Waddams says, the new rule determining enforceability is no longer presented as independent of the underlying reasons for it. Not only are unfair and grossly unreasonable – because unjustly disproportionate – clauses struck down as unenforceable penalties, but, at the same time, perfectly fair and reasonable clauses are upheld, even if they might have been voided under the older tests of genuine pre-estimate of loss or intended deterrent effect.[16] As formulated by the court, this new approach, Waddams argues, implies an inherent and general judicial power to modify contracts that, even though validly formed, are found to be highly unreasonable.

Sanctity of Contracts considers in-depth other parts of contract law which reflect courts' past and present recognition that, if a particular interpretation of, or a mode of enforcing, the terms of an agreement would result in a striking disproportion between the parties' benefits or burdens of performance, this calls for an explanation: one that can reasonably justify the disproportion on the basis of such factors as the contractually contemplated allocation of risk between the parties, the nature of the contract, the consideration given by both sides, the contract's surrounding circumstances, and so forth.[17] Absent such justification, the interpretation or enforcement of the agreement is liable to be

---

15 *Cavendish Square Holding BV v Makdessi*, [2015] UKSC 67 [*Cavendish Square*]. For discussions of the case, see Waddams, *Sanctity of Contracts*, supra note 3 at 3, 17–18, 118, 156–7, 199–200, 218–19, 223, 228 ff. Although *Cavendish Square* is not mentioned in his earlier books or in 'Unconscionability in Contracts' because it had not yet been decided, Waddams's own suggested analysis of the penalty doctrine in those prior works is precisely the approach which is later reflected in that decision.

16 Waddams notes that the clause at issue in *Cavendish Square* would have failed the older test. See Waddams, *Sanctity of Contracts*, supra note 3 at 225, n 27.

17 Importantly, this is also the very basis on which Bowen LJ grounds his analysis of presumed intent and reason in deciding whether to imply an obligation in a given transaction: *The 'Moorcock,'* (1889) 14 PD 64, 68 (UKCA).

rejected. Given the limits of space, I cannot discuss these other instances here.[18] What I do wish to consider, however briefly, is a major area of contract law that Waddams singles out and critically examines at length for *failing* to reflect this approach.[19] His critical discussion of the current treatment of mistake and frustration, at least by courts in the United Kingdom,[20] is important not only because it points persuasively to a more rational understanding of these key doctrines. In addition, it helpfully illustrates his view that the fusion/fission debate can and should be transcended in this contractual context and explains his call for a new concept of contractual enforceability that would place the perspective of fairness, along with the principles for formation, at its centre.[21]

C. Mistake and frustration

Agreeing with and, indeed, developing George Palmer's seminal analysis of mistake and unjust enrichment, Waddams argues compellingly that the doctrines of mistake in assumptions and frustration must rest on the very same juridical basis: the only difference between them is the timing of the event or facts – existing at or subsequent to the time of formation – about which one or both parties may be ignorant or

---

18 Some further instances discussed in detail in *Sanctity of Contracts* include: the analysis of remoteness, at 72–5; choice of remedies (specific performance, cost of reinstatement, gain-based damages) at 76–90; interpretation and implied terms at 53–69; the enforceability of boilerplate and documents in the digital age at 92–117; and good faith and abuse of rights at 121–7.

19 There are other areas that Waddams sees as also failing to do so. The most striking instance is the approach taken by the UK Supreme Court to contractual interpretation and fairness in *Arnold v Britton*, [2015] UKSC 36 (enforcing a compound escalator clause for calculating a proportionate share of maintenance expenses in long leases of very modest holiday homes). In all of his writings, no decision has been subjected to more devastating and sustained critique than is the majority's approach in that case. In *Sanctity of Contracts*, it attracts the same amount of discussion, though wholly negative, as does *Cavendish Square*.

20 The main target of his criticism is the reasoning (though not necessarily the outcome on the facts) in *Great Peace Shipping Co v Tsavliris Salvage (International) Ltd*, [2002] EWCA Civ 1407 [*The Great Peace*]. See Waddams, *Sanctity of Contracts*, supra note 4 at 35–8, 169–72, 179–80.

21 In-depth discussions of mistake and frustration are extensive in a number of Professor Waddams's writings. See, for example, the full discussions in Waddams, *Principle and Policy*, supra note 5 at ch 5; Stephen Waddams, 'Mistake in Assumptions' (2014) 51:3 Osgoode Hall LJ 749; Stephen Waddams, 'Mistake and Unfairness in Contract Law' in John Goldberg, Henry Smith & PG Turner, ed, *Equity and Law: Fusion and Fission* (Cambridge, UK: Cambridge University Press, 2019) 229. For further discussion, see Waddams, *Sanctity of Contracts*, supra note 3 at 32–8, 166–70, 179–80, 222 ff.

mistaken.[22] Their shared juridical basis, he contends, requires a power to excuse performance in some cases where, as a result of a mistake or ignorance, a party will be compelled to pay for something or to perform an obligation that turns out to be fundamentally different in value or kind from what they had reasonably supposed to receive or to perform and where, very importantly, that party cannot reasonably be held to have assumed the risk of this outcome under the terms of their contract. The underlying aim of both excusing doctrines is thus to avoid a contractually unjustified enrichment or disproportion that can result from mistake or ignorance in these kinds of circumstances. Whether unjust disproportion exists in this context will depend on factors that are specific to the operation of mistake and frustration. Thus, whether or not the contract allocates the risk of the existing or future event can here be decisive. By contrast, the factor of inequality or weakness of bargaining power may normally play little role, if any. Importantly, Waddams emphasizes that both mistake and frustration are best understood as excusing doctrines and, therefore, contrary to the dominant view of nineteenth-century and even some twentieth-century contract law, are distinct from, and cannot be assimilated to, the analysis of contract formation (or discharge). Both should at most render an otherwise enforceable agreement voidable, not void.[23]

Because, according to Waddams, identical normative considerations of justice between the parties underlie both doctrines, he urges that there should be a 'common framework of thought' that deals with both doctrines and integrates them fully with unfairness in contracts.[24] On this basis, he contends that the fact that relief for mistake as to existing facts was originally granted by the Chancery Court, whereas relief from ignorance or mistake as to future changes in circumstances via frustration was developed and refined by common law courts should not affect this basic point. Indeed, if anything, the 'equity-like' approach taken by modern formulations of frustration suggests the irrelevance of this historical difference.[25] For Waddams, the idea of separate and distinct lines of juridical analysis for these excusing situations, whether as between mistake and frustration or between a 'common law' versus an 'equitable' understanding, is untenable from the standpoint of

---

22 George Palmer, *Mistake and Unjust Enrichment* (Columbus: Ohio State University Press, 1962).

23 Waddams, *Sanctity of Contracts*, supra note 3 at 167–70. See his cogent criticism of the approach taken by Lord Atkin in *Bell v Lever Bros Ltd*, [1932] AC 161.

24 Waddams uses this term throughout *Sanctity of Contracts*, supra note 3. See ibid at 170.

25 Ibid at 222–3 ff.

a rational treatment of the relevant issues, at least one that is rooted in a concern to do justice between the parties.[26] 'A common framework of thought for mistake and frustration,' he concludes, 'can *only* be achieved by *transcending*, in this context, the distinction between law and equity.'[27]

D. Unconscionability

In all his writings, starting with 'Unconscionability in Contracts,' Waddams adduces equitable responses to grossly unequal exchanges as settled instances where courts have struck down or modified otherwise valid contracts on the basis of transactional unfairness. Here also, while the doctrine was originally developed by the Chancery Court, its rational basis, he contends, can and should be stated and understood in basic normative terms that need not refer to its historical jurisdictional pedigree. In this context as well, he suggests that the fusion/fission debate can and should be transcended. But he also thinks that certain features of equity's approach remain normatively important for, and should be reflected in, a modern framing of the principle: above all, the idea that unconscionability is a principle of fairness inherent to contractual enforceability which, while remaining irreducible to and distinct from the requirements for contract formation, must be fully integrated in modern contract law.[28]

Here, disproportion takes the specific form of a gross disparity in the values of the items exchanged. Assessing the contract terms in light of the contract's surrounding circumstances and their values relative to going market prices, a court must determine whether such disproportion exists. But this is only one of the prerequisites for deeming a transaction unconscionable. Such inequality of values

---

26 For criticism of *The Great Peace* on these points, see ibid at 35–8.

27 Ibid at 170 [emphasis added]. Note that Waddams's proposal in this book for transcending this distinction is made for these and related areas of contract law only.

28 In addition to the discussion of unconscionability in chapter 7 of *Sanctity of Contracts*, there is a superb account of the principle in Waddams, *Principle and Policy*, supra note 5 at 87–122 ('Unequal Transactions'). See also his short but helpful article: Stephen Waddams, 'Unconscionable Contracts: Competing Perspectives' (1999) 62:1 Sask L Rev 1. It is worth noting that in the recent landmark Supreme Court of Canada decision in *Uber Technologies Inc v Heller*, 2020 SCC 16 [*Uber v Heller*], the majority explicitly endorsed and applied Waddams's understanding of the principle.

is not by itself a sufficient ground for setting it aside.[29] A gross disparity in values exchanged calls for an explanation: can the disadvantaged party be reasonably held to have assumed the risk of the disparity or to have intended the difference as a part-gift? If so, neither equity nor modern contract law normally sets it aside. However, if the disadvantaged party has assented to the terms in a condition of ignorance as to the disparity or out of necessity, because they are lacking practical access to a more reasonable alternative, this will ordinarily negate an inference of assumed risk or part-gift, making the disproportion in values contractually unjustified. With this further factor of impaired bargaining power, the twin prerequisites for unconscionability will be met: there is a gross disproportion that cannot be contractually justified as between the parties. This is something that contract law will not coercively enforce (whether by damages or *in specie*). While the agreement will not be void *ab initio* – because there is consideration on both sides – it may be treated as voidable for unconscionability at the demand of the disadvantaged party.

There are certain core features of this analysis that should be highlighted. First, as Waddams emphasizes, unconscionability should be understood as a principle of fairness that governs the terms of a transaction, even where parties may have assented to those terms in a way that satisfies the doctrinal requirements of consideration and offer/ acceptance. In addition to the principle being distinct from the basic requirements for contract formation, wrongdoing or fault in the usual sense was never, and should not now be, a prerequisite for finding such unfairness. All that is necessary is that there be a gross disproportion that results from the disadvantaged party's impaired bargaining power (through being ignorant of, or not being able to access, a reasonable price generally available) rather than from what reasonably (objectively) appears to be her assumption of risk or donative intent. Where these prerequisites are satisfied, a modern court should not compel enforcement of the terms. In the earlier language of equity, it would be against conscience for the advantaged party to insist on

---

29 Equity sometimes viewed very unequal values as a basis for presuming equitable fraud which itself was an essential basis for giving relief against enforcement. And although such a presumption might be particularly strong, it was always open to the advantaged party to show that, when the transaction was properly and fully understood in context, the terms were in fact just and reasonable or that the disadvantaged party in fact had assumed the risk or intended a part-gift. See the discussion in Waddams, *Sanctity of Contracts*, supra note 3 at 30–2.

enforcement, and a court of equity could not do so for this would be for it to decree inequity.[30]

Thus understood, the aim of the principle is to relieve one party from a contractually unjustified enrichment at the expense of the other. It is not, and cannot be, to protect vulnerable individuals as such or to achieve a fairer distribution of assets and resources.[31] To see why not, it must be emphasized that bargaining impairment is only one of the prerequisites: there must also be a gross disproportion in the values exchanged. Further, and very importantly, impaired bargaining power, involving ignorance of, or lack of access to, the going market prices is contractually relevant not in itself but only insofar as it negates a reasonable inference that the party has assumed the risk of the disparity or intended it as a part-gift. Apart from this, it is normatively irrelevant as a matter of unconscionability. And, clearly, because the principle can at most deny enforcement to an unjustified disproportion between the values exchanged, it cannot change, let alone ameliorate, the pre-existing distribution of assets or resources between the parties: a disadvantaged party is protected only to the extent of not losing the reasonable value of whatever she began with, whether this is much or little or fairly determined when viewed from the standpoint of distributive justice. The principle aims at setting aside contractually unjustified enrichments by one at the expense of the other: not distributive justice but, rather, justice as between the two contracting parties.[32]

Throughout Waddams's scholarly work spanning five decades, the principle of unconscionability figures prominently as the exemplar of a requirement of fairness in modern contract law. As noted earlier, in *Sanctity of Contracts*, Waddams no longer suggests that the general power of modern courts to ensure fairness in contracts be framed abstractly as a power to set aside unconscionable transactions: avoidance for unconscionability now represents for him only a specific, even if a very clear, instance of a general power of relieving from contractually unjustified

---

30 This is how it was put in the anonymous *A Treatise of Equity* (Dublin, 1737), attributed to Henry Ballow, which Waddams refers to at many points throughout his writings. See e.g. Waddams, *Sanctity of Contracts*, supra note 3 at 23–4, 129, 232.

31 See the full discussion of this aspect in Waddams, *Principle and Policy*, supra note 5 at 117–21.

32 As Waddams notes, while consumers may often be vulnerable to unfair terms and bargaining impairment, this can also be true of small businesses, such as franchisees. The power to relieve against unfair contracts should be a general power that is not limited to only certain categories of parties or contexts. See Waddams, *Sanctity of Contracts*, supra note 3 at 128–9.

disproportionate terms.[33] This brings me to what is arguably the central claim throughout all his writing – namely, that such a general power in its many applications can and must be explained not as marginal or exceptional to a conception of contractual enforceability exclusively specified in terms of the principles of formation with their notion of mutual assent but, instead, as fully part of, and integral to, an idea of enforceability that coherently incorporates both aspects, without reducing one to the other.

In keeping with the overall aim of this volume, I wish now to take up this central contention and indicate how, in my view, it might be further worked out and vindicated. To show this effectively, however, it would be necessary to explain how this holds for each of the different manifestations of this general power, taking each in turn with its distinctive features and requirements. That would clearly be beyond the scope of this short article. Given the particular importance that Waddams attributed to unconscionability as an exemplar of this general power, I will do this by discussing the relation between unconscionability and the long-settled formation requirement of consideration. Can they be shown to cohere in a unified concept of contractual enforceability as he envisaged it? The next and final part attempts to provide the beginning of an answer.

III. Between unconscionability and consideration

It is by no means clear that the doctrines of unconscionability and consideration can fit together as inherently fundamental aspects of one integrated concept of contractual enforceability. Unconscionability, with its explicit focus on the fair proportionality between the two sides of the parties' exchange, and consideration, with its stated indifference to precisely such questions of adequacy and so to this entire dimension of fairness, would seem rather to be mutually exclusive or at least in basic tension with each other. Indeed, with the notable exception of Waddams and a handful of other contract scholars, this was and

---

33 In connection with Waddams's treatment of forfeitures and mistake/frustration, we saw that not all determinations of contractually unjust disproportion rest on the existence of impaired bargaining power as an essential or even a relevant factor. Hence, as he rightly concludes in his later work, a general power to set aside unfair transactions has to be characterized at a higher level of abstraction than in terms of unconscionability with its twin specific requirements of unequal values and bargaining impairment: unconscionability (and, for different reasons, good faith) cannot serve as the organizing idea for contractual unfairness. See ibid at ch 7.

continues to be, in some form or another, the prevailing assumption of most commentators and contract theorists.[34] To see why this prevailing assumption may be mistaken and how the two doctrines might be integrated into one conception of enforceability, it is essential to keep in mind what consideration requires and also the limits of what it requires.[35]

The prevailing assumption that the two doctrines are mutually incompatible presupposes that the prerequisite of consideration is to ensure that contractually enforceable agreements be bargains in the sense of being economic exchanges of values and that the role of contract law is to enforce such bargains.[36] Not only must all non-formal agreements (for example, those not under seal) satisfy consideration for there to be contract formation, but this requirement is viewed as sufficient for such agreements to be contractually enforceable. Consideration is thus taken to be not only a necessary but also a sufficient basis of enforceability. Thus, any principle of contractual fairness – whether deriving historically from equity or common law – must count as a derogation from – and, hence, as an exception to – this fundamental analysis. On this view, unconscionability would seem to set aside perfectly valid and fully enforceable agreements on the basis of a criterion that imposes what a court takes to be a fair exchange of values, not the exchange of values that was freely chosen by the parties themselves. Unconscionability inherently interferes with the parties' freedom of contract and the security of transactions freely entered into.[37]

It is unnecessary, however, to view the requirement of consideration in these terms. We know that non-commercial agreements that do not

---

34 Along with Professor Waddams, other prominent contract scholars who developed an alternative view of the nature and place of contractual fairness in the overall framework of contract law include John Dawson and James Gordley.

35 The following discussion draws in part on, but also tries to clarify, what I wrote about consideration and its relation with unconscionability in Peter Benson, *Justice in Transactions: A Theory of Contract Law* (Cambridge, MA: Harvard University Press, 2019) at ch 1, 4.

36 Both Lon Fuller and Charles Fried, perhaps the two most influential modern contract theorists, make this assumption explicitly. Fuller sees this as a reason for endorsing consideration, whereas Fried views it as a basis for rejecting it. For Fuller, see Lon Fuller, 'Consideration and Form' (1941) 41 Colum L Rev 799 at 815. For Fried, see Charles Fried, *Contract as Promise: A Theory of Contractual Obligation*, 2d ed (New York: Oxford University Press, 2015) at 29, 35ff.

37 Highly influential earlier statements of this view, critically discussed by Waddams, are those by Pollock and Anson. See Waddams, *Sanctity of Contracts*, supra note 3 at 164.

contemplate exchanges of economic equivalents can perfectly satisfy consideration. More fundamentally, this interpretation runs counter to the core of what that doctrine actually stipulates and does. While the doctrine of consideration requires that non-formal promissory relations satisfy a rigorous and definite kind of reciprocity between the parties, it ascertains whether this relation of *quid pro quo* obtains not merely without comparing the exchange values of what each side promises the other but, even more, without referring to and leaving wholly undetermined this entire dimension of exchange value. In short, the doctrine of consideration says nothing at all about the matter of relative values.

Stated positively, the doctrine requires merely that each party's promise be made for something requested by that party that is to be provided by the other party in return for the first party's promise. The consideration must be *substantively* some item (whether a thing, service, right, and so on) that the first party can reasonably be viewed, in the context of their interaction, as wanting to have or to enjoy in virtue of that item's particular concrete qualities. This is true even when the item requested and wanted is money – as in my promise of a horse for your one hundred dollars. Here, the money requested counts and functions as consideration because (and insofar as) it is wanted for its use as a universal means of purchase, as distinct from being a crystallization or measure of exchange value. When the doctrine refers to consideration as something having 'value' in the eye of the law, it is as such *use value* only.

Inasmuch as each party's promise must be made for consideration so understood, each party, in the standard scenario of mutual promising, is viewed as requesting and wanting the other's promise of something of value, which is moved by that other party in response to and in return for that of the first. Each side is viewed at formation as both receiving from the other the consideration that they have requested and also as moving to the other their own consideration which the other party has requested: each both receives and gives consideration as part of a unified two-sided movement. This is a strictly two-sided and purely reciprocal relation: neither side's promise has any contractual significance or effect as a promise unless it is joined with the other's promise in this way.

My major contention is that the role of consideration is simply and necessarily to establish this kind of intrinsically two-sided reciprocal promissory relation: this and nothing else or more. Now, for there to be two sides, the only comparison needed with respect to the substantive contents which each party promises the other as consideration is that the consideration promised by one must be qualitatively different from the consideration promised by the other party. Only thus can one party be reasonably viewed as having requested the substance of what the other promises as something wanted in return. But how large or small each side is in terms of any metric of value is irrelevant: what counts is simply that there be something promised for something else. This means that, so far as the requirement of consideration is concerned, it is both unnecessary and without any doctrinal basis to hold that its requisite relation of *quid pro quo* supposes that the parties view what each promises the other as being in any way equivalent in terms of exchange value. The latter dimension of exchange value is simply not part of the required analysis.[38] Thus, the kind of 'bargain' relation required by consideration is juridical, not economic.

The fact that the requirement of consideration does not ascertain or concern itself with the dimension of exchange value represents the doctrine's limited aim and scope. But this does not necessarily imply that this dimension must therefore be rejected or viewed as irrelevant within contract law's complete framework. Nor that it must be excluded by the doctrine of consideration itself. It means at most that such a concern is not part of determining whether there has been contract formation in the narrow sense of establishing that there is a potentially enforceable agreement, instead of a set of gratuitous promises that are simply void *ab initio*. Contract law may include other principles that make this dimension relevant and, indeed, essential from their own standpoint and role within the complete framework. Building on Waddams's scholarship, clearly unconscionability is one such principle. If so, how does it stand *vis-à-vis* consideration in light of our discussion of each of these doctrines and can the two fit harmoniously together? As I will now suggest, they work together jointly in tandem as distinct yet mutually compatible and fully integrated determinations of whether an agreement should be contractually enforced. Neither the contractual enforceability of an agreement nor even contractually effective mutual assent is reducible to what satisfies the requirements of contract formation alone.

Summarily stated, the requirement of consideration ensures that there is a certain kind of two-sided promissory relation which is then further specified by the principle of unconscionability so as to reflect

---

38 The leading nineteenth-century writers such as Pollock and Anson incorrectly imported this dimension of exchange value into the analysis of consideration, holding that the parties should be taken as viewing the considerations necessary to satisfy contract formation as equivalent in value. See Waddams, *Sanctity of Contracts*, supra note 3 at 164. This mistake is still sometimes made by contemporary writers.

more completely what the parties can reasonably be held to have intended in that promissory interaction. Let me briefly elaborate.

As already discussed, consideration determines that for any non-formal promise to be contractually binding, a party must make it for something else requested by her and coming from ('moved' by) the other party, and, further, this something else must be reasonably viewed as having value in the sense of being wanted by the first party for its particular qualities and uses. Thus, the immediate focus of this requirement is on this other thing which the promisor asks in return for her own promise, *not* on what she herself promises or gives up in turn for that other thing. Each side's promise is viewed and tested on this same basis. Where each party's promise satisfies this criterion, the promises count as mutual promises for consideration, and the two-sided relation required for contract formation is established.

Now, being two-sided, this contractual relation can be 'looked at from both sides at once': not only the other thing, requested by and given in return for the promise, but also and at the same time what the promisor gives for that other thing.[39] This direct relation between what each party gives up for what she gets – and, thus, between the two different considerations promised between them – is the specific focus of unconscionability. But, instead of viewing the two considerations in terms of their *qualitative features and differences*, as is done by the doctrine of consideration, it abstracts from this qualitative dimension and analyses them in the *quantitative terms of equivalence*.

What does this idea of equivalence entail? The general idea of equivalence views two different things as commensurable in some way, despite the qualitative differences between them. There must be two different things, of course. One thing cannot be viewed as commensurable with itself. Starting with this difference, the idea of equivalence then abstracts from the particular qualitative differences between them and supposes that they can be directly compared with each other (and, normally, other things) in terms of how much (quantitively) they embody a certain shared dimension that properly applies to both. In the contract doctrine of unconscionability, the idea of equivalence takes the specific form of commensurability between the two qualitatively different considerations construed in terms of their exchange value.

---

39 This is the way Waddams puts it in *Principle and Policy*, supra note 5 at 121, citing Ernest Weinrib, *The Idea of Private Law* (Cambridge, MA: Harvard University Press, 1995) – in my view, the single most important work in private law theory since Hohfeld. For discussion of Weinrib's work, see Arthur Ripstein's chapter in this volume.

For when viewed in the latter terms, the considerations are no longer analysed for their particular features and differences but, simply, as quantitatively determined embodiments of value that relates them to a common measure and dimension (for example, a going market price where this can be identified) and that holds, relationally, as between them.[40]

In doing this, the principle of unconscionability does not deny the work done by the doctrine of consideration. To the contrary, it presupposes and builds on it. First, the principle applies only if and where there is the requisite two-sided relation established by that doctrine. By viewing the two-sided promissory relation required by consideration under the aspect of equivalence, unconscionability takes it fully to be the kind of relation that it is: a direct relation between the two sides. Second, it builds on the fact that, so far as consideration is concerned, as long as each party promises just some thing for some other thing, it does not matter what in particular they choose to promise. In this way, the doctrine of consideration already construes the subject matter of an enforceable agreement in a way that facilitates the move to abstraction involved in the idea of equivalence. Third, by assessing this subject matter in terms of whether it comprises items that can be moved from one party to the other and that can be used or enjoyed by one party to the exclusion of the other, the consideration requirement characterizes the mutually related considerations as use values, requested and given each for the other, and, therefore, as amenable to being further specified in terms of exchange value. For the latter exists only where things with use value are given over and taken up consensually by and between persons.

But why should contract law, via a principle of unconscionability, presume that parties, as reasonable and rational, care about the comparative exchange values of what they are giving up in return for what they are receiving as between them? For it does seem to presume this. By way of an answer, first, each party can reasonably be presumed to view what she promises for the other's return promise as being a means, which is necessary, to obtain it: each must give up something to get the other's thing. In this way, each party can reasonably be presumed to regard what she promises as having certain purchasing power. This power, at least potentially, can be used to obtain different things, and, in this respect, an exchange value can be assigned to it, as to anything

---

40 In a case of pure barter where, by definition, there are no other comparable units, the terms are necessarily equivalents: each is the measure of the other's exchange value.

else, in relation to other things. But, second, it cannot be reasonably presumed of parties that they are indifferent as to whether they receive less than the value of the purchasing power that they give up. They cannot be presumed, as rational, to be indifferent as to whether they lose all or even some of their means to obtain other things. This is not something, therefore, that either party can reasonably presume the other intends in the circumstances of their relation. But, while this cannot be just presumed by either party of the other, it may be reasonably clear in their interaction that a party does so actually intend, whether by assuming the risk of this subtraction or by intending the difference as a part-gift. This intention, in turn, can only be reasonably inferred where it appears that the losing party knows that the terms are not equivalent in circumstances where she can practically access terms that would be. Where this is the case, the principle of unconscionability will not deny enforceability.

The relation between consideration and unconscionability can thus be put this way. Consideration requires that there is a two-sided promissory relation in and through which parties move from and to each other items that have use value. However, because the dimension of exchange value is irrelevant to satisfying this requirement, enforceable promises can comprise indifferently not only terms that are equivalent in exchange value but also those that are not. In short, any two-sided promissory transaction – but it must be two-sided – along a continuum from exchanges for equivalents to part-gifts can satisfy this requirement of contract formation and, not being void, is potentially enforceable.[41] But no one can reasonably be presumed to give away her own for nothing or for greatly less in return.[42] This is how intent must be viewed objectively or transactionally in two-sided transactions where parties give and take items having exchange value. Consequently, this is how the parties' intent must be viewed with respect to the relation between the considerations promised by each.

As for this relation between the considerations, the principle of unconscionability does not require equivalence per se. Instead, it determines whether a manifest lack of equivalence in exchange values can reasonably be viewed as having been intended by the losing

---

41 Notably, Waddams explicitly makes this very point. See Waddams, *Sanctity of Contracts*, supra note 3 at 38, 157, n 101. See also Waddams, *Principle and Policy*, supra note 5 at 108.

42 Throughout his later writings, Waddams emphasizes this fundamental assumption. For a particularly clear and forceful statement, see Waddams, *Principle and Policy*, supra note 5 at 87.

party. Impaired bargaining power in the form of ignorance or necessity negates such intent. But where the losing party can reasonably be viewed as having assumed the risk of the non-equivalence, or as having donatively intended it as a part-gift, or just affirmed it, the terms will not be avoided for unconscionability.[43] Because the unequal values do not result from bargaining impairment and can be reasonably viewed as intended by the losing party, the enrichment has been voluntarily conferred. There is no basis in justice to impugn it. Whereas promises that fail to meet the requirements of consideration are void because no contract is formed, unconscionability at most renders them voidable if this is necessary to avoid injustice between the parties.

We see, then, the following division of labour between the distinct roles of these two doctrines: on the one hand, consideration ensures just that there is a genuinely two-sided promissory transaction, the terms of which may be indifferently anything from equal exchanges to part-gifts, without determining whether it is any one of these; on the other hand, unconscionability takes the further step of specifying whether those terms can really count contractually (that is, as a two-sided promissory relation satisfying consideration) as either an equal exchange or a gift or some combination thereof, determining this on the basis of the reasonably construed manifest intent of the parties in the circumstances of their interaction. Together, consideration and unconscionability establish, respectively, the possibility and the actuality of two-sided promissory exchange and gift transactions.

To be fully enforceable, then, promises must be reasonably intended as one (or a mixture) of these basic categories of promissory transactions. An exchange of manifestly unequal values that cannot be reasonably viewed as intended because it has been transacted in circumstances of necessity or ignorance qualifies neither as an exchange nor as a gift and is not contractually enforceable against the disadvantaged party despite assents that satisfy the prerequisites for contract formation. As reflected in these fundamental doctrines of contract law itself, the mutual assents that are pertinent to contractual enforceability are thus the assents necessary to infer the genuine existence of the kinds of promissory transactions which both these doctrines of formation and fairness together make possible and ensure. The consensual basis of contract is not reducible to that entailed by the doctrines of formation alone. Even less, it is not some independently free-standing normative

---

43 This approach is explicitly adopted by the majority judgment of the Supreme Court of Canada in *Uber v Heller*, supra note 28.

ideal which contract law must satisfy. The relevant idea of consent in modern contract law – 'the concurrent intention of the parties … necessary to the validity of a contract' – is specified through its doctrines.[44] And these doctrines comprise both those going to contract formation and those ensuring fairness between the parties. Together, they allow contract law to fulfil the lofty claim: 'Qui dit contractuel, dit juste.'[45]

IV. Afterword

In one of his very last published pieces, a sensitive and thoughtful presentation of the life and scholarship of Brian Coote, the prominent New Zealand contract law scholar, Stephen noted that the fact that Coote could have written, but did not, a treatise on contract law was not 'entirely a matter of regret … because, freed from the treatise-writer's attempt (never completely successful) to be comprehensive, he was able, instead, to write more deeply and more cogently on particular issues that commanded his, and hence his readers' interest.'[46] He added that Coote's many articles and notes will be valued and cited long after treatises written during his time are forgotten. This assessment reflected Stephen's exceptionally great and genuine modesty. For he, himself, wrote many excellent and probing articles – too many to list here – not only on all aspects of contract law but also on other areas of private law. But beyond these, he was also the acclaimed author of two major treatises, five outstanding books on contract law and legal history, and more.[47] For me, what is truly remarkable about this monumental lifetime of work is that, through all his writing, which continued right up to the end, Stephen continued to deepen, clarify, and systematize ideas

---

44 From Lord Eldon's unpublished manuscript 'Of the Distribution of Justice in Courts of Equity with respect to Contracts,' quoted in Waddams, *Sanctity of Contracts*, supra note 3 at 27.

45 Originally stated by the late nineteenth-century French philosopher Alfred Fouillée and made famous by the early twentieth-century French contract theorist Emmanuel Gounot. See, Louise Rolland, '"Qui dit contractuel, dit juste." (Fouillée) … en trois petits bonds, à reculons' (2006) 51 McGill LJ 765 (Stephen referred to this adage, taking it seriously).

46 Stephen Waddams, 'Professor Brian Coote (1929–2019)' in James Goudkamp & Donal Nolan, ed, *Scholars of Contract Law* (Oxford: Hart Publishing, 2022) 331 at 348–49.

47 Mention should also be made here of his 'little book' (as he referred to it), Stephen Waddams, *Introduction to the Study of Law*, 8th ed (Toronto: Carswell, 2016), originally published in 1979, and his first book, Stephen Waddams, *Products Liability*, 5th ed (Toronto: Carswell, 2011), originally published in 1974.

that seem to have been with him from the start.[48] And he did so in a prose unmatched for its clarity and elegance. In my view, judged in terms of the depth, breadth, carefulness, and sheer excellence of work, Stephen's scholarly contribution to our understanding of the common law of contract must rank as among the greatest since those of Williston and Corbin.[49] This exceptionally accomplished scholar and thinker always spoke humbly, yet truly, of himself as a student of contract law and, as a professor of thousands as well as a prolific author, invited others to join with him in this shared lifelong endeavour of intellectual discovery which he so cherished. Whether or not we had the privilege of being his students, we can all continue to learn from and with him. His work and example, I am certain, will not be forgotten.

---

48 At the time of his passing in May 2023, Stephen was in the process of completing the draft of a new book, 'Continuity and Change in Private Law: The Equitable Perspective.' The present writer is currently editing the manuscript for publication.

49 Had Stephen's work been done in the United States or the United Kingdom, this would have been much more widely recognized. His *The Law of Contracts* (now in its 8th edition) is outstanding, perhaps the very best, among all the one-volume (that is, post-Williston and Corbin) common law treatises on contract law published anywhere, in virtue of the way it is at once comprehensive, conceptually ordered and analytical, and written with unmatched clarity, simplicity, and elegance.

7 The Law's Own Terms[†]

ARTHUR RIPSTEIN

Rereading Ernie Weinrib's remarkable book *The Idea of Private Law* thirty years after its publication, I found myself reminded of many of its virtues and struck by the various marks it bore of a book of enduring interest and importance.[1] One striking feature is the then prominent literature with which it sometimes engages as points of contrast. Many of those writers provided familiar signposts through which readers of 1995 could orient themselves; today, however, they are largely forgotten. By contrast, *The Idea of Private Law* remains as compelling and illuminating and important as ever.

That enduring importance reflects another mark of great legal, philosophical, and academic writing more generally: its relentless development of a single simple yet powerful idea. Although a wide range of issues figure as points of contrast and elucidation, they are illuminated by its organizing thought, which might initially strike the reader as unremarkable: the key to understanding private law is to focus on the relation between the plaintiff and the defendant. What else, it might be wondered, could be at the heart of private law? Strikingly, scholarship in 1995 (and far too much of it even today) offers any number of different explanations, focusing on the plaintiff alone, on the defendant alone, on third parties, and on broader social concerns. By redirecting attention to the parties before the court in a private law action, Weinrib redirects attention to the parties involved in a private legal transaction,

---

† I am grateful to Chris Essert and Jutta Brunnée for helpful comments, to audience members at the symposium Looking Forward by Looking Back for comments and questions, and, most of all, to Ernie Weinrib.

1 Ernest J Weinrib, *The Idea of Private Law*, 2d ed (Oxford: Oxford University Press, 2012) [Weinrib, *Idea of Private Law*].

the bearers of the rights and duties that are the ultimate subject of private law.

In this short article, I cannot do justice to all of the aspects of *The Idea of Private Law*, let alone to all aspects of the private legal relationship that is its subject matter. Instead, I limit myself to a brief description of the order in which these aspects of the relation develop before turning to a reflection on its distinctive 'internal' perspective. Many of the law's familiar distinctions can be made to look puzzling when an external perspective is assumed, even if it is the external perspective of one or the other of the parties to litigation. Many writers wonder how the law can treat economic losses differently than property damage, or differentially declare intention relevant or irrelevant to liability, or why the defendant's liability should depend on arbitrary factors such as the plaintiff's earning capacity. An internal perspective explains how the law's framing of a question can exhibit a rational form.

I. Plaintiff and defendant

The plaintiff/defendant pair appear together repeatedly throughout *The Idea of Private Law*: as the parties before a court adjudicating a private legal dispute; as the two poles of the relation at the heart of private law; as the bearer of a right and the party bound by a correlative duty; as the sufferer and the doer of a private wrong; as the one who loses and the other who thereby gains; as the thing overlooked by economic analysis and so much other private law scholarship; and as a recurring caution against the reductivist impulse at the heart of so much writing about law, in general, and private law, in particular. Weinrib does not just begin his analysis of private law with this relationship – although in 1995 that alone was a sufficiently novel and unorthodox position as to be noteworthy – but, rather, the entire book works out the implications of it.

By focusing on the relation between the plaintiff and the defendant, Weinrib provides a systematic alternative to the idea that the purpose of private law litigation is to give effect to some goal that can be specified without any reference to private law's distinctive concepts and doctrines. Some of Weinrib's provocative formulations – including the claim that 'the only function of the law of torts is to be the law of torts'[2]

---

2 Ernest J Weinrib, 'The Insurance Justification and Private Law' (1985) 14 J Leg Stud 681 at 686.

and the comparison of private law to love[3] – give expression to the irreducible nature of the law's distinctive concepts. Rather than attempting to explain remedies or court processes by identifying extra-legal goals to which they are conducive, Weinrib's account focuses on the bilateral nature of private law adjudication on the grounds that its subject matter – transactions between private persons – is itself bilateral in just the same way. It is not just that only two parties happen to be before the court; the court's exclusive concern is with those parties because they appear before the court with respect to a transaction involving the two of them. In so doing, he explains why private law has a distinctive mode of ordering that is proprietary to its distinctive subject matter; the grounds for private law claims and adjudication differ from those proper to other modes of legal ordering. The correlative nature of right and duty underlies the transactional nature of wronging, which in turn underlies the transactional nature of tort litigation and so explains why the particular plaintiff recovers from the particular defendant. Neither the plaintiff's entitlement to recover, nor the defendant's liability to pay, is in the service of any purpose other than remedying the wrong the defendant committed against the plaintiff.

Exhibiting the rational structure of private law litigation reveals its structure as a distinctive enterprise of justification. That enterprise in no way generates anything like a libertarian repudiation of any intervention in private law. It is entirely consistent with familiar features of contemporary legal systems, including such things as mandatory forms of social insurance replacing tort litigation and mandatory forms of consumer protection out of which the parties cannot contract. The distinctive enterprise of justification shows instead that these features of the contemporary legal landscape are distinct from private law. They can be assessed (and embraced or rejected) without supposing that private rights are in no way distinctive among the many items in the legislative toolkit, with no rational structure of their own.

Weinrib engages with both legal doctrine and prominent thinkers from the history of philosophy. The point of these discussions is not to contend that, as a matter of historical fact, the common lawyers of the seventeenth through twentieth centuries were secret readers of Aristotle or Immanuel Kant. It is quite the reverse: Aristotle, Kant, and many other writers took legal reasoning, and, specifically, reasoning about the adjudication of private disputes, as a central instance of a rational enterprise and sought to work through the presuppositions

---

3 Weinrib, *Idea of Private Law*, supra note 1 at 6.

and limitations of that enterprise. To assess whether private law has the rational credentials it purports to have, you must understand whether and how the parts of its justifications fit together.

II. The forms of justice

Building on vocabulary first introduced by Aristotle, Weinrib distinguishes between corrective justice and distributive justice. Consider the familiar thought that justice is giving each their due: anyone charged with doing justice is charged not with doing it in the abstract; instead, some particular person is charged with doing it ('giving') in relation to the person or persons ('each') to whom something is claimed to be 'due' on some particular basis. The question of justice is not the open ended 'who should have what?' The question of justice always concerns the task faced by some specific decision maker: on what grounds should that decision maker determine what is due to whom? John Rawls famously contended that 'justice is the first virtue of social institutions.'[4] He neglected to add that social institutions only operate through their officials, and many of those officials are charged with doing justice. The focus on someone making a decision on the grounds particular to some official role, in turn, draws attention to the difference between the two fundamentally different ways in which something can be due to a person and, thus, to two fundamentally different ways in which the person charged with giving someone their due could make a justifiable decision.

In Aristotle's terms, distributive justice is the task of some person charged with allocating some good or benefit (or burden) among the members of a specified group, seeing to it that each receives an appropriate share. Distributive justice can be characterized in purely formal terms as giving each member of the specified group their share in accordance with some criterion. What counts as an appropriate share depends on the criterion of distribution employed, but the concept of distributive justice does not tell you on its own what criterion to employ. Aristotle's own example is distributing offices based on merit. The point of the example is not to prefer merit as a criterion for distribution but, rather, to note the fact that distribution always divides or allocates based on some criterion. Distributing seating based on a person's place in line is an exercise in distributive justice; each person's claim to a seat follows from that person's place in line. So too with distributing medication based on need or merit pay based on course evaluations or

---

4 John Rawls, *A Theory of Justice* (Cambridge, MA: Harvard University Press, 1971) at 1.

publications; all of these are exercises of distributive justice, albeit with different people charged with the allocation, different subject matters, different collections of people to whom things might be due, and different criteria thought to be appropriate to them.

Crucially, distributive justice applies to all people in the relevant class, and so a just distribution is one that treats all members of the relevant unit relevantly alike, with the same ratio between the criterion and the amount due applied in each case. For example, assigning grades on the basis of the quality of the written work is an exercise in distributive justice; the faculty member is supposed to award each student a grade in proportion to the quality of that student's performance in the course, rather than on any other grounds, and to do so only with respect to the students who are enrolled in the class, rather than taking it upon themselves to assign a grade to someone who is not enrolled or who was enrolled in a different class. Aristotle characterizes this form of justice as 'geometric' because any number of people within the relevant group can stand in the same ratio of criterion and amount, each receiving an amount in proportion to their satisfaction of criterion.

Corrective justice is fundamentally different because it is concerned with transactions. It, too, is purely formal but in a different way. Rather than awaiting some principle of distribution appropriate to the things being distributed to some specific class of persons, corrective justice is formal because it attends only to a transaction between the defendant and the plaintiff. Corrective justice is the principle for determining what is due between two private persons based on what has transpired between them. The agent of corrective justice in a sophisticated legal system is the judge, who Weinrib, following Aristotle, characterizes as 'justice ensouled.'[5] The judge is the public official whose distinctive mandate is concerned with coherence, with (in a private law dispute) determining how things stand between the parties in order to determine how things stand with respect to the relief requested by the plaintiff. The judge who steps outside this role, who resolves the dispute on the basis of something loosely called 'policy' or arrogates to the judicial role the task of matters 'of public policy which we, as judges, must resolve,'[6] steps outside this role and so fails to act for proper purposes.

Weinrib elsewhere distinguishes between two conceptions of judicial decision making.[7] One view, common to Hans Kelsen and his followers

---

5 Weinrib, *Idea of Private Law*, supra note 1 at 218.

6 *Dorset Yacht Co v Home Office*, [1969] 2 QB 412 at 426, per Lord Denning MR.

7 Ernest J Weinrib, 'Civil Recourse and Corrective Justice' (2011) 39 Fla St UL Rev 273 at 274.

as well as to partisans of instrumentalist accounts and those defenders of civil recourse who contend it differs from corrective justice, supposes that a private injustice – a breach of contract, tort, or an instance of unjust enrichment – provides the occasion on which a judge or other decision maker is empowered to advance some range of what are thought to be desirable social purposes. The alternative, which Weinrib defends, sees instead the instance of the private injustice – once again, breach of contract, tort, or a case of unjust enrichment – as the reason for the judicial intervention and response. Because it is exclusively attentive to the transaction between the parties, corrective justice is therefore (notoriously) indifferent to concerns of need or merit; if a transaction is wrongful, corrective justice mandates its undoing even if that will lead to a transfer from a needy person to an affluent one or from a meritorious person to one who is not.[8]

The distinction between distributive justice and corrective justice is formal rather than material; they are different ways of reasoning about what some person or persons are due. Distributive justice divides something (whether benefit or detriment) among the members of the relevant group based on the criteria thought appropriate to it; properly allowing that different criteria are proper to different questions; corrective justice seeks to address a wrongful transaction, focused exclusively on the parties to it. This distinction between two different but both genuine forms of justice provides a caution against two troubling features of the contemporary legal academy. One of these, which Weinrib characterizes as instrumentalism, supposes that there are no distinctive private legal concepts, that interactions between private persons are something to be managed in pursuit of some broader social purpose. Instrumentalism of this kind is one of the explicit targets of *The Idea of Private Law*. Weinrib variously characterizes it as focusing on only one of the parties, as attending (however inadequately and incompletely) to distributive rather than corrective justice, and as failing to provide a coherent justification for the structure of private law litigation. Weinrib's rejection of instrumentalism is not, however, a rejection of distributive justice as such; the point of distinguishing between the forms of justice is to show the different ways in which they each manifest coherent modes of justification, neither of which is reducible to the other.

---

8 Aristotle notes that corrective justice requires the reversal of a transaction even in cases in which a 'decent' person is required to pay damages to a 'base' one. Aristotle, *Nicomachean Ethics*, edited R Crisp (Cambridge, UK: Cambridge University Press, 2004) book V, ch 4 at 87.

Looked at from the other direction, however, Weinrib's arguments also reveal the flaw in another prominent position in the contemporary legal academy (and political culture), according to which public law must be analysed through private legal concepts, as if every interaction between citizens and their government are to be analysed as a private transaction assessed by whether the citizen got what they paid for. Weinrib's emphasis on the forms of justice, with its recognition of more than one coherent form of justification, reveals how these seemingly opposed trends – the reduction of corrective justice to a tool in the service of some external goal, and the rejection of distributive justice in the name of a thoroughgoing idea of purely private interaction – are mirror images of each other and that a properly synoptic understanding of law sees that each has a place in a system in which public law and private law are coordinate rather than one being subordinated to the other.

III. Coherence

Weinrib expresses this focus on form in several overlapping vocabularies, including 'understanding law on its own terms,' of corrective justice and, strikingly, a further vocabulary of 'coherence' according to which a justification is coherent if its elements are properly related to each other. Weinrib's approach contrasts with other senses that might be attached to the word 'coherence' and other ways in which it might be thought of as an explanatory virtue. On one prominent understanding, coherence is a marker of explanatory power, the ability to unify as many seemingly disparate things as possible, either by seeking to explain an antecedently identified domain or, alternatively, by finding a single explanatory factor that figures in accounts of a broader range of phenomena. Some writers who emphasize coherence in this sense see it in terms of having as few principles as possible to explain either some doctrinal area of the law or the legal system taken as a (coherent) whole or of explaining the outcome of a particular case by situating it in a larger pattern, arguing that some general principle provides the best or simplest or most attractive explanation of that larger pattern and, therefore, of the particular case.[9]

---

9 See the discussion and sources cited in Julie Dickson, 'Interpretation and Coherence in Legal Reasoning' in Edward N Zalta, ed, *The Stanford Encyclopedia of Philosophy* (Winter 2016), online: <plato.stanford.edu/archives/win2016/entries/legal-reas-interpret/>.

Appeals to coherence in that sense treat questions of explanation and justification as a holistic exercise through which particular outcomes are explained or justified in terms of their relation to other broader elements of the legal system. Such an approach invites multiple challenges of application: identifying the relevant unit of coherence (the legal system as a whole, private law in particular, contract law alone, contracts for sales of goods); a separate class of disputes concerns the dimension along which an explanation might be judged to be best; whether it coheres with a broader range of facts or moral intuitions (whether, for example, the thing to be explained should be all of the ways in which a society deals with accidents or all of the ways in which it deals with economic transactions) or whether some other explanation might do better; and yet another class of disputes concerning the dimensions along which explanatory power is to be assessed and applied to the specific case of private law, whether binary adjudication of disputes might be conducive to other purposes or perhaps has only a historical explanation.

Weinrib's approach is different; the demand for coherence in private law comes from attention to private law's distinctive form of thought. Rather than a thoroughgoing holism, whether general or local, Weinrib's focus on form enables a synoptic vision of the differences between public law and private law without reducing both to a third structure or valorizing one at the expense of the other. In the case of private law, the plaintiff and defendant do not figure as two among a larger class of items that might be data for a broader explanation. Instead, the distinctive feature of private law both in its norms of conduct and in its structure of litigation is that the plaintiff and defendant always figure as a matched set. The plaintiff's claim always makes explicit reference to the defendant who is alleged to have breached the contract with the plaintiff or committed the tort against the plaintiff or been enriched at the plaintiff's expense; the plaintiff seeks a remedy from the defendant on the basis of that transaction.

The plaintiff comes before the court, demanding a remedy from the defendant who the plaintiff alleges to have wronged that very plaintiff in particular: the plaintiff, pointing at the defendant says: 'That person <breached a contract with/committed a battery against/converted property that belongs to/through their negligence injured /trespassed against/made a defamatory statement about> me.' The idea of form is already contained in the plaintiff's pleading. The prepositions (with, against, to, through, against, about) already contain the relevant form: what the defendant did to the plaintiff and what the plaintiff suffered from the defendant are the same thing. There is a unified relation, because each side of it is correlative to the other side.

The remedy received by the plaintiff and the remedy exacted from the defendant are correlative in just the same way. The remedy is taken from the defendant (in particular) and given to the plaintiff (in particular); the appropriate measure of coherence is not holistic but rather transactional because the explanation of the relief sought – the explanation of why this defendant must provide and why this plaintiff must receive the remedy in question – must pertain to both the plaintiff and the defendant. The reason for taking money from the defendant is the same as the reason for giving money to the plaintiff – that is, the sense in which plaintiff-focused and defendant-focused aspects of the analysis must cohere. Grounds that are particular to only one of the parties could at most explain why the defendant was fined or taxed or why the plaintiff received compensation; they do not explain why the plaintiff receives a remedy from the defendant tied to the specific wrong and its consequences of which the plaintiff complains.

Weinrib does not deny that there could be other bases for taking a sum of money from one person and an equivalent sum given to another; his claim instead is that a past transaction between those two persons provides a distinctive basis for taking from one and giving to the other. That distinctive ground is relational (as is the transaction). Because he does not operate with a holistic conception of coherence, Weinrib is not committed to any ambitious claims according to which corrective justice is the only possible basis or the best explanation for taking money from one person or giving an equivalent sum to another. Legal philosophy is not an exercise in abduction, trying to provide an inference to the uniquely best or only possible explanation of some observed event of a judge telling someone to pay money to someone else. Its aim instead is to elucidate a distinctive form of thought.

IV. Justification

At this point, you might be wondering whether legal doctrine is a promising starting point for either understanding or justifying the behaviour of legal actors. Perhaps it strikes you as especially unpromising with respect to the explanation of common law subjects, which are themselves products of a decentralized system of dispute resolution and filled with the contingencies and preoccupations of the parties to those disputes, parties who may well have spun all manner of webs of rationalization or acted on the basis of values or motives of a bygone age. To acknowledge that the law is a historical product (indeed, achievement) does not preclude an examination of its claim to be a rational enterprise in which parties come before the court and give arguments of recognizably distinctive forms, forms that are different in the case of private law than in public law. Such an examination need not prejudge the question of whether the law lives up to its self-presentation; no normative or conceptual inquiry could guarantee that a historical institution has never taken a wrong turn. That question could only be answered once the self-presentation is properly elaborated and examined to reveal its presuppositions and, in so doing, reveal its limitations.

Perhaps the concern is not with explanation but, rather, with justification, the concern about what Jeremy Bentham characterized as the perils of the 'quietism' that he saw in every attempt to invoke distinctively legal concepts in the justification of legal practice,[10] a charge reiterated by HLA Hart when he wrote of the 'the old confusions between law and the standards appropriate to criticizing the law.'[11] For Bentham and Hart, distinctively legal concepts have nothing to recommend them. They are products of a history riddled with contingency and with features that contemporary legal actors view with concern or even alarm. Bentham and Hart both also express concern that an appeal to familiar legal concepts will make their own justification too easy.

Weinrib's provocative formulations ('the function of private law is to be private law' or 'tort law is like love') have led some readers to suppose that he fails to take such a challenge seriously and so, in the words of one particularly hostile reviewer, thinks of law on the model of art for art's sake[12] and thinks of law as exercising an enormous coercive power apart from any engagement at all with anything that might matter to the human beings whose conduct is regulated and who are subject to its coercive enforcement. Worse yet, talk about justification, normativity, and freedom might be thought to impose the exact same type of extrinsic demands on the law that are imposed on it by human welfare, with the only credentials of that abstruse vocabulary being drawn from the fact that they are supposedly already in the law.

That is not it at all: the point of beginning with the law's own structure, with its correlativity between the plaintiff and the defendant and working out both the presuppositions and limitations of that correlativity – that is, the way in which it conceptualizes human agency

---

10 Jeremy Bentham, *A Fragment on Government*, edited by HLA Hart (Cambridge, UK: Cambridge University Press 1988) at 11.
11 HLA Hart, 'Introduction' in HLA Hart, *Essays on Jurisprudence and Philosophy* (Oxford: Oxford University Press, 1983) 1 at 11.
12 Robert Rabin, 'Law for Law's Sake' (1996) 105 Yale LJ 2261.

and interaction as well as the ways in which it engages with the contingent matter of choice and the range of things on which it can operate – is to understand how judges justifying their decisions in concrete disputes could do so as part of a rational enterprise, the results of which can be enforced consistent with, and give effect to, the rights of the parties. The answer is that they are doing what they say they are doing – namely, resolving a private matter between the parties before the court.

Weinrib's approach therefore avoids both the quietism and anarchism challenges bruited by Bentham as well as the 'old confusions' charge posed by Hart. It avoids the quietism charge because it does not say that the fact of being adopted into positive law provides a decisive or overriding normative justification or, indeed, any justification at all; it avoids the opposite charge of anarchism because it assigns an essential role for legal institutions and does not imagine that every private person is entitled to appoint themselves the agent of corrective justice. It avoids the 'old confusions' charge because it says only that a specific department of the law has a coherent way of doing things, which contains within it the resources to specify its operations and their scope, and so explains why distinctions that the law draws – such as that between nonfeasance and misfeasance, between injury to person or property and pure economic loss, between parties to a contract and strangers to it, between cases in which the plaintiff can recover for what seems to be the same factual injury under one cause of action but not under another, any one of which might appear to be troublingly formulaic from many other perspectives – are in fact the consistent working out of the set of private legal relationships.

In law, the question of justification is always the question of why some decision maker is properly empowered to decide with respect to some person. In the case of corrective justice, the judge is empowered to award (or decline to award) a remedy to the plaintiff based on the transaction between the plaintiff and the defendant. Justification connects the grounds of the decision to the grounds of the judge's power: the judge is empowered to resolve a private dispute between the plaintiff and the defendant and is charged with resolving it in private terms – that is, on the basis of the very matter that is in dispute, the plaintiff's contention that the defendant committed a legal wrong against that plaintiff in particular. The decision in favour of the plaintiff or defendant focuses exclusively on things involving the terms of the contract, the elements of the tort, and the transfer from one to the other without juristic reason.

V. Coherence among coherent forms

A coherent justification under distributive justice would connect the person (natural or artificial) making the distribution to the recipients by explaining why this specific distributor would use this specific criterion to distribute this specific benefit or burden to or among this specific group of persons. Whether concert tickets, grades, merit pay, taxes, health care, or social insurance is being given out or collected, to give each their due under a distributive scheme is for the person charged with doing justice to attend to the criteria in relation to the class of persons. Distributive justice is not a free-floating idea or description of an ideal end state but, rather, a formal feature of the way in which a distribution can be shown to be justified to those in the class of persons to which it applies or criticized for its failure to be justified. Failures of distributive justice will be failures of coherence in relation to its formal criterion: the wrong person taking it upon themselves to distribute things, or distributing it among the wrong class of persons, or using a criterion of distribution inappropriate to distributing the particular type of benefit and burden to that class of persons.

In *The Idea of Private Law*, Weinrib only mentions the concept of coherence appropriate to distributive justice in passing, remarking: 'For any such particular distribution one can require that its various elements fit with one another, but the notion of internal ordering is not sufficiently powerful to establish the boundaries or the criterion of the scheme.'[13] In *Reciprocal Freedom*, Weinrib elaborates further:

> The criterion acts as a unifying principle for linking the benefit to the persons, thereby relating every participant in the distribution to every other participant in an ordered way. The tighter the connection between the criterion, on the one hand, and the persons and benefits that it governs, on the other, the more coherent is the distributive arrangement. Conversely, a distribution is incoherent to the extent that it operates under-inclusively or over-inclusively, giving participants either more or less than they merit under the criterion of distribution, or dividing among the participants a benefit that fails to fulfil the criterion's purpose, or employing a criterion that does not felicitously link the benefit being distributed and the persons among whom it is being divided. Distributive justice is thus a structure through which persons can coherently be related to one another with respect to whatever is being distributed in accordance with its governing criterion.[14]

---

13 Weinrib, *Idea of Private Law*, supra note 1 at 210–11.
14 Ernest J Weinrib, *Reciprocal Freedom* (Oxford: Oxford University Press, 2022) at 95.

The demand for coherence, then, is a feature of the distinctively legal form of justification, of the demand for justification made by members of sophisticated legal systems, and of the types of justifications that can be given by agents within those legal systems. This structure within which justifications are demanded and given is a fundamental feature of legality and figures in different ways in corrective justice and distributive justice and, indeed, in the difference between justification in public law and in private law.

In private law litigation, a private party comes before a court complaining about the action of another private person (or a public authority acting within a certain kind of distinctively private-like context, whether because the public authority is engaged in a characteristically private activity such as operating a vehicle or because a public official has somehow stepped outside their public role in a way that is inconsistent with its public character). The basic principle of corrective justice governs the adjudication of such disputes because the plaintiff faces the task of establishing that the defendant's conduct was a wrong that was personal to the plaintiff. In public law, by contrast, the principle of distributive justice governs whether some official charged with some aspect of determining who gets what, or what gets taken from whom for some public purpose, was acting properly with respect to the relevant distributive criterion. In public law, the role of the official (other than a judge) is not as someone with an unfettered license to make the world better; rather, it is the very narrow role of acting within their proper mandate – that is, making decisions based on the grounds specified in that mandate. The distinction between corrective and distributive justice therefore informs the familiar difference between the position of a private person and a public official within a legal system. The distinction is crisply formulated in a remark attributed to Frank Scott:

> The first is that the individual may do anything he pleases, in any circumstances anywhere, unless there is some provision of law prohibiting him. Freedom is thus presumed, and is the general rule. All restrictions are exceptions. The second rule defines the authority of the state, and places the public official (including the policemen) in exactly the opposite situation from the private individual: a public officer can do nothing in his public capacity unless the law permits it. His incapacity is presumed, and authority to act is an exception.[15]

---

15 Frank Scott, unpublished paper, quoted in WS Tarnopolsky, 'Frank Scott: Civil Libertarian' (1981) 27 McGill LJ 14. See also *R v Somerset County Council, ex parte Fewings*, [1995] 1 All ER 513 at 524, per Laws J:

The different conceptions of coherence for corrective and distributive justice follow this distinction. The characteristic form of private wrongdoing is one person interfering with the object of another person's right. The question of whether the defendant has interfered with the plaintiff's right can only be answered through an examination of factors pertaining to both plaintiff and defendant because the plaintiff's right is a restriction on the conduct of the defendant. The question of whether a norm of conduct protecting the plaintiff restricts the defendant's freedom depends on whether it is a member of a set of limits protecting the capacity of other private persons to act; those who act within those constraints are permitted to do so for whatever purposes they might seek to advance. By contrast, a public official is not permitted to use their powers for their own private purposes, and the grounds on which they are permitted to exercise them are themselves constrained. The characteristic form of wrongdoing by a public official is a violation of distributive justice. Public wrongdoing is paradigmatically committed by a public official or a private person acting in an official or quasi-official capacity; the official is permitted to exercise the specified powers in a way that private persons are not, but only in accordance with their proper mandate. The characteristic content of the wrong is a violation of the criterion of distribution proper to that official capacity – that is, either distributing things on other than the specified grounds or other than the specified class of persons. Those acting in such capacities are required to exercise the powers that they have – to give to some, or to take from others – in accordance with the rationale for the particular official having the relevant power to give to, or take from, some legal person something on other than the specified grounds or grounds inconsistent with the role of the decision maker in question.

A different way of making this point is to say that the structure of justification that underlies legality always has in the background something that might be thought to be a 'by what right?' type of question: why am I ordered to pay this tax, why am I left with the cost of the injury

---

For private persons, the rule is that you may do anything you choose which the law does not prohibit. ... But for public bodies the rule is the opposite, and so of another character altogether. It is that any action to be taken must be justified by positive law. A public body has no heritage of legal rights which it enjoys for its own sake; at every turn, all of its dealings constitute the fulfilment of duties which it owes to others; indeed, it exists for no other purpose. ... It is in this sense that it has no rights of its own, no axe to grind beyond its public responsibility: a responsibility which defines its purpose and justifies its existence.

that I suffered, why am I being compelled to compensate this other person whom I injured or pay back the money that I received as a gift from someone other than the plaintiff? Such questions might be answered in a variety of ways, and different people might be satisfied with different types of answers. Attention to legal form reveals a distinctively legal way in which they can be asked and answered. In corrective justice, the answer is only sensitive to the question if it is coherent – that is, if the explanation of why the defendant has to pay, or, if the plaintiff's suit fails, why the plaintiff does not receive the remedy sought, refers to the relevant transaction. In distributive justice – that is, in exercises of public power – the only thing that is sensitive to the plaintiff's question is an answer that is coherent within the bounds of distributive justice, which is to say an answer that explains why the criterion in question – first-come-first-served, attention to need, grades on the basis of comparative academic merit within the student body – is appropriate for the official or quasi-official in question to be deploying in giving out the things being distributed. So, too, in the case of both distributive and corrective justice, there will be questions about the application of the relevant coherent principles to the particular instance.

In putting this point in terms of the demand for justification by the party seeking something from a public official or the parties before the court, I do not mean to be attributing to ordinary appellants or litigants a commitment to, or even a grasp of, corrective justice or Aristotelian form or any other degree of philosophical sophistication that is at odds with their own factual self-understanding. No doubt, many of them simply want the money; further, some – perhaps many – are engaged in opportunistic behaviour, pushing the margins of legal doctrine in the hope of securing something favourable to them. All of that is true. The point is not that people are engaged in an abstract philosophical activity of demanding justifications and that they will only go away happy if those justifications are coherent either as corrective or distributive justice. Many – perhaps most – people will go away satisfied if they win and disappointed if they do not, and they may not even be convinced by the reasons offered by the court or official. But the entire activity only makes sense against the background of the demand for an answer to the question 'why me?'

The role of coherence in legal justification reveals the problems of many attempts to shoehorn distributive concerns into private law litigation. Such attempts not only violate corrective justice – by looking outside of how things stand between the parties – but also are at odds with a coherent application of distributive justice. Consider the familiar suggestions that the point of tort litigation is compensation, or deterrence, or some balance of the two. Such proposals are distributive in character. Compensation proposals seek to distribute something – financial relief – based on the criterion of current loss. Such a proposal violates corrective justice because it looks only to the plaintiff, ignoring the situation or role of the defendant. As such it does not explain why the defendant, in particular, should be the one to finance the compensation. It does no better as distributive justice because it fails to explain why the rationale for current loss or need (or spreading losses or compensating those in need) should only apply on the occasion of a transaction involving some defendant.[16] If the distributive criterion is one of attention to need, or perhaps need incurred through no fault of those experiencing it, the scheme does not consistently apply it. The same point applies with respect to the criterion of deterrence. An exclusive focus on it attends only to the defendant (and other potential defendants not currently before the court) rather than to the plaintiff who is, after all, the one bringing the action. The rationale sounds in distributive, rather than corrective, justice but in a way that is at odds with a coherent understanding of its basis. Providing incentives to avoid socially unwanted behaviour is an intelligible and acceptable public purpose; singling out those who have caused injury in pursuit of that public purpose is arbitrary from the point of view of the purpose itself.

None of this is to say that more sophisticated versions of distributive justice could not be developed that would provide a rationale for a limited application of a distributive principle; the point is rather that such a rationale, to be adequate, would need to show itself to be coherent with respect to the criteria proper to distributive justice: that this is a properly public purpose and that those who are being singled out by the means taken to its pursuit are chosen in a non-arbitrary way, properly related to the criterion in question. Focusing on coherence does not on its own resolve questions of how public legal institutions should address problems of wrongdoing or loss or even whether they should be conceptualized under such headings or in some other way. Instead, it draws attention to the need for any legal justification to be coherent, for the person engaging in the justificatory activity – whether a judge deciding a private claim or a public official carrying out a mandate – to do so in a way that is properly attentive to the task at hand. Rather than seeing a private dispute as the occasion or opportunity to bring about some independently desirable result, the judge deciding such a dispute should address it on its own terms. The fact that other public

---

16 Weinrib, *Idea of Private Law*, supra note 1 at 213.

legal institutions are entitled to restrict the operation of corrective justice, even to the extent of moving some class of cases outside of private adjudication, as many jurisdictions have done for workplace injuries, does not show that private law adjudication is just a clumsy mechanism for addressing workplace injuries or that addressing transactional wrongdoing is simply a 'decision' that the legal system has made on ideological (that is non-rational) grounds. Corrective justice is a distinctive way in which law can be a rational enterprise in relation to private disputes.

Understood in these terms, the idea of legal form dispels the mistaken impression that a concern with corrective justice, or an insistence on the way in which it excludes distributive considerations, reflects a commitment to some form of libertarianism or, as Kelsen has sometimes suggested, a 'social decision' in favour of capitalism.[17] The distinction between the forms of justice, and the ideas of coherence proper to each of them figures in an explanation of how legal institutions – courts, in particular – can be engaged in fundamentally different forms of reasoning while, at the same time, being charged with doing justice on the terms in which the dispute or issue presents itself.[18] That there

---

17 Hans Kelsen, *Introduction to the Problems of Legal Theory: A Translation of the First Edition of the Reine Rechtslehre or Pure Theory of Law*, translated by Stanley Paulson (Oxford: Oxford University Press, 1997). Hans Kelsen's concern to 'overcome' the 'dualism' between public and private law leads him to represent the plaintiff's power to sue as a delegated public power, despite the obvious differences between them – notably, the fact that the plaintiff's decision about whether to exercise it is a purely private matter, one that the plaintiff can act on for any private purpose whatsoever. By contrast, the exercise of public powers is constrained, and a public official is not allowed to act for any private purpose whatsoever. No doubt, there is conceptual space for describing the power to decide whether to sue or settle as conferred with the proviso that it can be exercised on any grounds whatsoever, but any such conferral would need to be done by some higher level of the legal system that was already in possession of a power of untrammeled discretion. Otherwise, the delegation or conferral of such a power would confer more power than the conferring power had. The root of the difficulty is the 'decisionism' at the heart of Kelsen's account; the fact that private rights can be limited does not show that they are in no way distinctive.

18 Even HLA Hart, who, as we have seen, insists on the distinction between the law and the concepts proper to the criticism of it acknowledges this. His example is the tort of battery; he acknowledges that criminal law prohibitions of battery and compensation for injuries would be inadequate; the fact that one person intentionally hit another is a wrong as between those two persons. So, too, even in Hart's most conspicuous deployment of his distinction between the law's concepts and the proper grounds of criticism of it is the inadequacy of English law at the time in its failure to protect against invasions of privacy. Strikingly, in his discussion of battery, the law's own

are such different terms is the beginning of the understanding of law; that they all fit into a general idea of legality, on which all exercises of power are subject to requirements of justification, does not mean that the law is doing just one thing.

VI. Conclusion

As I have articulated it, Weinrib's distinctive contribution to both legal philosophy and the study of private law is the idea of form. As the legal realists and their contemporary followers will never tire of telling you, form is insufficient to decide cases. This is often announced with great confidence, and there is every reason to be greatly confident in such an obvious, even platitudinous, truth. But, for all that, its obviousness is not a thing that the formalist has overlooked but, rather, the formalist's key insight. Form is not sufficient to decide cases; it is necessary.

A focus on legal form also illuminates the sense in which private law is not an application of public law or distributive justice, but coordinate with it, without being a merely delegated public power. Precisely because the judge is not merely the official charged with doing justice between the parties but more generally an official of the legal system as a whole, there will be circumstances in which the demands of the legal system as a whole will require the limitation of the operation of corrective justice. In such circumstances, it is not that the apparatus of corrective justice fails to engage but, rather, that the legal system as a whole requires restricting its operation in some class of cases. Such limitations do not mean that there is somehow a general and open decision about whether to apply it; instead, there may be justifiable limits on the operation of corrective justice even if transactions otherwise fall within its scope.

---

concepts are brought forward in defence of the law's treatment of a particular social phenomenon; in discussing privacy, the law's own concepts are said to call for the giving effect to a right that was not recognized in English law at the time. Hart does not say (and, indeed, could not say with a straight face) that private rights of action are a particularly effective way of addressing an ongoing social problem of battery or interferences with privacy by advertisers. The problem is not just that public law prohibitions plus compensation would fail to consider the transaction between plaintiff and defendant in the way in which the law does in other cases; the deeper problem is that the relation between the plaintiff and the defendant seems not merely to be the focus of the court's attention. That is the point of Hart's example of invasions of privacy; his claim/complaint is that the law fails to attend to a transaction. It is because transactions are a fundamental form of justice. HLA Hart, *The Concept of Law*, 3d ed (Oxford: Oxford University Press, 2012) at 164.

Weinrib illustrates this coordinate structure in his ground-breaking 1976 article on illegality as a tort defence.[19] He notes that the illegality defence has its natural home in a contractual setting, refusing to enforce a right as dictated by the transaction between the parties because of the relation between doing so and the rest of the legal system. A court may refuse to give effect to an illegal contract on the grounds that the law of contract must not facilitate that which has been prohibited by the criminal law. Although Weinrib's discussion predates *The Idea of Private Law* by almost two decades, it shares the same attention to legal form in its caution about transplanting a defence from contract law into tort law. Most significantly, attention to the public law rationale for limiting the operation of private rights shows that, far from being the general defence it is sometimes taken to be, it is instead much more limited to the case in which the plaintiff seeks to recover damages that will give effect to an illegal enterprise. (Weinrib illustrates this idea with the example of a thief who is caught, convicted, and fined as a result of his fellow thief's negligence in a botched attempt to disable an alarm system. The thief would not be able to receive reimbursement of the expense incurred in paying the fine.)

The same point applies to the interaction between the law of defamation and the various privileges protecting defamatory statements. A statement made in judicial or parliamentary proceedings does not cease to be defamatory because of where it is made; it is subject to absolute privilege for systematic legal reasons. So, too, qualified privileges and the more recently developed law of responsible journalism restrict the operation of the law of defamation; they allow what would be a defamatory statement to stand without being either withdrawn or corrected because of the distinctive context in which it is made. Whether to treat something as a matter of public health or private law is not a question that concepts from private law could possibly be sufficient to answer, but this insufficiency does not show that they lack either a normative structure or conceptual contours. It shows instead that, in order to make a determination that they are to be or not to be operative with respect to some class of cases, one must first understand what they are and how they operate. That is the more general lesson of *The Idea of Private Law* and of corrective justice: legal forms are irreducible but not opposed, coordinating rather than conflicting. That is what it is to live under a system of law.

---

19 Ernest J Weinrib, 'Illegality as a Tort Defence' (1976) 26 UTJL 28.

8 Trebilcock and Trade-Offs[†]

EDWARD M IACOBUCCI

I. Introduction

Michael Trebilcock's impact as a legal academic is astounding. Along one dimension, he is one of Canada's foremost contributors to the world of legal ideas. He was a founder of law and economics, one of the most influential intellectual schools within the legal academy[1] and, indeed, was central to the development of the interdisciplinary study of law at the University of Toronto and around the world. He is an astonishingly prolific scholar and, moreover, one whose breadth is unmatched – he has written on competition law, consumer protection law, immigration law, trade law, contract law, law and development, regulation, legal institutions, and many other topics. Along another dimension, he has been a beloved and inspiring law teacher whose former students now populate the professoriate at the world's leading law schools.[2] To rely on a metaphor from his favourite sport, he is an academic all-star who could play whatever position one would ask him to, whether opening batsman, wicketkeeper, spin bowler, or fast bowler.

---

† Thanks to Arthur Ripstein and Michael Trebilcock for helpful conversations.

1 For example, he is the only scholar not based in the United States whose work was included in a collection of essays by the founders of law and economics. See Francesco Parisi & Charles Rowley, eds, *The Origins of Law and Economics: Essays from the Founding Fathers* (Cheltenham, UK: Edward Elgar, 2005). He is also the only non-US scholar to be president of the American Law and Economics Association.

2 To convey a sense of his impact as a supervisor and teacher, the Faculty of Law organized a conference in tribute to Trebilcock drawing significantly on the participation of his former students (including me and the other three co-editors) who became law professors. Anita Anand et al, eds, 'Law, Economics and Public Policy: Essays in Honour of Michael J Trebilcock' (2010) 60:2 UTLJ 1.

With this as a backdrop, it is daunting to contemplate how one could begin to select a single piece, or even a single area of law, to provide a focus for a retrospective on his work. Indeed, it is sufficiently daunting that I decline to do so. Instead, I will emphasize themes that permeate his work and isolate a few examples to illustrate his unique approach and contributions to legal scholarship. In his work within law and economics, Trebilcock was a trailblazer who amply demonstrated the power of careful economic thinking to respond to partial examinations of the economics pertaining to a question. An excellent illustration of his contributions within law and economics is found in his pathbreaking article 'The Doctrine of Inequality of Bargaining Power: Post-Benthamite Economics in the House of Lords.'[3] This article concerned a contract dispute that was resolved in the plaintiff's favour in the UK House of Lords. Trebilcock demonstrates convincingly that the House of Lords latched too easily onto a glib economic narrative of a battle between the little guy and the bad corporation and failed to take seriously both facts and economic arguments that offered strong support for the defendant corporation in this case. It was an important article both in its specific arguments and in its call for the law, when assessing the economic fairness of a contract, to take economic reasoning seriously. Part II discusses this article.

Trebilcock's enthusiasm for clear thinking over visceral reaction is also amply illustrated by his influential and important book *The Limits of Freedom of Contract*, which provides the focus for Part III.[4] While 'Post-Benthamite Economics' demonstrated the perils for the law of not appreciating competing economic arguments that push back on lazy economic thinking, *The Limits of Freedom of Contract* refuses to accept the lazy view that economics has all the answers to a range of difficult legal questions. For example, while economics may have something useful to say about thorny questions such as the enforceability of surrogacy or sex work contracts, other normative understandings, including those concerning the dangers of commodification, should also be taken seriously if law is to reflect society's values.

Part IV shifts gears to review a core element of much of Trebilcock's work: institutions matter. In particular, Part IV will relate Trebilcock's emphasis on institutional comparative advantage to competition law

---

3 Michael J Trebilcock, 'The Doctrine of Inequality of Bargaining Power: Post-Benthamite Economics in the House of Lords' (1976) 26 UTLJ 359 [Trebilcock, 'Post-Benthamite Economics'].

4 Michael J Trebilcock, *The Limits of Freedom of Contract* (Cambridge, MA: Harvard University Press, 1993) [Trebilcock, *Limits of Freedom of Contract*].

institutions. For example, for reasons both pragmatic and principled, Trebilcock has advocated for limited political oversight of competition reviews of mergers in critical infrastructure industries, such as transport and finance.[5] Part V concludes by discussing the theme that runs through Parts II–IV. Trebilcock's work takes trade-offs seriously, but he also takes the nature of the trade-off seriously in thinking about optimal institutional design. As Part V emphasizes, the nature of the legal question connects closely to the optimal institutional question: technocratic questions invite technocratic institutional authority, while questions that require consideration of a range of normative perspectives invite political oversight. Indeed, on some questions, there simply is no correct answer, and the appropriate response of the law is simply to assign authority for making the trade-off to the right institution.

In summary, as I hope to demonstrate, Trebilcock's work offers two approaches to trade-offs: substantive answers to particular trade-offs and institutional arrangements that respond optimally to the trade-offs. His institutional and substantive contributions are connected.

II. 'Post-Benthamite Economics': taking economic trade-offs seriously

In a seminal contribution to the law and economics of contracts, Trebilcock considers a UK House of Lords case about inequality of bargaining power and the enforceability of contracts.[6] *Macaulay v Schroeder Publishing* concerned a contract between a songwriter and a music publishing company.[7] The facts, in short, were as follows. An unknown songwriter entered into a contract with a music publisher. The contract was a standard form contract with a fifty-pound-sterling advance on royalties to the songwriter and a five-year term, renewable automatically for an additional five years if the royalties in the first five years exceeded five thousand pounds. The publisher could assign or terminate the contract without restriction, while the songwriter had no right to terminate and could only assign with the agreement of the publisher.

---

5 Michael J Trebilcock & Edward M Iacobucci, 'Designing Competition Law Institutions' (2002) 25 World Law and Economics Review 361 [Trebilcock & Iacobucci, 'Designing Competition Law']. I am a co-author of this article but recall only reluctantly including a role for political oversight in our institutional proposals for competition law enforcement. In hindsight, I have come to the conclusion that my reluctance was misguided.

6 Trebilcock, 'Post-Benthamite Economics,' supra note 3.

7 *Macaulay v Schroeder Publishing Co Ltd*, [1974] 1 WLR 1308 (HL).

A unanimous panel of three at the Court of Appeal, and a unanimous panel of five at the House of Lords, found the contract to be contrary to public policy in imposing unreasonable restraints on the songwriter's ability to market his work. They found that the contract was the product of unequal bargaining power and was unenforceable.

Trebilcock's article on this case was a foundational contribution to the economic analysis of law, in general, and of contract law, in particular. Trebilcock dismantles the simple-minded analysis of the House of Lords carefully and methodically. The House of Lords, to put it succinctly, had little theory behind its reasoning, nor did it have any evidence; it simply offered a conclusion that the contract was unfair to the songwriter.[8] One possible (though only possible) justification for the Court's conclusion would have been that the publisher had market power that allowed it to act independently of competitive pressures in offering one-sided terms to songwriters through its standard forms. To be sure, it is not obvious that market power would have justified the Court's conclusion. Competition law is, for the most part, highly reluctant to decide whether prices or other terms set by a monopolist are unfair – how is one to determine what a fair price or term is?[9] But following his own guidance that lawyers ought always to take the facts seriously, and making an early contribution to empirical law and economics, Trebilcock canvasses the market facts – from primary sources, given that the Court did not even nod in this direction – to demonstrate convincingly that market power was very unlikely to be present in this case.

For example, *Billboard's 1975-6 International Buyer's Guide* listed 428 music publishers in the United Kingdom, which hardly suggests a concentrated industry.[10] He also notes that music publishers and record pro-

---

8 As a student, I recall fondly Trebilcock's admonition, made with his distinctive giggle, that, when confronted with a 'fairness' question like the consistency of a contract with public policy, students ought to aspire to offer more than a 'visceral grunt.' Trebilcock demonstrates clearly that the House of Lords had little to offer but a visceral grunt.

9 Even after section 78 of the Canadian *Competition Act*, RSC, 1985, c C-34, was recently amended to allow the tribunal to find 'unfair' prices to be considered an abuse of dominant position, the Canadian Competition Bureau signaled its reluctance to enforce this strictly by requiring that the high prices somehow disadvantage a competitor before being considered an abuse. See 'Changes to the Provisions on Mergers and Restrictive Trade Practices in the Competition Act' (7 November 2024), online: *Competition Bureau* <competition-bureau.canada.ca/en/mergers-and-acquisitions/changes-provisions-mergers-and-restrictive-trade-practices-competition-act>.

10 Trebilcock, 'Post-Benthamite Economics,' supra note 3 at 367.

ducers were often integrated and that there were, according to the same source, 276 UK record and tape manufacturers/distributors/importers, and fifty-four independent record producers. Recognizing that similar patterns of concentration tend to arise across countries in similar industries, Trebilcock also canvasses US data, which revealed that the twenty largest record manufacturers held 81 per cent of the market in 1967 but that even this concentration ratio was overstated. As he colourfully puts it, '[b]ecause of the highly volatile nature of the industry, the effects of foreign competition and the presence of "pirates," "diskleggers," "rack jobbers," and other assorted forms of wildlife who apparently inhabit the music-industry's demi-monde, these figures undoubtedly understate the number of firms active in the industry.'[11] Moreover, as Trebilcock observes, the defendant publisher was literally a mom and pop operation, consisting of husband-wife 100 per cent shareholders of a US parent and the defendant UK subsidiary. It is not plausible that the publisher had market power. Given the presence of competition, there is little reason to suppose that publishers would be able to impose disproportionately profitable terms on songwriters, let alone ones that are so one-sided as to be problematic as a matter of public policy. Competitive firms will earn normal profits, which are profits that compensate its factors of production at competitive rates but not more than that.

Trebilcock does not rest on empirics alone, however. He also takes seriously the idea that even competitive firms might be able to impose onerous terms on their customers through the use of standard form contracts such as those found in this case. As he points out, any assumption that standard form contracts must reflect market power because they are presented on a take-it-or-leave-it basis is fallacious, despite the view of the House of Lords and a then common view in the legal literature to the contrary.[12] As an empirical matter, such contracts are common in a wide range of highly competitive industries in which exploitation of the customer is unlikely. The fact that restaurants offer a fixed menu, for example, is not evidence of the restaurant's market power. His careful analysis of the theoretical reasons why competitive firms are unlikely to be able to exploit customers through complicated standard form contracts was ahead of its time. Trebilcock points out the role of informed customers at the margin who keep sellers honest, as well as the incentives of competitors to call attention to their rivals' terms that would not be popular with customers. At the same time, he recognizes that

---

11 Ibid at 368.
12 Ibid at 364.

information is a public good, including information about the import of standard form contracts, and that it, in consequence, may be under-supplied. But the best explanation is that standard form contracts exist not to exploit but, rather, to save on transaction costs by short-circuiting an extensive back and forth over contract terms, an explanation that is now widely (though not universally)[13] accepted, even if Trebilcock was out of fashion at the time. In any event, as he observes, there was no question as a matter of fact in this particular case about how well informed the songwriter was about the contract; rather, he just did not like the substantive terms after he had become successful.

Perhaps the most profound contribution of Trebilcock's analysis of *Macauley* rests on a foundation that underlies all his scholarship: take trade-offs seriously. The House of Lords was naïve in its analysis of the fairness of the contract. In particular, the Court emphasized the fact that the publisher had termination and assignment rights, while the songwriter did not, without thoroughly considering the possibility that this asymmetry was best for both parties.[14] The House of Lords seemed to be concerned that the songwriter would not have an out even if the publisher failed to promote his songs appropriately. But, as Trebilcock points out, it is not obvious why the publisher would choose not to promote a song if it were profitable to do so, and, in any event, it appeared that the publisher did promote the songwriter: he was an unknown at the start of the contract but was well known by the time of the dispute; moreover, his royalties exceeded five thousand pounds in the first five years of the contract, which led to its automatic renewal.[15] In addition, the House of Lords found the asymmetry of termination and assignment problematic even while finding nothing problematic about the royalty terms themselves – as Trebilcock points out, how could it have reached a conclusion about one-sidedness without considering the benefits and obligations of each party? Finally, the Court decided that the contract was unfair without considering comparable contracts in the marketplace, which is another peculiar feature of its reasoning.

---

13 In a recent Supreme Court of Canada case, a significant majority of the Court expressed concern about standard form contracts, concern that contributed to their conclusion that a contract was unconscionable. *Uber Technologies, Inc v Heller*, 2020 SCC 16 [*Uber*]. It is unfortunate that Trebilcock's work on the question was not part of the majority's discussion.
14 See discussion in Trebilcock, 'Post-Benthamite Economics,' supra note 3 at 377.
15 Ibid at 377–8.

Even more importantly, Trebilcock calls attention to a fundamental oversight of many critics of 'unfair' market behaviour in a variety of settings: the distinction between *ex ante* and *ex post* profitability of a contract (or other action). It is worth reproducing Trebilcock's observations on this question:

> The validating condition hypothesized by Lord Reid – a right in a composer to terminate in the event of non-publication – also requires analysis. This appears to misunderstand the high-risk nature of the popular songwriting, music-publishing and recording industries. To quote some suggestive US figures, a music publisher in 1965 estimated that 30,000 songs are recorded and released on single records in the US each year. 85,000 musical compositions were deposited for copyright. ... In signing unknown songwriters, music-publishing and recording firms must therefore make risk calculations similar to those in the insurance business. In effect, what is the actuarial probability of an unknown songwriter later proving a commercial success? If the chance, for example, is only one in ten, then the terms offered all such songwriters will have to reflect the fact that with nine writers out of ten the publisher will incur evaluation and promotional expenses that will have to be recouped from the efforts of the one writer who proves a success. Given that in advance the publisher has no way of discriminating among unknown risks, he offers all unknown writers the same terms. To allow a writer to terminate his contract when success beckons is to ignore the risk-spreading nature of the enterprise. If successful writers could withdraw ... and take better terms elsewhere whenever prospects of entering the ranks of the 'established' looked good, a publisher would be left with unrecoupable losses on his other nine contracts. ... To allow withdrawal by the successful writer would be tantamount to an insured asking for his money back after the term of a life-insurance policy had expired on the grounds that he had not died during the period of the coverage. Presumably other risks had.[16]

As Trebilcock persuasively observes, if a songwriter becomes successful, it may well be true *ex post* that the publisher will earn a significant profit on the contract, in part because exclusivity prevents the songwriter from renegotiating. However, it is far from clear *ex ante* that the contract will be successful. To use Trebilcock's numbers, if there is a 90 per cent chance that the contract will be a money loser, it is important that profits 10 per cent of the time are large enough to offset the losses;

---

16 Ibid at 381.

otherwise, there is little point in entering into the contract in the first place.

In summary, the article makes several foundational contributions and exemplifies Trebilcock's scholarship. It provides an example of the importance of taking facts seriously – do not, for example, assert that a firm is able to exploit its customers without giving some attention to the competitive situation in which it finds itself and to the plausibility of an assertion that customers will be naïve about their options. This lesson continues to resonate, for example, with political discourse in recent years inaccurately blaming inflation on market power, contrary to the facts.[17] He also offers a careful and nuanced analysis of standard form contracts, one that might have benefited the Supreme Court of Canada in deciding a recent case involving standard form contracts, *Uber v Heller*, had it been cited.[18] Also, as in all his scholarship, his article takes economic trade-offs seriously: if the House of Lords lets the songwriter out of the contract, despite its riskiness, it is predictable that music publishers will be more reluctant to take on the risk of signing unknown songwriters. Indulging the songwriter in *Macauley*, in other words, would harm publishers and songwriters alike. This does not seem to be a sensible approach for the law to take. If courts are to engage in an economic analysis of contracts in order to conclude that they are one-sided, courts have to take the theory and evidence seriously. Trebilcock demonstrates convincingly that the House of Lords did neither.

The important distinction between *ex ante* and *ex post* perspectives matters not just for the analysis of this contract but is also relevant in a wide range of circumstances. For example, pharmaceutical companies are often in the crosshairs of critics for earning allegedly excess profits on patented drugs, but this is the same kind of situation as that in *Macauley*: while, *ex post*, the pharmaceutical company may earn significant profits on a particular drug, it may have required a large and very risky investment to develop the drug such that the expected profits from the drug from an *ex ante* perspective may be unremarkable even if *ex post* profits are significant. While the distinction between *ex post* and *ex ante* perspectives is now well known in legal analysis, this is in

---

17 See e.g. a recent Bank of Canada study showing that commonly made claims that recent increases in inflation were caused by sellers with market power were inaccurate. Panagiotis Bouras et al, 'The Contribution of Firm Profits to the Recent Rise in Inflation' (1 August 2023), online: *Bank of Canada* <www.bankofcanada.ca/wp-content/uploads/2023/08/san2023-12.pdf>.

18 *Uber*, supra note 13.

part because of Trebilcock's importation of economics into his analysis of *Macauley*.

III. *Limits of Freedom of Contract*: taking normative trade-offs seriously

'Post-Benthamite Economics' was a foundational contribution to the law and economics of contract. But Trebilcock is not at all an economic chauvinist. Rather, Trebilcock is generally ecumenical in his approach: while economic analysis of legal questions has something important to add to the conversation, depending on the issue, it ought not always to have the final word. At risk of committing academic malpractice, I will quote a source not generally known for its intellectual heft to capture this aspect of Trebilcock's work: a dustjacket blurb. Margaret Jane Radin, a major contributor to the literature on the perils of subjecting all aspects of human life to market transactions, contributed a blurb to *Limits of Freedom of Contract* that pithily identifies the distinctiveness of Trebilcock's scholarship. She observes:

> Trebilcock is unique among the adherents of the economic paradigm for the way he does justice to the complexities of views about the appropriate scope of the market domain. Even while defending the virtues of the market he takes seriously the arguments of feminists and communitarians who emphasize its vices. Above all, he takes seriously the overarching humanitarian agenda of ending deprivation and oppression.[19]

Radin is entirely correct in emphasizing both features of Trebilcock's work: he accepts that the market domain has its limits, but he also accepts that markets have virtues for human flourishing that ought to be a part of the inquiry.

In no work are both aspects of his approach more important than in *Limits of Freedom of Contract*. In a masterful study of the boundaries of contractual freedom, he considers a number of doctrinally and philosophically important questions: should surrogacy contracts be enforced; should sex work contracts be enforced; when is a contract coercive; when should asymmetries in access to information between parties vitiate a contract? Trebilcock's sensitivity to the importance of non-economic normative objectives, combined with his recognition of the importance of economic incentives, both predictively and

---

19 Trebilcock, *Limits of Freedom of Contract*, supra note 4, jacket cover.

normatively, set this book apart. An example illustrates. Trebilcock considers the legality of a surrogacy contract in which would-be parents enter a contract with a woman to have her become pregnant with the parents' embryo and carry the fetus until delivery, at which point the surrogate relinquishes any parental claim. These contracts are controversial, and Trebilcock considers the challenges to them respectfully and seriously.

He starts his analysis with the most straightforward observation from a law and economics perspective: if surrogate and would-be parents realize potential gains from entering into a surrogacy contract, there is an argument for enforcing the contract.[20] The would-be parents may have reasons to prefer surrogacy to adoption, including wishing to have a biological connection to their children, and surrogate mothers may have reasons to be willing to provide such services, including altruism and remuneration. But while the economic analysis of the contracts is relatively straightforward, there are objections to the contracts from outside economics that Trebilcock takes seriously.[21] For example, there is a concern that surrogacy contracts commodify a woman's reproductive faculties and allow the would-be parents to use the surrogate as a means to their ends. While acknowledging that the argument has force, Trebilcock provides a series of responses. For one thing, all contracts involve each party using the other for their own ends; this is, Trebilcock observes, simply another way of saying that both parties benefit from an exchange. For another, he also cites the feminist argument that, if women are to have full control over their own bodies and reproductive systems, it is not obvious why they should not be able to exercise a freedom to enter into a surrogacy contract.

Trebilcock also considers the risks of infirmities in the contracting process that may render the contract suspect. Surrogate mothers may, for example, underestimate the emotional costs of relinquishing parental rights. Surrogate mothers may also be vulnerable, perhaps with pressing financial needs, and the contract may be perceived as exploitative. Trebilcock ultimately takes a compromise position, rejecting the idea that surrogacy contracts ought to be unenforceable outright. He observes that a ban would 'risk infantilizing women and reinforcing perverse gender stereotypes.'[22] He also accounts for incentives, concluding that the ban would have harmful effects on both the demand

---

20 Ibid at 48–9.
21 Ibid at 49–53.
22 Ibid at 53.

and supply side: on the demand side, childless couples may resort to riskier fertility treatments, or may even abandon their relationship, if surrogacy were to be unavailable, while, on the supply side, would-be surrogates may be driven into impoverishment or demeaning alternative work options, or surrogacy may be driven underground where the birth mother might not have any legal protections at all. He does not, however, reject specific regulation of such contracts. Rather, he recommends regulation that would avoid some of the perverse incentive effects of a ban while avoiding or minimizing the potential harms of surrogacy contracts.

For example, to address the concerns that the birth mother may not appreciate the harms to her from giving up the child to the would-be parents, Trebilcock endorses Martha Field's suggestion that surrogacy contracts ought to be respected but should include a clause that allows the birth mother for a short period after birth to repudiate the contract and decide to keep the child.[23] He observes that such a rule would not only protect vulnerable surrogates from improvident agreements but would also create incentives for would-be parents to seek to ensure that a prospective surrogate is aware of the challenges, including the psychological challenges, of bearing and then giving up the child. At the same time, the grace period would clarify custodial rights, avoiding disputes and even destructive litigation over custody should the surrogate change her mind. As always, Trebilcock does not believe that decisions come without trade-offs and acknowledges that the grace period would raise risks for the commissioning parents and might lead them to back-end load any payments so as to diminish the risk of repudiation. But these costs, Trebilcock concludes, are worth the benefits. A regulated surrogacy contract is better than either no contract at all or an unregulated contract.

Trebilcock's approach to surrogacy contracts exemplifies what Radin calls his 'unique' approach to law and economics scholarship, one that takes incentives and welfare considerations seriously but, at the same time, respects and accounts for normative perspectives that give rise to very different understandings of justice. The grace period in which birth mothers may repudiate surrogacy contracts that Trebilcock would make mandatory, for example, comes with costs and benefits. When there are such trade-offs, law and economics would generally recommend leaving decisions about whether to include such a period up to

---

23 Martha A Field, *Surrogate Motherhood: The Legal and Human Issues*, expanded ed (Cambridge, MA: Harvard University Press, 1990).

the parties. His concern for the exploitation of a potentially vulnerable birth mother, however, causes him to recommend a mandatory grace period. His analysis is orthodox neither on a law and economics dimension, nor on any other; rather, he accepts that law ought to reflect a variety of normative perspectives, perspectives that inform our lives and choices in other domains. Human beings are not monomaniacally focused on living their lives by a single value, nor should the law be.

IV. Trebilcock and institutional analysis

In this part, I explore a different strain of Trebilcock's scholarship. Trebilcock is known not only for his contributions to the analysis of substantive law but also for his contributions to the study of institutions. He has written about the choice of policy instruments that governments ought to adopt, initially writing a stark public choice analysis[24] that evolved over time into one that reflected more confidence in the role of ideas rather than political self-interest in the choice of policy instrument.[25] Much of his work in law and development recognizes the importance of institutions for human flourishing.[26] And he has also written about specific institutional questions, such as a comparative study of, and the appropriate structure of, competition law institutions.[27] To illustrate Trebilcock's approach to institutional analysis, I will focus on his work on competition law institutions.[28] Competition law in Canada and elsewhere involves trade-offs within a standard economic framework as well as trade-offs that involve competing normative perspectives.[29] I will consider two examples: one is the now

---

24 Michael J Trebilcock et al, *The Choice of Governing Instrument* (Ottawa: Minister of Supply and Services, 1982).

25 Michael J Trebilcock, 'The Choice of Governing Instrument: A Retrospective' in Pearl Eliadis, Margaret M Hill & Michael Howlett, eds, *Designing Government* (Montreal and Kingston: McGill-Queen's University Press, 2014) 51.

26 See e.g. Mariana Mota Prado & Michael J Trebilcock, *Advanced Introduction to Law and Development*, 2d ed (Cheltenham, UK: Edward Elgar, 2021).

27 See e.g. Trebilcock & Iacobucci, 'Designing Competition Law,' supra note 5.

28 I do so with some trepidation as I was a co-author on some of his work in this area and would be loath to imply that his work in this area either required my input or reflects his most important work on institutions; neither implication is warranted. But his analysis of competition law institutions nicely illustrates his sensitivity to the importance of institutional design in relation to substantive law.

29 See e.g. Eleanor Fox & Michael J Trebilcock, *The Design of Competition Law Institutions: Global Norms, Local Choices* (New York: Oxford University Press, 2013); Francesco Ducci & Michael J Trebilcock, 'The Revival of Fairness Discourse in Competition Policy' (2019) 64 Antitrust Bulletin 79.

abolished efficiencies defence to mergers; the other is the role of Cabinet oversight of mergers.

On the first example, Canada until recently had an efficiencies defence to mergers in section 96 of the Competition Act.[30] This defence permitted mergers even if they substantially lessened competition as long as there were efficiency savings that were greater than, and offset, the merger's anti-competitive harms. However, the provision did not define anti-competitive harms, and there are different possibilities.[31] One possibility, which Trebilcock and I endorsed with our co-authors, is that both efficiency benefits and anti-competitive harms ought to be understood as relating to economic surplus: higher prices create efficiency losses, while cost savings create efficiency gains.[32] For a permissible merger, the latter effect should be greater than the former. A different possibility is that higher prices create concerns about distributive justice, not just efficiency losses. The Federal Court of Appeal, taking note of the Competition Act's statement of purpose in section 1.1, which identifies keeping prices low as an objective of the Act as well as efficiency, held that both efficiency and distributive concerns were relevant to the adjudication of section 96.[33]

Those who advocate for an efficiency approach to section 96, including Trebilcock, do not argue that distributive concerns have no place in law or policy. Rather they argue that competition law ought to focus on economic efficiency, while leaving critical questions of distributive fairness to other government instruments better equipped to address distribution, such as progressive taxation and government expenditures.[34] By focusing on instrument choice, the law can divide the policy objectives across instruments: competition law focuses on growing the size of the pie, while tax and expenditures help divide the pie. It might be easy to overlook an institutional foundation to this analysis. An

---

30 *Competition Act*, supra note 9.

31 See the discussion in Edward M Iacobucci, 'The Law's Answers to the Question: Why Competition?' in Randy Tritell, Daniel Crane & Damien Gérard, eds, *Why Competition? Voices from the Antitrust Community and Beyond* (New York: Concurrences, 2024) 43.

32 Michael J Trebilcock et al, *The Law and Economics of Canadian Competition Policy* (Toronto: University of Toronto Press, 2002) at 149–50 [Trebilcock et al, *Canadian Competition Policy*].

33 *Canada (Commissioner of Competition) v Superior Propane Inc*, [2000] CCTD No 15 (Comp Trib), [2001] FCJ No 455 (FCA); *Canada (Commissioner of Competition) v Superior Propane Inc*, [2002] CCTC No 10; *Canada (Commissioner of Competition) v Superior Propane, Inc*, [2003] 3 FC 529 [*Superior Propane*].

34 Trebilcock et al, *Canadian Competition Policy*, supra note 32 at 150.

efficiency approach to section 96 does not eliminate the need to weigh efficiency and distribution but merely punts the question to other legal instruments. The avoidance of the question within competition law, however, is entirely justifiable for institutional reasons.

If the trade-off between efficiency and distribution were both engaged in section 96 analysis, then the Competition Tribunal would have the responsibility to make a trade-off between two normatively incommensurable values, raising institutional competence questions (about which the tribunal itself expressed concern)[35] as well as questions about the determinacy of a law that depends fundamentally on a political choice by politically unaccountable tribunal members. On the other hand, by leaving distributional considerations to tax and expenditures, an efficiency approach to section 96 allocates responsibility for distributional questions to legislatures in setting tax and expenditure policy. This is wholly appropriate. Politicians ought to be better equipped to digest and consider questions about the overall level of economic fairness in a jurisdiction than a tribunal that specializes in technocratic competition law questions. Moreover, legislatures are accountable politically for their conclusions about how to resolve the efficiency-distribution trade-off.

The efficiencies defence example demonstrates an institutional constraint on the substantive law: even if multiple values are implicated by a legal question – in the case of the efficiencies defence, efficiency and distribution – this does not mean that a statute, or even an area of law, ought to account for a wide range of values. In the efficiencies defence context, rather than forcing the tribunal to answer political questions about what value to emphasize in a given case, it is better to have competition law focus on a single value, efficiency, and leave the choice of normative goals to other areas of law formulated by politically accountable legislatures. That is, institutional considerations push for substantive boundaries to competition law not because those boundaries have some Platonic, abstract meaning but, rather, because the institutional responsibility for answering some questions is better allocated to the legislature.

On a different matter, Trebilcock and I discuss political oversight of competition-related matters in a number of articles.[36] In Canadian

---

35 See *Superior Propane*, supra note 33.

36 Trebilcock & Iacobucci, 'Designing Competition Law,' supra note 5; Michael J Trebilcock & Edward M Iacobucci, 'The Design of Regulatory Institutions for the Canadian Telecommunications Sector' (2007) 33 Canadian Public Policy 127 [Trebilcock & Iacobucci, 'Telecommunications Sector']; Michael J Trebilcock & Edward M Iacobucci, 'Designing Competition Law Institutions: Values, Structure and Mandate' (2010) 41 Loy U Chicago LJ 455.

competition law, for example, mergers in transportation and finance are exempt from oversight by the Competition Tribunal and, instead, must be approved as being in the public interest, or disapproved, by the minister of transport and the minister of finance respectively.[37] Other sectors might also be subject to ministerial oversight but not explicitly. For example, the minister of industry, science and economic development must approve the transfer of any telecommunications licences, such as the licence to operate cellular services in a particular range of frequencies, which gives the minister as a practical matter the final say over a telecommunications merger. This was central to the Rogers-Shaw merger, which required both tribunal approval on pure competition law grounds, which was obtained,[38] and ministerial approval based on his assessment of the public interest to transfer spectrum licences, which was also eventually obtained with various conditions.[39]

It is not obvious that ministerial oversight of mergers in transport, finance, and telecommunications is institutionally appropriate. Indeed, I was initially sceptical of political oversight when we wrote our article together, worrying that the risks of self-interested politicking would outweigh the advantages of a broader perspective on a merger. Trebilcock persisted, however, and our article includes support for ministerial authority over mergers in sensitive industries. He wrote, and I co-signed, the following:

> Many competition law experts and commentators have decried the politicisation of merger review exemplified in the bank and airline mergers over the past three years and contrast the unruly, undisciplined, ill-informed and often unprincipled character of political debates and political decision-making, at least in a mega-merger context, with detached, expert review of mergers against a reasonably well-articulated set of principles by the Competition Bureau and the Competition Tribunal. We have noted that in practice decision-making in the Canadian competition context has not been as expert and well articulated as it might be, given the experience with the Tribunal, but these concerns raise two legitimate

---

37 *Competition Act*, supra note 9, s 94.

38 *Commissioner of Competition v Rogers Communications Inc and Shaw Communications Inc*, 2023 Comp Trib 1.

39 See 'Statement of Minister Champagne Concerning Competition in the Telecommunication Sector' (31 March 2023), online: *Government of Canada* <www.canada.ca/en/innovation-science-economic-development/news/2023/03/statement-from-minister-champagne-concerning-competition-in-the-telecommunication-sector.html>.

issues, one positive, one normative: (a) can a power of legal intervention for Cabinet Ministers be avoided? (b) is such a role undesirable?

We doubt that in a liberal democracy it is possible to avoid entirely a role for elected officials and Cabinet Ministers, in particular, in merger review. The range of interests, not all purely economic, affected by some mergers will invite intervention whether or not it is desirable from a competition perspective. Moreover, we doubt that it is desirable to exclude Cabinet Ministers entirely in this context. The difficulty, of course, is in determining when such involvement may be warranted.

In major national network infrastructure industries like banking, airlines, railroads, broadcasting and telecommunications where the federal government has pre-existing major regulatory responsibilities and where citizens coast-to-coast, in large communities and small, see themselves as potentially affected by mergers that may transform important elements of their communities' infrastructure, it is hardly surprising or unnatural that broad cross-sections of the citizenry and many organised interest groups will seek avenues to articulate their concerns and to seek reassurances that they will be addressed. Neither the Bureau's merger review process nor the merger review process currently undertaken by the Tribunal ... can accommodate this generalised form of civic engagement with the economic and social implications of mergers of this scale in national network infrastructure industries.[40]

That is, political oversight of mergers in such critical industries is both inevitable and normatively justifiable.

To be clear, Trebilcock is not in favour of a political free-for-all untethered to principled competition analysis. Rather, as in the Rogers-Shaw merger, there ought to be clear divisions of responsibility between competition enforcers and other bodies: the tribunal ought to have the authority to review the merger based on standard competition analysis, and, after obtaining approval, the minister or Cabinet ought to have authority to review the merger on public interest grounds. This, as in Trebilcock's work on institutions generally, exploits institutional comparative advantage by allocating technocratic decision making over competition matters to competition authorities, while leaving broad political concerns and protecting other normative values up to the politically accountable minister.[41]

---

40 Trebilcock & Iacobucci, 'Designing Competition Law,' supra note 5 at 385.

41 We elaborated on a similar institutional division of labour between competition authorities and the Canadian Radio-Television and Telecommunications Commission in Trebilcock & Iacobucci, 'Telecommunications Sector,' supra note 36.

V. Conclusion: institutions and trade-offs

Trebilcock takes trade-offs seriously. In his analysis of *Macauley*, he demonstrates that the House of Lords ignored trade-offs within its economic analysis of the contract, only considering the burdens of the contract to the songwriter. In *Limits of Freedom of Contract*, on the other hand, he also considers trade-offs, but trade-offs that often involve different normative perspectives, whether economic, feminist, communitarian, or others. The trade-offs in the *Macauley* kind of analysis are straightforward to resolve in principle: choose a legal approach to unfairness in contract that does not destroy mutually beneficial contracting. On the other hand, the trade-offs identified in *Limits of Freedom of Contract* are difficult, perhaps impossible, to resolve in principle. If economics points in one direction for a legal rule, while commodification concerns point in the opposite direction, there is no objectively correct way to resolve this trade-off: economic and commodification concerns are not subject to relative weightings that would allow a principled resolution of trade-offs between different values. Trebilcock wrestles with this incommensurability in *Limits of Freedom of Contract*, seeking to endorse legal approaches to difficult questions that respect different perspectives while accepting that it is impossible to satisfy the values of all perspectives simultaneously. He refuses to focus narrowly on a single value, insisting that this is not how society generally answers these difficult questions but, at the same time, does not provide a crisp answer to how we should address normative trade-offs.

Trebilcock's approach in *Limits of Freedom of Contract* to reject the primacy of any single perspective contrasts favourably with attempts to claim that one approach to law is superior to all others. Louis Kaplow and Steven Shavell, for example, reject any approach to law that does not seek to maximize welfare.[42] They rest this argument largely on the observation that, if a law fails to maximize welfare, it is possible for the law to make everybody worse off (a Pareto-inferior outcome). If everyone is as equally likely to be a tortfeasor as a tort victim, for example, inefficient tort law that seeks to promote fairness rather than maximize welfare would predictably make everybody worse off in expectation from a welfare perspective. But this conclusion is hardly surprising, nor does it do any work in rejecting non-welfarist approaches to law. If, for example, corrective justice demands a certain

---

42 Louis Kaplow & Steven Shavell, *Fairness Versus Welfare* (Cambridge, MA: Harvard University Press, 2002).

approach to tort law,[43] then the fact that it does not maximize welfare, and might even consequently reduce everyone's welfare, is not a reason to reject it – corrective justice is not seeking to promote welfare, and, thus, it is irrelevant that welfare considerations would demand an alternative approach.

While Trebilcock avoids Kaplow and Shavell's mistake, it is also fair to say that *Limits of Freedom of Contract* cannot prove that its recommendations provide the best approaches to questions subject to competing normative perspectives; without a single metric on which to measure the desirability of outcomes, it is impossible to do so. Trebilcock provides a wise, ecumenical, and thoughtful approach to different normative trade-offs in a wide variety of contexts in *Limits of Freedom of Contract*, but his conclusions are inevitably contestable. Trebilcock's full body of work, however, provides a different kind of approach to resolving trade-offs. Rather than attempting to resolve specific legal trade-offs substantively through defensible but contestable approaches to normative pluralism, his work on institutions provides a different perspective. Trade-offs within a particular normative framework are susceptible to objectively optimal resolutions, while other trade-offs with different values at stake do not have correct responses; rather, the question for the legal observer is simply to identify the appropriate institution to resolve the trade-off. For example, as discussed, before it was recently abolished, Trebilcock argued that the efficiencies defence ought to focus on efficiency while leaving distributional questions to other areas of law. This allocation of responsibility has an institutional foundation: legislatures are elected to advance law that reflects their vision of the values that matter most in society and are accountable for their choices, while competition authorities in contrast are expected to have and apply technocratic expertise. The law writ large does not avoid normative judgments about efficiency versus distribution – nor should it – but competition law in Trebilcock's ideal would focus on technocratic efficiency questions while leaving normative trade-offs to other institutions and the hurly burly of political debate.

The other institutional example discussed above of merger review in critical infrastructure industries pulls together the analysis in each section of this article. Trebilcock argues that competition authorities ought to review mergers in critical infrastructure industries such as transport and finance for competition questions, while leaving ultimate approval or rejection of the merger to political authorities. The review of a merger

---

43 Ernest J Weinrib, *The Idea of Private Law* (Oxford: Oxford University Press, 1995).

for its competition implications, whether in infrastructure or any other industry, is a technocratic question, one that involves difficult questions that turn on careful economic analysis of the competitive strengths and weaknesses of an acquisition. It is in this sense consistent with the economic analysis of the contract in *Macauley*: there were economic costs and benefits of the contract for both plaintiff and defendant, and the House of Lords's mistake was to focus excessively and mistakenly on the costs to the plaintiff. The Court was capable of appreciating some economic aspects of the contract and simply erred by not considering all of them. Just as courts are (or ought to be) equipped to consider the economic substance of a contract if they are adjudicating the economic fairness of the contract, competition authorities are capable of taking a careful look at competition economics in a merger.

The question of whether there are non-competition, public policy grounds to stop a merger in major infrastructure industries is a different kind of question. It does not involve analysis solely within an economic normative framework but, rather, might address questions about goals that are not economic, such as regional development, distributive justice, financial prudence, national security, technological development, and so on. Deciding whether a merger is in the public interest writ large is not a technocratic exercise but, rather, is an intensely political one that involves decisions about how much weight to put on different normative objectives. The analogue is not with the analysis of *Macauley* but, rather, with surrogacy in *Limits of Freedom of Contract*, an issue that invites consideration of not just economic incentive issues but also of issues that might include commodification, feminism, and autonomy. It is no surprise, then, that Trebilcock would rely on political oversight of politically significant mergers. While competition authorities may contribute to the analysis by assessing pure competition matters, institutional comparative advantage in deciding social policy questions that turn on a possible range of normative considerations are better left to political oversight.

One can now see the connections between Trebilcock's varied impacts on legal scholarship considered in this article. While, in principle, there is a correct, even if elusive, answer to an economic analysis, there is no correct answer in a contest between normative frameworks. 'Post-Benthamite Economics' got the economics right, while *Limits of Freedom of Contract* provided wise answers to difficult, polycentric problems, but there are no uncontroversially correct answers to these problems, even in principle. This is where Trebilcock's other swathe of scholarly contributions is relevant: institutions matter. Rather than merely addressing the polycentric problems in *Limits of Freedom of Contract* substantively, his body of work also offers an institutional way of thinking about poly-centric problems. Recognizing that institutional comparative advantage ought to be exploited, single-value problems, as in the economic analysis of contract in *Macauley*, or the competitive analysis of a merger, can be assigned to technocratic, expert institutions such as courts or tribunals to decide. Problems that invite multiple normative perspectives, on the other hand, ought to be decided by institutions equipped to weigh these competing normative perspectives and to be accountable for their ultimately political decisions. Thus, surrogacy contracts ought to be governed by mandatory regulations, and Cabinet ought to have the final say over mergers in infrastructure industries. There is an institutional armature that holds the stained-glass window of Trebilcock's scholarship together.

A final word about scholarly attention to institutions. While taking an entirely different intellectual approach to Trebilcock, his long-time University of Toronto colleague and leading private law theorist Ernest Weinrib has made arguments about private law and corrective justice that have a strong resonance with Trebilcock's thinking about institutions.[44] Weinrib accepts that there are entirely defensible – indeed, perhaps socially preferable – alternatives to tort law, such as government-administered no-fault insurance. If, however, society opts for the institution of tort law in which a plaintiff sues the defendant for a wrong, Weinrib argues that it has chosen an institution with a corrective justice foundation.[45] There is a strong connection between institutional choice and substantive law. The attention that scholars as brilliant and different as Trebilcock and Weinrib pay to the subject only reinforces the critical importance of the study of institutions and their relationship to substantive law.

---

44 See ibid.

45 See e.g. Ernest J Weinrib, 'The Insurance Justification and Private Law' (1985) 14 J Leg Stud 681 at 687 (who states in reference to a no-fault insurance scheme found in New Zealand: 'Now an assertion of the integrity of private law supplies no ground for preferring private to public law: both modes of ordering can have their own integrity. Affirmation of the coherence of private law in terms of corrective justice is in no way inconsistent with the advocacy of the replacement of tort law by a comprehensive compensation scheme on the New Zealand mode').

9 'More Legal Theory Than I Thought': Robert Sharpe and Legal Scholarship[†]

HAMISH STEWART

Robert Sharpe was a professor in the Faculty of Law at the University of Toronto from 1976 to 1988 and dean of the faculty from 1990 to 1995. He was appointed as a judge of the Ontario Court of Justice (General Division) in 1995; in 1999, he was elevated to the Court of Appeal for Ontario. Since retiring from the Court in 2020, he has returned to the Faculty of Law as a Distinguished Jurist in Residence and has been a very active member of the law school community as a teacher and a regular participant in seminars and workshops. Sharpe's works of legal scholarship fall into three categories. The first includes four works of doctrinal legal scholarship: *The Law of Habeas Corpus* (1976), *Interprovincial Product Liability Litigation* (1982), *Injunctions and Specific Performance* (1983), and *The Charter of Rights and Freedoms* (co-authored with Katherine Swinton in 1998).[1] Each of these books takes as its task to state a particular area of the law clearly, succinctly, and precisely but not uncritically. The second category includes several works of legal history, the most significant arguably being a magisterial biography of Brian Dickson (co-authored with Kent Roach).[2] The third category

---

† I am very grateful to Robert Sharpe, Chris Essert, David Dyzenhaus, and Gary Trotter for their comments on a draft of this article.

1 Robert J Sharpe, *The Law of Habeas Corpus* (Oxford: Clarendon Press, 1976) [Sharpe, *Habeas Corpus*]; Robert J Sharpe, *Interprovincial Product Liability Litigation* (Toronto: Butterworths, 1982); Robert J Sharpe, *Injunctions and Specific Performance* (Toronto: Canada Law Book, 1982) [Sharpe, *Injunctions*]; Robert J Sharpe & Katherine Swinton, *The Charter of Rights and Freedoms* (Toronto: Irwin Law, 1998). *Habeas Corpus* is in its third edition (with co-authors). *Injunctions and Specific Performance* has become a regularly updated looseleaf service available from Thomson Reuters. The *Charter* book is currently in its seventh edition, Kent Roach having replaced Katherine Swinton as co-author.

2 Robert J Sharpe & Kent Roach, *Brian Dickson: A Judge's Journey* (Toronto: University of Toronto Press, 2003). The others are Robert J Sharpe, *The Last Day, The Last Hour*

contains, so far, only one book: *Good Judgment* (2018), a series of reflections on judicial decision making, with specific reference to Sharpe's own experience as an appellate judge.[3]

Habeas Corpus, the book I will focus on, is a doctrinal analysis of an area of the law that had not previously received this type of treatment in book length. The ambition of a work of doctrinal legal scholarship, I take it, is to accurately state the law of a particular jurisdiction at a particular point in time. It has at least two positivistic features. First, it takes the law as a set of social facts to be described, at least initially; second, it has no difficulty conceptualizing a difference between the law 'as it is,' given the material at hand, and the law 'as it should be,' understood in light of some understanding of its purposes.[4]

Doctrinal legal scholarship may initially be contrasted with what I will refer to simply as 'legal theory.' I use that phrase to encompass any effort to understand what law in general is, how it differs (if at all) from other social phenomena and other ways of organizing human life, and, without necessarily accepting or even taking at face value its own normative claims, why (if at all) it has any normative hold over us. Legal theory in this sense includes many different approaches to, and understandings of, law. Some legal theorists try to make sense of the law's own concepts and categories, understanding them as coherent and mutually supporting expressions of a distinctive kind of normative claim,[5] or as normative constraints on the ways in which public

---

(Toronto: University of Toronto Press, 1988); Robert J Sharpe & Patricia I McMahon, *The Persons Case: The Origins and Legacy of the Fight for Female Legal Personhood* (Toronto: University of Toronto Press, 2007); Robert J Sharpe, *The Lazier Murder* (Toronto: University of Toronto Press, 2011).

3 Robert J Sharpe, *Good Judgment: Making Judicial Decisions* (Toronto: University of Toronto Press, 2018) [Sharpe, *Good Judgment*]. By my count, this book has already been cited twelve times by the Supreme Court of Canada, including by both the majority and the concurring judges in the landmark administrative law decision *Canada . (Minister of Citizenship and Immigration) v Vavilov*, 2019 SCC 65 [*Vavilov*]. Sharpe's forthcoming memoir may also fit into this third category. See Robert J Sharpe, *My Life in the Law: Lawyer, Scholar, Judge* (Toronto: Osgoode Society for Canadian Legal History and University of Toronto Press, 2025) [Sharpe, *My Life in the Law*].

4 'My aim in writing this book has been to provide an accurate account of the present state of the law with respect to injunctions and specific performance, and at the same time to contribute to the process of elaborating sound theoretical principes to govern the award of these remedies.' Sharpe, *Injunctions*, supra note 1 at v.

5 The University of Toronto Faculty of Law is well known for this style of legal theory. See, in particular, Ernest J Weinrib, *The Idea of Private Law* (Cambridge, MA: Harvard University Press, 1995); Arthur Ripstein, *Force and Freedom* (Cambridge, MA: Harvard University Press, 2008).

power can legitimately organize human activity,[6] or as particular ways of institutionalizing normative claims that are not distinctively legal.[7] Legal theorizing can also occur in a more sceptical register, treating legal concepts and categories as being, at best, distorted reflections of other more basic normative ideas[8] and, at worst, as ideological masks for operations of power,[9] of no normative significance in themselves. Doctrinal legal scholarship may also be contrasted with what I will simply call 'law reform' – that is, advocacy for change intended to improve the law with respect to some criteria, which may (or may not) themselves be connected with legal theory.

It is obvious that there are differences between these types of legal scholarship. Stating the test for an interlocutory injunction, on the basis of what courts have said when deciding whether to grant one, is one thing; advancing policy reasons for changing the test is another; and providing an account of why the test is what it is, or what it should be, in terms of a set of values that is hypothesized to underpin the law, is yet another.[10] Yet it is equally obvious that all these forms of legal scholarship are mutually interdependent. The dependence of legal theory and law reform on legal doctrine is plain enough: the doctrine is the thing (or at least one of the things) that the theory is supposed to be giving an account of (for better or for worse) and the thing that law

---

6 See e.g. David Dyzenhaus, *The Long Arc of Legality* (Cambridge, UK: Cambridge University Press, 2022).

7 See e.g. Joseph Raz, *The Morality of Freedom* (Oxford: Clarendon Press, 1986); John Gardner, *Law as a Leap of Faith* (Oxford: Oxford University Press, 2012).

8 This approach is characteristic of some strands of economic analysis of law and, in particular, of Ronald Coase's foundational 'The Problem of Social Cost' (1960) 3 Journal of Law and Economics 1 (which begins by debunking the legal concept of causation and, from there, attempts to subordinate all legal concepts to a particular conception of economic efficiency). Economic analysis of law, as practised at Toronto, has tended to be less sceptical than that. See e.g. Michael Trebilcock, *The Limits of Freedom of Contract* (Cambridge, MA: Harvard University Press, 1993).

9 This was the classic Marxist and socialist attitude to legal concepts, encapsulated in Karl Marx's dismissive reference to 'the narrow horizon of bourgeois right.' Karl Marx, 'Critique of the Gotha Program' in Robert Tucker, ed, *The Marx-Engels Reader*, 2d ed (New York: Norton, 1978) 531. It is also summed up in Frederick Engels's sketch of the process by which, he predicted, the state would wither away under socialism and communism because, being an instrument of class oppression, it would have no function in a classless society. Frederick Engels, *Herr Eugen Dühring's Revolution in Science*, 3d ed (New York: International Publishers, 1939) at 306–9.

10 In *Injunctions*, supra note 1, ch 2, Sharpe explicitly does the first two of these things, and the third, I would suggest, is implicit, having to do with the proper role of an interlocutory injunction in a legal system organized around ideas of right.

reform is supposed to be improving.[11] The dependence of legal doctrine on legal theory is perhaps less obvious. But recall the basic ambition of legal doctrinal scholarship: it is to state the law. What law does it state? Every body of law has within it themes and counter-themes, which is hardly surprising given the plurality of actors who have a hand in making it what it is: framers of constitutions, legislators, and judges, not to mention influential scholars such as Sharpe himself – all writing at different times, from different political persuasions, with different policy objectives, different social and economic backgrounds, and incompatible jurisprudential views.

I would guess that, for every proposition of law and for every attempt to 'state the law' on a particular point, no matter how uncontroversial it may seem, one could find in the relevant legal materials contrary propositions and counter-examples, which need to be explained as exceptions, written off as anomalies, or simply rejected as errors, if the stated proposition is to stand.[12] Of course, if no generalization was possible,

---

11 This point seems obvious. For a recent and more elaborate way of making it, see William Hamilton Byrne & Henrik Palmer Olsen, 'Doctrinal Legal Science: A Science of Its Own?' (2024) 27 Can JL & Jur 343. Yet the importance of legal doctrinal scholarship is still doubted in some quarters. See e.g. Geoffrey Samuel, 'Can Doctrinal Legal Scholarship Be Defended?' (2022) 4 Amicus Curiae 43 at 53 (describing legal doctrine as 'pseudo-scientific drivel' and, by extension, arguing that legal doctrinal scholarship has no value beyond assisting the legal profession in its presumably meaningless work).

12 The presumption of innocence is a good example. The 'golden thread' of English criminal law, as Viscount Sankey famously called it in *R v Woolmington*, [1935] AC 462, requires the Crown to prove all the elements of a criminal offence beyond a reasonable doubt. Thus, on a murder charge, the Crown has to prove both the unlawful act and the intention to cause death beyond a reasonable doubt. Yet, prior to *Woolmington*, it was very plausible to say that the Crown was required to prove only the *actus reus* and that the onus then shifted to the accused to demonstrate that he did not intend to cause death. Viscount Sankey writes several pages to refute a seemingly authoritative statement to that effect. Sir Michael Foster, *Crown Law* (Oxford: Clarendon Press, 1762) at 255. See also *Rex v Greenacre* (1837), 8 C & P 35 (disapproved in *Woolmington*) and, in Canada, *Girvin v The King* (1911), 45 SCR 167 (where the charge was arson). More recently, consider the bold statement in *R v Brown*, 2022 SCC 18 at para 90, that a precondition to the imposition of criminal liability, required by section 7 of the *Charter*, is proof of at least a marked departure from the standard of care that a reasonable person would have applied in the circumstances. *Canadian Charter of Rights and Freedoms*, Part 1 of the *Constitution Act, 1982*, being Schedule B to the *Canada Act 1982* (UK), 1982, c 11. But this holding is not consistent with the case law interpreting the offences involving operation of a conveyance under the influence of alcohol or drugs. The case law generally holds that, to prove the offence of 'over 80' operation of a conveyance causing death, the Crown need not prove any departure at all from the standard of care

then legal doctrinal scholarship would also be impossible. So would the rule of law because without some way of identifying what the law requires, there is no way of identifying what conduct counts as complying with it or departing from it. Nevertheless, the core demand of doctrinal legal scholarship – to state the law – cannot be answered without making choices (exercising judgment) about what to do with those counter-propositions and counter-examples: say they are not really part of the law; explain them as exceptions; assert that they are just wrong? And there is no way to do that, at least no way to do it coherently, without having at least implicitly a position on the values that the law should instantiate or promote – that is, without being a legal theorist, at least implicitly.[13] Thus, in addition to the two positivistic features I mentioned above, doctrinal legal scholarship necessarily has a normative orientation and, to that extent, is necessarily anti-positivist. A legal theorist might, for example, ask what the stresses that times of war and emergency place on the law tell us about the nature of law itself,[14] while a doctrinal legal scholar might find that they cannot tell us anything interesting about what the law is without taking a position, perhaps quite a strong one, on what its normative function is.[15] For both of them, making sense of the law requires attention to the justifications actually offered for specific legal decisions and the justifications that would make the whole set of legal decisions coherent.

Habeas Corpus illustrates these points. Though not explicitly a work of legal theory, it is an example of the way in which doctrinal legal scholarship and legal theory (at least in some of its forms) are engaged

---

applicable to either the activity of driving or the activity of drinking. See e.g. *R c Leblanc*, 2021 QCCA 1283 at para 105. Some courts have held that proof of impaired driving causing death does not require proof that the impairment caused the death, obviously making any inquiry into the manner in which the accused became intoxicated irrelevant to fault, and, while proof that the accused's actions were a significant contributing cause of death is required, that is not at all the same as proof of a marked departure from the standard of care expected of the reasonable driver (at paras 106–7). See also *R v Kelly*, 2025 ONCA 92; *R v Andre*, 2022 YKTC 9. In light of *Brown*, all of this case law appears quite anomalous and needs to be rationalized by anyone who wants to 'state the law' of criminal fault in Canada today.

13 For similar arguments along these lines, see Jan M Smits, 'What Is Legal Doctrine? On the Aims and Methods of Legal-Dogmatic Research' in Rob van Gestel & Hans-W Micklitz, eds, *Rethinking Legal Scholarship* (Cambridge, UK: Cambridge University Press, 2017) 207. See also Peter Benson's contribution to this special issue.

14 David Dyzenhaus, *The Constitution of Law* (Cambridge, UK: Cambridge University Press, 2006) [Dyzenhaus, *Constitution of Law*].

15 Sharpe, *Habeas Corpus*, supra note 1, ch 4.

in the same project: making sense of the phenomenon of law.[16] Sharpe describes the writ of *habeas corpus* as follows: '*Habeas corpus* is the common law remedy allowing anyone illegally imprisoned to petition the court for immediate release. The writ … commands the gaoler immediately to bring the prisoner before the court and to explain the reason for the imprisonment. If the judge finds the imprisonment to be unlawful, the prisoner is entitled to immediate release.'[17] Sharpe begins with a historical overview of the writ (chapter 1) and then goes through a whole series of doctrinal questions. What kind of review does the writ involve (chapter 2)? What kinds of facts are the proper subject matter of proof on an application and how does a party go about proving them (chapter 3)? How does the writ operate in times of actual or alleged emergency (chapter 4)? How does the writ operate in criminal law, and can it be used as a kind of appeal mechanism where there is no right of appeal or when the accused person's statutory rights of appeal have run out (chapter 5)?[18] How does it apply in civil commitment proceedings (chapter 6)? What is the temporal and geographical scope of the writ (chapters 7 and 8)? Sharpe's decision to organize the case law in this way was itself significant as no previous work on *habeas corpus* had done so.[19] All of this material is presented, as one would expect, succinctly and with the utmost clarity and precision. It is also, as one

---

16 It is, then, not surprising to learn from his other writings that Sharpe adopts a quasi-Dworkinian view of judicial decision making, requiring that a new decision make sense both in light of the existing legal materials and in light of the normative orientation of the legal order, though he does not claim to be an avatar of Ronald Dworkin's Hercules as he is less confident than Dworkin that he knows the unique right answer to any given legal question. See Sharpe, *Good Judgment*, supra note 3, chs 3, 5. Compare Ronald Dworkin, *Taking Rights Seriously* (Cambridge, MA: Harvard University Press, 1977), especially ch 4. While reading for the DPhil at Oxford in the mid-1970s, Sharpe attended a series of Dworkin's lectures, which he describes as a preview of *Taking Rights Seriously*. Sharpe, *My Life in the Law*, supra note 3, ch 5.

17 Robert Sharpe, 'Habeas Corpus' in Peter Cane & Joanne Conaghan, eds, *The New Oxford Companion to Law* (Oxford: Oxford University Press, 2008).

18 Compare *Forster v Canada (Correctional Service)*, 2019 ONCA 91, allowing an application for *habeas corpus* to proceed to determine the legality of the applicant's indefinite detention as a dangerous offender, which had been ordered more than thirty years earlier. The applicant's appeal from that order had been heard and dismissed, but the Court commented at para 20 that it was 'not a foregone conclusion' that the specific issue raised in his *habeas* application could have been a ground of appeal at that time. See also *Forster v Canada (Correctional Service)*, 2025 ONCA 40 (granting the application and ordering a new dangerous offender hearing).

19 An appellate judge (not Sharpe) once told me that the thing he liked most about a book I had recently written was the table of contents. At the time, I was taken aback by this remark, but I understand it now.

might expect, a little dry.[20] So it is startling to find, not in the main text but in a footnote, the word 'intolerable' used to describe a series of *habeas corpus* cases.[21] Where does that word come from? What is it doing in a book that is devoted to the seemingly positivistic project of stating the common law as of 1976?

Where it comes from, of course, is the normative orientation of the book. Although Sharpe does not put it quite this way, the book is about the role of the writ of *habeas corpus*, and, therefore, of judges, in a system of law that is oriented toward human freedom. The law of *habeas corpus* recognizes, in various ways, that depriving someone of one of the most basic freedoms – the freedom to move around in public and private spaces – by detaining or imprisoning them must, at least, be lawful.[22] No one would write a book like *Habeas Corpus*, a book that takes the writ seriously and tries to make sense of the disparate case law that is proper to it, without recognizing the values that the writ supports.

The word 'intolerable' occurs in the chapter titled 'Habeas Corpus and the Executive,' where Sharpe considers the use of the writ to test the legality of detentions under the executive's prerogative powers or under its special powers granted by the legislature in times of war and emergency. This is an area where 'stating the law' presents quite a challenge, as the reluctance of courts to second-guess the executive in troubled times creates results that cannot easily be squared with the law of *habeas corpus* or with general principles of public law. What Sharpe finds 'intolerable' is the refusal of courts to even consider the possible application of the writ in times of war and emergency by reading a statute empowering the executive to detain people so as to exclude it. Sharpe thinks that courts should do what they can to avoid such a result. They can do so not by inventing new legal doctrines or by going beyond their proper role as arbiters of the lawfulness of state action but by doing what courts normally do – reading a statute not only in light of its legislative purpose but also in light of the basic values of legal

---

20 Sharpe himself used this word when I told him that I was going to write about *Habeas Corpus*: 'It's a little dry, don't you think?'

21 Sharpe, *Habeas Corpus*, supra note 1 at 97, n 5.

22 In the *habeas corpus* entry cited in note 17 above, Sharpe puts it this way: '*Habeas corpus* is a cornerstone of the rule of law and a fundamental common law constitutional guarantee to ensure the liberty of the subject.' The law must, of course, also be justified by considerations that are appropriate to a free and democratic society. The writ of *habeas corpus* is not directly concerned with those considerations, but by requiring the person holding the applicant in detention to demonstrate the lawful basis for the detention, it can, in addition to requiring the detention to meet certain formal criteria of legality, bring them into focus.

order and so attributing a legislative intent to depart from those values only when other readings of the statute are unsustainable.

In doctrinal legal scholarship, there are three standard techniques for dealing with anomalies. The first is to show that the anomaly is only apparent because the seemingly anomalous case is an exception motivated by the same considerations as the rule itself: both the rule and the exception implement the same value or purpose.[23] The second is also to show that the anomaly is only apparent, this time because the apparently anomalous case does not really stand for the proposition that it is usually cited for because it has been systematically misread or because it can be satisfactorily explained on a different ground. The third method is to bite the bullet and say that the anomaly is real and that the decision in question is incorrect – not in light of some value or purpose that is external to the doctrine[24] but on the ground that it does not align with the values or purposes that the relevant area of the law is supposed to implement.

Sharpe uses some of these methods of explaining anomalies. He uses the second to explain away a series of cases in which prisoners of war and alien enemies were denied *habeas corpus*. These cases are often said to stand for the proposition that such detainees, and, in particular, prisoners of war, cannot apply for *habeas corpus* at all. Sharpe patiently shows that all of them can be explained on other grounds; therefore, they do not stand for that proposition. So, as Sharpe reads the law, a person held as a prisoner of war, like any other detainee, can contest the legality of their detention by way of *habeas corpus*.[25] For example, the *Kuechenmeister* decision is sometimes said to stand for the proposition that a person held as a prisoner of war or as an alien enemy in times of war cannot apply for *habeas corpus*.[26] But Sharpe shows that *Kuechenmeister* and the other relevant cases (at least, those from the era of World War II) in fact stand for the more modest proposition that a person who is 'properly considered a prisoner of war' is not entitled to release. But that is because the detention of a prisoner of war would be lawful under the executive's prerogative power to detain prisoners of war. If the detained person was not in fact a prisoner of war, or even if he was but had been released on license and subsequently detained for some other reason, or if the war was over, he could apply for *habeas*

---

23 That is the standard form of explanation for exceptions to the rule against hearsay.
24 There is nothing wrong with making such an argument, but it is not a legal-doctrinal argument.
25 Sharpe, *Habeas Corpus*, supra note 1 at 112–14.
26 *R v Bottrill, ex parte Kuechenmeister*, [1946] 2 All ER 434 (CA).

corpus to determine the legality of the detention: 'A more appropriate phrasing of the result would be: where someone held applies for habeas corpus, a complete answer to the writ will be that he is both in fact and law a prisoner of war detained by authority of the Crown.' If not, 'the court will investigate the propriety of the detention.'[27]

The issue in *Kuechenmeister* itself was whether the applicant's detention was still lawful given that, at the time of his application, active hostilities between the United Kingdom and Germany had ceased. The Court accepted a ministerial certificate stating that the United Kingdom and Germany were still in a state of war (Germany had surrendered, but a peace treaty had not yet been concluded) and so dismissed the application. Whether that was the right result or not, affording some deference to the executive's determination that a state of war continues to exist is a far cry from holding that a person who is held as a prisoner of war is not entitled to apply for *habeas corpus* at all. There is a world of difference between saying that a person who has been shown to be a prisoner of war is not entitled to release and saying that a person who happens to be in a prisoner of war camp is not even entitled to challenge the legality of their detention. *Habeas corpus* is the appropriate procedure for determining that issue. As Sharpe puts it, '[t]he danger in saying that a prisoner of war cannot apply for the writ is that it makes it appear that merely by being placed in an internment camp, an alleged alien enemy has had the legality of his detention conclusively determined.'[28]

The third method, as noted, is to say that the anomaly is real, meaning that the decision in question is wrong. Sharpe does not hesitate to do that either. He joins other critics in arguing that the House of Lords's well-known decisions in *Liversidge v Anderson*[29] and *Greene v Secretary of State for Home Affairs*[30] were wrongly reasoned. Both cases involved the interpretation of a war-time regulation giving the Home Secretary the power to detain 'any person' if the Home Secretary 'has reasonable cause to believe [the] person to be of hostile origin or associations, or to have been recently concerned in acts prejudicial to the public safety or to the defence of the realm.'[31] One might think, applying ordinary principles of statutory interpretation, administrative law, and criminal procedure, that a detained person could challenge the detention on two

---

27 Quotations in this paragraph are from Sharpe, *Habeas Corpus*, supra note 1 at 113.
28 Ibid at 114.
29 [1942] AC 206 [*Liversidge*].
30 [1942] AC 284.
31 *Defence (General) Regulations*, 1939, s 18B.

grounds: either the Home Secretary did not act in good faith (that is, he did not believe the facts supposedly justifying the detention), or the Home Secretary's belief in these facts was unreasonable. In either case, the statutory conditions justifying the detention would not exist. On that interpretation, the reasonableness of the Home Secretary's belief would be an issue for a reviewing court to determine. In *Liversidge v Anderson*, an action for false imprisonment against the Home Secretary, a majority of the House of Lords rejected that interpretation, holding that it was sufficient that the Home Secretary honestly believed that the facts justifying the plaintiff's detention existed.[32] As Sharpe puts it, the House of Lords held that 'the Home Secretary could judge for himself what was reasonable.'[33] Or, as Lord Atkin put it in his celebrated dissent, the majority held that 'the words "if the Secretary of State has reasonable cause" merely mean "if the Secretary of State thinks that he has reasonable cause."'[34] But, he insisted, these two expressions do not have the same meaning: thinking that one has something is not the same as having it.[35]

Sharpe summarizes all of this clearly and concisely.[36] Someone who thought that the function of doctrinal scholarship was merely to 'state the law' might have stopped there. But that would be, to say the least, unhelpful. The reasoning in *Liversidge v Anderson* is anomalous when compared to other common law doctrines that interpret similarly worded legal standards, such as the common law power of a constable to make an arrest.[37] The reader, even one who (probably mistakenly) thinks that they are only interested in what the law is, needs more. Sharpe gives us more. He supports Lord Atkin's dissent. He recognizes, of course, that what was '[a]t stake was the issue of the appropriateness of judicial

---

32 *Liversidge*, supra note 29 at 220, per Lord Maugham. The result in *Liversidge* was that the Home Secretary was not required to respond to the plaintiff's demand for particulars of the information that led to his forming the belief required by section 18A; the result in *Greene* was that the Home Secretary was not required to show that his grounds for detaining the applicant were reasonable, only that they were *bona fide*. Lord Atkin dissented in *Liversidge* but concurred in the result in *Greene* on the basis that the Home Secretary had shown reasonable grounds for the applicant's detention.

33 Sharpe, *Habeas Corpus*, supra note 1 at 99.

34 *Liversidge*, supra note 29 at 226, per Lord Atkin.

35 '"If A has a right of way" does not mean and cannot mean "if A thinks that he has a right of way."' Ibid at 227.

36 Sharpe, *Habeas Corpus*, supra note 1 at 98–100.

37 *Liversidge*, supra note 29 at 228–9, per Lord Atkin.

interference with the executive in time of war.'[38] But he insists that 'the interpretation of a statute can only take place in the broader context of the principles of constitutional and administrative law ... [which] Lord Atkin asserted, and [which] the majority chose to ignore.'[39] This conclusion can only follow from having a sense of the values of personal freedom that the law in general, and the writ of *habeas corpus* in particular, are supposed to protect: 'If [a] sacrifice [of personal liberty] is to be made to the public safety, then Parliament should say so in the clearest and most unequivocal language.'[40]

Yet it is not even these cases to which Sharpe applies the word 'intolerable.' That word appears in his critique of the Canadian authorities interpreting section 5 of the former War Measures Act.[41] That section provided that

> [n]o person who is held for deportation under this Act or under any regulation made thereto, or is under arrest or detention as an alien enemy or upon suspicion that he is an alien enemy, or to prevent his departure from Canada, shall be released upon bail or otherwise discharged or tried, without the consent of the Minister of Justice.[42]

The relevant cases generally hold that this section meant that a person detained under the War Measures Act could not challenge the legality of their detention even by means of an application for *habeas corpus*.[43]

---

38 Sharpe, *Habeas Corpus*, supra note 1 at 100.

39 Ibid at 102.

40 Ibid. For a more detailed discussion of the two cases, reaching a similar conclusion, see Dyzenhaus, *Constitution of Law*, supra note 14 at 149–60.

41 *War Measures Act*, SC 1914, c 2.

42 The section originally appeared as section 11 of the *War Measures Act*, ibid. In later versions of the Act, it appears as section 5 (see e.g. *War Measures Act*, RSC 1985, c W-2, s 5). I follow Sharpe in referring to it as section 5. The *War Measures Act* was repealed in 1988 by section 80 of the *Emergencies Act*, RSC 1985, c 22 (4th Supp).

43 The cases cited by Sharpe are *Re Beranek* (1915), 24 CCC 252 (Ont SC) [*Beranek*]; *Re Gusetu* (1915), 24 CCC 427 (Que Sup Ct) (holding that the applicant, an enemy alien held prisoner of war, could not succeed on a *habeas corpus* application because (a) as in *Beranek*, he had not obtained the minister's consent under section 5 of the *War Measures Act* and (b) prisoners of war cannot apply for *habeas corpus*); *Re Gottesmann* (1918), 29 CCC 439 (Ont SC) (same as *Beranek* and holding further that the privative clause in section 23 of the *Immigration Act, 1910*, 9 & 10 Edw VIII, c 27, precluded review of detention even by way of *habeas corpus*); *Re Sullivan* (1941), 75 CCC 70 (Ont SC), aff'd *loc cit* (Ont CA) (holding that a detention order of the Minister of Justice made under regulations enacted pursuant to the *War Measures Act*, RSC 1927, c 206, was not reviewable).

For example, in *Re Beranek*, a decision from World War I, the applicant was detained as an enemy alien. He asserted that he was not an enemy alien but had been naturalized as a British subject; if that was true, his detention would not be authorized by the Act. The Court refused to entertain his argument at all. Foreshadowing *Liversidge v Anderson*, the Court held that the only basis for review of the decision to detain would be bad faith,[44] but even that holding appears to be *obiter dicta* as the real basis of the decision is that the wording of section 5 meant that there could be no judicial proceedings at all without the consent of the Minister of Justice.[45] The same branch of government that had detained Rudolf Beranek thus had the power to decide whether there would be any review of its own decision to detain him. As the Court put it, 'if he be a British subject, he ought not to be detained as an alien enemy, whatever other charge might be laid against him: but all that is for the consideration of the Minister of Justice first.'[46]

Sharpe says: 'The result is intolerable.'[47] While he does not expand on the point, the word is apt because the basic personal freedom protected by the writ of *habeas corpus* is such an important element of the law of a free society that there must always be a forum to determine the legality of any detention. Moreover, the solution to this intolerable result, Sharpe suggests, is not hard to find. It lies well within the repertoire of basic common law principles: 'The reasoning used to evade the effect of privative clauses should be used.' That is, as in ordinary administrative law, so here, a clause purporting to oust judicial review of a decision by a public official should never be read as precluding review altogether but, instead, as signaling that a reviewing court should defer in certain respects to the decision maker whose decision is protected by the clause, thus limiting review to certain types of grounds or arguments.[48]

---

44 *Beranek*, supra note 43 at 253.

45 Ibid.

46 Ibid at 255.

47 All quotations in this paragraph are from Sharpe, *Habeas Corpus*, supra note 1 at 97, n 5.

48 The case law and academic literature on the effect of privative clauses is so vast as to defy easy summary, but see the discussion in *Vavilov*, supra note 3 at paras 210–29, per Abella and Karakatsanis JJ concurring in the result; Bora Laskin, 'Certiorari to Labour Boards: The Apparent Futility of Privative Clauses' (1952) 30 Can Bar Rev 986; David Dyzenhaus, 'Disobeying Parliament? Privative Clauses and the Rule of Law' in Richard Bauman & Tsvi Kahana, eds, *The Least Examined Branch: The Role of Legislatures in the Constitutional State* (Cambridge, UK: Cambridge University Press, 2006) 499. As Paul Daly puts it, the basic problem with a privative clause is that it renders the statute in question 'incoherent': the powers granted by a statute are necessarily limited by the statute itself, but the 'privative clause ... purports to render

If the power to detain had been exceeded – if, for example, it had been applied to a person who was clearly a British subject – then 'the prisoner would not be a person "held under this Act" and s. 5 would have no application.' On this reading, section 5 would not preclude *habeas corpus* but, instead, might require a reviewing court to afford some deference to the executive's determination that the person was not a British subject.[49] Without the possibility of any review whatsoever, the supposed power to detain enemy aliens without review would be in effect a power to detain anyone without review – not the power that the statute grants and an intolerable result indeed.[50]

Habeas Corpus is a finely crafted work of legal-doctrinal scholarship. It is also, not explicitly but implicitly, a work of legal theory in that its purpose is to state the law not just as a set of rules but also in a manner suitable for a society of free persons. Wartime anomalies in the availability of the writ are either explained as not so threatening to its essence as they appear to be or are frankly criticized for being wrong, even 'intolerable.' Summarizing the critical reception of *Habeas Corpus*, Sharpe notes that JAG Griffith had quoted from his discussion of *Liversidge v Anderson* in developing his own criticism of 'war-time internment decisions for ignoring legal considerations and deciding cases on the basis of politics.'[51] 'So,' concludes Sharpe, 'maybe there was more legal theory in my book than I thought.'[52]

---

these limits unenforceable by reviewing courts.' Paul Daly, *A Theory of Deference in Administrative Law* (Cambridge, UK: Cambridge University Press, 2012) at 65.

49 The Court thought this was a live issue on the facts of *Beranek*, but, given its interpretation of section 5, did not consider it. See *Beranek*, supra note 43 at 254–5.

50 The contemporary relevance of these issues is obvious. See *Abrego Garcia v Noem et al*, an unreported decision of the US Court of Appeals for the Fourth Circuit, released 17 April 2025, online: <s3.documentcloud.org/documents/25900477/25-1404-ruling.pdf>.

51 JAG Griffith, *The Politics of the Judiciary* (London: Fontana, 1977) at 79–83. As David Dyzenhaus pointed out to me, there is some irony here because Griffith was, from a democratic perspective, critical of the English judiciary as an institution, whereas Sharpe's account of *habeas corpus* contemplates a robust role for judges in a democracy.

52 Sharpe, *My Life in the Law*, supra note 3, ch 5.

10 On Living Federal Lives: Katherine Swinton's *The Supreme Court and Canadian Federalism* and the Future of Federal Imagination

JEAN-CHRISTOPHE BÉDARD-RUBIN

Does the law of federalism matter? In the middle third of the twentieth century, an increasing number of constitutional scholars, especially those with an ear for legal realism, started to doubt it. Courts appeared to retreat from a strict enforcement of the division of powers and allowed more overlap between federal and provincial jurisdiction. The increasing cooperation between the two orders of government through the enactment of interlocking legislation, intergovernmental agreements, and inter-delegation of executive powers suggested that the political process was better than courts at solving jurisdictional issues. When judges did enforce the federal division of powers, their jurisprudence seemed either incoherent or unprincipled, ultimately only delaying rather than blocking the optimal allocation of power. What use was there for a judicial arbiter of federal disputes that seemed useless at best and pernicious at worst?[1]

In her first book, published in 1990, *The Supreme Court and Canadian Federalism: The Laskin-Dickson Years*, Katherine Swinton took this realist challenge seriously.[2] The tensions that had accrued in the federation in the previous fifteen years – from the rise of Quebec separatism to

---

1 For the two most elaborate accounts of the Court's federalism jurisprudence along those lines, see Paul C Weiler, 'The Supreme Court and the Law of Canadian Federalism' (1973) 23:2 UTLJ 307; Paul Weiler, *In the Last Resort: A Critical Study of the Supreme Court of Canada* (Toronto: Carswell, 1974) [Weiler, *In the Last Resort*]; Patrick Monahan, 'At Doctrine's Twilight: The Structure of Canadian Federalism' (1984) 34:1 UTLJ 47 [Monahan, 'At Doctrine's Twilight']; Patrick Monahan, *Politics and the Constitution: The Charter, Federalism and the Supreme Court of Canada* (Toronto: Carswell, 1987).

2 'My objective is to respond to the critics of the Supreme Court who decry its role in federal-provincial disputes.' Katherine Swinton, *The Supreme Court and Canadian Federalism: The Laskin-Dickson Years* (Toronto: Carswell, 1990) at 5 [Swinton, *Supreme Court*].

Western alienation – had dealt an important blow to the smooth operation of cooperative federalism. Courts were thrust back into the constitutional spotlight as a result. Governments clashed directly or intervened to support private litigants in a sort of constitutional lawfare by proxy. By 1990, the Supreme Court of Canada had seen almost two decades of an unprecedented level of activity in federalism cases. Time was ripe for a reassessment of the question that the realist critics asked: does law matter to federalism?

Swinton's response was an emphatic 'yes.' This chapter explores her distinctive contribution to the study of federalism in Canada and some of the lessons one might draw from her work. Swinton's insistence on the importance of legal reasoning to the resolution of jurisdictional issues draws attention to the different imaginative possibilities that the law of federalism affords. Since federalism is a specific way of conceiving of the distribution of public power among different communities that coexist in a federation, Swinton underscores that the question of jurisdiction is one that citizens can validly make as they demand justifications from the governments who purport to exercise authority over them. Her work allows us to see competing constitutional visions staked out in the jurisprudence of the Supreme Court as judges tried to assess the constitutional soundness of the reasons presented in response. While the relatively consensual approach that seems to have characterized the Supreme Court's approach to federalism cases in the intervening decades might have attenuated those sharp contrasts, her work still reveals underlying federal logics in legal debates. It testifies to the enduring value of her work, even if some of her fundamental intuitions deserve to be further developed to speak meaningfully to some of today's most pressing legal challenges.

Part I of this article explains Swinton's distinctive contribution to the study of federalism in Canada and situates her work in the wave of scholarship of the 1990s that responded to the crisis of Canadian federalism. Part II expands on Swinton's fundamental insights to interpret other developments in the law of federalism in the context of constitutional reform. Part III looks forward and brings Swinton's pluralist sensibility to bear on the challenges that the recognition of Indigenous self-government poses for the Canadian federal imagination and its working conception of sovereignty.

I. Swinton's distinctive contribution to federalism

If one were to sum up Swinton's contribution to constitutional scholarship, a simple slogan might suffice: law matters. The statement seems banal, but Swinton's demonstration requires a sophisticated account of the judicial role in a diverse federation like Canada. She carefully reconstructs the distinct constitutional theories of three judges to show how they animate surface disagreement about the interpretation of the division of powers and the development of discrete doctrines in the law of federalism.[3] She argues that 'the judges in federalism disputes are engaged in a balancing exercise in which they are influenced by beliefs about the appropriate roles of federal and provincial communities in Canada, beliefs which are shaped, in part, by [values] such as tradition, efficiency, liberty, and functionalism.'[4] Swinton's book betrays a certain pluralist sensibility which this part will try to reconstruct through an examination of Swinton's central theses: a pluralism about constitutional values and a political pluralism about the different communities competing for the loyalties of citizens in the federal system.

Thus, to say that law matters first means that federalism is a distinct kind of political project that shapes the expectations of law's addressees. Courts 'must pay heed to the words of the [constitutional] document and past decisions, for courts have an obligation to the rule of law' and because '[g]overnments *and citizens* have expectations about the scope of federal and provincial jurisdiction based upon these sources.'[5] Courts offer a venue no less valuable than the political arena for the expression of competing views about the right allocation of jurisdiction in a federation. Throughout her analysis, Swinton underscores that courts can be more responsive to the diversity of interests and conceptions of citizenship than the political process. She starts from the fact that courts generally lack the expertise and democratic input necessary to make what are essentially marginal judicial amendments of the constitution. Nevertheless, Swinton traces the subtle acknowledgement by the Supreme Court of its policy-making role in federalism cases through the development of new judicial techniques that evince the Court's willingness to exercise its active virtues to bring it more closely into contact with citizens.[6]

For example, the Supreme Court of Canada relaxed its rules on standing in three cases in the late 1970s and early 1980s so as to 'recognize the

---

3 Ibid at 6.

4 Ibid at 5.

5 Ibid at 34 [emphasis added].

6 Ibid 62–8, 87–8. The contrast is with Alexander Bickel's praise for the 'passive virtues' of the US Supreme Court. Alexander M Bickel, *The Least Dangerous Branch: The Supreme Court at the Bar of Politics*, 2d ed (New Haven, CT: Yale University Press, 1986) at ch 4.

citizen's right to constitutional government in compliance with the distribution of powers [and] an individual interest in freedom from regulation by a government without jurisdiction to impose such restraints.'[7] Beginning with the *Anti-Inflation Reference*,[8] the Court also made greater use of legislative facts and social science evidence which 'signal[led] a judicial recognition that distribution of powers cases cannot be decided on the basis of cases and statute alone'[9] as well as its desire 'to obtain some sense of the impact that its own decisions may have.'[10] Around the same time, intervenors started playing a more active role in constitutional litigation.[11] Even if there was 'a real ambivalence in the Court about interest groups interventions,'[12] the general trend seemed to be an acknowledgement of the multi-polar nature of federalism disputes and the policy role of the Court in this context, 'a policy role that requires consideration of interests beyond those of the immediate litigants.'[13] Finally, the development of more flexible remedies, such as suspended declarations of invalidity, also suggested that the Court recognized that third parties as well as governments have a legitimate interest in the smooth operation of the federal system.[14] On the one hand, Swinton notes that '[t]he more the Court engages in consideration of evidence and the balancing of interests in the federal system, the more vulnerable the Court becomes to charges of illegitimacy and incompetence because it is seen to be second guessing elected legislators.'[15] But her demonstration also shows, on the other hand, that 'the[se] cases convey the belief that the Constitution belongs to the citizens of Canada, not the politicians who control federal and provincial governments from time to time.'[16] Many of the changes that are associated with the advent of a new constitutional culture and a 'citizens' constitution' with the

---

7 Swinton, *Supreme Court*, supra note 2 at 65–6; *Thorson v Attorney General of Canada*, [1975] 1 SCR 138; *Nova Scotia Board of Censors v McNeil*, [1978] 2 SCR 662; *Minister of Justice of Canada v Borowski*, [1981] 2 SCR 575.

8 *Re: Anti-Inflation Act*, [1976] 2 SCR 373.

9 Swinton, *Supreme Court*, supra note 2 at 80.

10 Ibid at 85.

11 See *Attorney General of Canada v Lavell*, [1974] SCR 1349; *Morgentaler v The Queen*, [1976] 1 SCR 616; Swinton, *Supreme Court*, supra note 2 at 70.

12 Ibid at 71.

13 Ibid at 75.

14 *Re Manitoba Language Rights*, [1985] 1 SCR 721 (on the suspended declaration of invalidity). See also *R v Mercure*, [1988] 1 SCR 234.

15 Swinton, *Supreme Court*, supra note 2 at 88.

16 Ibid at 65.

Canadian Charter of Rights and Freedoms can in fact be traced back to changes in federalism doctrines of the 1970s and early 1980s.[17]

Swinton visibly welcomes this transition. She proceeds to scrutinize the different 'values' that seem to inform the Supreme Court of Canada's more open approach to constitutional adjudication, be it based on text, history, or the balancing of competing economic interests. Overall, while she concedes that '[c]oncerns about tradition, liberty, and efficiency all play a role in constitutional interpretation,' she argues that 'none can provide a tool to resolve all disputes that reach the Court.'[18] Federal adjudication inevitably entails weighing a plurality of constitutional values and 'claims of federal and provincial communities for authority to act.'[19]

In fact, one of the most important points that Swinton makes is that governments that make claims on behalf of the communities they purport to represent compete for the divided loyalty of federal citizens. Other scholars similarly argued that judges bring to bear a 'background theory of the polity' in federalism cases, whether pan-Canadianist or provincialist, and that this theory often corresponds to a bias in favour of the interests of the federal or provincial governments.[20] But Swinton is more nuanced in her approach and captures the expression of more complex views of citizenship. She underscores that the federal system 'continues to respond to the diversity of the country and the demands of many of its elites *and citizens.*'[21] The positions articulated by governments are only imperfect proxies of the different conceptions of community held by citizens (even if they might be the only relatively reliable ones).[22] As a consequence, popular expectations matter in the interpretation of the federal division of powers.

In a nutshell, a 'judge's task is neither arbitrary and totally subjective … nor can it be seen as mechanical and totally objective, as

---

17 The idea of the 'Citizen's Constitution' is most closely associated with the work of political scientist Alan Cairns. See e.g. Alan C Cairns, *Disruptions: Constitutional Struggles, from the Charter to Meech Lake*, edited by Douglas E Williams (Toronto: McClelland & Stewart, 1991). Swinton also refers specifically to Cairns on this point and his assessment of the Meech Lake Accord in Katherine Swinton, 'Amending the Canadian Constitution: Lessons from Meech Lake' (1992) 42:2 UTLJ 139 at 152. *Canadian Charter of Rights and Freedoms*, Part I of the *Constitution Act 1982*, being Schedule B to the *Canada Act 1982* (UK), 1982, c 11.

18 Swinton, *Supreme Court*, supra note 2 at 195.

19 Ibid at 195.

20 See Monahan, 'At Doctrine's Twilight,' supra note 1.

21 Swinton, *Supreme Court*, supra note 2 at 201 [emphasis added].

22 Ibid at 207.

the form of many judgments might indicate. Judging is a human exercise disciplined by concerns for principle, respect for the constitutional text and for certainty, and yet also driven by vision of the "good" federal structure for this country at the time of the decision.'[23] The 'good' federal structure cannot be the actualization of the ideal federation for 'federalism itself is something of an indeterminate concept.'[24] Seen in this light, the apparent constraints that federalism doctrines impose on constitutional adjudication are evidence less of a reverence for legalism than a recognition that precedents and the rule of law are necessary to give due respect for the settled expectations of communities that have ordered their lives accordingly and those of governments that they feel loyal to.[25] The procedural reforms outlined above ensure that affected parties are afforded the opportunity to make representations and that their interests are taken into consideration when the Court considers the impact that its decisions might have on people living federal lives.[26]

By underscoring the inherently political but principled nature of constitutional decision-making, Swinton moves the debate about federalism into more philosophical terrain. She encourages judges to adopt a more self-reflexive approach and to cease to 'wear a mantle of neutrality' and hide behind a formalist facade: 'While the formalist style provides flexibility, in that it permits the Court to adapt the provisions of the constitution to changing circumstances, the result is, too often, an appearance of arbitrariness and confusion.'[27] The critics of the Court that Swinton is responding to adopt a broadly positivist conception of constitutional adjudication.[28] For them, law runs out when first-order rules are silent or indeterminate or when there is no precise second-order rule of interpretation to select between conflicting first-order rules. In these cases, judges 'are just making up the law as they go along.'[29] But Swinton encourages – and her scholarship in fact seeks to contribute to the development of – a richer conception of judicial interpretation that ties the inevitable policy element with a more explicit

---

23 Ibid at 200.
24 Ibid.
25 Ibid at 198.
26 According to Swinton, this is particularly true in the case of Brian Dickson. See ibid, ch 10.
27 Ibid at 87, 88.
28 See e.g. Weiler, *In the Last Resort*, supra note 1 at 173.
29 Swinton, *Supreme Court*, supra note 2 at 55 (criticizing Weiler's conception of constitutional adjudication in federalism cases).

acknowledgement of the background principles involved.[30] Swinton's reference to Ronald Dworkin suggests that she viewed constitutional interpretation as always, at bottom, both moral and legal theoretical and that there is no sharp dividing line between the two.[31]

This Dworkinian conception of constitutional adjudication is exploited most fruitfully in the three intellectual biographies of Bora Laskin, Jean Beetz, and Brian Dickson that Swinton uses to illustrate and contrast different principled approaches to constitutional adjudication. The decisions of Laskin, the functionalist; Beetz, the conceptualist; and – for lack of a better word – Dickson, the pragmatist, acquire an unexpected coherence thanks to the delicate brushstrokes with which Swinton paints their respective jurisprudential record. By bringing out the principled aspects of their decisions, Swinton connects seemingly discrete areas of constitutional law to draw the contours of relatively well-articulated alternative constitutional visions – from the status of superior courts to the federal criminal law power and the use of different modalities of constitutional interpretation.[32]

The assemblage brings out the differences of approach that lay behind the formal style of opinion writing and sharpens the contrast between their respective judicial philosophies. Her work on Beetz, in particular, remains quite helpful to constitutional scholars today.[33] Beetz was and remains a somewhat enigmatic figure.[34] On top of not being a particularly prolific academic – and a notoriously slow writer as a judge – most

---

30 She writes that 'constitutional adjudication is a creative enterprise that gives courts an important policy role in our federal system' (ibid at 31). Elsewhere, she writes that 'subjectivity cannot be avoided, for the judge must make a determination about the appropriate balance between federal and provincial governments in light of a variety of sources' (ibid at 210–11) and that 'there is no formula or grand theory which can explain or determine each case involving the distribution of powers, and it is unrealistic to search for one or to decry the judicial task as illegitimate because such a theory is lacking' (ibid at 216–17).

31 Swinton refers to Ronald Dworkin, 'Law as Interpretation' (1982) 60 Tex L Rev 527.

32 On modalities, see Philip Bobbitt, *Constitutional Fate: Theory of the Constitution* (Oxford: Oxford University Press, 1984).

33 Without detracting from Swinton's contribution, we now have excellent biographies of Bora Laskin and Brian Dickson. Philip Girard, *Bora Laskin: Bringing Law to Life* (Toronto: Osgoode Society for Canadian Legal History, 2005); Robert J Sharpe & Kent Roach, *Brian Dickson: A Judge's Journey* (Toronto: Osgoode Society for Canadian Legal History, 2003).

34 The reasons are explained in part in *Mélanges Jean Beetz* (Montreal: Themis, 1995). For another analysis of Beetz's judicial philosophy, see Andrée Lajoie, Pierrette Mulazzi & Michèle Gamache, 'Political Ideas in Quebec and the Evolution of Canadian Constitutional Law, 1945 to 1985' in Ivan Bernier & Andrée Lajoie, eds,

of Beetz's work before his appointment to the bench was written in French. There is thus less material to work with, even if Beetz had such a distinctive voice during his fifteen years on the Supreme Court of Canada. As she does for Laskin, Swinton helpfully brings out the connections between the different periods of Beetz's career and the different approach – one might call it cartesian or civilian – that Beetz and other Quebec judges like Louis-Philippe Pigeon brought to their work on the Court.[35] However, it is hard not to notice Swinton's penchant and sympathy for Dickson's 'jurisprudence of interests.' Dickson J's decisions seem to epitomize the open, prudent, and principled approach to federal policy-making that she thought the Court should adopt.[36] Those three intellectual biographies provide helpful resources to gain access to the constitutional visions that informed the federalism disputes of the 1970s and 1980s that were so formative in the development of modern federalism.[37]

Of course, Swinton's interest in federalism was not extraordinary. Despite the attractiveness of the new Charter, the study of federalism and Confederation also underwent a revival in the 1990s. The scholarship produced by historians and political theorists, in particular, contributed to the public discussion about mega-constitutional reform that spanned the decade between the Meech Lake Accord and the *Secession Reference*.[38] At a time when scholars were consumed by the light that

---

The Supreme Court as an Instrument of Political Change (Toronto: University of Toronto Press, 1985) 1.

35 It would be a worthwhile exercise to try to determine whether the distinctive approach of Quebec judges to federalism that Swinton discerned in the decisions of Jean Beetz and Louis-Philippe Pigeon continues to obtain on the bench since 1990. Unfortunately, it is not one I have space to pursue here.

36 See e.g. Swinton, *Supreme Court*, supra note 2 at 57–8.

37 To the extent that it can be used as a valid indicator, *The Supreme Court and Canadian Federalism* is featured more often than any other work of scholarship in the *Canadian Constitutional Law* casebook used across the country to introduce students to the mysteries of Canadian federalism – from the colour of margarine to the ineffable nature of emergency powers. Patrick Macklem & Carissima Mathen, eds, *Canadian Constitutional Law*, 6th ed (Toronto: Emond, 2023). As it happens, Swinton was one of the co-editors of the first edition.

38 *Constitutional Accord, 1987* (Ottawa: Government of Canada, 1987); *Reference re Secession of Quebec*, [1998] 2 SCR 217. For a discussion of the renewed interest in Confederation in the 1990s, see Janet Ajzenstat, *Discovering Confederation: A Canadian's Story* (Montreal and Kingston: McGill-Queen's University Press, 2014). From a contemporary perspective, see also Jeremy Webber, *Reimagining Canada: Language, Culture, Community, and the Canadian Constitution* (Montreal and Kingston: McGill-Queen's University Press, 1994).

history might shed on seemingly never-ending constitutional negotiations, Swinton's pivot to the present and the courts, motivated perhaps by her scepticism about the usefulness of text or history to resolve all the tensions that had accrued in the federal system, was noticeable. Swinton reasoned that, if Canadian experience taught anything, it is that there is no algorithm, no formula to derive law from text. The historical record of the intention of constitutional drafters, in this round of negotiation no less than in previous ones, was likely to yield only limited insight.

Instead of focusing on the initial allocation of power made by politicians, or the reallocation of those powers through formal constitutional amendments in executive-dominated talks, Swinton's work served as a reminder that citizens, lawyers, and judges participate on an ongoing basis in the redefinition of their federal project as they engage in principled disagreement about the nature of their communities and the proper roles and responsibilities of each. It is probably for this reason that she seemed particularly sceptical of the immense hopes put into the Meech Lake Accord by Quebeckers and critical of those who claimed it to be a threat to Canadian unity or Charter rights, as if the real consequences of the accord were foreordained. Swinton coolheadedly asserted that, come what may, the evolution of Canadian federalism would depend as much, if not more, on the judiciary interpreting the Constitution than on the words on paper of any single document.[39] Thus, the role of the constitutional scholar – exemplified in almost ideal form by Swinton's work on federalism – is perhaps less to influence those allocative choices than to fertilize the federal imagination and thus contribute to the imaginative possibilities that the law of federalism affords.

II. Federalism, constitutional reform, and the jurisprudence of interests

One of the underappreciated values of Swinton's work is that it allows us to connect judicial approaches in the law of federalism to broader debates in legal theory. Even if Swinton does not draw out

---

39 As she writes elsewhere, '[a] constitution is a living document which will inevitably change, and judicial interpretation will always be a creative component of that process.' Katherine Swinton, 'Federalism, the Charter and the Courts: Rethinking Constitutional Dialogue in Canada' in Karen Knop et al, eds, *Rethinking Federalism: Citizens, Markets, and Governments in a Changing World* (Vancouver: UBC Press, 1993) 294 at 309.

those connections explicitly, the intellectual filiation between Beetz's 'conceptualism' and the so-called *Begriffsjurisprudenz* or 'jurisprudence of concepts' in German legal theory is hard to miss.[40] So is the connection between Dickson J's 'jurisprudence of interests' and the *Interessenjurisprudenz* that emerged in Germany at the turn of the twentieth century as a school of thought critical of formalist conceptualism.[41] While the labels that she uses suggests a filiation with those traditions of legal thought, Swinton never ventures very deeply into intellectual history. Her work does not seek to elucidate the theoretical difficulties associated, for example, with the notion of community 'interests.'[42] Nevertheless, her fundamental insight can still help us understand constitutional puzzles that existed at the time of the publication of *The Supreme Court and Canadian Federalism* and that have persisted ever since.

Consider the example of the law of constitutional amendment. It is an area of law where the contested nature of communities and the representation of their 'interests' is particularly salient. The story starts in the late 1970s with *Attorney General of Quebec v Blaikie et al.*[43] The case concerned the power of Quebec's National Assembly to amend the language rights guaranteed in section 133 of the British North America Act, 1867.[44] The Attorney General of Quebec argued that section 133 relating to the use of English and French in courts and the legislature formed part of the 'Constitution of the Province.' As a consequence, it could be amended unilaterally by the provincial legislature.[45] The argument was rejected in a unanimous decision signed by 'the Court.' While the Court did not delimit precisely what is included or not in the 'Constitution of the Province,' it adopted the position of Chief Justice Jules Deschênes from the Superior Court on section 133 to the effect that it forms part of the Constitution of Quebec and Canada 'in an indivisible

---

40 In general, see Olivier Jouanjan, *Une histoire de la pensée juridique en Allemagne, 1800-1918: Idéalisme et conceptualisme chez les juristes allemands du XIXe siècle* (Paris: PUF, 2005).

41 For an introduction, see e.g. Lon F Fuller, 'Introduction' in M Magdalena Schoch, ed and trans, *The Jurisprudence of Interests: Selected Writings of Max Rümelin, Philipp Heck, Paul Oertmann, Heinrich Stoll, Julius Binder, Hermann Isay* (Cambridge, MA: Harvard University Press, 1948) xvii.

42 For a discussion, see e.g. Dwight Newman, 'Collective Interests and Collective Rights' (2004) 49:1 Am J Juris 127; Andrée Lajoie, *Quand les minorités font la loi* (Paris: PUF, 2002) at 26–31.

43 *Attorney General of Quebec v Blaikie et al*, [1979] 2 SCR 1016 [*Blaikie et al*].

44 *British North America Act, 1867* (UK), 30–31 Vict, c 3 [*BNA Act*].

45 Based on ibid, s 92(1). Now section 45 of the *Constitution Act, 1982*, being Schedule B to the *Canada Act 1982* (UK), 1982, c 11.

sense.'[46] As a consequence, it could not be modified unilaterally by the provincial legislature.

Presumably, the converse would also be true – that is, the federal Parliament could not unilaterally amend the parts of section 133 applicable to the federal government. But this question was not directly at stake in *Blaikie* because it was not controversial, the topic of language being explicitly excluded from the federal amendment power.[47] Indeed, the federal Parliament obtained the jurisdiction to amend 'the Constitution of Canada' with the British North America (No. 2) Act, 1949 (BNA Act, 1949). But this new federal amendment power, which now paralleled the provincial power over the Constitution of the province, was qualified by a list of excluded subjects, including 'as regards the use of the English or French language.'[48] The equivalent provincial power found in section 92(1) did not include such limitative language. Despite this asymmetry, the Supreme Court concluded that the provincial amendment power was just as limited as the federal one when it came to the language rights guaranteed in section 133 for they did not form part of the Constitution of the province only.

The Supreme Court of Canada picked up this line of argument again a year later in the *Reference re Upper House*.[49] The case concerned different proposals for Senate reform contemplated by the federal Liberal government at the time. Unlike 'the use of English and French,' the Senate was not specifically excluded from the federal amendment power in the BNA Act, 1949. Thus, while the question of what is included in the *'constitution* of Canada' for the purpose of the federal amendment power had long intrigued constitutional scholars, the case of the Senate turned on what is the 'constitution of *Canada*':[50]

> The Attorney General of Canada submitted that the power conferred upon Parliament by s. 91(1) is limited only by the specific exceptions contained in it. He contended that the very specificity of these exceptions pointed to the wide powers being conferred. If this approach were adopted, it would

---

46 *Blaikie et al*, supra note 43 at para 1025.

47 In *Jones v AG of New Brunswick*, [1975] 2 SCR 182 at 192–3, the Court recognized the validity of the federal *Official Languages Act* and that section 133 of the *Constitution Act, 1867*, or the *BNA Act*, supra note 44, is a floor, not a ceiling provision.

48 *British North America (No 2) Act, 1949* (UK), 13 Geo VI, c 81.

49 *Re: Authority of Parliament in Relation to the Upper House*, [1980] 1 SCR 54 [*Re: Upper House*].

50 See e.g. Paul Gérin-Lajoie, *Constitutional Amendment in Canada* (Toronto: University of Toronto Press, 1950) at xiv–xxxv.

mean that the Federal Parliament, acting unilaterally, could amend any part of the Act, subject only to the exceptions specified in s. 91(1). But s. 91(1) does not give power to amend the Act. Instead, the phrase 'Constitution of Canada' is used. In our opinion, the word 'Canada' as used in s. 91(1) does not refer to Canada as a geographical unit but *refers to the juristic federal unit*. 'Constitution of Canada' does not mean the whole of the British North America Act, but means the *constitution of the federal government*, as distinct from the provincial governments. The power of amendment conferred by s. 91(1) *is limited to matters of interest only to the federal government*.[51]

The interpretation that the Supreme Court puts on section 91(1) effectively confirmed the existence of a three-tiered constitutional structure in Canada. The jurisdictional space under the Constitution is not taken to be exhaustively distributed between the 'watertight compartments' of the provincial and federal governments.[52] What *Blaikie* and the *Reference re Upper House* suggest is that Canada as a whole or in an 'indivisible sense' transcends the mere aggregation of the jurisdiction or the interests of provincial and federal 'juristic units.' It suggests that 'the Constitution belongs to the citizens of Canada, not the politicians who control federal and provincial governments from time to time.'[53] If the basic units of federalism are communities instead of governments, the jurisdiction of the communities that citizens form from time to time may be hard to determine. But the notion of community interests proves to be much more amenable to the kind of analysis that the Court undertook in those two cases. Community interests, which are always imperfectly represented by the two orders of government, can still be reflected in the structure of institutions like the Senate. It is thus normal that those institutions should transcend the amendment jurisdiction allocated exclusively to either order of government. The modification of the Senate is thus not a 'matter ... of interests only to the federal government,' just like language was not of interest only to the provincial government.[54]

---

51 *Re: Upper House*, supra note 49 at 69–70 [emphasis added].

52 The nautical metaphor comes from *Canada (AG) v Ontario (AG)*, [1937] AC 326 (UKJCPC).

53 Swinton, *Supreme Court*, supra note 2 at 65.

54 There might even be instances, as the Meech Lake Accord exemplified, where the joint action of both levels of government might not be sufficient to garner the constitutional legitimacy requisite to bring about formal constitutional change and where it is necessary to find ways to engage these communities despite the government-centric amendment formula.

Swinton did not dwell on *Blaikie* and the *Reference re Upper House*.[55] But her work gives us analytical resources to grasp their underlying federal and admittedly pluralist logic. The interpretation of those two cases sketched here unfolded further in the two constitutional amendment cases of 2014. In the *Senate Reference*, a unanimous Supreme Court of Canada found that amendments affecting 'provincial interests' could not be adopted through the unilateral federal amendment power and added thus further limits to those already listed in Part V of the Constitution Act, 1982.[56] In the case of the Senate, this included 'provincial interests' affected even when the 'powers of the Senate and the method of selecting Senators,' which are protected by the general amending formula, are not at stake.[57] While the Court uses indistinctly the expressions 'provincial interests' and the 'interests of provincial governments' to characterize those aspects of the Senate that require use of the general amendment formula, the two need not be conflated. In fact, the Court recognizes that the Senate was often 'criticized ... for failing to provide meaningful representation of the interests of the provinces,' thus creating the weak political safeguards of federalism that Swinton also discussed.[58] After all, senators are entirely selected by the federal government without formal provincial input, a recurring source of complaint.[59] There are few eligibility requirements other than regional ones. The capacious notion of 'interest' thus allows the Supreme Court to look behind the mere interests of provincial governments to connect the role of the Senate to the interests of the provincial communities it represents. By using the notion of 'interests' in the law of constitutional amendment, the

---

55 Swinton mentions briefly *Blaikie* and *Re Upper House* to criticize the use of historical arguments in both cases. Also, she suggests that the argument in *Blaikie* is evidence of the 'compact theory' of Confederation. Insofar as *Re Upper House* extends (rather than departs from) the underlying logic of *Blaikie*, I think on the contrary that these cases exemplify the three-tiered structure of Canadian federalism that was taking shape at the time. Swinton, *Supreme Court*, supra note 2 at 114–17.

56 *Constitution Act, 1982*, being Schedule B to the *Canada Act 1982* (UK), 1982, c 11.

57 Ibid, s 42(1)(b).

58 *Reference re Senate Reform*, 2014 SCC 32 at para 17 [*Reference re Senate Reform*]; Swinton, *Supreme Court*, supra note 2 at 48.

59 In general, see David E Smith, *The Canadian Senate in Bicameral Perspective* (Toronto: University of Toronto Press, 2004). The extent of provincial involvement in Senate appointments has been a periodic matter of contention and debate. On this history and the contrast with the US Senate, see David Schneiderman, *Red, White, and Kind of Blue: The Conservatives and the Americanization of Canadian Constitutional Culture* (Toronto: University of Toronto Press, 2015) at ch 4.

Court moves away from a classical – one might say 'conceptualist' – understanding of federalism focusing on the exclusive 'jurisdiction' exhaustively divided between two orders of government and adopts a more modern understanding of federalism where it is the admittedly more amorphous 'interests' of the provincial or regional communities that are worthy of constitutional protection.

The 'provincial interests' and the 'interests of provincial governments' need not be understood as interchangeably as the Supreme Court of Canada's inconsistent use of those two expressions suggests. It might simply reflect the fact that, for most amendment purposes, only those two sets of constitutional actors are formally recognized to give expression to the multiple communities that Canada 'in an indivisible sense' is made up of. And, even then, the role of the Senate in the amendment process belies that characterization. It originally gave expression to regional and provincial communities, thus seemingly duplicating the role of provincial governments. But, over time, it also came to represent other communities as well. As the Court underscores, 'the Senate also came to represent various groups that were under-represented in the House of Commons. It served as a forum for ethnic, gender, religious, linguistic, and Aboriginal groups that did not always have a meaningful opportunity to present their views through the popular democratic process.'[60] Its role in the amendment process, even if admittedly modest, is thus an implicit recognition of the role of these communities otherwise than through provincial and federal governments.

Likewise, in the *Supreme Court Reference* decided a few weeks before, the Supreme Court of Canada concluded that three seats reserved for Quebec judges on the Court served to ensure 'not only civil law training and experience on the Court, but also to ensure that Quebec's *distinct legal traditions and social values* are represented on the Court, thereby enhancing the confidence of the people of Quebec in the Supreme as the final arbiter of their rights.'[61] While the Court did not go so far as Swinton in suggesting that Quebec judges like Beetz or Pigeon might have a distinctive legal approach,[62] its recognition of the importance of 'social values' was a clear move away from the facade of 'legalism' and 'neutrality' that she and other scholars decried little more than two decades before.[63] It was also a recognition that the Supreme Court, just like the

---

60 *Reference re Senate Reform*, supra note 58 at para 16.

61 *Reference re Supreme Court Act, ss 5 and 6*, 2014 SCC 21 at para 49.

62 Swinton, *Supreme Court*, supra note 2 at 268–9.

63 It is notable that Quebec scholars at the time tended to be much more praiseful of the Court's legalistic tendencies. See e.g. Gil Rémillard, *Le fédéralisme canadien: Éléments de formation et d'évolution* (Montreal: Québec Amérique, 1980) at 185.

Senate, 'represents' the interests of different communities in a way that does not fully correspond to those of their governments. As in the case of the Senate, the Quebec government has no formal role to play in the appointment process of judges of the Supreme Court, neither alone nor jointly with the federal government.[64] The social legitimacy that the Court was keen to preserve depends as much on federalism disputes between governments as it does on its adjudication of other cases brought by Quebec litigants.

III. Sovereignty and the future of federal imagination

The Supreme Court and Canadian Federalism remains quite helpful to understand legal developments since its publication. But the intervening thirty-five years have also revealed some of the ways in which Swinton's approach needs to be complemented. If it stays within the relatively well-defined terrain of the interpretation of the federal division of powers, federalism scholarship risks losing part of its critical bite. The law of federalism is then implicitly presented as a legal technique used to divide the plenary power of the Crown which is always assumed or taken for granted. Despite her pluralist sensibility, it seems that Swinton likewise presupposed that sovereignty is an ever-full reservoir of legal power. Yet federalism can also represent an alternative – or, at least, a challenge – to the 'sovereigntist' branch of the modern constitutional tradition when it speaks meaningfully to the question of the origin of sovereign power – rather than the way in which this power is distributed or exercised.[65] To be fair, it is also a topic that courts seem

---

64 Since this decision, the Quebec government reached an agreement with the federal government regarding the appointment of judges to fill the three seats reserved for Quebec lawyers and judges. See 'Protocole d'entente concernant le processus de nomination en vue de combler le poste qui sera laissé vacant à la Cour suprême du Canada à la suite du départ du juge Clément Gascon' (16 May 2019), online: *Government of Quebec* <www.sqrc.gouv.qc.ca/secretariat/salle-de-nouvelles /actualites/details.asp?id=108>. This being said, the National Assembly recently initiated the constitutional amendment process with a motion adopted unanimously requesting that judges from superior courts be appointed from among the candidates selected by the Quebec government. The proposed amendment would be inserted after section 98 of the *Constitution Act, 1867* as '98Q.1. Les juges des cours supérieures du Québec sont choisis parmi les membres du Barreau du Québec ayant été recommandés par le gouvernement du Québec.' Québec, Assemblée Nationale, *Procès verbal de l'Assemblée*, 43:1 (23 April 2025) at 3108.

65 See e.g. James Tully, *Strange Multiplicity: Constitutionalism in an Age of Diversity* (Cambridge, UK: Cambridge University Press, 1995). For a suggestion that there is inherent tension between federalism and sovereignty, see Olivier Beaud, *Théorie de la fédération* (Paris: PUF, 2008).

loath to enter and that scholars have explored in much more depth since 1990.[66] Swinton's analysis still offers intellectual resources to engage with these issues as well as with the opportunities and constraints that the Supreme Court's federalism jurisprudence presents for contemporary efforts to reconcile Indigenous and Crown sovereignty.

In the area of Aboriginal law, this question has become inescapable. The Supreme Court of Canada released its first decision on the rights protected by section 35(1) of the Constitution Act, 1982 – *R v Sparrow* – just as *The Supreme Court and Canadian Federalism* went to press.[67] The opinion of Dickson CJ and Justice Gérard La Forest in this case continues to reverberate thirty-five years later, especially their holding that 'there was from the outset never any doubt that sovereignty and legislative power, and indeed the underlying title, to such lands vested in the Crown.'[68] The literature on Crown-Indigenous relations has grown exponentially in the intervening years. It is fair to say that the Court has yet to catch up with it or that it is purposefully avoiding a direct engagement with the theory of Crown sovereignty undergirding its jurisprudence that scholars have subjected to scrutiny and criticism.[69] Either way, the situation in Aboriginal law is not unlike that which prevailed in the 1970s with regard to the inarticulate theory of federalism animating the Court's evolving and apparently wavering jurisprudence.

Despite the similarities, it would be harder today to do the kind of intellectual exercise that Swinton engaged in and flesh out relatively coherent and competing understandings of Aboriginal law espoused by different judges. In general, it seems that the Supreme Court of Canada

---

66 On the reasons why courts might not address directly the question of the origin of Crown sovereignty, see Kent McNeil, 'Crown and Indigenous Sovereignty' in Michael Asch, John Borrows & James Tully, eds, *Resurgence and Reconciliation: Settler-Indigenous Relations and Earth Teachings* (Toronto: University of Toronto Press, 2018) 292.

67 *R v Sparrow*, [1990] 1 SCR 1075.

68 Ibid at 1103.

69 To take just a few examples, see John Borrows, 'Sovereignty's Alchemy: An Analysis of *Delgamuukw v. British Columbia*' (1999) 37:3 Osgoode Hall LJ 537; Michel Morin, *L'Usurpation de la souveraineté autochtone: Le cas des peuples de la Nouvelle-France et des colonies anglaises de l'Amérique du Nord* (Montreal: Boréal, 1997); Joshua Nichols, *A Reconciliation without Recollection?* (Toronto: University of Toronto Press, 2019); Kent McNeil, 'La relativité de la souveraineté de jure au Canada: 1600–2018,' translated by Geneviève Claveau (2018) 49:2 Ottawa L Rev 305; Kent McNeil, 'Crown and Indigenous Sovereignty' in Michael Asch, John Borrows & James Tully, eds, *Resurgence and Reconciliation: Settler-Indigenous Relations and Earth Teachings* (Toronto: University of Toronto Press, 2018) 292. See also many of the texts in Joshua Nichols & Amy Swiffen, eds, *Indigenous Peoples and the Future of Federalism* (Toronto: University of Toronto Press, 2024).

has preferred the incremental approach of incompletely theorized agreements. It has allowed it to remain relatively unanimous rather than staking out opposite judicial approaches.[70] The well-trodden path of federalism jurisprudence has supplied the Court with ready-made arguments and modes of thought that tend to sidestep the direct confrontation of the question of the sovereignty of Indigenous peoples and the legal foundations of Crown sovereignty.[71] While this is a question that far exceeds the limits of this article, a few recent examples suffice to illustrate this recent tendency.

In the *Reference re An Act Respecting First Nations, Inuit and Métis Children, Youth and Families*, the Supreme Court upheld the impugned federal statute, the purpose of which is to 'affirm the inherent right of self-government, which includes jurisdiction in relation to child and family services.'[72] The Court upheld the statute, but it reached its conclusion by framing the issue as a strictly federal dispute, leaving by the wayside the Indigenous nations and organizations that were asking the Court to formally recognize an inherent right to self-government independent of the expression it finds in statute.[73] The Court avoided the issue and framed the case as concerning essentially the proper characterization of the federal statute under the 'pith and substance' test. What the statute presented as an affirmation was reinterpreted by the Court as an order issued by the federal Parliament and binding the federal and provincial executives – but not the courts – to its interpretation of the content of section 35(1) rights. This order to the executive branch, the Court concluded, is well within Parliament's jurisdiction under section 91(24) of the Constitution Act, 1867.[74] The expedients of federalism and a traditional understanding of the separation of powers allowed

---

70 On incompletely theorized agreements, see Cass Sunstein, *One Case at a Time: Judicial Minimalism on the Supreme Court* (Cambridge, MA: Harvard University Press, 2001). One notable exception is *Mikisew Cree First Nation v Canada (Governor General in Council)*, 2018 SCC 40, [2018] 2 SCR 765 [*Mikisew Cree First Nation*].

71 See e.g. *R v Pamajewon*, [1996] 2 SCR 821.

72 *Reference re An Act Respecting First Nations, Inuit and Métis Children, Youth and Families*, 2024 SCC 5 [*Reference re First Nations*]; *An Act Respecting First Nations, Inuit and Métis Children, Youth and Families*, SC 2019, c 24, s 8(a) [*Act Respecting First Nations*].

73 It is notable that the case was a reference question, a procedural mechanism though which governments can have a speedy resolution of their legal disputes. Indigenous peoples do not have such speedy access to courts and must go through protracted litigation to resolve their disputes with the Crown when out-of-court settlement is not possible.

74 *Reference re First Nations*, supra note 72 at para 118. The extent to which the statute in question does bind the provincial crowns remains uncertain, however.

the Court to circumvent the issue that seemed front and centre – that is, the effects that a statutory 'affirmation' might have on the sovereignty of the Crown and its potential relinquishment, even if only selectively, for the 'jurisdiction in relation to child and family services.'[75]

Likewise, in *Dickson v Vuntut Gwitchin First Nation*, the Supreme Court had to rule on the application of the Charter to an Indigenous government and the effect of section 25 of the Charter, which provides that '[t]he guarantee in this Charter of certain rights and freedoms shall not be construed so as to abrogate or derogate from any aboriginal, treaty or other rights or freedoms that pertain to the aboriginal peoples of Canada.' On the question of the application of the Charter, one preliminary question concerned the origin and nature of the legal authority of the Vuntut Gwitchin First Nation (VGFN) and the effect of the statute giving effect to their self-government agreement.[76] One view would be that the Vuntut Gwitchin exercise a form of delegated statutory authority, which is governmental by nature as its powers are analogous to those of a municipality. Another view advanced by some intervenors was that, since the VGFN's legal authority derives from an 'inherent' right to self-government, the powers of the Vuntut Gwitchin might be recognized by statute in Canadian law, but they do not originate from Canadian law and are thus excluded from the scope of the application of the Charter.[77] The question at stake in the background was the ascending or descending nature of sovereignty in Canada and the positivist assumption that all law-making power derives in one way or another from the state. In their opinion for the majority, Justices Mahmud Jamal and Nicholas Kasirer circumvented the issue by severing the two sources of authority of the VGFN and ruling that 'at least one source of the VGFN's lawmaking authority flows from Parliament, in that the VGFN exercises powers that Parliament otherwise would have exercised through its legislative jurisdiction under s. 91(24) of the *Constitution Act, 1867.*'[78] But the majority 'expressly refrain[ed] from commenting on whether the Charter would apply to an Indigenous government exercising an inherent self-government authority untethered from federal, provincial, or territorial legislation.'[79] By

---

75 *Act Respecting First Nations*, supra note 72, s 8(a).

76 *Yukon First Nations Land Claims Settlement Act*, SC 1994, c 34, s 6(1); *An Act Approving Yukon Land Claim Final Agreements*, RSY 2002, c 240, s 2.

77 *Dickson v Vuntut Gwitchin First Nation*, 2024 SCC 10 at para 74 [*Dickson*].

78 Ibid at para 82. See *Godbout v Longueuil (City)*, [1997] 3 SCR 844; *Eldridge v British Columbia (Attorney General)*, [1997] 3 SCR 624.

79 *Dickson*, supra note 77 at para 101.

thus severing the VGFN's legislative authority for the purpose of their analysis, Kasirer and Jamal JJ seemed to be of two minds about the nature of its powers – some of which having survived the assertion of Crown sovereignty and others being merely delegated by the Canadian Parliament as part of its jurisdiction in relation to 'Indians and lands reserved for Indians' – and the underlying conception of sovereignty that informs them.[80] As Martin Papillon rightly points out, these two cases 'tend to confirm the Canadian judiciary's unwillingness to address the issue of coexisting sovereignties head-on.'[81]

The question of the constitutional status of the legal instruments used in the process of reconciliation is bound to resurface in the future. Beyond formal treaties, modern land claims agreements, and self-government agreements, the relationship between the Crown and Indigenous peoples is now structured around increasingly diverse and complex forms of normative arrangements. While the specific duties that flow from the honour of the Crown in the context of these reconciliatory instruments may be hard to define, there is no doubt, for example, that some 'contracts between the State and Indigenous groups … are intended to foster the modern-day reconciliation of pre-existing Indigenous societies with the Crown's historic assertion of sovereignty.'[82] Seeing reconciliation as a process that is only gradually and partially achieved suggests that the 'assumed' sovereignty of the Crown flowing from 'de facto control of land and resources' cannot be conceived of in absolute terms – as an 'on-off' switch where only a treaty could conclusively remedy the Crown's sovereignty deficit.[83] But the bitterly divided case of *Mikisew Cree II* illustrates how challenging this understanding of sovereignty and reconciliation may prove to be in practice.[84]

---

80 *BNA Act*, supra note 44.

81 Martin Papillon, 'Book Review of Joshua Nichols & Amy Swiffen, eds, *Indigenous Peoples and the Future of Federalism* (Toronto: University of Toronto Press, 2024)' (2024) 54:3 Publius e49 at e50.

82 *Quebec (Attorney General) v Pekuakamiulnuatsh Takuhikan*, 2024 SCC 39 at para 13.

83 See *Haida Nation v British Columbia (Minister of Forests)*, 2004 SCC 73 at para 32. On the difficulty of defining 'reconciliation,' see Joshua Nichols, *A Reconciliation without Recollection? An Investigation of the Foundations of Aboriginal Law in Canada* (Toronto: University of Toronto Press, 2019). I would like to thank Eyal Wilke for drawing my attention to the complexity of this issue.

84 It seems that the uncertain footing of the sovereignty of the Crown explained why the four sets of opinions could not agree on the proper application of the doctrine of the sovereignty of parliament, even if the former is conceptually prior to the latter. See *Mikisew Cree First Nation*, supra note 70. I explore some of these issues in Jean-Christophe Bédard-Rubin, 'On the Subject of Constitutional Obligations: Provincial

The flexible federalism jurisprudence on delegation and inter-delegation of legislative and executive powers that characterized the rise of cooperative federalism might facilitate the 'braiding' of Canadian and Indigenous legal orders through reconciliatory instruments.[85] But, in these federalism cases, the Supreme Court of Canada was working with the 'old' conception of sovereignty, one where a sovereign parliament could delegate its powers, but where this delegation was always understood to be revocable as Parliament could not abdicate its sovereignty altogether.[86] Indigenous parties might not feel adequately protected if the case law that forms the legal basis for their relation with the Crown does not provide a firmer foundation. In other words, the flexibility that the case law on intergovernmental agreements affords might not hinder the development of new creative normative arrangements in the process of reconciliation. But it might not give these arrangements adequate constitutional protection either if Parliament is prevented from abdicating part of its 'assumed' sovereignty to give meaningful expression to 'asserted' constitutional rights such as the right to self-government.[87]

IV. Conclusion

To the extent that Canadian federalism is cyclical, one can fairly assume that the mid-2020s mark the beginning of a new cycle. Revisiting Katherine Swinton's *The Supreme Court and Canadian Federalism* helps us

---

States and Federal Crowns in the Charter Era' [unpublished manuscript on file with author]. On the duty to consult that flows from the honour of the Crown as a mechanism to mitigate the 'sovereignty deficit' in relation to Indigenous peoples, see Richard Stacey, 'Honour in Sovereignty: Can Crown Consultation with Indigenous Peoples Erase Canada's Sovereignty Deficit?' (2018) 68:3 UTLJ 405.

85 In general, on the braiding of legal orders, see John Borrows et al, eds, *Braiding Legal Orders: Implementing the United Nations of the Rights of Indigenous Peoples* (Montreal and Kingston: McGill-Queen's University Press, 2023).

86 See *In re Edwin Gray*, [1918] 57 SCR 150 at 157 (Fitzpatrick CJ) and at 176 (Anglin J). See also *PEI Potato Marketing Board v Willis*, [1952] 2 SCR 392 at 395; *Coughlin v Ontario Highway Transport Board et al*, [1968] SCR 569 at 574–5. On the contrast between the 'old' and the 'new' conception of sovereignty, the *locus classicus* is HWR Wade, 'The Basis of Legal Sovereignty' (1955) 13:2 Cam LJ 172.

87 I am thinking here, for example, of self-entrenched provisions that require special procedure for their own repeal. On this point, see Jeffrey Goldsworthy, *Parliamentary Sovereignty: Contemporary Debates* (Cambridge, UK: Cambridge University Press, 2010).

understand how we got where we are and calls our attention back to the fact that law will have a role to play in this new cycle no less than in previous ones. Constitutional lawyers and judges, like politicians, will find ways to give expression to the federal imagination of the different communities that Canada is made up of. Swinton's work serves as a helpful reminder that focusing on constitution makers can mask the iterative process of constitutional meaning making that occurs on an ongoing basis as individuals and communities who live federal lives bring their cases to courts and as judges try to respond to the claims made by different orders of government to represent and exercise authority over those individuals and communities. Power is constantly reallocated and redefined, and jurisdictions, rights, and responsibilities are clarified. But the process is never a completely political exercise either as it is constrained by the requirements of constitutional legality. Swinton's call to think carefully about the reallocation of powers through interpretation deserves to be heard and the pluralist sensibility that guides her analysis deepened if federalism is to speak meaningfully to the legal challenges that Canada faces in the twenty-first century. Can the law of federalism illuminate not merely the distribution of powers but also the very foundations of legal powers? If it can, it could contribute to the development of new forms of collective agency that confronting these challenges may require.

11 Denise Réaume and the Women's Court of Canada: Feminist Judgment Projects and Rewriting *Pierson v Post*[†]

ANGELA FERNANDEZ

I. Introduction

Denise Réaume published *Law v Canada (Minister of Employment and Immigration)* in a special 2006 issue of the *Canadian Journal of Women and the Law*, a rewrite of a decision denying the equality claim of a thirty-year-old woman denied survivor benefits under the Canada Pension Plan after the death of her spouse.[1] The special issue's collection of six rewritten decisions of the Supreme Court of Canada (SCC) introduced the world to the Women's Court of Canada (WCC), which was the brainchild of seventeen feminist lawyers, academics, and human rights activists.[2] These equality thinkers were looking for a way to object to what they perceived as 'grievous judicial backsliding on equality,' specifically what they viewed as an overly narrow approach to section 15 of the Canadian Charter of Rights and Freedoms, especially

---

[†] Many thanks to Animal Law Research Associates, Krystal-Anne Roussel, and Kira Berkeley.

[1] Denise Réaume, '*Law v Canada (Minister of Employment and Immigration)*' (2006) 18:1 CJWL 143 [Réaume, '*Law v Canada*']. The 2006 issue of the *Canadian Journal of Women and the Law* was released in 2008 due to a backlog at the journal. See Jennifer Koshan, 'Impact of the Feminist Judgment Writing Projects: The Case of the Women's Court of Canada' (2018) 8:9 Oñati Socio-Legal Series 1325, n 2 [Koshan, 'Impact']. *Law v Canada (Minister of Employment and Immigration)*, [1999] 1 SCR 497.

[2] The seventeen original members (in alphabetical order) were: (a) Gwen Brodsky; (b) Melina Buckley; (c) Marie Chen; (d) Rachel Cox; (e) Shelagh Day; (f) Mary Eberts; (g) Avvy Go; (h) Jennifer Koshan; (i) Sonia Lawrence; (j) Diana Majury; (k) Sharon McIvor; (l) Teressa Nahanee; (m) Margaret Parsons; (n) Dianne Pothier; (o) Denise Réaume; (p) Kate Stephenson; and (q) Margot Young. List taken from 'Your Honour, We Respectfully Disagree,' *Toronto Star* (8 March 2008), online: <perma.cc/43QX-WKCE> ['Your Honour'].

when it came to women's rights and gender equality issues.[3] This inaugural collection ushered in what has become an influential mode of legal scholarship – feminist rewrites of court decisions thought to be wrongly or over-narrowly decided – a movement that has 'swept the globe' in the last twenty years.[4] Cambridge University Press (CUP) has a series on US cases, entitled 'Feminist Judgment Series: Rewritten Judicial Opinions,' with thirteen installments to date and counting.[5] There are Feminist Judgment Projects (FJPs) currently operating in England, Australia, Ireland, New Zealand, and Scotland as well as in the United States, Central and Eastern Europe, India, Africa, and Pakistan.[6] There is a FJP in international law and one specifically on the International Criminal Court and its approach to sexual and gender-based crimes.[7] There is also a collection on children's rights.[8] Réaume, a faculty member in the Faculty of Law at the University of Toronto from 1982 to 2023, was a founding member of the WCC, and Toronto was the location of the launch of the inaugural project in 2008.[9] Hence, it is appropriate that this retrospective of faculty scholarship include Réaume's contribution to this highly successful global scholarly movement.[10]

From early on in her career, Réaume wrote extensively about women's equality and discrimination.[11] The WCC, premised as it was on

---

3 Diana Majury, 'Introducing the Women's Court of Canada' (2006) 18:1 CJWL 1 at 1 [Majury, 'Introducing the Women's Court']; *Canadian Charter of Rights and Freedoms*, Part 1 of the *Constitution Act, 1982*, being Schedule B to the *Canada Act 1982* (UK), 1982, c 11.

4 Denise Réaume, 'Rewriting Equality II' (2018) 30:2 CJWL i at I [Réaume, 'Rewriting Equality'].

5 See 'Feminist Judgment Series: Rewritten Judicial Opinions,' online: *Cambridge University Press* <perma.cc/H6FK-LCJJ>.

6 See Website of the Gilbert and Tobin Centre of Public Law, University of New South Wales, Australia, with links to materials on the projects in all these countries. 'Feminist Judgment Projects,' online: *Gilbert and Tobin Centre of Public Law* <perma. cc/W5N2-NVP5> ['Feminist Judgment Projects'].

7 Loveday Hodson & Trol Lavers, eds, *Feminist Judgments in International Law* (Oxford: Hart Publishing, 2017).

8 Helen Stalford, Kathryn Hollingsworth & Stephen Gilmore, eds, *Rewriting Children's Rights Judgments: From Academic Vision to New Practice* (London: Bloomsbury Publishing, 2017).

9 Jennifer Koshan et al, 'Rewriting Equality: The Pedagogical Use of Women's Court of Canada Judgments' (2010) 4 Canadian Legal Education Annual Review 121 at 122 [Koshan et al, 'Rewriting Equality'].

10 Thank you to Rebecca Cook for suggesting the inclusion of Denise Réaume's work on the Women's Court of Canada in this collection at our Faculty Retreat in 2024 and for her thoughtful comments on earlier drafts.

11 See e.g. Denise Réaume, 'Women and the Law: Equality Claims before Courts and Tribunals' (1979) 5 Queen's LJ 3; Denise Réaume, 'The Social Construction of

revisiting the Supreme Court of Canada's developing conception of equality, can be seen as a culmination of that part of her scholarship as distinct from other aspects of her work in the area of language rights.[12] Part II of this article will, first, provide some background on the WCC and the FJPs and the role that Réaume played in launching this initiative. Part III will focus on the SCC's decision in *Law* and offer some comments and reflections on Réaume's rewrite. Part IV pivots to 'looking forward by looking back,' exploring my own experience doing a feminist rewrite of the (in)famous property law decision *Pierson v Post*.[13] The conclusion will tie Réaume's work on the WCC to Karen Knop's on the Tokyo Women's Tribunal and Knop's insight that the work of imagined courts should be understood as acts of the imagination mixing historical fact and fiction: 'fact-ion,' pointing the way toward future work using the FJP model.

II. The Women's Court of Canada

In the introduction to the original six rewritten decisions of the WCC, Diana Majury explained that the idea for the WCC was born around a long table at an Italian restaurant in downtown Toronto in February 2004 after a day-long event talking about section 15 of the Charter.[14] The lawyers, activists, and academics assembled were specifically lamenting that 'politicians and Supreme Court of Canada judges alike seemed to think that women have largely attained equality and that other issues [for example,] balanced budgets[,] … should take priority over equality.'[15] Majury wrote: 'As we momentarily teetered on the

---

Women and the Possibility of Change: Unmodified Feminism Revisited' (1992) 5 CJWL 463; Denise Réaume, 'What's Distinctive About a Feminist Analysis of Law?: A Conceptual Analysis of Women's Exclusion from Law' (1996) 2 Legal Theory 265; Denise Réaume, 'Of Pigeon Holes and Principles: A Reconsideration of Discrimination Law' (2002) 47 McGill LJ 113; Denise Réaume, 'Comparing Theories of Sex Discrimination: The Role of Comparison' (2005) 25:3 OJLS 547.

12 Réaume wrote extensively in the area of language rights. See e.g. Denise Réaume, 'Language Rights, Remedies, and the Rule of Law' (1988) 1 Can JL & Jur 35; Denise Réaume, '*Beaulac* and the Demise of the Political Compromise Doctrine: Have Official Language Use Rights Been Revived?' (2002) 47 McGill LJ 593.

13 See Angela Fernandez, '*Pierson v Post*, 3 Cai R 175 (NY Sup Ct 1805), Justice Angela Fernandez, dissenting' in Eloisa C Rodriguez-Dod & Elena Maria Marty-Nelson, eds, *Feminist Judgments: Rewritten Property Opinions* (Cambridge, UK: Cambridge University Press, 2022) 98 [Fernandez, '*Pierson v Post*'].

14 See Majury, 'Introducing the Women's Court,' supra note 3 at 1, 5.

15 Ibid at 1.

brink of hopelessness, someone burst out with: "So why don't we show them it could have been done, what substantive equality would look like in those cases? Why don't we rewrite these decisions that are so wrong?"[16] The idea was 'to demonstrate that a formalistic turn in the doctrine was not inevitable ... to prove to ourselves as well as to others that our idealism [about substantive equality] could also be realistic.'[17]

Inspired by the WCC, a group of feminist socio-legal scholars published a book of twenty-three feminist rewrites of cases from England and Wales in 2010.[18] This collection introduced the idea that the judgments should be written as if they were taking place at the same time as the original case (rather than a later 'reconsideration' or appeal) as well as beginning the practice of pairing up a commentator for each rewritten decision.[19] The cases in this project spanned many different subject matters – parenting, property and markets, criminal law and evidence, public law, and equality. This differed from the WCC, which focused on the single idea of substantive equality. The UK approach also differed from the one taken a little later in the US FJPs published by CUP, an (ongoing) series that brings together multiple authors writing on different cases in one area of the law – for example, tax law (2017), reproductive health law (2020), family law (2020), trusts and estates (2020), employment and discrimination (2020), tort (2020), property (2022), health law (2022), criminal law (2023), corporate law (2023), and immigration law (2024).[20] The editors of the first collection in this series – rewrites

---

16 Ibid at 2.

17 Ibid at 6.

18 Rosemary Hunter, Clare McGlynn & Erika Rackley, eds, *Feminist Judgments: From Theory to Practice* (London: Bloomsbury Publishing, 2010) [Hunter, McGlynn & Rackley, *Feminist Judgments*].

19 See Linda Roland Danil, 'Review of *Feminist Judgments: From Theory to Practice*,' *Marx & Engels Philosophy, Review of Books* (7 July 2013), online: <perma.cc/25K7-YW6V>.

20 See Bridget J Crawford, ed, *Feminist Judgments: Rewritten Tax Opinions* (Cambridge, UK: Cambridge University Press, 2017); Kimberly M Mutcherson, ed, *Feminist Judgments: Reproductive Justice Rewritten* (Cambridge, UK: Cambridge University Press, 2020); Rachel Rebouché, ed, *Feminist Judgments: Family Law Opinions Rewritten* (Cambridge, UK: Cambridge University Press, 2020); Deborah S Gordon, Browne C Lewis & Carla Spivack, eds, *Feminist Judgments: Rewritten Trusts and Estates Opinions* (Cambridge, UK: Cambridge University Press, 2020); Ann C McGinley & Nicole Buonocore Porter, eds, *Feminist Judgments: Rewritten Employment and Discrimination Opinions* (Cambridge, UK: Cambridge University Press, 2020); Martha Chamallas & Lucinda M Finley, eds, *Feminist Judgments: Rewritten Tort Opinions* (Cambridge, UK: Cambridge University Press, 2020); Eloisa C Rodriguez-Dod & Elena Maria Marty-Nelson, eds, *Feminist Judgments: Rewritten Property Opinions* (Cambridge, UK:

of opinions of the US Supreme Court, published in 2016 – stated: 'Our project would not have been possible without the vision of the women who created the Women's Court of Canada and the UK Feminist Judgments Project.'[21]

The UK project showed that the rewriting approach worked for a wide range of legal areas, not just those one would immediately associate with women and inequality. It also made very clear that there was no single feminist perspective on any given case as (other feminist) commentors would sometimes take issue with the rewrite.[22] Lady Brenda Hale, who in 2010 was the only woman on the UK Supreme Court and a 'staunch supporter'[23] of the UK's FJP project – also wrote the foreword to the collection – emphasized this multiplicity, both of doctrinal legal areas and feminist perspectives.[24] Testifying before the Lords Constitution Committee inquiry into gender diversity in judicial appointments, Baroness Hale stated in response to a question whether women judges would decide decisions differently than their male counterparts that the FJP showed that 'where you start from can have an effect on where you end up. … That's the best answer I can give you. Go and read that book.'[25] When Rosemary Hunter, one of the editors and organizers of the project, was interviewed in a podcast, she said that the idea 'came from Canada, from the Women's Court of Canada.'[26]

Cambridge University Press, 2022); Seema Mohapatra & Lindsay Wiley, eds, *Feminist Judgements: Health Law Rewritten* (Cambridge, UK: Cambridge University Press, 2022); Bennett Capers, Sarah Deer & Corey Rayburn Yung, eds, *Feminist Judgments: Rewritten Criminal Law Opinions* (Cambridge, UK: Cambridge University Press, 2023); Anne M Choike, Usha R Rodrigues & Kelli Alces Williams, eds, *Feminist Judgments: Corporate Law Rewritten* (Cambridge, UK: Cambridge University Press, 2023) [Choike, Rodrigues & Williams, *Corporate Law Rewritten*]; Kathleen Kim, Kevin Lapp & Jennifer Lee, eds, *Feminist Judgments: Immigration Law Opinions Rewritten* (Cambridge, UK: Cambridge University Press, 2024) [Kim, Lapp & Lee, *Immigration Law Opinions*].

21 'Acknowledgements' in Kathryn M Stanchi, Linda L Berger & Bridget J Crawford, eds, *Feminist Judgments: Rewritten Opinions of the United States Supreme Court* (Cambridge, UK: Cambridge University Press, 2016) at xxxi [Stanchi, Berger & Crawford, *United States Supreme Court*].

22 See Rosemary Hunter, 'An Account of Feminist Judging' in Hunter, McGlynn & Rackley, *Feminist Judgments*, supra note 18 at 41–2 (explaining the 'anti-essentialism' in the collection).

23 'Feminism and the Law' (25 July 2011), 15:20, online: *Pod Academy* <perma. cc/9KDK-9ZYE>.

24 See Rosemary Hunter, 'The Power of Feminist Judgments?' (2012) 20:2 Feminist Legal Studies 135 at 138 [Hunter, 'Power of Feminist Judgments'].

25 See 'Constitution Committee' (2 November 2011), 00h:10m:37s, online: *Parliamentlive. tv* <perma.cc/DC27-3DJ6>.

26 Hunter, 'Power of Feminist Judgments,' supra note 24, 00h:01m:52s.

Hunter, whose professional ties were to Australia as well as to the United Kingdom, went on to co-organize FJPs in Australia and New Zealand.[27] She has supported and served as an advisor on FJPs in the United States, Northern/Ireland, Scotland, and Brazil.[28]

At the time the first set of WCC decisions were rendered, the *Toronto Star* published summaries of four of the judgments.[29] The article placed Réaume's rewrite of *Law* first, explaining that the discrimination at issue in the case was not just on the basis of age. The discrimination was also on the grounds of sex given the fact that younger women are more likely than younger men to earn less, shoulder more household responsibilities, and face more discrimination in the workplace and that they should not be treated the same as a younger male surviving spouse, who might need less government assistance when widowed.

III. *Law* and its rewrite

Nancy Law was thirty years old when her fifty-year-old husband passed away. He had been paying into the Canada Pension Plan (CPP) for twenty-two years at the time of his death, but the plan, at that time, did not provide benefits to a surviving spouse under the age of forty-five unless they had dependent children or a disability, neither of which applied to Law. Law argued that the age distinctions discriminated against her on the basis of age, contrary to section 15 of the Charter. The SCC dismissed her case, finding that the age distinction was not discrimination in a 'substantive sense.'[30] On behalf of the full court, Justice Frank Iacobucci found that adults under forty-five are not a 'discrete and insular' minority and that the legislative distinction did not violate Law's human dignity.[31] The disadvantage imposed by the law was 'unlikely to be a substantive disadvantage in the long term,'

---

27 See Heather Douglas et al, eds, *The Australian Feminist Judgments: Righting and Rewriting Law* (Oxford: Hart Publishing, 2014) [Heather Douglas et al, *Australian Feminist Judgments*]; Elisabeth McDonald et al, eds, *Feminist Judgments of Aotearoa New Zealand: Te Rino: A Two-Stranded Rope* (Oxford: Hart Publishing, 2017).

28 See 'Professor Rosemary Hunter KC (Hon.) FAcSS,' online: *University of Kent* <perma.cc/9G2X-3KRM>. See also Máiréd Enright, Julie McCandless & Aoife O'Donaoghue, eds, *Northern/Irish Feminist Judgements: Judges' Troubles and the Gendered Politics of Identity* (Oxford: Hart Publishing, 2017); Sharon Cowan, Chloe Kennedy & Vanessa E Munro, eds, *(Re)Creating Law from the Outside* (London: Bloomsbury Publishing, 2021).

29 'Your Honour,' supra note 2.

30 *Law v Canada (Minister of Employment and Immigration)*, [1999] 1 SCR 497 at para 38 [*Law*].

31 Ibid at para 95.

nor did it 'stereotype, exclude, or devalue adults under forty-five,' who have a greater chance than older adults to find long-term income replacement.[32]

Although Réaume did reverse the SCC decision in her rewrite, the 'Author's Note' introducing her judgment stated that, at least at first, she did not necessarily disagree with the decision, explaining that, before embarking on the project, she did not have 'strong views about the correct outcome. ... If anything, I thought that the Supreme Court of Canada has probably gotten the right answer.'[33] 'Initially,' she wrote, she 'did not have much sympathy for Nancy Law's claim.'[34] She wanted, however, to rewrite the decision in order to try and bring more rigour to the concept of dignity that had been developing in the SCC's jurisprudence since the 1990s.[35] Réaume had been writing about equality and dignity in the usual academic way.[36] She wanted to see what it would look like to apply the scholarship to a concrete case in the 'more "practical" form' of a judgment.[37]

Law's lawyers had not raised the possibility that the CPP's denial of benefits engaged sex/gender discrimination under the Charter. They likely thought that this was not a very strong argument as the 'under forty-five' age distinction applied equally to both male and female surviving spouses. However, formal equality (usually) does not result in substantively equal effects.[38] Interestingly, the SCC rejected the lens of formal equality and invoked the language of substantive equality.[39] They even seemed to be alive to the fact that the challenge had been put forward narrowly, noting that it would be 'open to a claimant to

---

32 Ibid at paras 104, 102.

33 Réaume, '*Law v Canada*,' supra note 1 at 143.

34 Ibid.

35 Justice Bertha Wilson first wrote about human dignity in her decision *McKinney* in 1990. *McKinney v University of Guelph*, [1990] 3 SCR 229 at 391, cited in *Law*, supra note 30 at para 47. Women's Court of Canada (WCC) member Melina Buckley served as project director to Wilson's Task Force on Gender Equality in the Legal Profession from 1991 to 1993. See 'Local Researchers – Canada,' *Global Access to Justice*, online: <perma.cc/35KT-V7FY>.

36 See e.g. Denise Réaume, 'Indignities: Making a Place for Human Dignity in Modern Legal Thought' (2002) 28 Queen's LJ 61; Denise Réaume, 'Discrimination and Dignity' (2003) 63 La L Rev 645.

37 Réaume, '*Law v Canada*,' supra note 1 at 143.

38 See the following famous graphic by Artist Angus Maguire made available by the Interaction Institute for Social Change, available at Interaction Institute for Social Change, 'Illustrating Equality vs Equity,' *Interaction Institute for Social Change* (13 January 2016), online: <perma.cc/W6VR-VMFB>.

39 See e.g. *Law*, supra note 30 at paras 38–9.

articulate a discrimination claim under more than one of the enumerated or analogous grounds' or on 'a combination of different grounds,' 'confluence of grounds,' 'or intersection of grounds' in section 15.[40] However, Iacobucci J wrote that '[t]he appellant is asserting her claim solely on the basis of age.'[41] 'Clearly a court cannot, *ex proprio motu*,' he continued, 'evaluate a ground of discrimination not pleaded by the parties and in relation to which no evidence has been adduced.'[42] There was no intervenor, such as the Women's Legal Education and Action Fund before the court representing the perspective of sex/gender discrimination.[43]

Réaume's rewrite addressed 'the claimant's failure to raise sex discrimination, and the absence of intervenors before the Court,' writing that it 'would have been wise to have appointed *amicus curiae* to present arguments about the gender implications of the progressive denial of benefits to those below age forty-five.'[44] 'The grounds of age and sex are intricately intertwined,' and the decision should have examined the legislative imposition of 'a male norm on women under the age of forty-five.'[45] Admitting that 'men under forty-five are also affected, women are more likely to find themselves in this situation [that is, widowed] and to suffer more from exclusion.'[46] The survivor benefit was 'originally designed with women in mind' and is paid more

---

40 Ibid at paras 93–4. Though it was not cited, the idea of 'intersectionality' was made famous by Kimberlé Crenshaw's writing on the double bind of simultaneous racial and gender prejudice in the early 1990s. See e.g. Kimberlé Crenshaw, 'Mapping the Margins: Intersectionality, Identity Politics, and Violence against Women of Color' (1991) 42 Stan L Rev 1241. See also Elizabeth V Spelman, *Inessential Woman: Problems of Exclusion in Feminist Thought* (Boston: Beacon Press, 1988).

41 *Law*, supra note 30 at para 95.

42 Ibid at para 58.

43 Of the seventeen founding WCC members, many were affiliated with the Women's Legal Education and Action Fund (LEAF). Shelagh Day was the founding president ('Shelagh Day,' online: *Canada's Human Rights History* < perma.cc/4EFT-HXK2>). Mary Eberts was also a founding member ('Mary Eberts,' online: *Wikipedia* <perma.cc/5LJV-GX9M>). Others who worked with LEAF at some point in their careers include: Melina Buckley (see note 35 above); Avvy Go ('Avvy Go,' online: *Wikipedia* <perma.cc/3JUP-HJRD>); Jennifer Koshan ('Jennifer Koshan,' online: *University of Calgary* <perma.cc/F9ZE-J4QB>); Diana Majury ('Diana Majury,' online: *Community First* <perma.cc/H7K5-PPV9>); and (now deceased) Dianne Pothier ('Remembering Dianne Pothier,' online: *Women's Legal Education & Action Fund* <perma.cc/4PCH-VYZ5>).

44 Réaume, '*Law v Canada*,' supra note 1 at 149.

45 Ibid at 150.

46 Ibid at 173.

frequently to women (90 per cent of the recipients were women in 1997) given the fact that women are more likely to survive a male spouse than the other way round.[47] Because women's earning power is usually 'considerably lower than that of men,' Réaume wrote, 'the expectation that young widows can and should be instantly self-sufficient is clearly unsound.'[48] The scheme recognized this reality for women with dependent children or those with a disability; however, especially if there was a heavy mortgage on the family home or other significant debt, 'a spouse's death might well throw [even an able-bodied woman without children] into complete financial chaos, leading to the loss of home or apartment and a downward spiral into poverty out of which it would be difficult to climb.'[49]

Today, the survivor's benefit continues to be framed in gender neutral terms, with the amount differing depending on the age of the surviving spouse. However, the 'younger/older' distinctions were eliminated in 2018.[50] Currently, all surviving spouses under sixty-five receive a flat rate plus a percentage of the contributor's retirement pension – hence, the only age distinction is between those over and under the age of sixty-five.[51] If the Supreme Court of Canada was wrong to deny that younger women were being discriminated against in a way that violated their dignity as connected to prejudice, stereotyping, or exclusion, today, they are no longer singled out in that way under the CPP. However, women are still much more likely to be widowed than men because they live longer, and, in heterosexual marriages or common law unions, men are still often older than their wives, despite the fact that fewer younger women are widowed today than they were in the 1990s (due mostly to longer life expectancies for men).[52]

Réaume did not discuss the assumption that the SCC made about younger women remarrying in her rewrite. The judgment quoted from the minister responsible for the implementation of the CPP in 1964, the Honourable Judy LaMarsh, who stated in the parliamentary debate about the reduced benefits to those under forty-five and the ineligibility

---

47 Ibid at 175; see also at 183–5.
48 Ibid at 181.
49 Ibid at 182.
50 *Canadian English Dictionary*, 4th ed (June 2024) (online) at para 13, 'Survivor's Benefits – Survivor's Pension' [*CED*].
51 See 'Survivor's Pension' (24 May 2024), online: *Employment and Social Development Canada* <perma.cc/4Q76-YXLQ> ['Survivor's Pension'].
52 See Nathan Battams & Sophie Matthieu, 'Families Count 2024' (2024), online: *Vanier Institute of the Family* <perma.cc/7AGC-NUNX>.

of those under thirty-five: 'Young widows in their twenties and early thirties usually have little difficulty in finding employment, and of course many of them remarry.'[53] Remarriage has not disentitled a surviving spouse from receiving the survivor's benefit since 1987.[54] Presumably, Réaume would have said that the idea that younger women will likely remarry is not a stereotype in a problematic sense unless it is an 'inaccurate generalization.'[55] I query it because it seems like a stereotype, not unlike the idea that it is justifiable to pay married women less than married men for the same work as they are less likely to be the family's breadwinner or the argument that it would be better to hire a man than a woman for a job since they might be more likely to need parental leave. Generalizations that may be accurate because they are likely can still be problematic stereotypes that pave the way to gender discrimination. As Rebecca Cook puts it, '[o]ne of the continuing challenges with gender discrimination is to show how it is hidden, camouflaged, and normalized.'[56]

Réaume described rewriting *Law* as 'a profound learning experience – both my understanding of the issues in the case and aspects of my general account of equality changed in the process.'[57] This 'creative form of critique' turned out to be 'a great teacher.'[58] She made the original six rewritten decisions the basis of a course called 'Rewriting Equality' in 2008–9.[59] In a later interview, she stated that she thought the *Law* rewrite 'would make for great teaching materials.'[60] She characterized her 'main ambition' as getting students 'to see "the fork in the road," the point at which, and the reasons for which, the WCC decision took a different direction from the SCC decision.'[61] Why? Identifying this crossroads was 'crucial to disrupting the impression typically conveyed by judgements that the result was inevitable.'[62]

---

53 *Law*, supra note 30 at para 97.

54 See 'Survivor's Pension,' supra note 51; *CED*, supra note 50.

55 Réaume, '*Law v Canada*,' supra note 1 at 166.

56 Rebecca J Cook, 'Introduction' in Rebecca J Cook, ed, *Frontiers of Gender Equality: Transnational Legal Perspectives* (Philadelphia: University of Pennsylvania Press, 2023) 1 at 2 [Cook, *Frontiers of Gender Equality*].

57 Réaume, '*Law v Canada*,' supra note 1 at 143.

58 Ibid at i, vi.

59 Koshan et al, 'Rewriting Equality,' supra note 9 at 137; see also at 146, Appendix 2 (for the course syllabus).

60 Diane Peters, 'The Women's Court of Canada: A Group of Female Academics, Activists and Litigators Have Joined Together to Literally Rewrite Charter Equality Cases from a Feminist Perspective,' *University Affairs* (12 September 2011), online: <perma.cc/762G-9LDJ>.

61 Koshan et al, 'Rewriting Equality,' supra note 9 at 139.

62 Ibid.

The problem with equality at the time was not really the test, Réaume explained, it was the inability of the (mostly male) judges to understand how the context of the reality of women's lived experiences should impact the outcome.[63] Using a rewrite in a classroom shows that there are, as Réaume put it, 'usually two sides of every story' and that '[t]he shadow judgment has done the filtering work, pulling together the data and academic insights relevant to the case. And then it goes one better, by applying that knowledge to the actual facts. As a way of modelling critical legal analysis, this is as rich as it gets.'[64] In terms of dignity, '[w]ithout the back story,' the actions in the WCC cases 'can be presented as isolated decisions that are mere instances of group members just not getting everything they would like. ... Placed properly in context, the implication of disrespect and lesser worth is not so easily denied.'[65]

Other FJP editors and commentators have echoed Réaume's points about modelling and disruption as well as plausibility.[66] The editors of the first US collection identified the purpose of their FJP as showing '*in a practical and realistic way*, that US Supreme Court decisions could have been decided differently had the justices approached their decisions from a more complex and contextualized vantage.'[67] Baroness Hale emphasized the plausibility of the UK FJP in her foreword to the work.[68] The UK editors wrote that, since their purpose 'was to demonstrate how cases could have been written and decided differently, it was important to make our judgments as *plausible* as possible to sceptical lawyers and judges.'[69] They also wrote that one of their aims was 'to *disrupt* [the] process of gender construction, and to introduce different accounts of gender that might be less limiting for women.'[70] Commenting on the International Law FJP, Hilary Charlesworth, today a judge at

---

63 Denise Réaume, 'Turning Feminist Judgments into Jurisprudence: The Women's Court of Canada on Substantive Equality' (2018) 8:9 Oñati Socio-Legal Series 1307 at 1310–11.

64 Ibid at 1313.

65 Ibid at 1319.

66 See e.g. Réaume, 'Rewriting Equality,' supra note 4 at vi (the judgments of the WCC are 'not just what the SCC should have said but what it could have said,' i.e., plausibility).

67 Kathryn M Stanchi, Linda L Berger & Bridget J Crawford, 'Introduction' in Stanchi, Berger & Crawford, *United States Supreme Court*, supra note 21 at 9 [emphasis added].

68 'Foreword' in Hunter, McGlynn & Rackley, *Feminist Judgments*, supra note 18 at v.

69 'Feminist Judgments: An Introduction' in Hunter, McGlynn & Rackley, *Feminist Judgments*, supra note 18 at 6 [emphasis added].

70 Ibid at 7 [emphasis added].

the International Court of Justice, wrote about the rewrites 'unsettling the determinacy of law' and also 'prefiguring' what that law could be.[71]

IV. Rewriting *Pierson v Post*

Here, I will switch gears a bit and describe my own experience doing a rewrite for an edited collection on rewritten property law decisions published in 2022.[72] Specifically, I contributed a rewrite of *Pierson v Post*, a case concerning a hunted fox, often used in property law classrooms to introduce students to the concept of possession.[73] I initially wanted to write the judgment from the perspective of the fox, allowing 'Reynard J' to speak in their own voice.[74] However, there could only be one opinion, and it had to come from me as the judge. Denise and I discussed the challenge of trying to figure out how to present the fox's perspective in this exercise. She suggested using the framework of a dream, which the editors of that collection were open to.[75] However, in the end, we settled on a compromise, with me, as Justice Angela Fernandez, imagining what the fox would say and with Fernandez J explaining two points that she felt 'the Fox herself (or a lawyer acting on her behalf) would point out if she were permitted to speak.'[76] Denise and I did not talk about changing the fox from a 'he' to a 'she,' but it seemed like an appropriate choice for a feminist rewrite that she would have agreed with.[77]

---

71 Hilary Charlesworth, 'Prefiguring Feminist Judgment in International Law' in 'Feminist Judgment Projects,' supra note 6 at 491. See also Davina Cooper, 'Enacting Counter-States through Play' (2016) 15:4 Contemporary Political Theory 453 [Cooper, 'Encountering Counter-States'].

72 Fernandez, '*Pierson v Post*,' supra note 13.

73 See Angela Fernandez, *Pierson v Post, the Hunt for the Fox, Law and Professionalization in American Legal Culture* (Cambridge, UK: Cambridge University Press, 2018) at 1–4 [Fernandez, *Pierson v Post*].

74 I dedicated the book 'To poor Reynard' in a way that was initially meant to mirror the mock seriousness I would be talking about but which was also heartfelt in the sense that I was aware of the debt I owed this animal, myself also being one on a long list of legal professionals to benefit from their (violent) death.

75 This is similar to advice Réaume gave to Jennifer Koshan when she was wrestling with how to respond to reviewers' comments that would have forced her to change her original rewritten decision too much. Réaume suggested to Koshan that she write her response in the form of an after-dinner speech from her retired self. See Réaume, 'Rewriting Equality,' supra note 4; Koshan et al, 'Rewriting Equality,' supra note 9.

76 Fernandez, '*Pierson v Post*,' supra note 13 at 107.

77 I was originally alternating between 'he' and 'she' when referring to the fox, and the editors suggested going only with 'she' despite the fact that, in the original

The age of the case, which dates from 1805, posed an issue as it required quite a lot more time travel than the WCC cases and those in many of the other collections, which dealt with more modern cases.[78] It was difficult to find feminist references from the period, and Rosemary Auchmuty, a UK FJP contributor, pointed me to the work of Australian feminist Dale Spender.[79] Unlike the days of the WCC's 'Author's Note,' which prefaced a rewritten decision, there was nowhere to acknowledge that debt as the judge doing the rewrite cannot provide any commentary/explanation or even use footnotes.[80] The thinking in the UK collection was that judgments do not contain footnotes and 'authenticity' required a preclusion on explanations because '[j]udgments in the real world do not come accompanied by exegeses, and we wanted the reasoning in the feminist judgments, too, to stand up on its own.'[81]

An additional point that caused some trouble was that I had written a whole book about my case, and it was going to be difficult to track or flag the additional facts coming from that research without footnotes or explanation.[82] I did attempt to alert the reader to the basic fact by writing: 'I can write a whole book about this case and have done so.

---

judgment, Reynard was a 'he.' See the dissent by Livingston J in *Pierson v Post*, 3 Cai Rep 175 (1805) at 180:

> a fox is a "wild and noxious beast." Both parties have regarded him, as the law of nations does a pirate. … His depredations on farmers and on barn yards, have not been forgotten; and to put him to death wherever found, is allowed to be meritorious, and of public benefit. … [O]ur decision should have in view the greatest possible encouragement to the destruction of an animal, so cunning and ruthless in his career.

See Eliot Schrefer, *Queer Ducks (and Other Animals): The Natural Work of Animal Sexuality* (New York: HarperCollins, 2022) at 28 (exploring whether animals have gender or whether it is 'just a human thing').

78 The oldest case in the UK collection was 1925, and the oldest in the first collection of US Supreme Court cases was 1873.

79 At Rosemary Auchmuty's suggestion, I used Dale Spender's books on women writers and philosophers such as Mary Astell, Lady Mary Wortley Montague, and Mary Hays. See Dale Spender, *Women of Ideas and What Men Have Done to Them* (New York: HarperCollins, 1982); Dale Spender, *Feminist Theorists: Three Centuries of Women's Intellectual Traditions* (New York: Pantheon, 1983). See Fernandez, '*Pierson v Post*,' supra note 13 at 115–17.

80 Réaume's approach in *Law* of writing a 'reconsideration' of the Supreme Court of Canada (SCC) decision (rather than a concurring or dissenting opinion at the same time) would also not have been allowed under the rules as they developed. See Réaume, '*Law v Canada*,' supra note 1 at 148.

81 See 'Feminist Judgments: An Introduction' in Hunter, McGlynn & Rackley, *Feminist Judgments*, supra note 18 at 16, 27.

82 Fernandez, '*Pierson v Post*,' supra note 13.

Nonhuman animals ... are given no such chance to have their voices heard.'[83] Thankfully, the editors did not take a strict approach to the 'first hearing rule,' which has been interpreted in other FJPs as precluding reference to anything the two sides would not have had access to at the time.[84] Where there was a relevant later legal development, I tried to work it creatively into the decision.[85] And even factual future states could be handled obliquely. For example, responding to the characterization of the beach in the case as 'waste land,' Fernandez J wrote that '[t]his area of the country is so beautiful, it is bound to become very valuable real estate' when currently this part of Long Island, the Hamptons, contains some of the most expensive properties in the United States.[86]

I made the reasoning very Lockean as this would have made the most sense at the time.[87] And it was John Locke, after all, who maintained that individuals own their own bodies, supportive of the claim that Fernandez J made that 'the Fox owns herself' and that 'all nonhuman animals arguably own themselves in the same way [as you and me].'[88] My rewrite was in flagrant violation of what I now learn was the KISS command: 'Keep It Short and Simple' or 'Keep It Simple Sister.'[89] However, I felt that the elaborateness of the original decision demanded an equally elaborate mirroring on my part. Given that much of that style of legal learnedness operated to exclude women and other 'outsiders' from the profession, I felt it was necessary as a female judge, about whom people would have been sceptical (to say the least) in 1805, to show – yes, Fernandez J could speak in that style – the mock seriousness of the original decision.[90] However, I also needed to make some kind of comment about how the time travel felt very forced to me, not just as a woman but also as a racialized female, something that would have been literally impossible in that time and place.

---

83 Ibid at 116.

84 Heather Douglas et al, *Australian Feminist Judgments*, supra note 27 at 12.

85 For example, I gave some options for avoiding the gross disproportion between costs and amount awarded in *Pierson* ($126.37 in costs for the seventy-five-cent jury award) and included among them one I knew would be adopted three years later by the New York legislature – namely, to cap costs at twenty-five dollars under the small claims statute, which only allowed for claims up to twenty-five dollars. See Fernandez, *'Pierson v Post,'* supra note 13 at 104–5; Fernandez, *Pierson v Post,* supra note 73 at 191.

86 See Fernandez, *'Pierson v Post,'* supra note 13 at 111.

87 Ibid at 100, 112–13.

88 Ibid at 98, 110.

89 Heather Douglas et al, *Australian Feminist Judgments*, supra note 27 at 12.

90 See Fernandez, *'Pierson v Post,'* supra note 13 at 99–102.

Fernandez J writes that what she finds so unsettling is 'the attitude that underlies the behavior of the lawyers and my male colleagues, namely, that the Fox, a sentient fellow creature, can be treated as a mere plaything in a debate about an intellectual question that interests them.'[91] While noting that 'I realize I risk being attacked as a humorless feminist,' Fernandez J calls out 'the profound disrespect' that judges and lawyers exhibit toward the hunted animal, acting 'as if it were perfectly acceptable for her torture and death to serve as the occasion for an elaborate debate with the exchange of some learned authorities and the occasional witty repartee, all of which presupposes rather than argues for the legitimacy of her status as property.'[92] Their behaviour demonstrates a presumption of superiority over the animal and an attitude of entitlement, leaving to one side the fox who 'has no voice and cannot speak for herself and no one represents her interests.'[93]

This part of the rewritten decision became something of a composite about points relating to women's disrespectful treatment in the law and professional legal life, a concern that Réaume shared.[94] For example, I was thinking about Justice Bertha Wilson and how she felt excluded by her male colleagues at the SCC, who were making alliances on the golf course or tennis court, sports she did not play, when I had Fernandez J criticize her male colleagues, writing:[95]

> [T]here is nothing funny about the male clubbiness that has swirled around the decisions to frame, argue, and decide the case as it has been done. I have been party to none of them, and I would like to know when and who decided that the case would be treated ... so that the lawyers could have their State of Nature debate. I am unable to obtain a satisfactory answer from my male colleagues ... Did it happen in the men's robing room or washroom? Perhaps it was during a hunting or a fishing outing ... As a female member of this bench, I often feel excluded from the male fraternity of judges and lawyers who are often unwelcoming (not unwittingly) and who make many assumptions I find to be problematic. I am

---

91 Ibid at 114.

92 Ibid.

93 Ibid.

94 For an early publication, see e.g. Denise Réaume, 'Review of *Women in the Law* by J Brophy and C Smart eds' (1986) 93 Queen's Quart 417.

95 See Ellen Anderson, *Judging Bertha Wilson: Law as Large as Life* (Toronto: University of Toronto Press, 2001) at 257 [Anderson, *Judging Bertha Wilson*].

not entirely sure that they do not often make jokes about me, something
which they obviously would not share with me.[96]

This last part of the quote is harsh but fair given how male judges at the
time would have reacted, and, in the case of Bertha Wilson, did react, to
a woman among them as an equal and a peer.[97]

Our colleague Karen Knop used to emphasize what Patricia Williams wrote about *Pierson*, feeling an identification with the fox and her
enslaved great-great-grandmother when she studied the case in law
school.[98] With this in mind, Fernandez J wrote:

> At any rate, I have not felt the exclusion from their fraternity in so poin-
> ted a way as I have over this fox case, as I find myself identifying with
> the Fox, the slave, the dispossessed, rather than my colleagues, the White
> privileged men, who are supposed to be my professional peers but, yet,
> who act here in such an unprofessional way. I fear that the exclusions
> in my case have been exacerbated by being not only a woman but also
> a racialized female in a country where human beings are routinely and
> callously enslaved by virtue of their ethnicity and skin color, brought
> here from other countries where they have been colonized by different
> forms of occupation or born into a slave system which turns them into
> property.[99]

Slavery in Eastern Long Island, where the case took place, was com-
monplace – and, indeed, most of the people connected to the *Pierson*
case were slaveowners (for example, the families of the two litigants,
the Justice of the Peace who tried the matter, and the owner of the house

---

96 Fernandez, '*Pierson v Post*,' supra note 13 at 114–15. My best guess is that the
    decision to publish *Pierson* was the Reporter George Caines and the judges and
    lawyers did not expect for it to appear in print. See Fernandez, *Pierson v Post*, supra
    note 73 at 223–51.

97 For example, when Bertha Wilson was appointed to the Ontario Court of Appeal and
    a special meeting was called to discuss her appointment and the fact that she was a
    woman, one of the most senior judges apparently blurted out: 'No woman can do
    my job.' See Anderson, *Judging Bertha Wilson*, supra note 95 at 88. Wilson felt more
    welcome and respected when she was a lawyer working at a big downtown Toronto
    law firm than at the Supreme Court of Canada. See Angela Fernandez & Beatrice
    Tice, 'Bertha Wilson's Practice Years (1958–1975): Establishing a Research Practice and
    Founding a Research Department' in Kimberly Brooks, ed, *One Woman's Difference: The
    Contributions of Justice Bertha Wilson* (Vancouver: UBC Press, 2009) 15.

98 See Fernandez, *Pierson v Post*, supra note 73 at 130.

99 Ibid at 114–15.

where the jury trial took place).[100] This connection to slave owning is not something that is usually (if ever) discussed in connection to the case.

In addition to sexism and racism, there is also the issue of brute physical violence. Here, it is highly gendered not just because we decided to make the fox a 'she' but also due to the connection between perhaps the decision's most famous phrase – the 'saucy intruder' – and the rape and mutilation of Lavinia in Shakespeare's play *Titus Andronicus*.[101] It is a tricky matter to point out the dark underside of such a beloved case and how it is premised on lethal occupation and even sexual violence. Joining in the mock tone but making opposite arguments was one way to do it that was both true to the time and place but also provided a needed 'update' with respect to both animals and feminism.[102] Using some 'solemn foolery' of my own was the way out that I was looking for.[103] As Jessica Eisen put it, writing specifically about the rewrite, 'jumping into the comedic fray serves as such a powerful repudiation. Hers is not the droll mockery of the comfortably superior. It is wit used to hold a mirror up to power.'[104] In a world where legal power was 'crafted in social clubs and robing rooms, often by those sharing a joke,' Eisen continued: '[G]etting in on the law means getting in on the joke.'[105]

What would Réaume think about the rewrite providing updates regarding both animals and feminism? I think I can safely say that she would have been empathetic about the latter goal, researching and writing as extensively as she did about women and intimate partner violence.[106] She might also have agreed with the former. Réaume

---

100 But not the twelve men in the jury pool (except one), who were generally of less wealthy means. See Fernandez, *Pierson v Post, supra* note 73 at 157, 167–8 (the families), 46 (the Justice of the Peace), 160 (the house owner), 306.

101 Ibid at 115–24. I benefited from discussions about this damned-if-I-do, damned-if-I-don't problem with Deborah Dinner.

102 See Kunal Parker, 'The Hunt as History and as Game,' *Legal History: Jotwell* (9 December 2019), online: <perma.cc/AS6X-YRL8>.

103 Andrea Freeman not only sent me the call to participate in the project rewriting property decisions, but she encouraged me to use some solemn foolery of my own making. On legal solemn foolery, see Fernandez, *Pierson v Post,* supra note 73 at 3–34, 75–106, 302–3, 315–16.

104 Jessica Eisen, 'Of Linchpins and Bedrock: Hope, Despair, and Pragmatism in Animal Law' (2022) 72:4 UTLJ 468 at 483.

105 Ibid.

106 See e.g. Denise Réaume & Shauna Van Praagh, 'Family Matters: Mothers as Secondary Defendants in Child Abuse Actions' (2002) 17 SCLR 179. She also, along with Janet Mosher and Martha Shaffer, produced materials on wife assault to include in law school courses across Ontario as well as a separate course on the topic in 1992.

supervised a directed research project written by University of Toronto doctorate of law student Camille Labchuk, which examined arguments for veganism as a protected creed under the Ontario Human Rights Code circa 2010.[107] While this topic relates to the protection of humans against discrimination on the basis of sincerely held beliefs, it also suggests a certain amount of respect toward these beliefs. There are direct connections between the protection of women in situations of domestic violence and the protection of animals. Topics here include domestic violence survivors being permitted to take their companion animals into shelters, the inclusion of companion animals in protective orders, and the alarmingly high numbers of abusers who target a survivor's companion animal in order to exert 'coercive control' over the survivor.[108] Care must be taken connecting the idea that those who abuse animals will 'graduate,' as it were, to harming people.[109] However, there are overlapping considerations when considering the vulnerabilities

---

107 See Krystal-Anne Roussel & Camille Labchuk, 'A Single Black Bean: Discrimination and the Protection of Ethical Vegans in Canada' in Jeanette Rowley & Carlo Prisco, eds, *Law and Veganism: International Perspectives on the Human Right to Freedom of Conscience* (Lantham, NY: Lexington Books, 2022) 27. The case of a vegan firefighter named Adam Knauff, which Labchuk helped bring forward, is still being litigated. See *Animal Law Digest: Canada Edition*, online: <perma.cc/NKN7-X3Q6>. *Human Rights Code*, RSO 1990, c H.19.

108 See e.g. Rochelle Stevenson, Amy Fitzgerald & Betty Jo Barnett, 'Keeping Pets Safe in the Context of Intimate Partner Violence: Insights from Domestic Violence Shelter Staff in Canada' (2018) 33:2 Feminist Inquiry in Social Work 236; Amy Fitzgerald, 'Animals as Covictims and More-Than-Property: The Inclusion of Companion Animals in Protective Order Statutes at the State Level in the United States' (2024) 40:1 Violence and Victims 110; Amy Fitzgerald, 'Animal-Inclusive Protection Order Statutes: A Powerful Tool for Addressing and Mitigation Coercive Control' (2025) 0:0 Violence Against Women.

109 I recall Denise warning me to heed the research on domestic violence, which cast doubt on the wisdom of using a highly punitive approach that blew back on survivors themselves financially and otherwise, particularly if there were children from the union. This question is highly relevant to the animal protection movement, which gravitates, especially in the United States, toward carceral solutions to social problems. Yet the animal movement is also a civil rights movement, which one would think would not be in the business of advocating for incarceration that ruins people's lives. See Justin F Marceau, *Beyond Cages: Animal Protection and Criminal Punishment* (Cambridge, UK: Cambridge University Press, 2019). The alignment of animal law with the left or the right is complicated. For example, the White Coat Waste Project in the United States advocates for the reduction or elimination of animal testing on the basis of reducing government waste. See *White Coat Waste Project*, online: <perma.cc/MK5U-M4SG>.

involved with both non-human animals and women.[110] Arguably, Réaume's work on language rights could be connected to her general commitment to the situations and perspectives of minority groups who have less power and their social recognition and legal rights are precarious as a result.[111] 'Why do men abuse women?' I once asked her: 'Because they can,' she replied, a chilling answer that is perhaps even more applicable to animals.[112] Réaume published numerous pieces in volumes edited by Will Kymlicka relating to multiculturalism, whose work on animals, along with Sue Donaldson, has been pathbreaking.[113] Other WCC members worked in areas such as disability studies and queer theory that are also being explored in critical animal studies.[114]

Although I was not able to rewrite the *Pierson* judgment exactly as I wanted, I liked the result. Some of the constraints actually helped me express things that were difficult, if not impossible, to write about ordinarily. There was something about occupying such an impossible subject position that created a channel to express outrage, not just about how women are treated but also about non-human animals, and

---

110 See e.g. Ani B Satz, 'Animals as Vulnerable Subjects: Beyond Interest-Convergence, Hierarchy, and Property' in Martha Fineman & Anna Grear, eds, *Vulnerability: Reflections on a New Ethical Foundation for Law and Politics* (Burlington, VT: Ashgate, 2013) 65; Maneesha Deckha, 'Vulnerability, Equality, and Animals' (2015) 27:1 CJWL 47.

111 See e.g. Denise G Réaume, 'Fairness and Equal Recognition' in Sergi Morales-Gálvez & Nenad Stojonovi, eds, *Equal Recognition, Minority Rights and Liberal Democracy: Alan Patten and His Critics* (London: Routledge, 2017) 63.

112 Criminal law, federal and provincial, is very dependent on a third party reporting (for example, a neighbour who hears the abuse) as there is no way for animals to self-report, although a vet might alert police or animal welfare authorities of abuse if they were to observe it. Removal, charges, or arrests can follow when (usually) a man is recorded by a bystander with a cell phone beating his dog on the street or in a condominium elevator or lobby video camera that he (usually the boyfriend of the female owner) is clearly not aware is recording him. Women are also often involved in animal abuse cases, either as part of a couple or on their own. Cases run the gamut. See the 'Enforcement Updates' of issues in *Animal Law Digest*, Canada edition, online: <perma.cc/6388-4DZK>.

113 Réaume's work appeared in a volume that Will Kymlicka co-edited with Ian Shapiro, *Ethnicity and Group Rights, NOMOS XXXIX* (New York: New York University Press, 1997), one he edited *Diverse Societies: Theory and Practice* (New York: Oxford University Press, 2000), and another co-edited with Alan Patten, *Language Rights and Political Theory* (Oxford: Oxford University Press, 2023). See also Sue Donaldson & Will Kymlicka, *Zoopolis: A Political Theory of Animal Rights* (Oxford: Oxford University Press, 2017).

114 See e.g. Nik Taylor & Richard Twine, eds, *The Rise of Critical Animal Studies: From the Margins to the Centre* (London: Routledge, 2014) at 4.

these not just a historical matter but also continuing and currently. I took the liberty to make a few references to things that would not have made sense to a nineteenth-century reader – for example, writing about women writers at the time who might 'take to their pens to make "me too" demands for liberty and equality.'[115] The UK editors acknowledged that, 'in relation to some of the older cases, it was impossible to eliminate all traces of an early twenty-first-century feminist judicial sensibility.'[116] Was it even desirable really to do that when the point was to create a judgment that, yes, 'plausibly' reads like it was written in 1805 but was in actuality for twenty-first-century readers?

V. Conclusion

Majury wrote that the WCC method would 'grow and change, and perhaps morph into something quite different.'[117] That has been happening over the last twenty years. Collections in 2023 and 2024 have included male authors and editors.[118] There have also been very deliberate departures from the 'fair hearing rule'[119] as well as more experimental FJPs.[120] Jennifer Koshan, an original WCC member, did an analysis of citations to the WCC's judgments, finding that, after ten years, the feminist judgments were not cited very extensively by other academics or courts or lawyers making arguments to courts, tribunals, or administrative bodies.[121] Rosemary Hunter, one of the editors of the UK collection and consultant on other FJPs, is not aware of any court citations.[122] Koshan

---

115 Fernandez, '*Pierson v Post*,' supra note 13 at 116.

116 'Feminist Judgments: An Introduction' in Hunter, McGlynn & Rackley, *Feminist Judgments*, supra note 18 at 15.

117 Majury, 'Introducing the Women's Court,' supra note 3 at 5.

118 See Kim, Lapp & Lee, *Immigration Law Opinions*, supra note 20; Choike, Rodrigues & Williams, *Corporate Law Rewritten*, supra note 20.

119 See e.g. Charles G Ngwena & Rebecca J Cook, 'Restoring Mai Mapingure's Equal Citizenship' in Cook, *Frontiers of Gender Equality*, supra note 56 at 411 ('[w]e recognize that we are departing from the rules of other rewriting projects that require judgments to be written only according to the law the time').

120 See e.g. Daniel Del Gobbo, 'Finding Equality: A Creative Take on Feminist Judgment Projects and the Criminalization of HIV Non-Disclosure' (2025) 20:1 JL & Equality 183 [Del Gobbo, 'Finding Equality'] (providing an example of a 'found' poem created from a judgment); see also 194–5 (describing how the Aotearoa/ New Zealand, Australian, Northern/Irish, and Scottish FJPs deviated from the 'conventional methodology'), 190–1 (describing critical race, queer, Indigenous, Earth law, and Anthropocene FJPs).

121 See Koshan, 'Impact,' supra note 1.

122 Email to the author, 21 July 2024.

noted that '[i]t is perhaps no coincidence that scholars of literature are among those who have deeply engaged with' the WCC judgments.[123] This feedback suggests that the original aim of having the judgments operate 'as if' they were real and using the 'realistic' and 'plausible' benchmark might have been off the mark, at least approaching it in an overly narrow sense.

Around the same time that Réaume was working on the WCC, our colleague Karen Knop started thinking deeply about the Tokyo Women's Tribunal.[124] This tribunal was positioned by the various women's and non-governmental organizations from across Asia who organized it as an actual judgment of the International Military Tribunal for the Far East sitting in the year 2000 'as if' it was 1946.[125] Knop pointed to the 'time machine' problem that this tribunal created.[126] Likely thinking also about the WCC, Knop identified the tribunal as a work of 'fact-ion,' the deliberate mixing of fact and fiction that opts for a 'usable past' over a technically accurate one.[127] By using the concept of 'sexual slavery' (a term that would not become common until the 1990s), the tribunal sought, in Knop's words, 'to consolidate feminist gains in current international law by constructing a fictional precedent.'[128]

These 'as if' performances are not just 'elaborate works of fiction'; they are also works of 'alternative history' – that is, the 'serious play' of prefigurative politics.[129] Yet their fictional aspects put them at risk of not being taken seriously, something those who speak up for women's rights and non-human animals must contend with regularly. For

---

123 Koshan, 'Impact,' supra note 1 at 1334.

124 See Karen Knop, 'The Tokyo Women's Tribunal and the Turn to Fiction' in Fleur Johns, Richard Joyce & Sundhya Pahuja, eds, *Events: The Force of International Law* (New York: Routledge, 2011) 145 at 149, 160, n 1 [Knop, 'Tokyo Women's Tribunal'].

125 Ibid at 146.

126 Ibid at 153, 146.

127 Ibid at 149, 158. Knop borrowed the term 'usable past' from John J Su, 'Fantasies of (Re)collection: Collecting and Imagination in A.S. Byatt's *Possession: A Romance*' (2004) 45:4 Contemporary Literature 684 at 704. I find some similarities between Knop and the tall Maude Bailey, walking with a generous stride and 'dressed with unusual coherence for an academic.' AS Byatt, *Possession: A Romance* (London: Vintage, 1990) at 43. There was literally a hardcover copy of the novel in my office in the renovated Attic of Flavelle House when I moved in there in 2005, and Karen and I used to speculate about why the office's previous occupant had left it there.

128 Knop, 'Tokyo Women's Tribunal,' supra note 124 at 158.

129 Cooper, 'Encountering Counter-States,' supra note 71 at 457. See also the posthumously published piece, which calls the Tokyo Women's Tribunal 'performative fiction' or 'law-adjacent performance art.' Karen Knop & Annelise Riles, 'My Own Pink World: Feminist Diplomacy after Culture' (2024) 74:1 UTLJ 186 at 17.

example, when the (now late) animal lawyer Steven Wise first began practising animal law in 1981, he used to be barked at when he entered a courtroom.[130] When Réaume wrote about dignity, she had human, not non-human, dignity in mind.[131] However, much of what she said about dignity could apply to non-human animals.[132] With that in mind, one of the ways I will be playing forward Réaume's work on the WCC is a project bringing together rewrites of cases involving animals, which incorporate scientifically informed perspectives on their situations. It

130 See Steve Jacobs, 'The 30-Year Fight for Chimps' Rights,' *Sydney Morning Herald* (3 May 2015), online: <perma.cc/Q465-9TBQ>. When I first met Steve and interviewed him in Oxford, England, in 2017, he immediately understood the connections between disrespect, legal solemn foolery, and the *Pierson* case. This conversation helped make the point explicit for me in a way that I then brought into the rewritten decision. See Angela Fernandez, 'Legal History and Rights for Nonhuman Animals: An Interview with Steven M Wise' (2018) 41:1 Dal LJ 197. I connect Denise to this conversation because I also met up with her in Oxford on this occasion as she was still traveling to her house there in the summertime at that time. Wise died at the age of seventy-three on 15 February, 2024. See 'Steven M Wise, Legal Force for Animal Rights, Dies at 73,' *Washington Post* (20 February 2024), online: <perma.cc/7C7N-RAH6>.

131 See e.g. Denise Réaume, 'Dignity, Choice, and Circumstances' in Christopher McCrudden, ed, *Understanding Human Dignity* (Oxford: Oxford University Press for the British Academy, 2013) 539 at 540 [Réaume, 'Dignity, Choice, and Circumstances'].

132 Knop worked closely with Anne Peters on a symposium for the *American Journal of International Law Unbound*. See Anne Peters, 'Introduction to Symposium on Global Animal Law (Part I): Animals Matter in International Law and International Law Matters for Animals' (2017) 111 AJIL Unbound 252. I recall Karen was particularly excited about a paper in that issue on the military use of dolphins. See Jérôme de Hemptinne, 'The Protection of Animals during Warfare' (2017) 111 AJIL Unbound 272. Peters wrote a note she included in a copy of her book *Animals in International Law* (Leiden: Brill/Nijhoff, 2021), which she sent to Karen, writing that she was looking forward to Karen taking up the Max Planck Fellowship, which of course Karen's death prevented. This fellowship is 'the highest honour that the Max Planck Law network can confer on scholars working outside Germany's Max Planck Society.' See 'In Memoriam: Professor Karen Knop (1960–2022),' University of Toronto, Faculty of Law, online: <perma.cc/54AL-V7YB>. When she was the editor of the *University of Toronto Law Journal*, Knop also curated the Focus Feature, 'Foxes, Seals, Whales and the Rule of Capture: Animals in the Law and Legal History' (2013) 63 UTLJ 97. Karen's December 2021 private international law exam included a question relating to a US court's recognition of a 'community of hippopotamuses living in the Magdalena River' in Colombia as 'interested persons' in a foreign lawsuit. See 'Landmark Animal Personhood Case Proceedings from US and Colombia,' *Brooks Animal Law Digest: Canada Edition* (2021), online: <perma.cc/UMG2-GZHQ>. Karen recommended we subscribe to the farmed animals section of *The Guardian* to locate international stories for the digest.

is what Knop identified as 'informed invention.'[133] Also taking a lesson from Réaume about the pedagogical value of rewritten judgments, David Sandomierski and I have curated a collection of student-written canonical contract law cases, which explicitly combine the rewritten judgment approach with legal archaeological studies in order to see the difference that these materials make to understanding these landmark contract law cases.

It seems likely that, as legal scholars become comfortable with innovating the 'conventional methodology,'[134] the fictional aspects of the 'fact-ional' genre will grow and acquire a wider range of readers. Imagination will be needed in order to decide project by project what factual constraints will continue to provide the loose guardrails within which to play in this serious way. Judgment writers and editors will need to ask themselves how strictly they should be guided by conventional norms given to whom they want the decisions to be realistic and plausible and for what purpose. In the animal case, it will be in part to make a collective argument about, to use Réaume's words, 'recogniz[ing] the capacity for agency that people have at whatever level they have it.'[135] In a world where the law mostly facilitates the use of non-human animals, powerful imagination is needed to imagine another, better world, one in which human law recognizes the intrinsic worth of other animals and bends toward meaningfully protecting them. This requires positioning non-human animals as subjects (rather than mere objects) of the law with representable interests and a way to have their voices heard. Neither the animal nor the contracts project is explicitly feminist, but both will contribute to the kind of disruptions which are a hallmark of the critical legal approaches within which Réaume located the WCC, thereby carrying on the fertile tradition she created in different ways.

---

133 See Knop, 'Tokyo Women's Tribunal,' supra note 124 at 151.
134 Del Gobbo, 'Finding Equality,' supra note 120.
135 Réaume, 'Dignity, Choice, and Circumstances,' supra note 131 at 540.

12 Transforming Spousal Support from the Ground Up: Carol Rogerson and the Development of the Spousal Support Advisory Guidelines†

MARTHA SHAFFER

It is not often that one can say that a colleague's work has had a profound real-world impact on a body of law, much less on a body of law that is likely to touch the lives of many Canadians. But one can say that about the work of Carol Rogerson. In addition to writing numerous articles that made her the most prominent Canadian scholar on the law of spousal support (more on that later), Carol was one of the two creators of the Spousal Support Advisory Guidelines (SSAGs), a set of informal and non-binding guidelines that have fundamentally reshaped the law of spousal support in this country.[1] The importance of the SSAGs to Canadian family law is impossible to overstate. The guidelines have given coherence and structure to an area of law that, in the 1980s and 1990s, had become uncertain and unpredictable. They have provided a framework for determining the amount and duration of spousal support obligations that can be easily accessed by judges, lawyers, mediators, and former spouses. Not only have the SSAGs made spousal support orders more consistent and more principled, but the clarity that the guidelines provide has also improved access to justice by encouraging negotiation and settlement. Despite being informal

---

† The author would like to thank Carol Rogerson, Arnold Weinrib, and David Dyzenhaus for their very helpful comments. Special thanks go to Rollie Thompson for discussing the process of creating the Spousal Support Advisory Guidelines (SSAGs) and for his help throughout.

1 Carol Rogerson & Rollie Thompson, *Spousal Support Advisory Guidelines* (Ottawa: Department of Justice, 2008) [*SSAGs*]. The other co-author of the guidelines was Rollie Thompson of the Schulich School of Law at Dalhousie University. The authors of the guidelines worked extensively with a working group of family law experts, including judges, lawyers, and mediators from across Canada. The process of developing the guidelines will be discussed in greater detail in notes 46–8 below and the accompanying text.

and advisory, the SSAGs have been described as the most ambitious spousal support guidelines in the common law world.

Of all of Carol's scholarship, I have chosen to highlight the SSAGs because, in addition to their enormous importance in their own right, the SSAGs can also be seen as the culmination of Carol's academic writings in family law. From the very start of her academic career, Carol's work as a family law scholar focused on the economic consequences of marriage breakdown, with a particular emphasis on the effects of marriage breakdown on women and children.[2] Throughout her career, Carol explored the ways in which the law could structure post-marriage economic arrangements between the spouses to ensure fairness for the former spouses and their children. Although she wrote about child support[3] and domestic contracts,[4] Carol's work on spousal support is particularly noteworthy. In a series of articles in the 1990s and early 2000s, Carol wrote about the evolution of the spousal support obligation and its place in a modern no-fault divorce regime.[5] Her scholarship combined an understanding of the theoretical models underlying competing conceptions of the modern spousal support obligation with a highly nuanced understanding, gleaned from her comprehensive knowledge of

---

2 See e.g. Carol Rogerson, 'Winning the Battle, Losing the War: The Plight of the Custodial Mother after Judgment' in Margaret E Hughes & E Diane Pask, eds, *National Themes in Canadian Family Law* (Toronto: Carswell, 1988) 21; Carol Rogerson, 'The Causal Connection Test in Spousal Support Law' (1989) 8 Can J Fam L 95; Carol Rogerson, 'Women, Money and Equality: The Background Issues' in Karen Busby et al, eds, *Equality Issues in Family Law: Considerations for Test Case Litigation* (Winnipeg: Legal Research Institute of the University of Manitoba, 1990) 97; Carol Rogerson, 'Judicial Interpretation of the Spousal and Child Support Provisions of the Divorce Act, 1985: Part 1' (1991) 12 Adv Q 377; Carol Rogerson, 'Judicial Interpretation of the Spousal and Child Support Provisions of the Divorce Act, 1985: Part 2' (1991) 7 Can Fam LQ 155.

3 Carol Rogerson, 'Child Support under the Guidelines in Cases of Split and Shared Custody' (1998) 15 Can J Fam L 11; Carol Rogerson, 'The Child Support Obligation of Step-Parents' (2001) 18 Can J Fam L 9.

4 Carol Rogerson, '"They Are Agreements Nonetheless" Case Comment on *Miglin v. Miglin*, 2003 SCC 24' (2003) 20 Can J Fam L 197; Carol Rogerson & Martha Shaffer, 'Contracting Spousal Support: Thinking through *Miglin*' (2003) 21 Can Fam LQ 49; Carol Rogerson, 'Spousal Support Agreements and the Legacy of Miglin' (2012) 31 Can Fam LQ 13.

5 Carol Rogerson, 'Spousal Support after *Moge*' (1997) 14 Can Fam LQ 281; Carol Rogerson, 'Spousal Support Post-*Bracklow*: The Pendulum Swings Again?' (2001) 19 Can Fam LQ 185; Carol Rogerson, 'Developments in Family Law: The 2001–2002 Term' (2002) 18 SCLR (2d) 335; Carol Rogerson, 'Developments in Family Law: The 2002–2003 Term' (2003) 22 SCLR (2d) 273; Carol Rogerson, 'The Canadian Law of Spousal Support' (2004) 38 Fam LQ 69 [Rogerson, 'Canadian Law of Spousal Support'].

the case law, of how these theoretical models play out in a world marked by gender inequality, both within the paid labour force and within marriage. Carol's carefully reasoned articles were regularly cited by courts throughout the country, including the Supreme Court of Canada, which relied heavily on Carol's work in its major spousal support decisions rendered in the 1990s. Carol's unique scholarly and practical perspective provided the necessary foundation for the development of the SSAGs.

To explain the significance of the SSAGs, I start by situating the guidelines in the context of the development of the spousal support obligation in the no-fault divorce era. I then discuss the advisory guidelines themselves as well as the process that Carol engaged in to create them. I end by discussing the impact of the guidelines on Canadian family law.

I. Spousal support in the age of no-fault divorce

The story of spousal support is the story of a modern statutory obligation derived from historical common law roots. At common law, before the advent of judicial divorce, marriage was viewed as a relationship for life which could only be dissolved through annulment, the death of one of the spouses, or by going to Parliament and petitioning for a private act of divorce.[6] However, courts could grant a *'divorce a mensa et thoro'* – a separation of bed and board – an order that did not dissolve the marriage but merely proclaimed that the spouses were no longer legally obligated to live together. In the event of a separation of bed and board, husbands were required to pay 'alimony' to their wives simply by virtue of their continuing status as husband and provider so long as the wives were not guilty of marital misconduct. After the recognition of judicial divorce in various provinces, alimony, as a gender-specific remedy, continued to exist, and it was intertwined with notions of matrimonial fault: alimony was payable by husbands who were guilty of matrimonial offences to 'innocent' former wives, but women who had committed matrimonial offences lost their right to alimony.[7] The link between fault and alimony was consistent with the grounds for judicial divorce. Under the various provincial divorce statutes, divorce was

---

6 Rollie Thompson, 'Ideas of Spousal Support Entitlement' (2014) 34 Can Fam LQ 1 [Thompson, 'Ideas of Spousal Support']; Christine Davies, *Power on Divorce and Other Matrimonial Causes*, 3d ed (Toronto: Carswell, 1980), vol 2, ch 9; Jim Phillips, *I Did Not Commit Adultery: Marital Conflict and the Law in Ontario in the 1870s* (Toronto: University of Toronto Press, 2025).

7 Thompson, 'Ideas of Spousal Support,' supra note 6.

fault based and could only be granted where one spouse was guilty of a matrimonial offence.[8]

In 1968, Parliament passed Canada's first national Divorce Act, making judicial divorce available on a uniform basis across the country.[9] While this statute retained fault as a basis for divorce,[10] it also permitted, for the first time in Canada, divorce to be granted on a no-fault basis where the spouses had been living separate and apart for a period of not less than three years.[11] Canada's next Divorce Act,[12] enacted in 1985, went one step further and made marriage breakdown the sole ground for divorce.[13] Marriage breakdown could be established in two distinct ways: by showing that the spouses had lived separate and apart for at least one year[14] or by showing that the spouse against whom the divorce proceeding had been brought had committed adultery or

---

8 Although divorce is a matter of federal jurisdiction under section 91(26) of the *Constitution Act, 1867* (UK), 30 & 31 Vict, c 3, divorce laws that were on the books at the time a province entered into Confederation remained on the books until Parliament passed the *Divorce Act* of 1968. All of the provincial divorce statutes were fault based and contained a gendered double standard: a husband could be granted a divorce on the basis of his wife's adultery alone, but a woman was not entitled to a divorce unless she could show that her husband was guilty of adultery plus an additional matrimonial offence.

9 *Divorce Act*, RSC 1970, c D-8.

10 Section 3 of the 1968 *Divorce Act* stated:

Subject to section 5, a petition for divorce may be presented to a court by a husband or wife, on the ground that the respondent, since the celebration of the marriage: (a) has committed adultery; (b) has been guilty of sodomy, bestiality or rape, or has engaged in a homosexual act; (c) has gone through a form of marriage with another person; or (d) has treated the petitioner with physical or mental cruelty of such a kind as to render intolerable the continued cohabitation of the spouses.

11 Section 4(1)(e) of the 1968 *Divorce Act* provided:

In addition to the grounds specified in section 3, and subject to section 5, a petition for divorce may be presented to a court by a husband or wife where the husband and wife are living separate and apart, on the ground that there has been a permanent breakdown of their marriage by reason of one or more of the following circumstances as specified in the petition, namely: ... (e) the spouses have been living separate and apart (i) as on other than that described in subparagraph (ii) for a period of not less than three years, or (ii) by reason of the petitioner's desertion of the respondent, for a period of not less than five years, immediately preceding the presentation of the petition.

12 *Divorce Act*, RSC 1985, c 3 (2nd Supp).

13 Ibid, s 8(1).

14 Ibid, s 8(2)(a).

treated the other spouse with physical or mental cruelty of such a kind as to render intolerable the continued cohabitation of the spouses.[15] Under both the 1968 and 1985 Divorce Acts, spousal support could be claimed by either spouse, regardless of gender. The 1985 Divorce Act also expressly disentangled the historical link between spousal support and conduct, providing in section 15.2(5) that, in making an order for spousal support, 'the court shall not take into consideration any misconduct of a spouse in relation to the marriage.'

These developments produced a seismic challenge for the law of spousal support. If support was no longer rooted in the status of being an 'innocent' wife, what was its justification? To go a step further, no fault divorce meant that marriage was no longer a commitment for life and signalled that former spouses should be free to move on with their lives and to form new relationships following the end of their marriage. Why, then, should a divorced person be burdened with the obligation to support a former spouse? These legal changes were also taking place alongside significant social changes. Traditional gender roles were beginning to break down, and women were entering the paid labour force in greater numbers. In this changed legal and social landscape, what was the role of spousal support? If there was a continuing role for spousal support, what were the objectives of this modern spousal support obligation? In the era of no-fault divorce and movement toward gender equality, had spousal support become, as Carol once put it, a 'remedy without a rationale'?[16]

While the 1968 Divorce Act was silent on the justifications for spousal support, Parliament addressed the purposes of the obligation in the 1985 Divorce Act. Section 15.2(6) provided that the objectives of spousal support were fourfold: (a) to recognize any economic advantages or disadvantages to the spouses arising from the marriage or its breakdown; (b) to apportion between the spouses any financial consequences arising from the care of any child of the marriage over and above any obligation for the support of any child of the marriage; (c) to relieve any economic hardship of the spouses arising from the breakdown of the marriage; and (d) in so far as practicable, to promote the economic self-sufficiency of each spouse within a reasonable period of time.[17] Even on a cursory reading of this provision, it is clear that

---

15 Ibid, s 8(2)(b).

16 Rogerson, 'Canadian Law of Spousal Support,' supra note 5 at 72.

17 Parliament went on to set out, in section 15.2(4), various factors that courts were to consider in making orders for spousal support: '15.2(4) In making an order under subsection (1) or an interim order under subsection (2), the court shall take into

Parliament did not endorse a single theory of spousal support but, instead, embraced multiple objectives. To quote again from Carol, the 1985 Divorce Act

> establishes multiple objectives for spousal support – compensating spouses for the economic impact of the marriage and marital roles, meeting post-divorce economic needs, and encouraging spousal sufficiency after divorce, to identify three. Although in some cases these objectives can work together and reinforce one another, in other cases, depending on which is emphasized – compensation, need, or self-sufficiency – they can suggest very different understandings of the purpose of the support obligation and lead to very different support outcomes.[18]

The inclusion in the 1985 Act of multiple, and potentially conflicting, spousal support objectives was a double-edged sword. On the one hand, it had the benefit of creating a legal framework that was capable of being applied to a wide range of marital relationships of different structure and duration. But, by the same token, the inclusion of multiple support objectives effectively gave courts broad discretion to make spousal support orders based not simply on the facts of the case before them but also on the individual judge's view of the purpose of the modern spousal support obligation.

Throughout this period, and even with the additional guidance provided by the 1985 Divorce Act, courts struggled to articulate an overarching framework to guide the making of spousal support orders. Crafting a spousal support order required consideration of three questions: (a) was a spouse entitled to support; (b) if so, what should the amount, or quantum, of the order be; and, finally, (c) what should the duration of the order be or, to put that question differently, how long should support payments last? Judicial understandings of how these three questions were to be answered fluctuated dramatically, reflecting the lack of social consensus on the role of spousal support in the no-fault divorce age. By the middle of the 1980s, the prevailing view – articulated by many lower courts and by the Supreme Court of Canada in three important cases known as the *Pelech* trilogy – was that spousal support orders should be short term and 'rehabilitative,' with the goal

---

consideration the condition, means, needs and other circumstances of each spouse, including (a) the length of time the spouses cohabited; (b) the functions performed by each spouse during cohabitation; and (c) any order, agreement or arrangement relating to support of either spouse.'

18 Rogerson, 'Canadian Law of Spousal Support,' supra note 5 at 76.

of making the formerly dependent spouse – almost always the woman – self-sufficient as quickly as possible.[19]

Spousal support was frequently referred to in disparaging terms as an impediment to promoting a former wife's self-sufficiency and as placing unfair burdens on former husbands. For example, an Ontario Court cautioned against making support awards that would create 'a comfortable pew' from which the recipient would have trouble removing herself.[20] The Court awarded the applicant wife, who had married at the age of seventeen and had been a traditional homemaker for the following twenty-seven years, four years of spousal support in declining amounts, starting at six hundred dollars per month.[21] The court explained this support award in the following way: 'The judgment should provide some stimulus to prevent the order from becoming considered a permanent pension.'[22] Similarly, in comments that clearly reflect a negative view of ongoing spousal support orders, the majority of the Supreme Court of Canada in *Messier v Delage* was quick to explain that its refusal to terminate spousal support following the wife's completion of a retraining program did not mean that

> the obligation of support between ex-spouses should continue indefinitely when the marriage bond is dissolved, or that one spouse can continue to be a drag on the other indefinitely or acquire a lifetime pension as a result of the marriage, or to luxuriate in idleness at the expense of the other, to use the expressions one finds in some discussions of the subject.[23]

Two important Supreme Court of Canada decisions in the 1990s rejected this narrow vision of spousal support, but they also served to render the framework for assessing spousal support increasingly amorphous and hard to apply.

---

19 The three cases making up the trilogy are: *Pelech v Pelech*, [1987] 1 SCR 801; *Richardson v Richardson*, [1987] 1 SCR 857; *Caron v Caron*, [1987] 1 SCR 892. While the cases involved applications to vary separation agreements, the Court's discussion of the requirement for a spouse's financial need to be causally connected to the roles assumed during the marriage was generally interpreted as setting out a narrow 'clean break' model of spousal support.

20 *Karlovcec v Karlovcec* (1986), 50 RFL (2d) 259.

21 Juliana Karlovcec had few skills, having only worked outside of the marriage as a cleaner and babysitter. The court found that her employment 'was never intended to be anything more than a supplement to the income earned by her husband.' Ibid at 267.

22 Ibid at 268.

23 *Messier v Delage*, [1983] 2 SCR 401 at 416–17, per Chouinard J. Justice Lamer (as he then was), dissenting, would have terminated spousal support.

In the landmark 1992 decision in *Moge v Moge*,[24] the Court resoundingly rejected the view that the primary goal of spousal support orders should be to foster a clean break between the spouses, replacing it instead with the view that the four statutory objectives of spousal support should be interpreted 'as an attempt to achieve an equitable sharing of the economic consequences of the marriage or marriage breakdown.'[25] The Court embraced a 'compensatory model' of spousal support in which the 'focus of the inquiry when assessing spousal support ... must be the effect of the marriage in either impairing or improving each party's economic prospects.'[26] On this model, courts were to craft spousal support orders to compensate the lower income spouse for the reduction in earning power sustained as a result of the roles they assumed during the marriage and as a result of any ongoing childcare role they assumed after marriage breakdown. Seven years later in *Bracklow v Bracklow*,[27] the Supreme Court of Canada revised its view and held that, in addition to the compensatory model, the 1985 Divorce Act also encompassed a non-compensatory model of spousal support.[28] The non-compensatory model permitted courts to order spousal support based on a spouse's economic need alone, even where that need did not arise from the roles the spouses assumed during the marriage.

The effect of *Moge* and *Bracklow* was to create an expansive basis for entitlement to spousal support. But the models of support espoused in the judgments also spawned a host of problems. The compensatory model was often difficult to apply, potentially requiring the admission of expensive expert evidence to quantify the economic loss sustained as a result of the roles assumed during the marriage.[29] There was also the

---

24 [1992] 3 SCR 813.

25 Ibid at para 77.

26 Ibid at para 43.

27 [1999] 1 SCR 813.

28 Ibid at para 49. Justice Beverley McLachlin also recognized a third model of spousal support, a contractual model, in which valid agreements between spouses regarding their support obligations should generally be respected. The Court stated that '[c]ontractual support obligations ... were given new emphasis by statutory stipulations that the courts take into account support agreements, express or implied, between the parties.' Ibid at para 18. This contractual model has been all but ignored in the post-*Bracklow* case law.

29 The model could also be highly speculative, as in the case of marriages where the lower income spouse did not have an established career path before undertaking household or childcare roles. For a more sustained discussion, see Rogerson, 'Canadian Law of Spousal Support,' supra note 5 at 84.

problem of trying to quantify loss in traditional marriages, where often women had married young and did not have an established career path prior to the marriage. For non-compensatory support, one of the more challenging problems was quantifying 'need.' Should a spouse be seen to need support only when they were unable to meet their basic needs or should the assessment of need be linked to the standard of living that the spouse had enjoyed during the marriage? More fundamentally, however, the Supreme Court of Canada provided no guidance to lower courts on the relationship between the competing models of spousal support or on how to determine which model of spousal support would be appropriate in individual cases. The basis for entitlement – whether compensatory or non-compensatory – bears upon the determination of the two key features of a spousal support order: the quantum and duration of the award.

By the end of the 1990s, the law of spousal support had become, to use Carol's description, 'discretionary and uncertain as judges and lawyers struggled with broad and vague concepts of compensation and need.'[30] The uncertainty and unpredictability made it difficult for lawyers to negotiate settlements, which was a serious concern in family law where most cases are resolved through settlement rather than going to trial. Carol summed up the situation in the following way:

[T]he lack of clear guiding principles and the highly discretionary nature of the current law have resulted in an unacceptable degree of uncertainty and lack of predictability. Similar fact situations can generate a wide variation in results. There are significant variations in understandings of appropriate spousal support outcomes between individual judges, and moreover significant regional differences in spousal support cultures across the country. Individual judges are provided with little concrete guidance in determining spousal support outcomes, and their subjective perceptions of fair outcomes inevitably play a large role in determining the spousal support ultimately ordered. Lawyers in turn have difficulty predicting outcomes, thus impeding their ability to advise clients and to engage in cost-effective settlement negotiations. And for those without legal representation or in weak bargaining positions, support claims may simply not be pursued. Despite an expansive

---

30 Carol Rogerson, 'Child Support, Spousal Support and the Turn to Guidelines' in John Eekelaar & Robert George, eds, *Routledge Handbook of Family Law and Policy* (Cambridge, UK: Cambridge University Press, 2014) 153 at 167 [Rogerson, 'Child Support'].

basis for spousal support under current Canadian law, many women do not pursue their claims. The uncertain and controversial nature of the spousal support obligation means that it is often one of the first items taken off the bargaining table. [31]

In 2001, in an effort to bring clarity and predictability to spousal support law, the federal Department of Justice decided to investigate the possibility of creating informal, non-binding spousal support guidelines. In part, this project was motivated by the success of federal Child Support Guidelines which had been enacted as regulations to the 1985 Divorce Act and had become law in 1997.[32] The Child Support Guidelines, though very different from the informal guidelines contemplated for spousal support, had made family law lawyers accustomed to resolving some financial matters based on formulas rather than on judicial discretion.[33] But the project was also prompted by scholarship – including Carol's – which suggested that patterns for typical cases were beginning to emerge from the morass of spousal support case law. To undertake this project, the Department of Justice turned to the two leading scholars of spousal support in Canada, Rollie Thompson of the Dalhousie Law School and Carol. Carol and Rollie were given the task of exploring the possibility of developing informal guidelines that would function as 'a practical tool to assist family lawyers, mediators and judges' in their assessment of spousal support in individual cases.[34] The hope was that advisory guidelines would have a disciplining effect on post-*Bracklow* spousal support and improve the law in four ways: (a) by reducing conflict over spousal support and encouraging settlement; (b) by creating consistency and fairness within spousal support law; (c) by reducing the costs of resolving spousal support claims and improving the efficiency of the process; and (d) by 'kick starting' the process of common law development of spousal support law by providing a structure for judicial elaboration.[35] These potential benefits became the objectives of the advisory guidelines project.[36]

---

31 Rogerson, 'Canadian Law of Spousal Support,' supra note 5 at 96.
32 *Federal Child Support Guidelines*, SOR/97-175, as amended, enacted as regulations pursuant to the *Divorce Act*, supra note 12.
33 The *SSAGs* are not 'guidelines' in the true sense since they do not merely provide guidance but are mandatory.
34 Carol Rogerson & Rollie Thompson, *Spousal Support Advisory Guidelines: A Draft Proposal* (Ottawa: Department of Justice, 2005) at v [*Draft Guidelines*].
35 *SSAGs*, supra note 1 at 11–12.
36 Ibid at 11.

II. The creation of the Spousal Support Advisory Guidelines

The task that Carol and Rollie were charged with was a formidable one. The project faced a core challenge: whether it was even possible to create guidelines to regulate an area as complex and as varied as spousal support. To be successful, the guidelines would have to be applicable to the many ways in which married couples structure their home and labour market responsibilities. They would also have to be able to account for the many points at which marriages end in divorce – from long-term traditional marriages, to medium-term marriages with minor children, to short-term, childless marriages, and everything in between. Previous Canadian studies had rejected spousal support guidelines as unworkable, concluding that it would be impossible to draft guidelines with sufficient flexibility to apply to the diversity of marriages within Canadian society.[37] The lack of social consensus surrounding the justification for spousal support and the existence of multiple competing support objectives compounded the concerns that guidelines would be impossible to devise.[38] Ideally, guidelines would provide guidance on the duration of the support obligation as well as the amount to be paid, issues that are difficult to address without at least a general agreement on the goals that support awards are designed to achieve. There were also no direct precedents to draw from. Although a handful of US jurisdictions had experimented with spousal support guidelines, these guidelines were generally limited to very localized areas of practice – frequently limited to individual counties – and for a range of reasons were not readily transferable to the Canadian context.[39]

Despite these challenges, draft guidelines were released in 2005, less than four years after the start of the project, and a final, slightly modified

---

37 Carol cites several of these studies in Carol Rogerson, *Developing Spousal Support Guidelines in Canada: Beginning the Discussion* (Ottawa: Department of Justice, 2002), n 7 [Rogerson, *Beginning the Discussion*]. These include a study prepared for the Department of Justice by Danreb Incorporated; a report prepared by the Alberta Law Reform Institute; and a study prepared for the Department of Justice by the Canadian Research Institute for Law and the Family. See ibid.

38 Rogerson, 'Child Support,' supra note 30 at 165.

39 Carol provides a thorough discussion of the US spousal support guidelines in Rogerson, *Beginning the Discussion*, supra note 37 at 33–56. The American Law Institute also proposed the adoption of spousal support guidelines in the family law project that it released in 2002. American Law Institute, *Principles of the Law of Family Dissolution: Analysis and Recommendations* (Toronto: LexisNexis, 2002).

version of the SSAGs followed three years later.[40] The SSAGs consist of two formulas, a 'without-child-support' formula to be used in cases in which there are no dependent children and a 'with-child-support' formula for cases in which there were dependent children and where child support was being paid.[41] While both formulas are based on a model of income sharing, they are underpinned by different concepts. Without getting too deep into the specifics, the without-child-support formula is rooted in the notion of 'merger over time' in which the length of the relationship plays a central role in determining both the amount and duration of support.[42] The with-child-support formula springs from the principle of 'parental partnership,' in which post-separation child-care responsibilities are the most important determinant of spousal support.[43] More complex than the without-child-support formula, the with-child-support formula is more accurately described as a cluster of formulas that address different parenting arrangements.[44] Reflecting the primacy that Canadian family law accords to the child support obligation, spousal support is assessed under the with-child-support formula after the child support obligations of both spouses have been determined.[45]

---

40 For a discussion of the process leading up to the creation of the guidelines, see Rollie Thompson, 'Canada's Spousal Support Advisory Guidelines: A Half-way House between Rules and Discretion' (2010) International Family Law 106; Carol Rogerson & Rollie Thompson, 'The Canadian Experiment with Spousal Support Guidelines' (2011) 45:2 Fam LQ 241 at 250–1 [Rogerson & Thompson, 'Canadian Experiment']; *SSAGs*, supra note 1 at 16–20.

41 Both formulas require the use of software – forms of which are available free of charge on the Internet – to generate results. Commercial versions of this software are also available, including DIVORCEmate, Childview, and Aliform.

42 *SSAGs*, supra note 1 at 32. At the upper limit, after very lengthy marriages, the without-child formula would result in the equalization of the spouses' net incomes. The formula is summarized as follows:

The amount of spousal support is 1.5 to 2 percent of the difference between the spouses' gross incomes for each year of marriage, to a maximum range of 37.5 to 50 per cent of the gross income difference for marriages of 25 years or more (The upper end of this maximum range is capped at the amount that would result in equalization of the spouses' net incomes – the net income cap. ... Duration is 0.5 to 1 year of support for each year of marriage, with duration becoming indefinite (duration not specified) after 20 years or, if the marriage has lasted 5 years or longer, when the years of marriage and age of the support recipient (at separation) added together total 65 or more (the "rule of 65"). Ibid at 32.

43 Ibid at 32–3.

44 Ibid at 33.

45 Ibid. For a detailed explanation of the with-child-support formula, see *SSAGs*, supra note 1, ch 8.

Why were Carol and Rollie able to create advisory guidelines notwithstanding the complex and multiple hurdles inherent to the endeavour? The success of the SSAGs can be attributed to three decisions related to the process of creating the advisory guidelines and to the content of the guidelines themselves. First, the SSAGs were the product of a highly consultative process. Carol and Rollie did not see the creation of guidelines as a 'top-down' law reform project. Instead, working from the premise that the guidelines should reflect the best practices in the existing case law, Carol and Rollie sought to build guidelines 'from the ground up.'[46] This process required distinct sets of skills. There needed to be a 'big picture' understanding of the theories of spousal support and an understanding of the real-world consequences that result from the different theories given the gendered context in which, for the most part, family law operates. There needed to be a very practical sensibility, drawn from experience, that paid careful attention to what would constitute a fair outcome in individual cases. And there needed to be the ability to combine these skill sets to create a framework for simplifying the process of determining the amount and duration of spousal support.

To complement the academic and policy skills that they brought to the project, Carol and Rollie worked with an advisory group composed of thirteen experienced family law judges, lawyers, and mediators from across Canada.[47] This group played a crucial role in the development

---

46 Rogerson, 'Beginning the Discussion,' supra note 37 at 7. In the *Draft Guidelines*, supra note 34, Carol and Rollie explained their reasons for choosing this methodology at 13:

> The inspiration for the process chosen for the development of these advisory guidelines came from the experience of many of the American jurisdictions that have adopted spousal support guidelines. In the American context, spousal support guidelines have generally been the product of bench and bar committees of local bar associations. They were created with the intention of reflecting local practice and providing a more certain framework to guide settlement negotiations. ... A similar process was adopted for the development and implementation of these advisory guidelines. They have been created through a process that involves working with judges, lawyers and mediators who have expertise in family law. The goal of the process has been to articulate informal guidelines based on emerging patterns embedded in current practice.

47 The members of the group were: Justice David Aston (London, ON), Lonny Balbi (family lawyer, Calgary, AB), Julia Cornish (family lawyer, Dartmouth, NS), Justice Robyn Diamond (Winnipeg, MB), Philip Epstein (family lawyer, Toronto, ON), Rhonda Freeman (Director, Families in Transition, Toronto, ON), Marie Gordon (family lawyer, Edmonton, AB), Miriam Grassby (family lawyer, Montreal, QC), Justice Richard LeBlanc (Corner Brook, NL), Justin Levesque (mediator, Montreal, QC), Justice Jennifer Mackinnon (Ottawa, ON), Justice Donna Martinson (Vancouver,

of the guidelines. Since the vast majority of spousal support claims – like all other family law claims – are resolved outside of court through negotiation or mediation, the members of the advisory group contributed insights garnered from experience in legal practice that could not have been gleaned by reading reported cases. They also functioned as a kind of highly skilled sounding board, providing reactions and opinions on the amount of support they believed would be appropriate in typical family law scenarios. Their intuitions as to how claims should be fairly resolved were essential to the construction of the guidelines.

The SSAGs were created through this consultative process. Carol and Rollie identified emerging patterns in typical spousal support cases by undertaking a comprehensive review of reported case law and by checking the results against the on-the-ground experience of the advisory group members about settlements.[48] Carol and Rollie then worked backwards from these patterns to develop mathematical formulas that generated results consistent with the clusters they had identified. Then they engaged in further consultation by workshopping the formulas to groups of judges, lawyers, and mediators across the country and refining the formulas in light of the feedback they received. These formulas became the core of the SSAGs, with various grounds for departures from the formula ranges.

Second, as mentioned earlier, the SSAGs consist of two formulas, differentiated by the presence or absence of minor children at the point where spousal support is awarded. Carol and Rollie realized that spousal support guidelines would not work without making this distinction. A without-child-support formula and a with-child-support formula would be necessary to create guidelines capable of being applied to all – or at least most – marriages. Third, to make it possible for the guidelines to apply to a diverse range of marriages, the SSAGs were constructed with a degree of discretion and flexibility. Flexibility and discretion were built into the advisory guidelines in two ways. First, rather than generating a single fixed sum of spousal support payable in a given case, the SSAGs generate ranges. Judges, mediators, and lawyers can exercise their discretion as to where within the range support should fall based on various factors, including 'the strength of any compensatory claim, the recipient's needs, the age, number, needs and standard of living of any children,

---

BC), Barbara Nelson (family lawyer, Vancouver, BC), Jocelyn Verdon (family lawyer, Quebec City, QC), and Justice Donna Wilson (Regina, SK).
48 Rogerson & Thompson, 'Canadian Experiment,' supra note 40 at 251.

the needs and ability to pay of the payor, work incentives for the payor, property division and debts, and self-sufficiency incentives.'[49] The existence of ranges allows for individualized decision making that is absent from rigid guideline models. The second way in which the SSAGs incorporate discretion and flexibility is that they expressly contemplate exceptions and departures from the formula ranges for less typical spousal support cases.[50] These three decisions as to the process and substance of the guidelines were instrumental to the success of the project.

III. Transforming spousal support: the guidelines and their impact

The SSAGs have been enormously successful. They were rapidly adopted by lawyers and judges across Canada, with the exception of Quebec.[51] A mere eight months after the release of the draft version in 2005, the BC Court of Appeal endorsed the guidelines,[52] and they have since been endorsed by appellate courts across the country. The draft guidelines were downloaded over fifty thousand times in the first year following their release;[53] in March 2010, the Department of Justice informed Carol that she had a 'bestseller' on her hands as the SSAGs had been the most downloaded document on the Justice website so far that year. By February 2008, over four hundred judicial decisions had considered the SSAGs,[54] and, by April 2016, the SSAGs had been cited by 230 appeal court decisions and over twenty-nine hundred trial decisions.[55] The use of the SSAGs is now so widespread that a prominent Toronto family law lawyer recently remarked that, despite being only advisory, the guidelines have become, in reality, an obligatory starting point in spousal support determinations.

---

49 *SSAGs*, supra note 1 at 34.

50 Ibid, ch 12, 'Exceptions'; ch 14, 'Variation, Review, Remarriage, Second Families.'

51 For a discussion of the reluctance to embrace the *SSAGs* in Quebec, see Rollie Thompson, 'Spousal Support Eh? Sorry, Not Your American Alimony' (2019) 41 Hous J Intl L 641 at 654–5; Jodi Lazare, 'Spousal Support in Quebec: Resisting the *Spousal Support Advisory Guidelines*' (2018) 59 C de D 929.

52 See *Yemchuk v Yemchuk*, 2005 BCCA 406.

53 *SSAGs*, supra note 1 at 21.

54 Ibid at 23.

55 Carol Rogerson & Rollie Thompson, *Spousal Support Advisory Guidelines: The Revised User's Guide* (Ottawa: Department of Justice, 2016). By Rollie Thompson's count, by November 2024, the SSAGs had been cited in over 425 appeal decisions and over fifty-two hundred trial decisions. Email from Rollie Thompson, 25 March 2025 [on file with the author].

The SSAGs have become ubiquitous for good reason. By making the calculation of spousal support more straightforward and the steps involved more transparent, they have transformed the way in which spousal support is determined. By using income sharing as a starting point, they have eliminated the need to introduce complex (and often speculative) evidence of a spouse's economic loss or career trajectory. A 2012 study commissioned by the Department of Justice found that, by 'providing an objective starting point and narrowing the range of possible outcomes of spousal support cases,' the SSAGs had reduced conflict, made the negotiation of spousal support easier, and encouraged settlement.[56] The study also found that the advisory guidelines had made spousal support more consistent and predictable: 'All lines of evidence indicate that … couples in similar situations are more likely to receive similar support awards; the range in which spousal support awards are made has become narrower; and spousal support awards are becoming more consistent across the country.'[57] The SSAGs have also increased access to justice by making it easier for spouses to resolve spousal support without retaining lawyers[58] and by increasing the incidence of spousal support claims among low-income recipients.[59] Finally, the SSAGs have provided a structure to spousal support analysis with the result that both lawyers and judges tend to be more careful about the steps in the analysis, making the decisions they reach more logical and transparent.[60] Equally important, the SSAGs have provided judges across the country with a common language and a common set of concepts, thereby facilitating the development of the law. While they have not solved all of the tough issues that arise in spousal support, overwhelmingly, the SSAGs have accomplished their objectives.

The SSAGs have also earned Carol well-deserved recognition. In 2015, she received the Carolyn Tuohy Impact on Public Policy Award, an award given by the University of Toronto to a faculty member whose scholarship has had a significant impact on public policy. The award citation stated not only that Carol had played 'a pivotal role in

---

56 Prairie Research Associates, *Assessing the Impact of the Spousal Support Advisory Guidelines (SSAG)* (30 January 2012) at 37 [on file with the author].
57 Ibid at 38.
58 Rogerson, 'Child Support,' supra note 30 at 169.
59 Rogerson & Thompson, 'Canadian Experiment,' supra note 40 at 262. The authors explain that 'lawyers for lower-income recipients now make spousal support claims, when they might not have in the past, as the courts will generally award at least the low end of the ranges with little need for sophisticated argument.'
60 Ibid at 263.

shaping family law' but that 'no legal academic in Canada has had a greater impact on the development of Canadian family law and policy than Professor Carol Rogerson.'[61] In 2019, the Law Society of Ontario awarded Carol the Law Society Medal, which is given to lawyers who have made outstanding contributions to the profession. The Law Society noted that Carol's work in 'developing the Spousal Support Advisory Guidelines has had a profound impact on the operation of the family justice system across Canada' and that Carol had played 'a pivotal role in shaping family law and policy in Canada.'[62]

IV. Conclusion

It is not an exaggeration to say that Carol Rogerson has been instrumental in shaping Canadian family law. In particular, the SSAGs that she and Rollie Thompson created are a remarkable achievement. By creating guidelines that have brought greater predictability, certainty, and clarity to the law of spousal support, Carol has not only transformed the law, but she has also improved the process for all Canadians involved in spousal support claims. There is a tendency in academic circles to celebrate certain forms of scholarship that verge toward the highly theoretical. The significance and impact of the SSAGs are an essential reminder of the importance of scholarship that marries normative approaches with practical results.

---

61 The full citation for this award can be found at 'Awards of Excellence 2015 Recipients,' online: *University of Toronto* <alumni.utoronto.ca/community/awards/awex/recipients-2015#winners>.

62 This description was contained in the program prepared for the medal ceremony [on file with the author].

13 Individual Freedom and the Supremacy of Law: Alan Brudner on Criminal Justice

MALCOLM THORBURN

Alan Brudner is one of the pioneers of legal philosophy in the Faculty of Law at the University of Toronto. He began his career at the faculty in the fall of 1984, having recently graduated from the faculty and not long after completing his doctorate in political theory on the world historical role of GWF Hegel's *Phenomenology of Spirit*, also at the University of Toronto. At the time, legal philosophy across the English-speaking world was a thriving and growing field. In England, the work of Oxford theorists HLA Hart, Joseph Raz, and John Finnis dominated the field. In the United States, Ronald Dworkin as well as proponents of established traditions such as American legal realism, the legal process school, and growing fields such as critical legal studies and law and economics dominated the scholarly scene. In Canada, however, legal scholarship was still dominated by traditional common law doctrinal scholarship. There were a few political theorists and philosophers, working mostly in political studies and philosophy departments, who took an interest in the philosophical foundations of the law, but the systematic study of legal doctrine through the lens of philosophy was still virtually unheard of.

When Brudner arrived at the Faculty of Law, he and a small group of philosophically inclined scholars worked together to create a new school of legal theory, which was explicitly at odds with the main currents of legal philosophy in both England and the United States, founded not on the utilitarian liberal tradition of Jeremy Bentham and John Stuart Mill but, rather, on the idealist philosophy of German scholars Immanuel Kant and GWF Hegel. They applied this lens to a range of disciplines: constitutional law, criminal law, administrative law, and a host of private law subjects. Together, they built a vibrant intellectual community for the philosophical study of law, hiring more young legal philosophers to join their ranks, publishing influential books and articles, creating a legal philosophy reading group and a legal theory workshop, and turning the *University of Toronto Law Journal* into the internationally significant site of legal scholarship that it is today. Together, they made the 'Toronto school' of legal theory one of the leading accounts of law in the English-speaking world.

It has now been about half a century since Brudner began his career at the Faculty of Law. Over that time, he has also been an active contributor to important Canadian legal debates. In the years following the adoption of the Canadian Charter of Rights and Freedoms in 1982, as Canada was searching for a normative framework by which to make sense of key provisions, such as section 7 and section 1, Brudner had a comprehensive account at the ready.[1] He worked out these larger constitutional doctrines in great detail as a general theory of the Constitution,[2] and as they applied to defences such as necessity and to the fault standard for crimes.[3] But Brudner's most lasting contribution as a legal scholar is his bold, ambitious, and comprehensive work to reframe thinking about criminal law in the English-speaking world – a framework that he brought to the classroom every day to make sense of the thicket of doctrines and institutions that normally baffle a first-year criminal law student.

Brudner's theory of criminal law draws deeply from the work of the nineteenth-century German philosopher GWF Hegel.[4] Even in choosing Hegel's *Philosophy of Right* as his framework, Brudner already set himself apart from the received wisdom in Anglo-American criminal law theory. The field over many decades has been split between two rival camps, both of which operate within the standard Anglo-American starting points in legal theory: the tradition that sees law and legal institutions as a set of tools for bringing about valuable outcomes of one kind or another. The first camp – legal moralism – assumes that

---

1 *Canadian Charter of Rights and Freedoms*, Part I of the *Constitution Act 1982*, being Schedule B to the *Canada Act 1982* (UK), 1982, c 11.

2 Alan Brudner, *Constitutional Goods* (Oxford: Oxford University Press, 2004).

3 Perhaps Alan Brudner's most celebrated article in criminal law is Alan Brudner, 'A Theory of Necessity' (1987) 7:3 Oxford J Leg Stud 339.

4 Alan Brudner's Hegelian jurisprudence has been developed in counterpoint to the Kantian framework adopted by many of his Toronto colleagues. He writes: 'I must also acknowledge a debt of gratitude to the participants in the law and philosophy reading group of the Faculty of Law, University of Toronto. By making the strongest possible case for Kant's theory of justice, they contributed to my appreciation of the unsurpassed power of Hegel's.' Alan Brudner, *Punishment and Freedom: A Liberal Theory of Penal Justice* (Oxford: Oxford University Press, 2009) at xi [Brudner, *Punishment*].

criminal law is justified insofar as it gives moral wrongdoers the treatment they deserve in virtue of their wrongdoing. The second camp – what I call 'generic instrumentalists' – argue that criminal law is just another state institution that should be justified by showing that it brings about valuable social outcomes at a reasonable cost and subject to certain fairness and other constraints.

Brudner's Hegelian account rejects the founding assumptions behind both of these accounts, on two levels. On the most fundamental level, he rejects their understanding of the place of criminal law in legal ordering. Both moralists and generic instrumentalists assume that we can make sense of criminal justice as a tool for bringing about some pre-legal good: giving moral wrongdoers the response they deserve or bringing about valuable policy outcomes. Brudner, following Hegel, insists that we cannot make sense of criminal law except as an essential building block of legal ordering itself. Its point is to secure the authority of law and the state's exclusive right to rule – a point that we cannot make sense of except as a constituent part of legal ordering. On a second level, however, Brudner also disagrees with the moralists and the generic instrumentalists about the correct normative account by which to justify the operation of criminal justice institutions. Neither the moralist nor the generic instrumentalist account, Brudner insists, treats legal subjects in a way that is consistent with their status as free persons; but his Hegelian account, he insists, does.

Put in this way, it might sound as though Brudner's account is derivative, simply a retelling of a familiar (if complex) Hegelian story. But that would be quite wrong. In fact, Brudner's Hegelian take is very much his own. Although there have been Hegelian accounts of criminal law in the German-speaking world for many years (as developed most recently by Günther Jakobs and Michael Pawlik),[5] and there has been a resurgence recently of Hegelian criminal law scholarship in the United States (most notably, in the writings of Joshua Kleinfeld),[6] Brudner has developed Hegel's legal and political theory in his own distinctively liberal way, quite apart from these other traditions. As Douglas

---

5   See Michael Pawlik, *Person, Subjekt, Bürger* (Berlin: Duncker & Humblot, 2004); Günther Jakobs, 'Das Strafrecht zwischen Funktionalismus und "alteuropäischem" Prinzipiendenken' (1995) 107 Zeitschrift für die gesamte Strafrechtswissenschaft 843; Michael Pawlik, *Das Unrecht des Bürgers* (Tübingen: Mohr Siebeck, 2012); Michael Pawlik, 'Norm Confirmation and Identity Balance: On the Legitimacy of Punishment' (2020) 7:1 Critical Analysis of Law 1 [Pawlik, 'Norm Confirmation'].

6   Joshua Kleinfeld, 'Reconstructivism: the Place of Criminal Law in Ethical Life' (2016) 129 Harv L Rev 1485 [Kleinfeld, 'Reconstructivism'].

Husak puts it, Brudner has been a 'lone wolf crying in the wilderness' of Anglo-American criminal law theory, working out, step by methodical step, his own intricate and ambitious Hegelian vision.[7] As I argue in this short article, Brudner's argument about the place of criminal law in legal ordering is important, deep, and (I believe) correct. His liberal account of criminal law, too, has much to recommend it. The full power of his argument does not always shine through, however, because he insists on making these two quite distinct arguments in tandem. As a result, those who do not share his particular brand of liberalism are tempted to reject his conceptual claim about the place of criminal justice in legal ordering. But these are concerns about presentation: Brudner's writings on criminal justice are some of the most thoughtful and illuminating contributions to Anglo-American criminal law theory in decades.

In this article, I consider Brudner's contribution to criminal law theory in three parts. In Part I, I set Brudner's Hegelian account of criminal law into the larger context of criminal law scholarship that dominated the debate in the English-speaking world over the last fifty years. In Part II, I consider the connection between criminal justice and the authority of law that stands at the centre of Brudner's Hegelian account. This, I argue, is a deep and important insight not only into the point of criminal justice but also into the point of legal ordering more generally. In Part III, I consider the significance of Brudner's insistence that his is a distinctively liberal account of criminal law. Since Hegel's legal theory is often connected to illiberal tendencies, Brudner can be excused for insisting that his is not such an account. Nevertheless, by focusing so closely on the normative work of justifying his account as properly liberal, he draws attention away from the force of his analytical account of criminal law and its connection to legal ordering. I conclude with some thoughts on the centrality of political authority as an organizing idea in criminal law and in legal thinking more generally. We need not go as far as Hannah Arendt and insist that 'authority has vanished from the modern world,' but it has largely disappeared from discussions of

---

7 Douglas Husak, 'Review of *Punishment and Freedom: A Liberal Theory of Penal Justice* by Alan Brudner' (2010) 120:4 Ethics 841 at 846 [Husak, 'Review of *Punishment*'].

criminal law, and the subject is much the poorer for that.[8] Brudner's work leads the way to a recovery of recentring authority in our account of the field.

I. Thinking about criminal law

Brudner stands emphatically apart from both of the great traditions of Anglo-American criminal law theory of the past century. As Mariana Valverde said of *Punishment and Freedom*, his major book on the topic, '[i]t is sure to alienate mainstream liberals, conservative moralists, and postmoderns alike – not a small feat for a single book.'[9] Although he has developed his objections to their accounts of all the major doctrines of the general part of criminal law, his fundamental disagreement with them comes from their limited vision of the importance of the field as a whole. On one side of the Anglo-American debate are the legal moralists who insist that the institutions of criminal justice should be in the business of giving moral wrongdoers the response they deserve for their wrongdoing. On the other side are the generic instrumentalists who see criminal law as just one state tool among many for encouraging subjects to act in pro-social ways. Although these two camps have been warring with each other for well over a century, they both share a founding assumption that Brudner fundamentally rejects. They both assume that we can think meaningfully about criminal law largely in isolation from the larger structures of legal ordering. For Brudner, however, criminal law is an irreducible feature of legal ordering itself. That is, criminal law is a constituent part of a larger whole, and, as such, we cannot make sense of it without understanding the part it plays within that larger whole.

A. *Criminal law as a moral practice*

When Brudner joined the field of criminal law theory in the mid-1980s, accounts of criminal law as a moral practice were on the ascendant. Many of Brudner's contemporaries in the United Kingdom and the United States – legal scholars such as Michael Moore, Larry Alexander, and Andreas von Hirsch, and philosophers such as Douglas Husak, Antony Duff, Jean Hampton, and Jeffrie Murphy – saw themselves as

---

8 Hannah Arendt, 'What Is Authority?' in Hannah Arendt, ed, *Between Past and Future: Six Exercises in Political Thought* (New York: Viking Press, 1968) 91 at 91.

9 Mariana Valverde, 'Comment on Alan Brudner's Punishment and Freedom' (2011) 14:3 New Criminal Law Review 486 at 487; Brudner, *Punishment*, supra note 4.

radical reformers, attacking the orthodoxy that dominated the field at the time. Whereas, for decades before the 1970s, criminal law scholarship and policy had been dominated by a vision of the field as a tool of social policy (designed to deter undesirable conduct, to rehabilitate those who carry out that conduct, and, in some cases, to incapacitate those who cannot be deterred), these bold, (then) young scholars insisted that such policy-focused thinking failed to take seriously the moral language of the criminal law. In criminal law, we do not merely impose costs in order to deter conduct (as we do, say, when we impose excise taxes), and we do not merely educate citizens (as we do when we create public schools, colleges, and universities); we condemn individuals for their wrongdoing, we refer to their conduct as wrong, we talk of punishing them, and we have a whole host of practices that make clear that a central part of the institution is making moral judgments about conduct.

If we take this insight into the criminal law seriously – that it is not just a set of morally neutral institutional practices but also a system for making and enforcing authoritative moral judgments – then (the moralists insist) any account of that practice must seek to justify it as a moral practice. And, thus, based on this insight, moralist accounts of criminal law worked on the assumption that criminal justice institutions are simply scaled-up versions of inter-personal practices of holding one another accountable for moral wrongdoing. Some writers (mostly in the United States) have insisted that these practices are mostly oriented toward imposing retributive punishment on wrongdoers; others (mostly in the United Kingdom) have insisted that the practice follows a less punitive conception of our moral life, holding moral wrongdoers to account, engaging in meaningful moral debate, making moral judgments, and making room for moral education, 'secular penance,' or other morally appropriate responses to moral wrongdoing.

In the decades that have followed, this moralized account of criminal law and its institutions has come to dominate the theoretical literature on both sides of the Atlantic. There are ever more detailed discussions of what forms of wrongdoing deserve criminal punishment; what sorts of limits we might impose on these moral practices, given our liberal commitments; precisely how we should grade different moral wrongs and how we should calibrate deserved suffering to fit the crime; and so on. In *Philosophical Foundations of Criminal Law*, an important survey of theoretical work on criminal law published in 2011,[10] virtually all of

---

10 RA Duff & Stuart Green, *Philosophical Foundations of Criminal Law* (Oxford: Oxford University Press, 2011).

the contributors aligned with one version or another of this moralist account of the field.

B. *Criminal law as a generic policy tool*

In recent years, the theoretical literature on criminal law has moved away from the moralized picture that gained such prominence in the 1970s and has returned to the (generic instrumentalist) policy thinking that dominated the field at mid-century. Criminal law theory has taken a 'political turn.' Now, leading legal scholars such as Vincent Chiao, Bernard Harcourt, and Alice Ristroph, as well as prominent philosophers such as Philip Pettit and Matt Matravers, are putting forward accounts of criminal law as a distinctively political institution. Although they introduce a number of important sophisticated adjustments to the account (introducing considerations of republican freedom, Rawlsian difference principles, and so on), they represent a return to mid-century criminal law instrumentalism. Many of these writers also couple this insight with an aperçu developed most fully by criminologist David Garland: that criminal punishment is but one tool among many for addressing anti-social conduct, alongside informal social pressure, education, and welfare state programs, and we are usually well advised to pursue those other means because they are generally more effective and more humane.[11]

C. *Brudner and the two schools*

From a distance, Brudner's account looks like just another version of the 'political' school of thought. He insists in the very first pages of his criminal law theory monograph, *Punishment and Freedom*, that 'penal law theory … is a branch of political and constitutional rather than moral theory.'[12] This is a distinction that is especially important to political philosophers writing over the past half-century in the shadow of John Rawls's *Theory of Justice*.[13] Whereas utilitarians drew no sharp distinction between the principles that apply to inter-personal morality and those that apply to the conduct of state institutions, Rawls insisted that liberals

---

11 David Garland, *The Culture of Control: Crime and Social Order in Contemporary Society* (Chicago: University of Chicago Press, 2001) at 34.

12 Brudner, *Punishment*, supra note 4 at ix.

13 Katarina Forrester, *In the Shadow of Justice: Postwar Liberalism and the Remaking of Political Philosophy* (Princeton, NJ: Princeton University Press, 2019); John Rawls, *Theory of Justice*, rev ed (Cambridge, MA: Belknapp Press, 1999).

should care deeply about that distinction. States are special actors that tell us what to do and demand with coercive force that we comply with those demands. That means that we should pay careful attention not only to when the state uses coercion but also to the way in which it justifies doing so. Its reasons must be public ones that subjects could not reasonably reject. As Brudner puts it, his account of criminal law 'is primarily a theory about when it is permissible to restrain and confine a free agent, not a theory about when it is appropriate to blame and make suffer an individual moral will or character.'[14] Accordingly, the justification of criminal punishment is something quite special: '[P]enal action by public officials is permissible force rather than wrongful violence,' Brudner insists, 'only if it could be accepted by the sufferer, considered as a free and independent person, as being consistent with his or her freedom.'[15] In this way, then, Brudner is firmly in the second 'political' camp in Anglo-American criminal law theory, insisting that it is a political institution that must be justified in terms that are appropriate to such an institution. Because Brudner was writing at a time when the moral account was on the ascendant, he often puts this feature of his account at the fore:[16] his is a liberal account, concerned with the justification of coercion, through the use of public reason, and so on. What sometimes gets lost in the shuffle is just what sort of political account it is.

Brudner's account is distinct from the broader 'political turn' in criminal law theory in two important ways. First, it is distinctive because he insists that it is a theory of punishment and not just a theory of state coercion. As Brudner puts it, 'penal law theory is not coextensive with political theory. Rather, it is … a narrow theory about just punishment (and penalization) rather than a broad theory of the legitimate state authority to coerce.'[17] Many of the most prominent exponents of the political turn in criminal law theory today reject this distinction. For Vincent Chiao, for example, criminal punishment is better understood as a 'generically coercive rule-enforcement mechanism,'[18] and, for Alice Ristroph, rejecting 'criminal law exceptionalism' (based in large part on the specialness of criminal punishment) is a central plank of her

---

14 Brudner, *Punishment*, supra note 4 at ix.

15 Ibid at 2.

16 It is not only prominent in his presentation of the argument; it is how he characterizes and qualifies his conception. The subtitle of the book is 'A *Liberal* Theory of Penal Justice' [emphasis added].

17 Brudner, *Punishment*, supra note 4 at 16.

18 Vincent Chiao, *Criminal Law in the Age of the Administrative State* (Oxford: Oxford University Press, 2018).

political vision.[19] For Brudner, however, criminal punishment is indeed special. There are many ways besides punishment that states coerce us: when the state takes our money in taxes to pay for the provision of public goods, when we are subject to medical quarantine, or when we are required to submit to vaccination or public education. But these are merely the coercive incidents of the state's pursuit of a valuable policy of some kind. Criminal punishment, by contrast, is the deliberate infliction of suffering as suffering and in order to communicate censure. This calls for a different sort of justification that goes beyond merely justifying the coercion that is at play within it.

The most important distinguishing feature of Brudner's account, however, is one that is clearly at work within it, but which (I believe) he undersells. His account is fundamentally different from most other 'political' accounts because it ties the very point of criminal law and punishment to the existence of legal order itself. In one of the few places where Brudner makes this explicit, he does so in the following terms:

> The theory of punishment I have presented so far may be called classical legal retributivism. It is classical in that it stems from the writings of the great philosophers who, present at the birth of the liberal Rechtsstaat, first articulated (though differently) its theoretical foundations. I mean, of course, Hegel's *Philosophy of Right* and Kant's *Doctrine of Right*. It is legal retributivism in that it justifies judicial punishment as vindicating the authority of Law rather than as giving evil its just deserts.[20]

This legal retributivism – the irreducible connection between criminal law and punishment and vindicating the authority of law – is the most radical and most mysterious aspect of his account. It is here, more than his insistence that we should provide a liberal justification for state coercion, that Brudner's intellectual courage and insight shine through most clearly. It is worthwhile, then, to take a moment to dwell on what is at stake in this claim.

II. Punishment and the authority of law

The two accounts of criminal law that have dominated the theoretical literature of the English-speaking world for decades, if not centuries,

---

19 See Alice Ristroph, 'The Wages of Criminal Law Exceptionalism' (2023) 17 Crim L & Phil 5; Alice Ristroph, 'Criminal Law as Public Ordering' (2020) 70:64 UTLJ 64.
20 Brudner, Punishment, supra note 4 at 48.

have tried again and again to justify the basic practices of criminal punishment – trials, verdicts, sentences, and the like – as ways for the state to carry out some valuable task. They have ignored the strategy to which Brudner, following Hegel, draws our attention: criminal justice is an irreducible part of the very idea of living under the law. Indeed, as Douglas Husak makes clear, it is not just that this strategy is largely left out of the discussion, it is rejected as utterly mysterious. Typical Anglo-American criminal law theorists do not so much reject the Hegelian picture of legal retributivism as fail utterly to understand what it is all about: 'Attendees at conferences that include representatives from each tradition,' Husak suggests, 'usually stare blankly at one another.'[21] So let's take a moment to see what might motivate something like the Hegelian 'legal retributivist' view that Brudner espouses. It is an account that I have championed in my own writing, giving it the moniker: the 'right-to-rule' account of criminal law.[22]

A. Criminal law and the right to rule

At the heart of the right-to-rule account is a certain understanding of the normative structure of legal ordering more broadly. In any legal order, the state claims to be something more than just one tool among many for delivering good results. It has a special standing to make and to impose legal terms on its subjects with coercive force because it, and only it, is the mechanism through which a people makes laws for itself. Nowadays, that idea is usually understood in democratic terms: the state's laws are our laws insofar as they were voted on by democratically elected legislators,[23] and institutions of the executive branch speak in our name insofar as their enabling statutes have the proper democratic pedigree, their rule-making bodies engage in appropriate notice-and-consent procedures, and the officials who administer them do so according to the terms of a public office,[24] appropriately separating their

---

21 Husak, 'Book Review of *Punishment*,' supra note 7 at 841.

22 Malcolm Thorburn, 'One Right to Rule them All' in Philipp-Alexander Hirsch & Elias Moser, eds, *Rights in Criminal Law: Studies on a New Paradigm in Criminal Law and Procedure* (Oxford: Hart Publishing, 2025).

23 Tom Christiano, *The Constitution of Equality: Democratic Authority and Its Limits* (Oxford: Oxford University Press, 2008); Jeremy Waldron, *The Dignity of Legislation* (Oxford: Oxford University Press, 1999).

24 The idea of public office, where decisions can be attributed to the office and not to the private person who inhabits it, is crucial to the legitimacy of many public institutions, including the police. Malcolm Thorburn, 'Policing and Public Office' (2020) 70 UTLJ 248.

public role from their private preferences and discretion. It is because we think of our laws and public institutions as speaking in our name that we can think of them as legitimately imposing burdens upon us and enforcing them with coercion.[25]

In an earlier, less democratic age, the supremacy of the law over the wills of private actors had a different flavour – but it was no less important. The supremacy of the king's writ is an idea with a history in the common law, stretching back at least to the time of King Henry II in the twelfth century.[26] Whether we are zealots for democracy or believers in the divine right of kings, the question of who is entitled to set the terms under which we relate to one another is fundamental, and the supremacy of our shared law over anyone's private preference is a founding principle of any legal order. So long as we take the legal order to be a legitimate one, we have reason to resist efforts to displace the law in favour of terms set according to anyone's private preferences.[27] Nevertheless, it is perhaps no surprise to find that the most passionate advocates for the right-to-rule account are the eighteenth-century pioneers of the social contract tradition for whom the idea of self-government through law was of central importance.[28]

Most of the time, of course, we take the supremacy of law and the authority of the state for granted and just get on with the day-to-day business of governing. When we relate to the state in this way, it is from within an existing and secure governance relationship. Within that

---

25 Precisely what is required to satisfy the demand that our laws and institutions speak in our name is a vexed question on which the literature is voluminous. Three treatments of this question that are sympathetic to my position are Jon Michaels, *Constitutional Coup: Privatization's Threat to the American Republic* (Cambridge, MA: Harvard University Press, 2017); Alon Harel & Avihay Dorfman, *Reclaiming the Public* (Cambridge, UK: Cambridge University Press, 2024); Chiara Cordelli, *The Privatized State* (Princeton, NJ: Princeton University Press, 2020).

26 Sir Frederick Pollock, 'The King's Peace in the Middle Ages' (1899) 13 Harv L Rev 177 at 179–80 ('[t]he king takes up the charge on behalf of his own peace, as he well might and ought, for the words of the appeal are that the act complained of was done "wickedly and in felony against the peace of our lord the king"'). See also Elizabeth Papp Kamali, *Felony and the Guilty Mind in Medieval England* (Cambridge, UK: Cambridge University Press, 2019) [Kamali, *Felony*].

27 I have explored the incompatibility of vigilantism with the rule of law. See Malcolm Thorburn, 'Justifications, Powers, and Authority' (2008) 117 Yale LJ 1070.

28 I have set out my debt to Jean-Jacques Rousseau and Immanuel Kant on this point before. See Malcolm Thorburn, 'Punishment and Public Authority' in Antje du Bois-Pedain, Magnus Ulväng & Petter Asp, eds, *Criminal Law and the Authority of the State* (London: Bloomsbury, 2017) 7. Brudner makes clear that this connection is present in the writings of Kant and Hegel as well.

relationship, the state sets down rules of conduct of various kinds and simultaneously puts in place a variety of measures designed to induce subjects to comply with those rules: licenses, positive incentives, education and other training schemes, the design of the built environment, and much more. If we simply ignore the question of how we got into that sort of relationship and how it might be maintained, it is easy to think of all our relations to the state (and, indeed, all our legal relations more generally) as reducible merely to this vertical relationship between established sovereign and subject. It is tempting simply to take for granted the existence of such a relationship of authority between state and subject and to think that questions of legal and political theory are just a matter of taming this apparently oppressive vertical relationship. Here, we are concerned with the state's pursuit of valuable public purposes according to certain political constraints of efficiency, fairness, and the like. The various generic instrumentalist accounts of criminal law present fairly plausible accounts of the regulatory state, but it is not nearly so obvious that they provide a plausible account of criminal law and punishment. The right-to-rule account of criminal trials and punishments, which is at the heart of Brudner's Hegelian account, recognizes that we cannot simply take this stable and enduring relationship of authority between state and citizen for granted. In order for the state to carry out its governance functions, it must retain its position of exclusive law-making authority in the jurisdiction. The state cannot regulate – indeed, it cannot do much of anything – unless it is secure in its exclusive right to rule. Recognizing this, the right-to-rule account insists that criminal trials and punishments are not just another governance tool through which the state pursues its public policies. Instead, they play a role in the legal order that goes largely unnoticed by advocates of both the generic instrumentalist and moralist conceptions: they concern the exclusive authority of the law and the wrongfulness of any subject's attempt to substitute his own private will for the valid law within the jurisdiction. The legal right that is at issue in the criminal trial – the right which is the object of the criminal defendant's alleged wrong – is the state's exclusive right to set the legal terms within the jurisdiction.

Many advocates of the two dominant traditions in Anglo-American criminal law theory (the generic instrumentalist and moralist accounts) might respond to the foregoing by conceding that, of course, there is an important difference in kind between valid legal rules issued by properly authorized state organs and the unilateral imposition of terms by private actors. But vindicating the validity of the former and condemning the latter as wrongs against the state's exclusive right to rule, they would insist, is not the business of the criminal law. That is because, however important the state's exclusive right to rule might be, it is simply not a justiciable matter. The state's exclusive authority to make the law is something that we must simply assume in order to get on with the business of governing. Where the state's authority itself is directly challenged, they would argue, the only plausible reply is to 'keep calm and carry on' – that is, we should simply continue engaging in governance and allow the fact of its continued effectiveness to be our reply. By carrying on and continuing to act as the exclusive legal authority in the jurisdiction and to maintain general habits of deference from subjects, they would argue, a state most effectively vindicates its exclusive right to rule. It is a category mistake, then, to think that states can establish their exclusive law-making authority by bringing a case to court. In matters of fundamental legal authority, as HLA Hart so pithily put the point many years ago, 'all that succeeds is success.'[29]

In one sense, of course, Hart and the defenders of the instrumentalist picture are entirely right. Criminal trials and punishments cannot possibly be the causal mechanism through which a state maintains its exclusive right to rule. In confronting large-scale insurrections against its right to rule, it would be absurd for a state to rely exclusively on a set of criminal proceedings against the rebels. Indeed, even in cases of one-off criminal wrongdoing, the causal mechanism through which the state pre-empts efforts to substitute private will for state law is direct coercive action: police intervention to resist the criminal act and to arrest the individuals carrying them out. But putting down rebellions and arresting criminal offenders in the act – meeting force with force – is not the end of the affair. At that point, all that we have done is defeat someone's efforts to impose his will by force by showing that our force is greater. But states claim not merely to be the most powerful agent in the jurisdiction; they crucially claim legitimacy, to be acting out of legal right. And that is why, once the imminent threat to the state's position of authority has been staunched with coercive force, principles of legality call for a forum in which the state's right can be vindicated through an authoritative legal judgment of wrongdoing against those who sought to substitute their will for the law we all share: *ubi jus ibi remedium* (wherever there is a right, there is a remedy).

B. *The place of criminal punishment*

So far, we have seen that any legal system must have an institution for recognizing crimes as wrongful and for vindicating the law as the only

---

29 HLA Hart, *The Concept of Law*, 2d ed (Oxford: Oxford University Press, 1961) at 153.

legitimate authority on how we may relate to one another. But why should a legal system require anything more than this? Why is it not enough to have a court with the authority to pronounce on the abiding authority of the law and on the illegitimacy and legal nullity of unilateral coercion? Brudner addresses this concern in an especially eloquent passage, as follows:

> Perhaps the lesson taught by punishment could be taught in school if the intentional interloper asserted his claim in the classroom. But he did not. He interfered with someone's agency, and his interference, because of its intentionality, expressed a right-denying principle. By actualizing a right-denying principle, however, the wrongdoer gave that principle an appearance of worldly authority, of existential force. He gave it, that is, the appearance of a law. That appearance would be allowed to stand if the nemesis of his principle were demonstrated by speech alone. ... So, by visiting the self-destructive consequence of the wrongdoer's principle upon him, punishment removes the appearance of its worldly validity and vindicates the worldly authority of Law.[30]

This is an evocative passage, but its concrete meaning is not immediately obvious. What does it mean to talk of punishment removing 'the appearance of worldly validity' from the offender's act and restoring it to the law? We might wonder about at least two aspects of this claim. First, this talk of removing the appearance of worldly validity might sound like metaphysical mumbo jumbo, simply obscuring the obvious and quite practical task of punishment: to deter undesirable conduct by raising its cost to the actor. But Brudner is alive to that worry. He recognizes that real, live offenders may be deterred by the prospect of punishment and that deterring criminal conduct is an important practical concern. But, he insists, that cannot be all there is to punishment. He has two parallel arguments for this: the first is a conceptual claim about the place of criminal punishment in legal ordering, and the second is a normative argument about the demands of liberalism on the institution of punishment. The conceptual argument is the one we have just seen: the survival of the legal system as a genuine system of authority, and not just coercive threats, relies on the institution of punishment to communicate that the law retains its worldly validity, and the offender's conduct does not. In order for that argument to succeed, however, Brudner needs to make clear that punishment is not just the imposition of coercion; it must be a communicative act. And this means

---

30 Brudner, *Punishment*, supra note 4 at 47.

that the procedures through which punishment is invested with such meaning – the criminal verdict and sentencing decision – play a crucial role in the Hegelian account of criminal law. Because of his liberal concern with justifying the use of state coercion against free persons, however, Brudner remains focused on the coercive element of punishment and pays little attention to the institutions that fill punishment with semiotic significance.[31]

Brudner's second argument is that any properly liberal justification for punishing must be one that treats the offender as a free person. This means that we should not merely threaten him like a dog with harm; instead, we should address him as an agent whose conduct is of the sort that has the potential to impose a system of authority on others. For that reason, we cannot treat the offender merely as (what Brudner calls) the empirical person, who is amenable to deterrent threats, but also as (what Brudner calls) the thinking agent,[32] who is a potential rival source of authority. But even once we have made sense of criminal punishment, there is another difficulty for Brudner's Hegelian account: the semiotic significance of crime itself. It does not seem obvious that crimes themselves challenge the system of authority at all. Most offenders would likely say that they had no interest in the authority of law; they just wanted to take the thing they stole or to harm their victim. Indeed, they would probably be quite happy to enjoy the protection of the legal system after having gotten away with their singular transgression. But to put things in that way is to miss the point altogether. Although individual offenders might want only to get away with a particular act, the law must conceive of us in a different way. Since the law makes a universal claim of exclusive legal authority (to protect all rights to property or to personal autonomy), the offender's negation of that claim, even in a single instance, has a systematic effect. The law's promise is not to protect this or that right; it is to protect all rights, systematically – to replace the world of lawless violence altogether

---

31 Alan introduces the idea of the semiotics of punishment in Alan Brudner, 'The Contraction of Crime in Hegel's Rechtsphilosophie' in Markus Dubber, ed, *Foundational Texts in Modern Criminal Law* (Oxford: Oxford University Press, 2014) 141 at 160–1 [Brudner, 'Contraction of Crime'].

32 Alan's introduction of 'the thinking agent' is one technique he uses to explain the meaning of Hegel's notoriously dense text. It allows him to make an important conceptual distinction, but it sometimes confounds readers who are not familiar with Hegelian metaphysics. See Dudley Knowles, 'Alan Brudner, Punishment and Freedom' (2012) 3:1 Jurisprudence 229 at 232 ('there is no thinking agent in Hegel's *Philosophy of Right*').

with a world of shared legal rules and procedures. It is because law makes this systematic claim that we must treat the acts of those who choose to impose their own terms in its place as systematic enemies of legal order.[33]

Of course, implicit in this conception of crime is a robust *mens rea* requirement. On the Hegelian account, the very essence of crime is the offender's putative exercise of authority in deciding on the terms under which they shall interact with others.[34] This means that the core of crime is their intention to act according to a rule of some kind and to impose that on others in the jurisdiction, the law's demands to the contrary notwithstanding. All this might seem like an alien imposition – a bit of nineteenth-century German metaphysics imposed on the pragmatic English common law – but that would be quite wrong. In fact, subjective *mens rea* has been the key distinguishing feature of crime for centuries in the common law tradition, and it has long been concerned with the supremacy of law and the state's exclusive right to rule. In her important study of felony in medieval England, Elizabeth Papp Kamali points out that '*mens rea* played a crucial role in jury considerations from the earliest days of the criminal trial jury. Although the formal law ... did not routinely invoke the language of *mens rea*, the idea of criminal intent lay at the heart of the word "felony".' And she quickly adds that '[t]he feudal meaning of felony drew upon notions of disloyalty or treason, the ultimate breach of fealty.'[35] Indeed, this idea that serious crime is not just a rule violation but also constitutes a wrong against the state's right to rule – that it is akin to an act of rebellion

---

33 Brudner, *Punishment*, supra note 4 at 81 ('because the reality of rights may be said to depend on the rule of law. A knowing breach of a statute involves a choice to which a denial of law's authority may be imputed').

34 Pawlik, 'Norm Confirmation,' supra note 5 at 16 ('criminal wrongdoing involves the perpetrator opposing the prevailing criminal norms and regulations, and showing, through his actions, that he gives this counter-norm precedence over the norm of the law. ... The expression of power on the part of the perpetrator ... is understood in this conception as the implementation of a normative program, a program that can reasonably be interpreted as nothing other than *a rebellion against the authoritative norms that apply to the perpetrator*. This normative self-elevation, or rather presumption, by the perpetrator is the source of the added significance of his action, which justifies finding him criminally responsible') [emphasis added].

35 Kamali, 'Felony,' supra note 26 at 36, 45. This insistence that subjective *mens rea* is so inherent in the idea of crime that it need not even be mentioned in the statute is still alive in contemporary criminal law jurisprudence. *Morissette v United States*, 342 US 246 (1952) ('[a]s the states codified the common law of crimes, even if their enactments were silent on the subject, their courts ... merely recognized that intent was so inherent in the idea of the offense that it required no statutory affirmation').

against the state's authority – not only has roots stretching back to the twelfth century; it is still an important part of the common law today, even though contemporary statutory law often disregards it.[36]

But, of course, the presence of *mens rea* alone is not enough to constitute a crime. Since the law does not merely make a verbal claim to authority – it puts in place a system of rights in the world – its denial cannot consist merely in a verbal claim denying its authority. A crime occurs only when someone imposes his view of how things should stand between himself and others through a coercive act – taking or damaging property, injuring another's person, and so on. But this connection to how things stand in the world (rather than just a merely verbal claim) in both law and crime is also what calls for the coercive element in the legal system's response to crime. Criminal punishment is accompanied by a verdict and a sentence, which give it a particular semiotic importance, but it is necessarily coercive, affecting the way in which things actually stand as between subjects of the law.

All this means that punishment must be coercive, but it does not mean that it must be the same in severity as the wrong to which it is a response. Neither does it mean that every criminal offender must be prosecuted and punished. The point of criminal punishment is systematic: to vindicate the law's authority in the face of challenge. This will survive a number of specific challenges, and so there might be good reasons not to pursue specific cases of criminal wrongdoing. What the legal retributivism of Brudner's Hegel requires, though, is that such a system exists and that it is put into operation in at least some cases. The severity of sanctions, too, is not something that is determined in any absolute way; rather, it is a matter of imposing sanctions that are sufficient to ensure the general authority of law in the jurisdiction. Brudner puts the point in the following terms:

> [A]s long as the inherent lawfulness of the social world is actualized in a well-functioning criminal justice system, it does not matter that this or that criminal occasionally escapes retribution. Secondly, ... as civil society grows stronger and the rule of law becomes as secure in political reality as it is in the nature of things, the importance of punishment as a way of dealing with convicted offenders diminishes. ... Thus, as civil society matures and the semiotic function of punishment recedes in importance, we see accused and convicted persons increasingly diverted from the justice

---

36 On the collapse of many longstanding principles in contemporary criminal law, see Andrew Ashworth, 'Is the Criminal Law a Lost Cause?' (2000) 116 Law Q Rev 225.

system to the welfare system. Conditional sentences, probation orders, and restorative justice programs belong to this picture.[37]

III. Liberal and illiberal criminal law

Brudner's Hegelian account of criminal law, like Hegel's, takes for granted that the point of the institution is to vindicate the supremacy of law. But Brudner does not stop there. Indeed, the vast majority of the argument in *Punishment and Freedom* is focused not on justifying this conception of criminal law's role but, rather, on putting forward a particular brand of Hegelian liberalism as the best way to justify the operation of such an institution. Since Brudner slides quite quickly over the argument about the place of criminal law in legal ordering and spends most of his time promoting his favoured liberal account of the enterprise, it is easy to take the former for granted and to focus almost exclusively on the success or failure of the latter. But that, I believe, would be a serious mistake. For whether or not we buy Brudner's particular brand of Hegelian liberalism, his account of criminal law's place in legal ordering is worth dwelling on for it is here that Brudner's account really opens up possibilities for new and productive ways of thinking about criminal law.

A. Illiberalism – Hegelian and otherwise

Why does Brudner frame his account so squarely as a distinctively liberal account of criminal law, taking attention away from the larger, more ecumenical account of the nature of criminal law and its place in legal ordering? The answer, I believe, lies in the long shadow of illiberal Hegelian accounts of many legal institutions, especially criminal law. In an important article in the 2018 issue of the *Harvard Law Review*, Joshua Kleinfeld puts forward an explicitly Hegelian account of criminal law: what he called 'reconstructivism.' On that account, criminal law's fundamental role is deeply illiberal: 'Reconstructivism's lodestar normative concept,' Kleinfeld writes, 'is not ... liberty; it is solidarity.'[38] Indeed, to mark that point, he cites Lord Devlin – the same Lord Devlin who insisted that 'society is justified in taking the same steps to preserve its moral code as it does to preserve its government'[39] – as one of

---

37 Brudner, 'Contraction of Crime,' supra note 31 at 161.

38 Kleinfeld, 'Reconstructivism,' supra note 6 at 1492.

39 Patrick Devlin, *The Enforcement of Morals* (Oxford: Oxford University Press, 1965) at 13.

the standard bearers of the reconstructivist account. Its central focus is not on the preservation of individual freedom or on the vindication of the legal order and the structure of rights and duties it sets out. Rather, the Hegelian vision that Kleinfeld details is concerned with the set of moral norms that lie deep beneath the surface in our society. He writes:

> The essential thought is this: criminal law has a distinctive role to play in the social world, a function that gives it a different center from other areas of law, because criminal law is the primary legal institution by which a community reconstructs *the moral basis of its social order*, its ethical life, in the wake of an attack on that ethical life.[40]

That is, criminal law is distinctive because, unlike other areas of law, it transcends the normal frame of law and reaches back to the deep moral principles on which the society is based. And, as Kleinfeld correctly points out, there is a long tradition of reading Hegel in this deeply illiberal way, focused on the shared 'ethical life' (Sittlichkeit) of a political community – most dramatically, in recent times, in the writings of Günther Jakobs and his concept of the 'criminal law of the enemy' (Feindstrafrecht).[41]

In light of this illiberal Hegelian tradition on both sides of the Atlantic, it is entirely understandable why Brudner might take such pains to insist that his is a liberal Hegelian account of criminal law.[42] The opening sentence of *Punishment and Freedom* is that '[t]his book sets out an understanding of the general part of the penal law of a liberal legal order. By a liberal legal order I mean one based on a fundamental belief common to all denominations of philosophical liberalism: that the individual agent is, by virtue of its capacity to set ends for itself, a locus of inviolable worth.'[43]

---

40 Kleinfeld, 'Reconstructivism,' supra note 6 at 1489 [emphasis added]. He adds:
    '[S]ince the message of a crime is a social one – a proposal submitted to the community
    that can become true as a description of social life only if the community approves it –
    punishment by the community genuinely undoes the crime.' Ibid at 1518.

41 Günther Jakobs, 'Bürgerstrafrecht und Feindstrafrecht' (2004) 21 Ritsumeikan Law
    Review 93. See also Daniel Ohana, 'Trust, Distrust and Reassurance: Diversion and
    Preventive Orders through the Prism of Feindstrafrecht' (2010) 73:5 Modern L Rev 721.

42 Squaring this circle – reaffirming a society's deeply held moral values and
    maintaining a commitment to liberalism – is a challenge that many criminal law
    scholars have faced. Antony Duff's 'liberal communitarianism,' set out most fully
    in *The Realm of Criminal Law* (Oxford: Oxford University Press, 2018), is perhaps the
    most prominent recent example.

43 Brudner, *Punishment*, supra note 4 at ix.

B. *Liberal and illiberal criminal law*

Brudner insists that both of the dominant accounts of criminal law today – moralist and generic instrumentalist alike – are inconsistent with the respect due to each person as free and independent members of the political community. Against moralist accounts, he insists that criminal law is the state at its most coercive and, therefore, calls for the most robust public justification. As Brudner puts the point, '[t]he forcible restraint of an individual's liberty by equal human beings requires a justification of an order altogether different from one suitable for expressions of condemnatory moral opinion, which the addressee is free to internalize or deflect.'[44] Against other political accounts that try to reduce criminal law and punishment to a generic institution of governance, Brudner insists (with Hegel) that we cannot impose criminal punishment merely as a deterrent against socially undesirable conduct because doing so would 'subordinate individual autonomy to the general happiness.'[45] The only consistently liberal account of criminal law and punishment, then, must be one that imposes punishment in a way that is consistent with the punished person's own choices. This Hegelian argument is notoriously elusive. Ristroph captures the puzzlement of non-Hegelians to this thought nicely in the following terms:

> Punishment, at least in its most familiar forms, is not freedom. Nearly all of the world's prisoners know this, as do most ordinary individuals. But philosophers are not ordinary individuals, and a strand of philosophy maintains that punishment is indeed a kind of freedom, if only we understand punishment, and freedom, properly. This is Alan Brudner's project.[46]

Although I am much more sympathetic than Ristroph to Brudner's project of vindicating the institution of criminal law and punishment as consistent with liberal freedom, it is clear that over the roughly two hundred years since Hegel set forth this argument, it has won only a small – if remarkably determined – set of adherents. But whether we accept Brudner's Hegelian liberal account of criminal law and punishment or not, his larger project must be recognized as a great achievement. Criminal law theorists in the Anglo-American tradition have

---

44 Ibid at 17.
45 Ibid at 182.
46 Alice Ristroph, 'When Freedom Isn't Free' (2011) 14 New Criminal Law Review 468.

been trying without success to make sense of the institution without reference to its essential role in vindicating the authority of law and the state's exclusive right to rule. As a result, they have failed in innumerable ways to make sense of key features of our criminal law doctrine and institutional set-up. By reconnecting criminal law to the larger rule-of-law project, Brudner has opened up much more productive ways of thinking about criminal law that had hitherto been largely ignored in the Anglo-American debate.

V. Conclusion

In recent years, criminal law theorists have started to think about how we might make sense of criminal law outside the confines of liberal political theory. How, for example, can we make sense of our own common law tradition in centuries past when states professed no liberal ambitions?[47] And how might we try to make sense of the role of criminal law and punishment in modern, functioning legal systems that simply do not share our most basic liberal commitments?[48] There is plenty of value in setting forth an account of criminal law that is most in line with our favoured political principles, but this should not preclude us from trying to make sense of the role of criminal law in legal orders that do not share those values. Brudner's legal retributivism, shorn of its particular brand of Hegelian liberalism, opens up the door to exciting new ways of thinking about criminal law.

---

47 Making sense of criminal law in the common law tradition at a time when we did not embrace recognizably liberal principles has been a focus in some of my own recent writing. See Malcolm Thorburn, 'Criminal Punishment and the Right to Rule' (2020) 70 UTLJ 44; Malcolm Thorburn, 'Old Fashioned Criminal Law Minimalism' [unpublished manuscript]. Peter Ramsay has also set out an account of this sort of pre-liberal criminal law in Peter Ramsay, 'Rights of the Sovereign: Criminal Law as Public Law' (2025) 36 King's LJ 70.

48 Hend Hanafy, 'Public Wrongs and Power Relations in Non-Democratic and Illiberal Polities' (2023) 18:3 Criminal Law and Philosophy 709.

14 Gender Equality, AI, and the Future of Human Rights

ANNA SU

I. Introduction

In a 1993 article entitled 'Women's International Human Rights Law: The Way Forward,' Rebecca Cook wrote succinctly that 'international human rights law has not yet been applied effectively to redress the disadvantages and injustices experienced by women solely because of their gender.'[1] Cook, a pioneering scholar and prolific advocate, has had a towering career in the field of women's health and the advancement of women's rights and gender equality through international human rights law and has spent years since that article indefatigably arguing how women's rights – including gender equality and women's health – should and could be protected through the international human rights system. And while women's rights have advanced since then – indeed, the issue is now a central pillar in international policy-making circles – old challenges remain in new guises even as entirely new problems have sprouted.

Cook's steadfast faith in the ability of international human rights law and its institutions to recognize, reconceptualize, and vindicate injustices against women amidst a complex and pluralistic global setting remains remarkable, especially given all the critiques that the edifice of human rights has received in the past several decades. Among the most influential pieces of her scholarly oeuvre are two edited collections that bring together lawyers and scholars from different parts of the world and aim to assess the progress and identify challenges to this project,

---

1 Rebecca J Cook, 'Women's International Human Rights Law: The Way Forward' (1993) 15:2 Human Rights Quarterly 230 [Cook, 'Women's International Human Rights Law'].

to recognize and guarantee specific human rights of women, and to make the human rights system more effective for women. The first, on women's rights, published in 1994, seeks to examine how human rights apply to women across different societies and cultures.[2] The second, on the frontiers of gender equality, published in 2023, expands the discourse surrounding gender equality law by considering a variety of approaches to correcting or righting gendered wrongs in domestic, regional, and international human rights systems.[3] Both collections speak to the continuing promises of human rights to vindicate equality rights in a way that responds to women's and gender minorities' experiences of various wrongs. They are also notable for their global character. After all, international human rights advocacy was at one point criticized for being too Western-centric. Although thirty years apart and dealing with distinct and slightly evolved challenges, Cook's message remains the same. International human rights law should and could do more to address the predicament of discrimination and the broader structural injustices that are produced by it, including pervasive economic inequality and physical violence.[4]

It would be useful to have some of Cook's faith at the moment as we confront current existential crises – the emergence of the algorithmic society and global climate change immediately comes to mind – and what they portend for international human rights. Each of these relatively siloed discussions have experienced a human rights turn in recent years.[5] Whatever the causes of such a turn, it makes it now possible to place these twin challenges in conjunction with other rights given the principle of universality, indivisibility, and interdependence of rights.[6] This means that all human rights – be they economic, social, or political and civil rights – must be treated equally, and none can be enjoyed fully without the others. It also places each of them within a broad, polycentric framework that is simultaneously an idea, a

---

2 Rebecca J Cook, ed, *Human Rights of Women: National and International Perspectives* (Philadelphia: University of Pennsylvania Press, 1994) [Cook, *Human Rights of Women*].

3 Rebecca J Cook, ed, *Frontiers of Gender Equality: Transnational Legal Perspectives* (Philadelphia: University of Pennsylvania Press, 2023) [Cook, *Frontiers of Gender Equality*].

4 Cook, 'Women's International Human Rights Law,' supra note 1 at 261; Cook, *Frontiers of Gender Equality*, supra note 3 at 2.

5 There are recent exceptions that bridge the two, but, for the most part, the separate human rights turns in each field have bloomed organically.

6 Vienna Declaration and Programme of Action, Doc A/CONF.157/24 (Part I) (1993), section 1, para 5.

movement, and a language as well as a legal regime that is buttressed by a deep history.[7] In light of these dimensions, human rights provide an accessible vocabulary and a useful coordinating framework that offers tools to accommodate the varied human interests implicated in these areas.[8] At the same time, there remains a burgeoning body of critique from various perspectives that questions the appropriateness of this framework for these emergent issues.[9]

In this article, I want to examine Cook's work and to situate it at a new frontier: the social, material, and technical realm of artificial intelligence (AI). Gender equality, a well-established and traditional human right, that has a robust and sophisticated body of case law and scholarship that is still evolving, provides a useful case study to highlight the panoply of intersecting human rights concerns around AI throughout its lifecycle. It also allows us to view the human rights turn in action in order to help us understand the myriad ways this framework may surface or obscure certain concerns and, more importantly, illuminate some of its limitations. Given their significant impact on the full spectrum of human interests and needs from education and health to employment and the maintenance of democratic society, it makes sense nevertheless to put human rights front and centre in regulatory discussions around AI systems. And yet, even though one of the promises of international human rights law (IHRL) is that of a deeper and fuller means of analysing the overall effects of the use of algorithms, this kind of study is not yet prevalent in the literature. Beyond listing what human rights or needs are implicated, we need to see how human rights are incorporated in the life cycle of AI systems, for example, and we also need

---

7 Philip Alston, 'Does the Past Matter?' (2013) 126:7 Harv L Rev 2043 at 2078.

8 Anna Su, 'The Promise and Perils of International Human Rights Law for AI Governance' (2022) 4:2 Law Technology & Humans 166; Vinodkumar Prabhakaran et al, 'A Human Rights-Based Approach to Responsible AI' (2022), online: *arXiv* <arxiv.org/abs/2210.02667>.

9 Sue Ann Teo, 'Artificial Intelligence and Its "Slow Violence" to Human Rights' (2024), online: *AI Ethics* <doi.org/10.1007/s43681-024-00547-x> [Teo, 'Slow Violence']; Sue Ann Teo, 'How Artificial Intelligence Systems Challenge the Conceptual Foundations of the Human Rights Legal Framework' (2022) 40:1 Nordic Journal of Human Rights 216; Barrie Sander, 'Freedom of Expression in the Age of Platforms' (2020) 43:4 Fordham Intl LJ 939; Nathalie Smuha, 'Beyond a Human Rights-Based Approach to AI Governance: Promise, Pitfalls, Plea' (2021) 34:S1 Philosophy and Technology 91; Rachel Griffin, 'Rethinking Rights in Social Media Governance: Human Rights, Ideology, and Inequality' (2023) 2:1 European Law Open 30 [Griffin, 'Rethinking Rights']; Hin-Yan Liu, 'AI Challenges and the Inadequacy of Human Rights Protections' (2021) 40:1 Criminal Justice Ethics 2.

to account for the prevailing critiques as we adopt the human rights language in evaluating the efficacy of these systems to achieve our desired outcomes moving forward. As historian Reinhardt Koselleck stated in 1965, '[t]he future … is characterized by two main features: first, the increasing speed with which it approaches us and second, its unknown quality.'[10] But it is not so much a path as a device with which we organize our thoughts about the present and choose our path for the future. The focus on AI as an important challenge in the future of human rights may force us to develop a new account that is attuned to its novel technological characteristics as well as its surrounding digital political economy.

Gender equality is as much a frontier of the human rights turn in AI as much as AI is a new frontier of gender equality. At this intersection, the future of human rights hangs once again in the balance. To what extent does Cook's faith in the international human rights system continue to be warranted? As AI systems increasingly shape and influence various areas of decision making in our society, the imperative to safeguard human welfare and values remains higher than ever. We certainly have to contend with the capacity of the discriminatory impacts of AI to amplify our existing biases even deeper into the world's bones,[11] but AI also puts to the test our collective decision to maintain the international human rights system as the predominant, moral, legal, and political framework to promote welfare and preserve values in the age of algorithms and machines. In other words, a concern is that the human rights turn in AI governance risks displacing other potentially more powerful and emancipatory language in dealing with the novel social, political, and economic challenges brought about by this technology.[12]

Overall, Cook's carefully curated volumes encompassing the advocacy of women's rights as human rights, the use of existing international legal and political institutions to address this problem, and the highlighting of a variety of voices on the ground manage to keep us tethered to some sources of optimism. This brief account of AI as a frontier of gender equality hopes to build on the clarity that we have thus far gained about the strengths and limitations of international human

---

10 Reinhardt Koselleck, *Futures Past: On the Semantics of Historical Time* (New York: Columbia University Press, 2004) at 22.

11 Ruha Benjamin, *Race after Technology: Abolitionist Tools for the New Jim Code* (Cambridge, UK: Polity Press, 2019); Timnit Gebru, 'Race and Gender' in Markus Dubber & Frank Pasquale, eds, *Oxford Handbook of Ethics in AI* (Oxford: Oxford University Press, 2020) 252.

12 Griffin, 'Rethinking Rights,' supra note 9.

rights law as a tool to advance important cross-cutting purposes that are not confined to gender-based injustices alone. In the process, it aspires to be generative in terms of reimagining voices, vocabularies, structures, and world-views in a way that reckoning with an uncertain future should rightfully demand.

II. From 'women's rights are human rights' to gender equality

Cook's influential work may be considered part of the 'women's rights are human rights' campaign in the 1990s during which leaders of various women's movements worked to establish women's rights as human rights by attending United Nations (UN) conferences, drafting documents, and demanding media attention, building on networks and ideologies that local activists had put in place. The 1993 Vienna Conference on Human Rights marked the first substantial recognition of women's rights by the UN human rights system.[13] This idea was accepted only after massive mobilization by women's groups around the world. In turn, this campaign was formalized in the international system. Legal anthropologist Annelise Riles categorized Cook, alongside a few others, as one of several academic practitioners sharing an interest with global women's organizations in influencing UN processes to gain acceptance and enforcement of 'women's rights as human rights' and in providing a detailed knowledge of UN procedures and actors such as the implications of different theories of government accountability in human rights law, the possible uses of reporting systems under the various relevant treaties, and the institutional politics of UN bodies.[14]

Although the principle of equality between the sexes has long been enshrined in basic human rights instruments, in practice, the interpretation and implementation of these instruments by UN bodies had fallen short in ensuring their full applicability to women until the adoption of the Convention on the Elimination of Discrimination against Women (CEDAW) in 1979.[15] Even then, the campaign only achieved prominence with then US First Lady Hillary Clinton's speech in Beijing in

---

13 Donna J Sullivan, 'Women's Human Rights and the 1993 World Conference on Human Rights' (1994) 88:1 Am J Intl L 152.

14 Annelise Riles, 'Rights Inside Out: The Case of the Women's Human Rights Campaign' (2002) 15:2 Leiden J Intl L 285.

15 *Convention on the Elimination of All Forms of Discrimination against Women*, 18 December 1979, 1249 UNTS 13, [1982] Can TS no 31 (entered into force 3 September 1981) [*CEDAW*].

1995, as she famously proclaimed 'women's rights are human rights.'[16] A full accounting of the history of the campaign is beyond the remit of this article, but, suffice it to say, that Cook's scholarly work is among those that provided the necessary legal foundations.

It is important to note that the problem of women's equality and empowerment has not always been framed in terms of international human rights. In fact, the key move in the 'women's rights are human rights' campaign was to elevate these challenges as a matter for international attention and enforcement. But, at the time, it was far from an obvious choice. For structural and historical reasons, international law has not been hospitable to issues affecting women. International law is and has always been state centred. That also meant that international law reinforced the division between public and private, insulating private relations such as family life from legal scrutiny and therefore ignoring the unequal distribution of power in these arrangements. International human rights law thus could only deal with public affairs. But many self-avowed feminists also came to the view that human rights discourse offers a recognized vocabulary to frame political and social wrongs. In other words, the advantage it offered was visibility. In Cook's introduction to her 1994 edited collection, she quotes then-professor-turned-ICJ-judge Hilary Charlesworth defending human rights as a vehicle to protect women's rights because, among other things, it is also a language spoken by the powerful.[17] Decades of political mobilization by women's groups eventually bore fruit in Vienna in 1993.

This was the historical and political moment in which Cook's own scholarship and facilitation of work by different women's rights advocates and scholars throughout the world must be situated. Cook took notice of the state of women in the international legal and political order as essentially invisible at that time: 'While women were not necessarily ignored, they were spoken for by men and by agencies and institutions that catered to men's interests in which men prevailed. ... States do not usually seek a woman's perspective in policymaking, and women do not rely on or trust states to serve their interests.'[18] The problem then was how to make the international legal system recognize wrongs against women as a human rights violation given the structural, conceptual, and social barriers to doing so. In her article 'State Responsibility

---

16 Hillary Rodham Clinton, *Remarks to the UN 4th World Conference on Women Plenary Session* (delivered 5 September 1995, Beijing, China).

17 Cook, *Human Rights of Women*, supra note 2 at 4.

18 Rebecca J Cook, 'State Responsibility for Violations of Women's Human Rights' (1994) 7 Harvard Human Rights Journal 125 [Cook, 'State Responsibility'].

for Violations of Human Rights,' published a year before her 1994 volume, Cook considered different ways of reformulating existing international legal doctrines to account for this deficit. She wrote, for instance, that customary law doctrines could be made applicable to violations of women's rights, which is important because this obliges even countries that have not ratified human rights treaties. According to the International Law Commission's (ILC) Draft Articles on State Responsibility, a conduct is considered an internationally wrongful act of a state when the 'conduct consist[s] of an action or omission attributable to the State under international law; and that conduct constitutes a breach of an international obligation of the State.'[19] International law makes it possible that these acts or omissions, even those committed by private parties not acting on behalf of a state, may nevertheless be attributed to the state either through the principle of state complicity in wrongs or through state failure to exercise due diligence in control of private persons.[20] This type of analysis eliminates the distinction between public and private and makes violations of women's rights susceptible to recognition and remediation as human rights violations, assuming that local remedies have been exhausted.

Similarly, even under human rights treaties, Cook wrote that states may nonetheless be held responsible for the actions of private persons or agencies for failures to exercise due diligence to eliminate, reduce, and mitigate violations of international human rights law – for example, incidences of private discrimination under CEDAW.[21] This view was supported by a 1988 decision of the Inter-American Court of Human Rights – a frequent forum for many of Cook's legal interventions throughout her career – in *Velasquez-Rodriguez*, which imposed liability on the government of Honduras for its lack of due diligence in preventing unexplained disappearances.[22] Apart from reinterpreting international law doctrines in order to make them amenable to seeing rights violations against women, Cook made the question of how to make international human rights law more gender conscious central in her 1994 volume. By identifying available avenues in international human rights – for example, the use of general comments to develop interpretations of a treaty or the use of general recommendations issued

---

19 International Law Commission, *Draft Articles on Responsibility of States for Internationally Wrongful Acts, with Commentaries*, 53rd Sess, UN Doc A/56/10 (2001), ch IV, art 3.

20 Cook, 'State Responsibility,' supra note 18 at 143.

21 *CEDAW*, supra note 15, art 2(e).

22 *Velásquez Rodríguez Case (Honduras)* (1988), Inter-Am Ct HR (Ser C) No 4 at 92.

by the committee established by different human rights conventions, she brought together lawyers who could then debate different understandings of discrimination and the appropriate test to be employed by human rights tribunals.[23] Finally, a notable thing about the volume was that it was cognizant that the protection of women's rights is a complex issue, often encountering legislative barriers that reflect cultural and religious biases from a variety of national settings. The question that Cook posed for the contributing authors – 'how can universal human rights become legitimized in radically different societies without succumbing to either homogenizing universalism or paralysis of cultural relativism?' – remains a challenge that resonates until today. A later review of the edited volume characterized it as a 'beacon of some hope' and giving 'a glimpse into how international law will have a critical role in creating a brighter future for women, not just in the theory of international law, but also in the communities in which they live.'[24]

A little over thirty years later, Cook replicated her strategy of reviewing the past, reinterpreting existing rules and cases, and thinking about the future with respect to gender equality and international human rights law. By this time, 'women's rights are human rights' was a firmly entrenched pillar of the international human rights system. The UN Entity for Gender Equality and the Empowerment of Women, also known as UN Women, was established in 2010 and was the central UN body charged with advocating for the rights of women and girls.[25] The shift toward gender equality traces its roots to the same international human rights instruments that undergirded the 'women's rights are human rights' campaign, such as the Universal Declaration on Human Rights and CEDAW.[26] In 1995, the Platform for Action adopted at the end of the Beijing Fourth World Conference on Women – the same conference in which Hillary Clinton uttered the famous phrase – included the objective to 'take all necessary measures to eliminate all forms of discrimination against women and the girl child and remove all obstacles to gender equality and the advancement and empowerment of women.'[27]

---

23 Cook, *Human Rights of Women*, supra note 2 at 11.

24 F Pearl Eliadis, 'Review of Rebecca J Cook, ed, *Human Rights of Women: National and International Perspectives*' (1996) 34:2 Alta L Rev 485.

25 GA Res 64/289, UN GAOR, 64th Sess, UN Doc A/RES/64/289 (2 July 2010).

26 *Universal Declaration of Human Rights*, GA Res 217A (III), UNGAOR, 3rd Sess, Supp No 13, UN Doc A/810 (10 December 1948).

27 *Beijing Declaration and Platform for Action*, adopted at the Fourth World Conference on Women, UN Doc A/CONF.177/20/Rev.1 (17 October 1995).

Like her 1994 volume, the 2023 volume *Frontiers of Gender Equality* provides a close illustration – thanks to contributors all over the world who, in Cook's own words, were chosen by her because they think differently from her and have had a variety of experiences – of how gender discrimination against women and other sexual minorities continues to be normalized and puts the theory and practice of gender equality law in various legal forums together into a conversation so that they can inform one another.[28] *Frontiers of Gender Equality* takes for granted that international human rights law is the proper framework for the protection of gender equality even as Cook writes that 'international law continues to reflect gender biases in its structure, thus requiring feminist reenvisioning to prefigure gender equalities in particular contexts.'[29] Unlike its predecessor, the problem of the public-private divide does not loom as large in the background. The chapters do not address any structural barriers to using human rights law to achieve its goals, focusing instead on reinterpreting existing instruments such as CEDAW or analysing decisions of various human rights tribunals.[30] It is similarly admirable for its structural and intersectional focus, identifying and developing interpretive legal methods for determining what might constitute gender and intersectional discrimination. More importantly, the volume recognizes that addressing gender equality requires dealing with both legal and political dimensions and that doing so remains an ongoing struggle. In the chapter on African gender equalities, lawyer Faréda Banda acknowledges, for instance, that, while many gender violence cases have featured intersectional analysis that offers insights into both causes and consequences of problems, ultimately, transformed gender relations 'require changes in attitudes and societal values.'[31]

Cook's introduction to *Frontiers of Gender Equality* reveals both a personal and professional aspect to this chosen topic. She notes that, early in her professional career, she was part of a team in a school of public health working to address preventable causes of maternal death but that these deaths were not legally recognized as discriminatory wrongs, only unfortunate tragedies. She has since spent time and effort on scholarship as well as legal interventions or 'friends of the court' briefs so that she could persuade tribunals to favour interpretations conducive to gender equality. She admits that failure on that front was

---

28 Cook, *Frontiers of Gender Equality*, supra note 3.

29 Ibid at 4.

30 Ibid.

31 Faréda Banda, 'African Gender Equalities' in Cook, *Frontiers of Gender Equality*, supra note 3, 259 at 265.

her motivation to convene a group that could think about more persuasive ways to improve theory and practice surrounding gender equality law.[32] In a later interview, Cook notes the afterlife of the collection, stating that, since its publication, she has been collaborating with some of the chapter authors on how the volume could inform practice, such as organizing webinars and particularly working with advocates on 'how to expose the gender dimensions of adolescent rape and sexual abuse by reading in "defilement status" as a ground of discrimination,'[33] which was already noted by Banda in the African chapter. The question of how the prevailing theoretical and doctrinal innovations on this front will help gender equality in other contexts presents the next challenge.

III. Gender equality and AI

If Cook's commitment to refining the tools of the international human rights system – the doctrinal output of its institutions enriched by the theoretical and practical contributions of practitioners and academic scholars who all participate in the development of the human rights project – shone brightly in her two volumes, the aim of this section is to evaluate that commitment. Cook's overall message that international human rights should and could do more in terms of promoting the welfare of women and fostering a culture of gender equality is a timely one in light of the gender equality challenges posed by the emergence of AI and AI-based technologies.

An AI system has been defined as a machine-based system designed to operate with varying levels of autonomy, potentially exhibiting adaptiveness after deployment, which infers how to generate outputs (predictions, content, and so on) from its input for specified objectives.[34] The human rights implications of such systems are, by now, well documented. A recent report by the B-Tech Project under the auspices of the UN Office of the High Commissioner on Human Rights provides a detailed taxonomy of human rights risks associated with the use of generative AI – a subset of AI that uses models to produce text, images, videos, and other content. Among the risks that impact gender equality

---

32 Cook, *Frontiers of Gender Equality*, supra note 3 at 1,

33 Author's interview with Rebecca Cook, *Frontiers of Gender Equality* (31 August 2023), online: <blog-iacl-aidc.org/just-published/2023/8/31/frontiers-of-gender-equality #:~:text=This%20book%20project%20had%20challenges,prioritarian%20account%20 of%20gender%20equality>.

34 Council Regulation (EU) 2024/1689 Laying Down Harmonised Rules on Artificial Intelligence, [2024] OJ L2024/1689, art 3 [AI Act].

was the tendency of current generative AI models to over-represent culturally hegemonic groups which may lead to misrepresentation or under-representation of other groups at scale.[35] AI-generated stories, for example, tend to reinforce gender stereotypes by producing stories about women, associating them with working in domestic roles four times more often than men.[36] Another oft-cited example is the tendency of these models to be used in applications that monitor, among other things, employee performance, which could introduce existing biases based on gender, race, and age.

Most problems concerning gender inequality in AI have been currently identified in the context of the problem of algorithmic bias, which is defined as 'the application of an algorithm that compounds existing inequities in socioeconomic status, race, ethnic background, religion, gender, disability, or sexual orientation and amplifies inequities in … systems.'[37] For example, a prominent study by researchers Joy Buolamwini and Timnit Gebru found that commercial facial recognition software significantly misgenders women and darker-skinned individuals.[38] Search engine results likewise return prejudiced representations, adversely affecting women and members of minority groups.[39] Gender bias and discrimination in AI can occur at various stages in an algorithm's development process, but the first overlooked field where inequality is rife is the lack of women researchers and developers in this area.[40] The under-representation means that there is a high risk of developing technologies that do

---

35 Marie Lamensch, 'Generative AI Tools Are Perpetuating Harmful Gender Stereotypes' (14 June 2023), online: *Centre for International Governance Innovation* <www.cigionline.org/articles/generative-ai-tools-are-perpetuatingharmful -gender-stereotypes/>.

36 'UNESCO Finds Pervasive Gender Bias in Generative AI Tools' (7 March 2024), online: *CIO* <www.cio.com/article/1312311/unesco-finds-pervasive-gender-bias-in -generative-ai-tools.html>.

37 Trishan Panch, Heather Mattie & Rifat Atun, 'Artificial Intelligence and Algorithmic Bias: Implications for Health Systems' (2019) 9:2 Journal of Global Health 1.

38 Joy Buolamwini & Timnit Gebru, 'Gender Shades: Intersectional Accuracy Disparities in Commercial Gender Classification' (2018) 81 Proceedings of Machine Learning Research 1.

39 Latanya Sweeney, 'Discrimination in Online Ad Delivery' (2013) 56:5 Communications of the Association for Computing Memory 44; Safiya Umoja Noble, *Algorithms of Oppression: How Search Engines Reinforce Racism* (New York: New York University Press, 2018).

40 Sarah Myers West, Meredith Whittaker & Kate Crawford, 'Discriminating Systems: Gender, Race and Power in AI' (2019), online: *AI Now Institute* <ainowinstitute.org /wp-content/uploads/2023/04/discriminatingsystems.pdf>.

not meet the needs of half the population. Much of the work on gender biases of AI systems, for example, has emerged from women and women-led programs. It is thus imperative to have women in various kinds of decision-making capacities so that they can help shape meaningful decisions toward a shared digital future.

A recent paper showed that Stable Diffusion, a popular generative AI application that produces images from text prompts, returns predominantly Western, light-skinned men when prompted for a 'person' and that it has a tendency to sexualize images of women of colour.[41] Alongside inert patterns in available datasets and training data, the algorithms themselves might worsen inequalities by perpetuating stereotypes, such as often portraying women in domestic settings engaged in kitchen or housework because of aggregation or learning bias. Search engines have also been found to filter out images of female bodies, often mischaracterizing them as inappropriate or 'racy.' This perpetuates bias as these results are often coded based on the viewpoint of a male designer or engineer. It also produces direct harm by hindering access to vital information about health and medical research.[42] The current move to AI-driven health-care services may likewise cement these biased representations based on historic data that misses women's illnesses, thus resulting in poor diagnostic outcomes for women, especially women of colour.[43]

As philosopher Carla Fehr has observed, 'AI is a predominantly white and male domain and there is a pressing need for work on race, gender, disability and social issues related to AI.'[44] Some scholars have argued that these kinds of less visible and apparent impacts may cause more harm than overt discriminatory effects because it is much easier to spread these seemingly innocuous biases.[45] Consider the tendency to feminize AI tools that mimic and reinforce structural hierarchies in

---

41 Sourojit Ghosh & Aylin Caliskan, '"Person" = Light-Skinned, Western Man, and Sexualization of Women of Color: Stereotypes in Stable Diffusion' (2023), online: *arXiv* <arxiv.org/abs/2310.19981>.

42 Gianluca Mauro & Hilke Schellmann, 'There Is No Standard: Investigation Finds AI Algorithms Objectify Women's Bodies,' *The Guardian* (8 February 2023), online: <www.theguardian.com/technology/2023/feb/08/ai-algorithms-objectify-women>.

43 Caméron Celeste et al, 'Ethnic Disparity in Diagnosing Asymptomatic Bacterial Vaginosis Using Machine Learning' (2023) 6 NPJ Digital Medicine 211.

44 Wendy Philpott, 'What Would It Mean to Have Feminist AI?' (10 April 2023), online: <uwaterloo.ca/artificial-intelligence-institute/news/what-would-it-mean-have -feminist-ai>.

45 Fabian Lutz, 'Gender Equality and Artificial Intelligence in Europe: Addressing Direct and Indirect Impacts of Algorithms on Gender-Based Discrimination'

society such as the use of female voices and names for digital assistants and the use of a female voice – infamously, the voice of the actress Scarlett Johansson, for ChatGPT – in order to perform subservient and affective labour.[46] Several studies have examined stereotyping in large language models and have observed that these gender stereotypes could pose significant risks by, among other things, facilitating downstream effects such as technology-facilitated gender-based violence.[47] Given the widespread use of generative AI, it thus directly participates in the creation and distribution of biased or stereotyped content that may indeed have broad societal consequences such as the further disempowerment of girls and women.

Finally, AI makes it easier to commit technology-facilitated gender-based violence – that is, any act that is committed, aggravated, or amplified by the use of technologies which results in different kinds of harms including physical, sexual, or psychological harm. This kind of violence includes cyber harassment and stalking, the creation of deepfake porn, and online sexual assault. These types of online violence disproportionately impact women and girls on an intersectional basis, taking into account factors such as race, age, and sexual orientation. In 2023, for instance, most deepfakes were pornographic in nature, and 99 per cent of those videos targeted women.[48] Many jurisdictions have since adopted various measures that aim to address this phenomenon such as requiring digital platforms to prohibit the posting of unwanted intimate images depicting individuals, whether real or synthetic.[49]

All these aforementioned harms against women and gender equality have been largely couched in the language of human rights and for good reason. The entire human rights edifice – whether it be its legal, moral, or political dimensions – offers a ready-made vocabulary and set of institutional arrangements that are already legible to a broad global audience. Concerns about gender equality in the digital space have

---

(14 April 2022), online: *ERA Forum* <link.springer.com/article/10.1007/s12027 -022-00713-w>.

46 Laila Brown, 'Gender, Race and the Invisible Labor of Artificial Intelligence' in Simon Lindgren, ed, *Handbook of Critical Studies of Artificial Intelligence* (Cheltenham, UK: Edward Elgar, 2023) 575.

47 UNESCO & International Research Center on Artificial Intelligence, *Challenging Systemic Prejudices: An Investigation into Bias against Women* (2024) UNESCO, online: <unesdoc.unesco.org/ark:/48223/pf0000388971>.

48 Chandra Steele, 'The Internet Is Full of Deepfakes – and Most of Them Are Porn' (18 October 2023), online: *PC Mag* <www.pcmag.com/news/the-internet-is-full-of -deepfakes-and-most-of-them-are-porn>.

49 Benjamin Sobel, 'A Real Account of Deep Fakes,' Mich L Rev [forthcoming].

already been enshrined in the relevant documents such as the Global Digital Compact (GDC) and the Framework Convention on AI and Human Rights, Democracy, and the Rule of Law (AI Convention).[50] The GDC, a UN-led initiative to ensure that digital technologies are used to promote sustainable development goals, advance human rights, and promote global digital cooperation, was adopted in September 2024. Among its guiding principles is that 'gender equality and the empowerment of all women and girls and their full, equal, and meaningful participation in the digital space are essential to close the gender digital divide and advance sustainable development.'[51] The same principle also emphasizes the encouragement of leadership by women, the mainstreaming of a gender perspective, and the elimination of all forms of violence, including sexual and gender-based violence, that occurs through, or is amplified by, the use of technology. Meanwhile, the AI Convention, a binding treaty that obligates its signatories (ten countries, so far) to ensure that activities within the AI lifecycle are consistent with, among other things, human rights, also includes a provision on equality and non-discrimination.[52]

The efficacy of gender equality provisions in these AI-focused documents thus rests on the same assumptions and aspirations that underlie the whole international human rights system, including the insights that have been generated from past decades of scholars such as Cook and her contributors that have grappled with gender equality in a variety of legal, geographical, and cultural contexts. For example, it is by now widely documented that gender stereotypes harm women by devaluing them and sharply limiting their ability to autonomously design their lives. In her 2010 monograph, entitled *Gender Stereotyping*, Cook argues that naming a gender stereotype and identifying its harm is critical to its eradication.[53] She sets up this problem in the context of CEDAW and the various obligations of both the state as well as influential non-state actors under the convention that are crucial for the perpetuation and reinforcement of these stereotypes and their elimination.

In addition to the international human rights system serving as a repository of gender-responsive insights that have been generated

---

50 United Nations, *Global Digital Compact*, UN Doc A/RES/78/1 (22 September 2024), Annex [*GDC*]; *Framework Convention on Artificial Intelligence and Human Rights, Democracy and the Rule of Law*, CETS No 226 (2024) [*AI Convention*].

51 *GDC*, supra note 50.

52 *AI Convention*, supra note 50.

53 Rebecca J Cook & Simone Cusack, *Gender Stereotyping: Transnational Legal Perspectives* (Philadelphia: University of Pennsylvania Press, 2010).

along a spectrum of legal and political contexts, it also has the capacity to incorporate distinct perspectives and epistemologies. As shown earlier in this article, while feminists in the past have challenged human rights orthodoxies – particularly, their androcentric construction and the centrality of the public-private distinction – they were nonetheless defended for the broad visibility that they confer on problems experienced by women. The ensuing dialectic between critique and response, for the most part, has proven fruitful as human rights consequently became a vehicle for the vindication of women's rights as they took on the challenge of investing the vocabulary of rights with meanings that would confront the persistent problem of the highly unequal distribution of economic, social, and political power between men and women. Today, in the field of gender equality and AI, a promising example is a collective project and community associated with the term 'Feminist AI,' which has recently coalesced in order to create a new body of knowledge and models focused on the global South.[54] Feminist AI is deeply rooted in the critical perspectives of feminist science and technology studies which emerged in the 1970s and 1980s as it began to examine the exclusion of women's knowledge and perspectives in scientific discourse. Its main contribution is characterized by a structural approach that identifies and recognizes multidimensional and intersectional harms, especially those affecting marginalized populations throughout the AI lifecycle such as digital colonialism and environmental degradation.[55] In this way, the human rights approach becomes a complementary way of addressing gender inequality either caused or enshrined by AI-based systems because it allows for feminist struggles and insights to be incorporated in interpreting and realizing the relevant human rights.

IV. Are human rights enough?

While it is clear that international human rights law provides many advantages as a vehicle for advancing the various goals of gender equality within the AI context, it is also easy to see its limitations. The most obvious one is that, while the GDC commits UN member states

---

54 Tamar Sharon Wellner & Talia Rothman, 'Feminist AI: Can We Expect Our AI Systems to Become Feminist?' (2020) 33:2 Philosophy and Technology 191; Jude Browne et al, eds, *Feminist AI: Critical Perspectives on Algorithms, Data, and Intelligent Machines* (Oxford: Oxford University Press, 2024).

55 Sophie Toupin, 'Shaping Feminist Artificial Intelligence' (2023) 26:1 New Media and Society 580.

principally, its practical realization rests in large part in the hands of private technology corporations that own, develop, and operate these AI systems. To be sure, this is a concern that is not limited to technology – business and human rights has been a lively field of study and practice for the past decade or so. However, the novel political economy surrounding AI systems has cast technology corporations in a very central and prominent role because the ability to use and enjoy digital services that are powered by AI and to exercise various digital freedoms depend largely on the relationship between individual users and the technology companies to an extent that is significantly different from that of a user *vis-à-vis* their state.[56]

As a general matter, Principle 11 of the UN Guiding Principles on Business and Human Rights (UNGP) states that 'business enterprises should respect human rights.'[57] The accompanying commentary to this principle states that the responsibility to respect human rights is a global standard of expected conduct for all business enterprises wherever they operate.[58] Many have criticized the voluntary nature of the UNGP. Alongside efforts toward a legally binding business and human rights treaty,[59] many companies have nonetheless made efforts to align their policies and practices with these principles, and the UNGP have been used in many jurisdictions to support national actions to protect human rights. Large technology companies such as Meta have also experimented with self-regulatory mechanisms that incorporate and implement these principles, in addition to the rest of international human rights instruments such as CEDAW, in their own corporate human rights policy.[60] In terms of concrete regulations, the European Union's (EU) Digital Services Act makes a reference to the UNGP, among others, as it requires risk assessments from very large online platforms when it comes to recommender systems.[61] Similarly,

---

56 Yuval Shany, 'Big-Tech Companies' Obligations under International Human Rights Law' (2024) 58 Israel L Rev 3.

57 *Guiding Principles on Business and Human Rights: Implementing the United Nations 'Protect, Respect and Remedy' Framework, annexed to the Report of the Special Representative of the Secretary-General on the Issue of Human Rights and Transnational Corporations and Other Business Enterprises*, UN Doc A/HRC/17/31 (2011).

58 Ibid.

59 Olivier De Schutter, 'Towards a New Treaty on Business and Human Rights' (2016) 1:1 Business and Human Rights Journal 41.

60 'Corporate Human Rights Policy' (March 2021), online: *Meta* <about.fb.com/wp-content/uploads/2021/03/Facebooks-Corporate-Human-Rights-Policy.pdf>.

61 Council Regulation (EU) 2022/2065 on a Single Market for Digital Services and amending Directive 2000/31/EC, [2022] OJ L277/1, arts 34–7.

Article 27 of the EU's AI Act mandates a fundamental rights impact assessment of AI systems for deployers of high-risk AI systems.[62] The Council of Europe has provided some non-legally binding guidance to both public and private actors on how to carry out such human rights risk and impact assessments.[63] Pending dramatic regulatory advances beyond these, however, international human rights norms and institutions suffer from significant structural deficits that could limit their ability to protect rights, including gender equality rights, from infringing practices of major technology corporations.

Another limitation in employing a human rights lens in advancing gender equality concerns the nature of AI itself and its surrounding political economy. Susan Marks has critiqued human rights frameworks for their inability to address the structural causes of human rights violations such as poverty and economic oppression.[64] While I would argue that developments in human rights frameworks have addressed this critique in part, there is much room left for improvement. A human rights approach to AI is likewise an imperfect tool to address the gendered harms of AI because its norms and institutions may not be able to fully address what Sue Anne Teo calls the 'slow violence' being wrought by AI.[65] It is not obvious, for example, how representational harms such as the stereotyping that occurs within black-box AI systems could be directly addressed. And this concern is especially prominent because it is already quite difficult to spell out the contours of the harm these systems cause at an individual level. As Teo argues,[66] individuals more often than not are unaware of their own condition – often lacking the tools and concepts to make sense of their world within systems mediated by AI, thus resulting in their own disempowerment. The nature of AI as a technology essentially makes it difficult for individuals to know that their rights are being violated.

Relatedly, the construction and maintenance of an algorithmic society is facilitated in large part by the surveillance capitalism business model which continuously extracts data from a multiplicity of sources

---

62 AI Act, supra note 34, art 27.

63 Committee on Artificial Intelligence, 'Methodology for the Risk and Impact Assessment of Artificial Intelligence Systems from the Point of View of Human Rights, Democracy and the Rule of Law' (28 November 2024), online: *Council of Europe* <www.coe.int/en/web/artificial-intelligence/huderia-risk-and-impact -assessment-of-ai-systems>.

64 Susan Marks, 'Human Rights and Root Causes' (2011) 74:1 Mod L Rev 57.

65 Teo, 'Slow Violence,' supra note 9.

66 Ibid at 5.

around the world that are then commodified.[67] To be sure, the human rights framework can address some of the harms flowing from this – for example, through different iterations of the right to privacy, as articulated in the EU's General Data Protection Regulation or reinvigorating traditional freedoms such as the right to freedom of expression and the right to transparency and due process.[68] The UN special procedures have also been hard at work in elaborating human rights standards and monitoring as they relate to technology companies and their products, although the effectiveness of such efforts remains to be seen.[69]

V. Conclusion

The international human rights system as we know it today was primarily developed to limit state power.[70] The state-centric configuration is evident from its law and structures, which explains some of the tensions and questions of fit between what the IHRL regime does and how it relates to existing social conditions around the world. Alongside climate change, the rise of AI in the past few years and the ensuing societal and individual implications have put the international human rights regime front and centre again as a key piece of the regulatory puzzle. Cook's scholarly body of work, which has ranged from advocating for the sexual and reproductive rights of women to women's rights in general, has been dedicated to making this kind of use of this system. Her work is foundational in nature. Her two edited collections laid the groundwork for, first, integrating gender into the practice and doctrine of international human rights law and, second, consolidating cutting-edge insights from the theory and practice of gender equality for use in human rights tribunals all over the world.

This short article has situated her scholarship and its faith in international human rights law and has expanded on this project to examine gender equality in an age of AI systems. While her work has not

---

67 Shoshana Zuboff, *The Age of Surveillance Capitalism: The Fight for a Human Future at the New Frontier of Power* (New York: Public Affairs, 2018).

68 Council Regulation (EU) 2016/679 on the Protection of Natural Persons with Regard to the Processing of Personal Data and on the Free Movement of Such Data, [2016] OJ L119.

69 United Nations Office of the High Commissioner for Human Rights, 'Allegation Letter to Microsoft, GitHub, and OpenAI,' online: <spcommreports.ohchr.org/TMResultsBase/DownLoadPublicCommunicationFile?gId=28221>.

70 Ed Bates, 'History' in Daniel Moeckli, Sangeeta Shah & Sandesh Sivakumaran, eds, *International Human Rights Law*, 2d ed (Oxford: Oxford University Press, 2014) 15.

specifically addressed the intersection of gender equality and AI, it has contributed the building blocks necessary to understand and address the challenges that women and other sexual minorities face in the digital age. The hope is that this article can provide a starting point on how we can harness the human rights framework that Cook has spent her career championing in this particular area. It is important to reiterate that Cook's faith in international human rights is not a blind one. All her work is critically attuned to the shortcomings of international human rights law and international law in general. Throughout her work, Cook has repeatedly referenced the male-centric presumptions and Western-centric bias that permeates international law as the context within which her work should be situated, even as she acknowledges that there have also been promising developments such as the emergence of Third World Approaches to International Law and anti-imperialist feminisms that have spurred welcome debates in the field.[71]

Similarly, whether the human rights regime can transcend the above-mentioned limitations, among others, and also address the formidable challenges presented by the algorithmic society is a question that scholars, practitioners, and supporters of this project should deem worth confronting with the same clarity that Cook has confronted the questions presented before her and her generation of feminists and human rights advocates. Because, while it appears formidable, it is not impossible. Consider the critiques levelled at human rights in the past, such as by Marks – particularly, that we cannot talk about redressing gender equality without talking about the systems that perpetuate gender injustices and violence in the first place. The intersectional approach to gender equality that characterizes Cook's *Frontiers of Gender Equality*,[72] now a mainstream position, is crucial for understanding how AI systems can perpetuate existing inequalities. Moreover, to the extent that contemporary equality and anti-discrimination law now possesses a 'common core' (that is, a convergence on certain normative principles),[73] the presence of the core's various components in current human rights institutions and its case law – in no small part, spurred by Cook and her scholarship – provides a promising basis for stakeholders to build on in the variety of soft law and best practices surrounding the development and use of AI-based systems.

---

71 Cook, *Frontiers of Gender Equality*, supra note 3 at 2.

72 Shreya Atrey, 'Frontiers of Gender Equality' in Cook, *Frontiers of Gender Equality*, supra note 3, 55.

73 Francesca Pou Gimenez, 'Taking Stock of Gender Equality' in Cook, *Frontiers of Gender Equality*, supra note 3, 430 at 437.

Another development that might address the limitations of a human rights framework concerns rethinking the foundations and conceptualizations of rights themselves. The relationship between technology and society is seldom reflected in rights discourse. Some scholars have begun to argue that the unique challenges posed by AI toward the human rights framework risk undermining the very framework itself by disempowering individuals since they are less able to understand the algorithmic mediations enabled through datafication or because of the inability of the human rights frame to truly encompass, not to mention address, its harms.[74] As Cook herself wrote with respect to state responsibility for women's rights violations, rights are not meaningful unless the institutional environment affords those wronged with the practical ability to claim and vindicate these rights. A similar dynamic is in play with Julie Cohen's idea of 'rights as affordances.'[75] Until relatively recently, rights discourse has operated with a set of unstated and often under-examined assumptions about physical constraints which technological advances have since called into question. But the imperceptibility of decisions made by AI systems essentially allows individuals only circumscribed room to maneuver to exercise their rights without them being fully aware of these limitations. This structural perspective is built into new rights that have surfaced in recent proposals such as the 'right to a human decision-maker,' the 'right to cognitive liberty,' the 'right not to be forgotten,' and the 'right to data protection.'

In a recent book, Shannon Vallor characterizes AI as a mirror because it reflects our individual and collective appearances, including the ugly realities about how humans interact with one another.[76] As AI systems increasingly shape and influence various areas of decision making in our society, the imperative to safeguard human welfare and values remains higher than ever. If we intend to maintain the international human rights system as the predominant legal, moral, and political framework to protect rights, including gender equality rights, we need to ensure that it is up to the task by continuously innovating its doctrines, strengthening its institutions, and reckoning with and working around its limitations, as the work of Rebecca Cook has shown us.

---

74 Teo, 'Slow Violence,' supra note 9.
75 Julie Cohen, 'Affording Fundamental Rights' (2017) 4:1 Critical Analysis of Law 1.
76 Shannon Vallor, *The AI Mirror: How to Reclaim Our Humanity in an Age of Machine Thinking* (New York: Oxford University Press, 2024).

15 A Rule-of-Law Compliant Reading of Section 33: The Continuing Relevance of Lorraine Weinrib's Public Law Scholarship

RICHARD STACEY

Section 33 of Canada's Constitution Act, 1982, is the focal point of what Lorraine Weinrib has called our 'unique and distinctively Canadian' version of rights protection.[1] Subsection (1) – the 'notwithstanding' clause – empowers Parliament and the provincial legislatures to declare that provisions in a statute 'shall operate notwithstanding' certain rights enshrined in the Canadian Charter on Rights and Freedoms.[2] The effect of including a notwithstanding declaration in a statute, as subsection (2) contemplates, is that statutory provisions protected by the declaration 'shall have such operation' as they would have had 'but for' the Charter rights identified in the declaration (the 'effects' clause). Subsection (3) provides that such a declaration shall expire after five years (the 'sunset' clause), while subsection (4) allows that a legislature may re-enact a declaration. Subsection (5) provides that any re-enactment will also be subject to the sunset clause.

Section 33 straddles the watershed moment of Canada's two constitutional identities: our typically Commonwealth system of parliamentary supremacy prior to the adoption of the 1982 Constitution Act and our commitment to constitutional supremacy thereafter.[3] While section 52(1) of the Constitution Act, 1982, affirms that statutory provisions

---

1 Lorraine E Weinrib, 'Learning to Live with the Override' (1990) 35 McGill LJ 541 at 544 [Weinrib, 'Learning to Live'].

2 *Canadian Charter of Rights and Freedoms*, Part I of the *Constitution Act 1982*, being Schedule B to the *Canada Act 1982* (UK), 1982, c 11.

3 Lorraine E Weinrib, 'Canada's Constitutional Revolution: From Legislative to Constitutional State' (1999) 33 Israel L Rev 13 [Weinrib, 'Canada's Constitutional Revolution']; Eric M Adams, '*Ford* Focus: Constitutional Context and the Notwithstanding Clause' (2023) 32 Const Forum Const 33 at 35; Henri Brun & Guy Tremblay, *Droit constitutionnel* (Cowansville, QC: Éditions Y Blais, 1982) at 419.

inconsistent with the Constitution are 'of no force or effect,'[4] section 33 appears to preserve a vestige of parliamentary supremacy by giving legislatures the option to override (or sidestep, supersede, circumvent) the substantive limits that the Charter puts on their legislative authority. Section 33 is sometimes referred to as the 'override' provision. A common understanding of Canada's Constitution in light of section 33 is that it does not attempt to balance the sometimes competing imperatives of constitutionalism and democracy so much as weight the scales in favour of democracy. The version of constitutional democracy that section 33 brings to Canada is perhaps better understood in reverse lexical order: as a primarily democratic constitutionalism.

Weinrib's scholarship and litigation on section 33, however, presents an alternative reading of the Constitution.[5] What makes section 33 distinctively Canadian is its capacity to bring constitutional values and democracy together through public discourse and deliberation about how our political community (or communities) should evolve. Section 33 does not compel a zero-sum choice between democracy and constitutional rights. On the contrary, it invites and encourages the Canadian and provincial publics to think deeply and make electoral choices about precisely those matters of principle that arise when constitutional rights and public policy collide. For section 33 to live up to that promise and to fit into Canada's deeper constitutional infrastructure, then, governments and legislatures invoking section 33 must meet obligations of publicity and explanation. This has been a constant theme of Weinrib's contributions to understanding section 33, and it continues to inform contemporary debates. Moreover, her work in connecting democracy and constitutional rights – two foundational pillars of Canada's legal order – emphasizes the importance

---

4 Section 52(1) of the *Constitution Act, 1982*, being Schedule B to the *Canada Act 1982* (UK), 1982, c 11, provides: 'The Constitution of Canada is the supreme law of Canada, and any law that is inconsistent with the provisions of the Constitution is, to the extent of the inconsistency, of no force or effect.'

5 See e.g. Weinrib, 'Learning to Live,' supra note 1; Lorraine E Weinrib, 'Of Diligence and Dice: Reconstituting Canada's Constitution' (1992) 42 UTLJ 207 [Weinrib, 'Of Diligence and Dice']; Lorraine E Weinrib, 'The Canadian Charter's Override Clause: Lessons for Israel' (2016) 49 Israel L Rev 67 [Weinrib, 'Canadian Charter's Override Clause']; Lorraine E Weinrib, 'The Supreme Court of Canada in the Age of Rights: Constitutional Democracy, the Rule of Law and Fundamental Rights under Canada's Constitution' (2001) 80:1 Can Bar Rev 699 at 720–8; Lorraine E Weinrib, 'Canada's Charter of Rights: Paradigm Lost' (2001) 6 Rev Const Stud 119 at 132–50; Lorraine Weinrib, 'The Canadian Charter's Transformative Aspirations' (2003) 19:2 SCLR (2d) 17 at 18–33.

of a third pillar: the rule of law. As Canada's public law jurisprudence has become increasingly oriented to the rule of law since the constitutional transformation in 1982, Weinrib's work on section 33 has re-emerged as critically relevant.[6]

At the same time, provincial governments' discussions and uses of section 33 since 2018 have extolled its democracy-enhancing characteristics in a way that refashions it into a tool of majoritarian and populist policy-making. An emerging line of academic commentary supports these political views, understanding legislation protected by section 33 that is enacted for the 'common good' to be entirely freed from any obligations of curial or public justification[7] or otherwise operative notwithstanding its constitutional invalidity.[8] These approaches are deeply problematic. The rule of law demands that those who hold public power account for their uses of it and explain why each exercise of power is consistent with previously declared rules.[9] To be consistent with the rule of law – and, thus, consistent with the fundamental architecture of the Canadian constitutional order – a government invoking section 33 must at least make an attempt to explain why provisions facially inconsistent with Charter rights should nonetheless be considered valid by virtue of their consistency with our most deeply held normative principles. To fail to do so is to sacrifice the rule of law at the

---

6 A smattering of cases suffices to illustrate the deep resonance of the rule of law in Canada's post-1982 constitutional jurisprudence. See e.g., *Re BC Motor Vehicle Act*, [1985] 2 SCR 486 at 512; *Reference re Secession of Quebec*, [1998] 2 SCR 217 at para 32 [*Secession Reference*]; *Dunsmuir v New Brunswick*, 2008 SCC 9 at para 27; *Canada (Minister of Citizenship and Immigration) v Vavilov*, 2019 SCC 65 at paras 2, 17, 53–72 [*Vavilov*]; *Canada (Attorney General) v Power*, 2024 SCC 26 at para 5.

7 See e.g. Stéphane Sérafin, Kerry Sun & Xavier Foccroulle Ménard, 'Notwithstanding Judicial Specification: The Notwithstanding Clause within a Juridical Order' (2023) 110 SCLR (2d) 135 [Sérafin, Sun & Foccroulle Ménard, 'Notwithstanding Judicial Specification']; Maxime St-Hilaire & Xavier Foccroulle Ménard, 'Nothing to Declare: A Response to Grégoire Webber, Eric Mendelsohn, Robert Leckey, and Leonid Sirota on the Effects of the Notwithstanding Clause' (2020) 29 Const Forum Const 37; Maxime St-Hilaire, Xavier Foccroulle Ménard & Antoine Dutrisac, 'Judicial Declarations Notwithstanding the Use of the Notwithstanding Clause? A Response to a (Non-)Rejoinder' in Peter Biro, ed, *The Notwithstanding Clause and the Canadian Charter* (Montreal and Kingston: McGill-Queens University Press, 2024) 132 [Biro, *Notwithstanding Clause*].

8 Grégoire Webber, 'Notwithstanding Rights, Review, or Remedy? On the Notwithstanding Clause and the Operation of Legislation' (2021) 71 UTLJ 537 [Webber, 'Notwithstanding Rights'].

9 Lon Fuller, *The Morality of Law*, rev ed (New Haven, CT: Yale University Press, 1969) at 209–10.

altar of a purely majoritarian and grotesquely impoverished conception of democracy. At a more pragmatic level, offering a justification to
voters preserves the very purpose of the sunset clause – namely, to put
the people in a position to make an informed democratic choice about
what values and norms they want their governments to uphold.

Weinrib's work offers a path to a rule-of-law compliant reading of
section 33 and, in turn, illuminates how contemporary invocations
and populist readings of the section threaten to undermine our commitment to the rule of law. Her work is as critical now as when she
put her submissions before the Supreme Court of Canada in 1988.[10] In
Part I of this article, I outline the first of three limbs of Weinrib's body
of scholarship on section 33: the historical context in which the clause
was developed, how its inclusion in the Charter was the political compromise that convinced the provinces to agree to constitutional reform
in the first place, and the implications that it had for the override provision early on.[11] In Part II, I connect this history to the development
of what has become known in Canada and across the Commonwealth
legal systems as 'dialogue theory' and to Weinrib's own conception of
dialogue. Central to that theory is the idea that, since rights are contestable and there is deep disagreement in a pluralistic and multicultural
society about what they mean (and what we mean to protect by con-
stitutionalizing them), courts should not have a monopoly over their
interpretation. Rather, courts and legislatures should work through the
meaning of rights together in a dialogic and iterative process. The third
limb of Weinrib's work concerns the idea that the mere existence of section 33, despite its rare use for most of the last forty years, has fostered
deep reflection about the fundamental values on which Charter rights
rest and to which they give expression. In Part III, I present the core of
the argument that Weinrib's work remains crucial: only by maintaining
a substantive debate about how invoking section 33 upholds Canadians' normative commitments can section 33 remain consistent with the
fundamental principle of the rule of law.

I. The terms of the debate

The parliamentary supremacy that section 33 of the Constitution Act,
1982, appears to affirm raises a question about how to understand the
affirmation of constitutional supremacy in section 52(1) of the same

---

10 Weinrib acted for Ontario in *Ford v Quebec (Attorney General)*, 1988 SCC 19 [*Ford*].
11 Weinrib, 'Of Diligence and Dice,' supra note 5; Weinrib, 'Canada's Constitutional
    Revolution,' supra note 3.

document. Some understand section 33 to make 'invalid' legislation operative, notwithstanding its unconstitutionality.[12] Others understand section 33 to render legislation consistent with the Constitution as a whole, notwithstanding its inconsistency with certain Charter rights.[13] With these two views laid out upfront, it is useful to recount the origin story of section 33, both because it puts this question in historical context and because the 'dialogue theory' that helps to resolve it is closely connected to that story.

A. Override or limitation: locating legislative supremacy

The idea of constitutional democracy is inherently paradoxical. For the people in a political community to commit to a set of rules for how political power is to be exercised necessarily limits the way in which the people, or their representatives, can subsequently exercise power. Until the adoption of the Charter in 1982, provincial legislatures and Parliament were constrained only by the distribution of legislative competences in sections 91 and 92 of the Constitution Act, 1867.[14] Within their respective jurisdictions, legislatures and Parliament faced no substantive limits on legislation. Weinrib details how this lack of constraints allowed legislatures to pander to electoral majorities, uphold ideological ideals, or simply reward political patronage without concern for the minorities to whose interests its legislation was disadvantageous or hostile.[15] Even so, the provinces did exceed their jurisdiction, and the courts did declare offending legislation *ultra vires* and invalid on federalism grounds. By the time debates about the patriation of the Constitution and the adoption of a bill of rights had become serious in the 1970s, the provinces had already experienced about one hundred years of constitutional limits on their legislative authority. A charter of rights would impose new, substantive limits on their legislative power, and it was perhaps no surprise that the provinces were reluctant to adopt one.

One idea that the provinces floated for watering down constitutional constraints on legislative supremacy in 1980 and 1981 was to tie the justification of statutory rights limitations directly to legislative sovereignty and so to infuse the rights debate with popular, or at least legislative,

---

12 Webber, 'Notwithstanding Rights?,' supra note 7.
13 Robert Leckey & Eric Mendelsohn, 'The Notwithstanding Clause: Legislatures, Courts, and the Electorate' (2022) 72 UTLJ 189.
14 *Constitution Act, 1867* (UK), 30 & 31 Vict, c 3.
15 Weinrib, 'Canada's Constitutional Revolution,' supra note 3 at 16–22.

opinion.[16] The provinces did not win this battle, and subsequent drafts of the Charter embraced the primacy of rights over legislative opinion and were oriented toward substantive, demonstrable justification of rights limitations on the basis of the values underlying the Constitution as a whole.[17] This textual reorientation had two effects. First, as Weinrib observes, it 'eliminated the possible misunderstanding ... that the entrenchment of rights left parliamentary sovereignty intact.'[18] Second, it pushed the provinces' efforts to maximize legislative authority out of the limitations clause and into an override provision.[19] Section 33 emerged both as the textual home for legislative supremacy in the Charter and the concession that the federal government had to make to get the provinces on board.

B. *The first phase of section 33's story: political costs and rare use*

Quebec remained opposed in principle to the idea of a Charter, however, and used the override both pre-emptively and comprehensively to opt out of the Charter for most of the 1980s.[20] The Supreme Court of Canada upheld these moves in *Ford v Quebec*, declaring that all section 33 requires of a legislature invoking it is that it expressly identifies the rights or sections of the Charter that the legislation is overriding.[21] The postscript to the *Ford* decision highlights Weinrib's understanding of section 33 as imposing primarily political restraints on legislatures. The Court found in *Ford* that Quebec's Charter of the French Language imposed unjustifiable limits on the right to freedom of expression protected by section 2(b) of the Canadian Charter.[22] Since the original invocation of the override had run past the sunset period, the Court declared the offending provisions of the statute to be of no force or effect. Emboldened by the Court's formal reading of section 33, Premier Robert Bourassa's government simply amended the Charter of the

---

16 Weinrib, 'Of Diligence and Dice,' supra note 5 at 218–21.

17 Lorraine E Weinrib, 'The Supreme Court of Canada and Section 1 of the *Charter*' (1988) 10 SCLR 469.

18 Weinrib, 'Of Diligence and Dice,' supra note 5 at 220.

19 Weinrib, 'Canada's Constitutional Revolution,' supra note 3 at 31; Weinrib, 'Of Diligence and Dice,' supra note 5 at 221; Eric M Adams & Erin RJ Bower, 'Notwithstanding History: The Rights-Protecting Purposes of Section 33 of the Charter' (2022) 26 Rev Const Stud 121 at 134 [Adams & Bower, 'Notwithstanding History'].

20 Weinrib, 'Learning to Live,' supra note 1 at 544.

21 *Ford*, supra note 10.

22 *Charter of the French Language*, CQLR, c C-11.

French Language to include a fresh invocation of section 33. Weinrib notes that, while Bourassa faced no immediate political blowback for the move in Quebec, it was not popular in the rest of Canada, and any pan-Canadian support his government had enjoyed for constitutional recognition of Quebec's distinct society evaporated.[23]

Quebec soon after faced a decision from the United Nations Human Right Committee that the Charter of the French Language was inconsistent with international law.[24] At the expiry of the sunset clause in the early 1990s, and worried about losing international sympathy for Quebec's independence aspirations, the Quebec government did not re-invoke section 33. Instead, it amended the statute to make it Charter compliant.[25] Later Quebec governments, at least before 2018, were similarly wary of invoking section 33.[26] Weinrib details how Alberta's experience with section 33 traces a similar pattern of initial enthusiasm followed by reflection and restraint. In the first example, Alberta proposed legislation that would limit the government's financial liability for the non-consensual sterilization of people institutionalized for mental illness and developmental disabilities between 1928 and 1972. The provincial government announced that it would invoke section 33 to ensure the legislation's operation notwithstanding any Charter rights violations. What Weinrib calls a 'firestorm of criticism' persuaded the government to reverse course.[27] Premier Ralph Klein admitted that his 'political radar' had failed him and that he had underestimated the depth of Albertans' feelings that it would be fundamentally unjust for the government to limit or discourage remedies for its own wrongs.[28] In short, Premier Klein realized that he could not justify overriding rights to Albertans.

Much the same story played out when Premier Klein chose not to invoke section 33 to protect Alberta legislation that the Supreme Court of Canada found inconsistent with the Charter's equality guarantees.[29] Assessing the calls to invoke section 33 as coming from a minority of Albertans, Premier Klein insisted that he would never invoke section

---

23 Weinrib, 'Canada's Constitutional Revolution,' supra note 3 at 35–6.
24 *Ballantyne et al v Canada*, Case no. CCPR/C/47/D/359/1989, Communication nos 385/1989/Rev.1, 359/1989 (31 March 1993).
25 Weinrib, 'Canadian Charter's Override Clause,' supra note 5 at 85–6.
26 Weinrib, 'Canada's Constitutional Revolution,' supra note 3 at 36; Weinrib, 'Canadian Charter's Override Clause,' supra note 5 at 85–6.
27 Ibid at 87.
28 Ibid.
29 *Vriend v Alberta*, [1998] 1 SCR 493.

33 without 'widespread public support.'[30] These examples show that governments have been wary of stoking the public opprobrium that comes from overriding rights in controversial circumstances. Indeed, governments appear loath to deploy section 33 unless they are confident that they will enjoy significant public support in doing so. Successful invocations of section 33 remain relatively uncontroversial: consider that 69 per cent or eighteen out of twenty-six invocations of the notwithstanding clauses tabled in legislatures between 1982 and 2024 eventually became law,[31] while government attempts to justify rights limitations under section 1 succeed at the Supreme Court in only 30 per cent of cases.[32] When the section has been successfully invoked, certainly up until about 2018, it has generally not sparked public controversy.[33] Then Justice Minister Jean Chrétien anticipated that this would be the case when he set out the 'rare-use' norm in 1981, assuring Parliament that the override would be used only in 'non-controversial circumstances' or to correct 'absurd situations.'[34]

For a paradigmatic example of the kind of meaningful dialogue that Weinrib anticipated would happen in controversial cases, consider Ontario's responses to an education workers' strike in October 2022. Anticipating that a statute requiring striking teachers to go back to work would unjustifiably infringe the Charter's collective bargaining rights, the statute invoked section 33.[35] Justifying the move, Premier Doug Ford argued that a strike 'affects the whole economy' and would be 'more devastating' than overriding collective bargaining rights.[36] The preamble to the Keeping Students in Class Act offered a further

---

30 Sheila Pratt, 'Klein Swayed a Divided Tory Caucus Not to Override Top Court's Decision,' *Edmonton Journal* (30 March 2008) E4.

31 Caitlin Salvino, 'Notwithstanding Minority Rights: Rethinking Canada's Notwithstanding Clause' in Biro, *Notwithstanding Clause*, supra note 7, 401 at 401.

32 Lorrian Hardcastle, 'Proportionality Analysis by the Canadian Supreme Court' in Mordechai Kremnitzer, Talya Steiner & Andrej Lang, eds, *Proportionality in Action: Comparative and Empirical Perspectives on the Judicial Practice* (Cambridge, UK: Cambridge University Press, 2020) 134 at 152.

33 Guillaume Rousseau and Francois Côté suggested in 2017 that all uses of section 33 until then had had 'so little impact that we can question their significance.' See Guillaume Rousseau & Francois Côté, 'A Distinctive Quebec Theory and Practice of the Notwithstanding Clause: When Collective Interests Outweigh Individual Rights' (2017) 47 RGD 343 at 349 [Rousseau & Côté, 'Quebec Perspective'].

34 *House of Commons Debates*, 32:1, Vol 12 (20 November 1981) at 13042–3.

35 *Keeping Students in Class Act*, SO 2022, c 19.

36 Liam Casey, 'Ontario Government Repeals Anti-strike Law for CUPE Education Workers' (14 November 2022), online: *CBC News* <www.cbc.ca/news/ algar/ algary /ont-government-repeals-education-bill-1.6650584>.

justification, adverting to the negative impact of school closures during the pandemic and the urgency of restoring regular and stable schooling. The invocation of section 33, the preamble went on, was intended to avoid the 'destabilizing uncertainty' that legal challenges would create. Teachers were not compelled by the government's reasoning. Despite the passage of the Act, fifty-five thousand teachers stayed away from the classroom. Facing unequivocal and united opposition, 'the government blinked' and repealed the Act.[37] The following day, a vote on Ontario's Bill 37, the Notwithstanding Clause Limitation Act, 2022, was successfully carried after its first reading in the legislature. Among other restrictions, the bill requires a report from the attorney general explaining how the use of the override can be demonstrably justified in a free and democratic society and requires the adoption of a notwithstanding declaration by a two-thirds majority of the legislature.[38] Although the bill died on the order paper when the legislature dissolved prior to the 2025 provincial election, it is nonetheless indicative of the idea that invoking section 33 requires good reasons and widespread support.

In the same vein, Alberta Premier Danielle Smith has indicated that she views section 33 as a means for a government to express substantive disagreements with courts about the justifiability of rights limitations. Speaking about Alberta's legislation restricting gender-affirming health care, Premier Smith said she would invoke section 33 only as a last resort and after having had an opportunity in court to argue that the statutory measures are 'reasonable, proportionate and evidence-based.'[39] Much of the discussion about inter-institutional dialogue is rooted in this first phase of section 33's story and in the rare-use norm. However, since 2018, provincial governments have proven more willing to invoke section 33 and to court controversy in doing so.[40] As this

---

37 '"The Government Blinked": Union to End Ontario Education Walkout after Ford Promises to Repeal Strike Law' (7 November 2022), online: *CBC News* <www.cbc .ca/news/algar/ algary/cupe-strike-labour-board-ruling-expected-1.6642824>. The repeal was effected by the *Keeping Students in Class Repeal Act*, SO 2022, c 20.

38 *Keeping Students in Class Act*, supra note 35.

39 Lisa Johnson, 'Alberta Premier Smith Willing to Use the Notwithstanding Clause on Trans Health Bill' (15 December 2024), online: *CBC News* <www.cbc.ca/news/algar /algary/alberta-premier-smith-willing-to-use-the-notwithstanding-clause-on-trans -health-bill-1.7411263>.

40 Caitlyn Salvino, 'A Tool of the "Last Resort": A Comprehensive Account of the Notwithstanding Clause Political Use from 1982–2021' (2022) 16 JPPL 11 at 58; Tsvi Kahana, 'The Notwithstanding Clause in Canada: The First Forty Years' (2023) 60 Osgoode Hall LJ 1; Adams & Bower, 'Notwithstanding History,' supra note 19 at 140.

has happened, dialogue has become a less accurate description of how governments relate to the Charter.

II. Democracy and dialogue theory

The rare-use norm is consistent with the idea that Canada's constitutional system rests on a set of fundamental values. While the Charter entrenches a handful of rights explicitly, those rights are best understood as instantiations of these deeper values. In turn, those values inform the scope and content of those rights and give them meaning.[41] While courts have on occasion enumerated fundamental values and expounded on them,[42] the work of doing so is not exclusively judicial. What ordinary people think about these values and how they should shape and inform public policy is just as important – at least – as what judges think.[43] When a legislature invokes section 33 pre-emptively and without facing opposition or public blowback, we might conclude that its reasons for overriding a right are acceptable to the voting public. Similarly, where there is no backlash to an invocation of section 33 responding to a court ruling, we might conclude that the public thinks, along with the government, that the court made a mistake in its assessment of the scope of the rights at stake or of the balance between rights and government policy objectives.

It is a core aspect of Weinrib's position on section 33 that the non-controversial cases are non-controversial precisely because they are the product of a normative consensus that overriding rights will advance the values underlying the constitutional project better than blocking legislation in order to uphold a right. The government, in other words, has made a successful pitch to a public generally committed to a set of normative values that the override is substantively consistent with those values, even though it has infringed a Charter right. This picture

---

41 *R v Keegstra*, [1990] 3 SCR 697 at 726a–728f (quoting Ford); *Loyola High School v Quebec (Attorney General)*, 2015 SCC 12 at para 36; *Commission scolaire francophone des Territoires du Nord-Ouest v Northwest Territories (Education, Culture and Employment)*, 2023 SCC 31 at paras 65–76.

42 *R v Oakes*, [1986] 1 SCR 103 at para 64.

43 Jeremy Waldron, 'The Core of the Case against Judicial Review' (2005–6) 115 Yale LJ 1346; Jeremy Waldron, 'Can There Be a Democratic Jurisprudence?' (2008) New York University School of Law, Public Law and Legal Theory Research Paper Series, Working Paper No 08-35, online: <http://ssrn.com/abstract=1280923>; Jeremy Waldron, *Law and Disagreement* (Oxford: Oxford University Press, 1999) at 149–63. For a reply, see Richard Stacey, 'Democratic Jurisprudence and Judicial Review: Waldron's Contribution to Political Positivism' (2010) 30 Oxford J Leg Stud 749.

of what is going on when a government invokes section 33 is what drove the dialogue literature of the 1990s and 2000s.

A. Deliberative dialogue

When a court finds that a statute has unjustifiably limited a Charter right, Peter Hogg and Allison Bushell argue in their seminal article from 1997 that the enacting legislature has a number of options by which to respond.[44] These 'legislative sequels' are the legislatures' contributions to the dialogue about rights. When the legislative sequel is an invocation of section 33, much of the dialogue literature understands the legislature to be expressing its disagreement with the court on matters of constitutional interpretation.[45] Indeed, this is the view that the Supreme Court of Canada committed to in 2021: 'Where, therefore, a court invalidates legislation using ... the Charter, the legislature may give continued effect to *its* understanding of what the Constitution requires by invoking s. 33.'[46] In circumstances where people disagree reasonably about the content of rights, there is no reason that the courts should be the only institution empowered to weigh in on what the Charter allows or prohibits. So, for a legislature to invoke section 33 in response to a court ruling is merely for the legislature to disagree with the court, substantively, on either of two questions.

In the first place, the legislature might have a different view of whether its statute limits a right at all. In the face of a court's conclusion that a right protects an activity that a statute prohibits, for example, a legislature may invoke the override to codify its view that the right does not protect that activity and that the statute does not limit that right. Second, whether or not a rights limitation is justified under section 1 – and, more specifically, whether it meets the 'minimal impairment' and 'proportionality in the strict sense' tests of the *Oakes* analysis – involves difficult value judgments over which courts, legislatures and people may reasonably disagree.[47] In this regard, if the Charter is primarily a

---

44 Peter W Hogg & Allison A Bushell, 'The *Charter* Dialogue between Courts and Legislatures (or Perhaps the Charter of Rights Isn't Such a Bad Thing After All) (1997) 35 Osgoode Hall LJ 187.

45 Dwight Newman, 'Canada's Notwithstanding Clause, Dialogue, and Constitutional Identities' in Geoffrey Sigalet, Grégoire Webber & Rosalind Dixon, eds, *Constitutional Dialogue: Rights, Democracy, Institutions* (Cambridge, UK: Cambridge University Press, 2019) 209.

46 *Toronto (City) v Ontario (Attorney General)*, 2021 SCC 34 at para 60 [emphasis in original].

47 See *R v KRJ*, 2016 SCC 31 at para 79; *Alberta v Hutterian Brethren of Wilson Colony*, 2009 SCC 37 at paras 191–9, per LeBel J, dissenting; *R v Oakes*, [1986] 1 SCR 103.

document protecting liberal individual rights, a government may want to lean on communitarian or cultural values in explaining that it needs to invoke section 33 in order to protect broader social interests that are themselves elements of Canada's constitutional system.[48] The heart of either of these dialogic exchanges is a disagreement about whether the impugned statute actually contravenes the Charter at all. When a legislature invokes section 33 at the conclusion of such a dialogue, the effect is not just to render the statute operative but to assert its validity on the back of reasoned and deliberate consideration about what rights actually protect or whether rights limitations are actually justified. A reasoned and deliberate invocation of section 33 allows a legislature to articulate its substantiated opinion that the statute at issue is not inconsistent with the Charter and is thus both valid and operative.

Moreover, from Weinrib's perspective, this dialogue is precisely how section 33 brings democracy and constitutional rights together. Even though it is settled that courts cannot call into question a government's reasons for invoking section 33, the 'manner and form' requirements that the Supreme Court of Canada set out in *Ford* nonetheless require a legislature to make it plain that they are enacting a law notwithstanding a court's actual or potential concerns about its consistency with Charter rights. Even a purely formal override of a right will, Weinrib observes, 'attract attention from those who value the Charter's application generally' and compel a government to explain – not to the courts but to the voting public – why the override is normatively acceptable. The normativity of the Charter, she goes on, 'will continue to have force in the political arena.'[49] As Guillaume Rousseau and Francois Côté say in setting out what they see as Quebec's distinctive approach to section 33, 'Weinrib is one of the few Anglo-Canadian authors to consider that the notwithstanding clause could legitimately be used to promote majority values. For Weinrib, the legislator could be morally justified in setting aside *Charter* rights to protect a piece of legislation from constitutional scrutiny, as long as it remains convinced that it respects the spirit of the *Charter*.'[50] Justice Minister Jean Chrétien thought the same way about section 33 in 1981, telling Parliament that 'it will be very difficult for a government to introduce without a very good reason a measure [invoking section 33].'[51]

---

48 Rousseau & Côté, 'Quebec Perspective,' supra note 33 at 400–13.
49 Weinrib, 'Canada's Constitutional Revolution,' supra note 3 at 33.
50 Rousseau & Côté, 'Quebec Perspective,' supra note 33 at 360.
51 *House of Commons Debates*, supra note 34 at 13042.

A practice of deliberative dialogue thus ensures that Canada is neither rocketed back to the pre-1982 era of legislative supremacy nor subjected to the juristocracy of super-courts. Rather, section 33 cements 'a complex partnership through institutional dialogue between super-courts and superlegislatures.'[52] Unfortunately, this is not the only form of dialogue in town.

B. *Majoritarian monologuing*

A government will feel compelled to offer justifications for invoking section 33 if it has a sense that it will pay an electoral price for failing to do so. Where a government has no reason to worry about electoral consequences, either because its majorities are secure or voters are apathetic and generally disengaged from constitutional politics, it is much less likely to engage in the kind of deliberative dialogue that Weinrib describes. In such a situation, a government need offer nothing more to justify invoking section 33 than the plain fact of its legislative majority. The normativity of the Charter plays no role in the dialogue: the government is not disagreeing with a court or with the public about the scope of rights or the justifiability of their limitation and, thus, about whether it has breached the Charter at all, so much as asserting that the Charter does not matter in the face of a popularly elected government's choices. In these circumstances, the government invoking section 33 is implicitly admitting that its conduct is invalid because of its inconsistency with Charter rights and section 52(1) of the Constitution Act, 1982, but that it is nonetheless 'operative' under section 33. It is effectively a suspension of the Charter.

There is a tendril of contemporary academic thought in Canada that tends to affirm or at least to clear a pathway for majoritarian deployments of section 33.[53] The thought here is that Charter rights should not be conceived of as subjective entitlements borne by individuals against the world but, rather, as a system of objective duties owed between individuals and institutions that meld together and, when enforced by public institutions, should promote 'the common good.'[54] Now, if all these authors were suggesting is that legislatures are better placed than courts to reason toward the common good and that section 33 merely

---

52 Weinrib, 'Learning to Live,' supra note 1 at 565–6.

53 See the sources cited in note 7 above.

54 The lawyers and academics in this group draw heavily on John Finnis, *Natural Law and Natural Rights*, 2d ed (Oxford: Oxford University Press, 2011) and on Adrian Vermeule, *Common Good Constitutionalism* (Cambridge, UK: Polity Books, 2022).

authorizes legislatures to specify the content of Charter rights based on reasoned arguments about the common good, we would still be in a world where substantive reasoning and argument matters. A government invoking section 33 in defence of the common good would still be required to explain on substantive grounds why overriding Charter rights is nonetheless justified. Indeed, these authors say as much: '[A] legislature's invocation of the notwithstanding clause need not be taken as the imposition of brute majoritarian preferences, but as a reasoned choice made for the common good.'[55]

But we should be wary of this tendril of common-good constitutionalism. By beginning with a conception of rights that has no place in the text of the Charter – that is, a 'classical natural law' idea that rights 'exist prior to any positive enactment'[56] – common-good constitutionalism invites a legislature to adopt specifications of rights that are 'not constrained by either the enumerated provisions [of the Charter] or the judicial interpretations thereunder.'[57] It is one thing to acknowledge that the text of the Charter is incomplete or ambiguous as to the scope or extent of rights and that people, courts, and legislatures can reasonably disagree as to what the Charter does protect. It is quite another thing to claim that the Charter is not exhaustive of our rights and that there are other rights, not specified in the Charter, that only a legislature is capable of discovering because 'it is entitled to promote a vision of the good that transcends individual interests taken subjectively.'[58]

Having thus removed the textual foundations of any dialogue between courts, legislatures, and the public, it is unclear on what normative foundation a legislature is meant to stand when specifying this common good. Once the constitution is off the table, what normative justification is a legislature supposed to give for an override other than its democratic mandate? And if this tendril of thought disavows brute majoritarianism, then we are left with a government entirely unbound from normative constraints and accountable to nothing and no one for its views about rights. By inviting this peculiar idea of the common good into the discourse, the tendril invites governments to fall back on a hollow claim to the authority of their electoral mandate as a proxy for any substantive argument about the common good. Instead of presenting reasoned and considered accounts of what the rights set out in the

---

55 Sérafin, Sun & Foccroulle Ménard, 'Notwithstanding Judicial Specification,' supra note 7 at 165.
56 Ibid at 146.
57 Ibid at 164.
58 Ibid at 160–1.

Charter should be understood to protect in light of the common good, or even of why a policy promotes the common good notwithstanding the limits imposed by rights, governments need only assert that their policies promote the common good precisely because a majority in the legislature said so.

This disdain for the reason-giving obligations that Weinrib understands Charter dialogue to involve is easily discernible in politicians' public comments on section 33 or about the relationship between courts and legislatures since 2018. When the Ontario government's decision to shrink the size of the Toronto City Council was found by a Superior Court to unjustifiably limit freedom of speech rights, Premier Ford described his willingness to invoke section 33 as nothing less than a clash of might between courts and legislatures: 'He's the judge. I'm the Premier. He gets to use his tools, I'll use every single tool to stand up for the people of Ontario.'[59] In 2025, reacting to a Superior Court injunction against removing bicycle lanes from Toronto streets pending a Charter challenge,[60] Premier Ford railed against 'bleeding heart' judges on openly populist grounds:

> We were democratically elected, as a government, and I always say … the legislature is supreme, the people are supreme. When you get a mandate to do something, you can't have judges constantly overruling government. … We get democratically elected and some judge slaps an injunction on bike lanes. … What right do they have, unelected, politically appointed judges determining our budgets? … We get elected democratically. Last time I checked, there hasn't [*sic*] been any judges elected. Maybe that's the problem. We should do what the US does: let's start electing our judges.[61]

In 2023, again pending a Charter challenge, a Saskatchewan Court enjoined the provincial government from enforcing legislation requiring teachers to inform parents of their children's preferred pronoun choices.[62] Premier Scott Moe justified his government's decision to

---

59 'Doug Ford: Notwithstanding Clause Will Be Used to Push Council Cuts' (10 September 2018), online: *CBC News* <youtu.be/oHXsVJKOWIs?si=Wf-e _TvoeR0NloCt>.

60 *Cycle Toronto et al v Attorney General of Ontario et al*, 2025 ONSC 2424.

61 'Ford Rants against "Bleeding Heart Judges" That Go against Province's Mandate' (30 April 2025), online: *CBC News* <www.cbc.ca/player/play/video/9.6743154>.

62 *UR Pride Centre for Sexuality and Gender Diversity v Saskatchewan (Education)*, 2023 SKKB 204.

re-enact the legislation with a notwithstanding declaration by asserting that the policy had 'the strong support of a majority of Saskatchewan residents, in particular, Saskatchewan parents.'[63] In none of these comments is there any justification for invoking section 33 other than an unvarnished claim to be acting 'for the people.' Perhaps the most telling example comes from the Ontario government's re-enactment of electoral spending limits following a Superior Court judgment that the statute unjustifiably limited the Charter right to freedom of expression.[64] The government recalled the legislature from recess to table the bill, and the debate following its second reading began just after midnight, early in the morning of Saturday, 12 June 2021.[65] Apart from the serious transparency and publicity issues that come from debating a matter of public importance under the cover of night, the record of the debate reveals no engagement on the part of the government with the content, scope, or appropriate limits of Charter rights, nor with the court's reasoning. There is nothing in the way of a substantive 're-specification' of the right to freedom of expression from the Attorney General.

Rather, what the Attorney General offered was a claim to the authority of the people, as wielding section 33 against the limits of Charter rights on the strength of an electoral mandate:

> Section 33, commonly referred to as the 'notwithstanding' clause, allows democratically-elected governments to declare that legislation applies, notwithstanding certain limited sections of the *Charter*, for a renewable five-year term. This entrusts the ultimate responsibility with the elected representatives of the people.
>
> It [section 33] was intentional and principled in its inclusion. The final say needs to lay with democracy, and the vote of the people needs to be respected.
>
> [Section 33] is core to the balance that was struck in favour of democracy and the special role the Legislatures play in our federation as the embodiment of the will of the people.
>
> There has to be a balance, and where that balance is, is a policy decision ultimately entrusted to the Legislature through section 33.[66]

---

63 Jason Warick, 'Sask. Premier to Use Notwithstanding Clause to Veto Judge Ruling on School Pronoun Policy' (29 September 2023), online: *CBC News* <www.cbc.ca/news/canada/saskatchewan/judge-grants-injunction-school-pronoun-policy-1.6981406>.
64 *Working Families Ontario v Ontario*, 2021 ONSC 4076.
65 *House of Commons Debates*, 42:1, No 273A (12 June 2021) at 14097–14126.
66 Ibid at 14101.

The difference between this invocation of section 33 and the government's attempts to justify back-to-work legislation in 2022 is stark not only because in 2022 the government made a meaningful attempt, in the daytime, to convince the public that it was worth it to override rights but also because of the result. By refusing to offer substantive justifications for its electoral spending limits and relying instead on the vaguely defined idea that a democratically elected government necessarily acts for the common good no matter what it does, the Ontario government avoided exposing the substance of the bill to public scrutiny and enacted it without public outcry. It is worth noting that the Supreme Court's view of this legislation, which the government described as a product of the democratic will, is that it imposed unjustifiable limits on democracy rights, which are not overridable under section 33.[67]

Finally, consider Quebec's explosive experience with Bill 21, an Act Respecting the Laicity of the State, passed in 2019.[68] In many ways, the bill is the culmination of Quebec's longstanding commitment to secularism, beginning with the Quiet Revolution in the 1960s, but the journey has not been without hiccoughs. A 2006 court challenge to the prohibition of religious garb in schools led to the recommendation of the Bouchard-Taylor Commission in 2008 that restrictions on religious symbols be limited to officers of the state who exercise coercive authority over the public: judges, crown prosecutors, police officers, and prison guards.[69] These recommendations were largely uncontroversial in Quebec, perhaps precisely because they reflected the views of the public with whom the commission had engaged and consulted on this question. When Bill 21 was tabled in the National Assembly in 2019, however, public school teachers had been added to the list of officials for whom the display of religious symbols would be prohibited. The public outcry about Bill 21 has focused on this departure from the consensus reflected in the Bouchard-Taylor Commission, and the controversy has only been stoked by the government's refusal to offer any substantive reasons for why. Rather, the premier and members of his government have explained only that invoking the override in Bill 21 is necessary both to ensure that the will of the majority prevails and to avoid lengthy court battles.[70] At the time of writing in mid-2025, the

---

67 *Ontario (Attorney General) v Working Families Coalition (Canada) Inc*, 2025 SCC 5 at para 13.

68 *Act Respecting the Laicity of the State*, SQ 2019, c 12.

69 *Multani v Commission scolaire Marguerite Bourgeoys*, 2006 SCC 6.

70 Louis-Philippe Lampron, 'La Loi sur la laïcité de l'État et les conditions de la fondation juridique d'un modèle interculturel au Québec' (2021) 36 CJLS 323 at 332.

Supreme Court is poised to hear arguments about Bill 21 and the implications of its invocation of section 33 for judicial review.

III. The threat to the rule of law

That governments are reverting to purely majoritarian and populist justifications for invoking section 33 should worry us, in the first place, because of what it means for democracy. The conception of democracy at work here is one in which, as long as the people get to vote in elections from time to time, the government they elect will have a mandate to act howsoever they determine to be in the common good.[71] There is a second concern, though, which is that unsubstantiated, non-reasoned invocations of section 33 pose a grave danger to the rule of law. Moreover, since it is adherence to the rule of law that allows section 33 to bring together our commitments to democracy and to constitutional rights, undermining the rule of law strips everything that is 'distinctively Canadian,' to invoke Weinrib's phrasing, from section 33.[72]

In *The Long Arc of Legality*, David Dyzenhaus argues forcefully that, for every legal system to make a meaningful claim to legitimate authority in the exercise of public power – that is, power exercised in the name of a people – its officials must be able to provide an answer to every single subject of the legal system when they ask the question: 'but, how can that be law for me?'[73] It is not enough, in answering that question, to point mutely at the raw numbers of a recent election. To rely on nothing more than the authority that comes from an election is to reduce the political system to a fiefdom where whomever holds power can do as they please, even if power is acquired through a free and fair election. Such a system runs on the whims of officials. It is not a system of the rule of law.

If we are to be a system of the rule of law, then, officials must explain why a rule has been formulated in a particular way, why rules are applied in particular ways, and why it is acceptable to depart from the

---

71 I have lamented this 'Porky Pig' version of democracy – because you get to vote and 'That's all, Folks' – elsewhere. Richard Stacey, 'Is TRS Allan Really That Popular? Sovereignty, Democracy and the Rule of Law' in Geneviève Cartier & Mark Walters, eds, *The Promise of Legality: Critical Reflections on the Work of TRS Allan* (Oxford: Hart Publishing, 2025) 337 at 339–43.

72 Weinrib, 'Learning to Live,' supra note 1.

73 David Dyzenhaus, *The Long Arc of Legality: Hobbes, Kelsen, Hart* (Cambridge, UK: Cambridge University Press, 2022) at 2.

constraints imposed by constitutionally entrenched rights in order to achieve some other objective. The answer to the question 'but, how can that be law for me?' involves officials explaining both that each specific exercise of power is contemplated by a previously established rule and why each specific exercise of power is congruent with the substance of that rule. The Supreme Court of Canada has emphatically and enthusiastically embraced this 'culture of justification' in public law.[74] In easy cases, there is a clear rule with definable limits and uncontroversial content to which an official can point to justify their actions. But, in hard cases, where it is not obvious what limits previously declared rules set or what the precise content of those rules is, officials will have to search further and deeper for the normative resources against which they can justify their conduct. In hard cases, officials committed to the rule of law must make an argument that explains that their decision is legitimate because it is congruent with the values that underlie our political community.

In hard cases involving Charter rights, it is often the values that underlie the rights and give them meaning that will do this interpretive work. In this light, excepting the government from the constraints set out in the Charter – itself a reflection of those deeply held values – will require a deeper and more compelling explanation than any other exercise of public power. Asserting that a decision is best for the people because the people voted for the person making the decision is question begging at best and authoritarian at worst.[75] A claim to democracy, without more, is not enough. In the *Secession Reference*, the Supreme Court articulated four fundamental principles of the Canadian constitutional order, of which democracy is but one.[76] In resolving the question of what an affirmative answer to a provincial referendum on secession would mean, the Court understood democracy and federalism to be equally important to the very existence of Canada. Neither principle is superordinate over the other, and Canada exists as it does because of the interaction between these two principles.[77]

---

74 *Vavilov*, supra note 6 at para 2.
75 Thomas Hobbes puts it thus: 'For he that doth any thing by authority from another, doth therein no injury to him by whose authority he acteth: But by this Institution of a Commonwealth, every particular man is Author of all the Soveraigne doth; and consequently he that complaineth of injury from his Soveraigne, complaineth of that whereof he himself is Author.' Thomas Hobbes, *Leviathan*, edited by Richard Tuck (Cambridge, UK: Cambridge University Press, 1996), ch XVIII.
76 *Secession Reference*, supra note 6 at paras 48–9.
77 Ibid at paras 87–8.

But they were not the only principles the Court articulated. It also listed respect for minorities and the rule of law. Just as the unwritten principle of federalism will temper the implications of an exercise of democratic power in the context of a secession referendum, it must follow that the democratic impulses protected by section 33 must be balanced against the principle of the rule of law. At the very least, the rule of law demands that legislatures, seeking to invoke section 33 to override the constraints of Charter rights, offer a substantive explanation for why doing so is a good thing. Section 33's sunset clause means nothing unless governments explain to voters why they are invoking the notwithstanding clause. The voters then get to decide at the ballot box whether that explanation does answer the question 'but, how can that be law for me?'

It may be democratic – in a very thin sense – to refuse to offer these explanations and bang the drum of an electoral mandate. But to do so abandons the commitment to the rule of law and subjects us to exercises of raw power unmoored from the very values and principles that make us Canada. Weinrib has argued for nearly forty years that the architecture of Canada's constitutional system requires a government invoking section 33 to offer public, open, transparent, and, above all, substantive justification for doing so, not to the courts but to the people themselves. It is that very same requirement that will safeguard Canada's commitment to the rule of law in an era when that principle is ever-increasingly imperilled.

IV. Conclusion

I grew up in South Africa in the 1990s when the country was emerging from apartheid and embracing the values of dignity, equality, and social justice explicitly entrenched in its 1996 Constitution. As a law student, I read the Supreme Court of Canada's Charter decisions and articles by Weinrib and others, alongside the nascent case law of the newborn South African Constitutional Court.[78] I thought hard about how Canadian values of minority rights protection, multiculturalism, and equality could guide South Africa's journey of constitutional transformation.[79] As a naturalized Canadian, I am proud to have dedicated

---

78 Weinrib delivered the tenth Oliver Schreiner Memorial Lecture in South Africa, entitled 'Constitutionalism in the Age of Rights: A Prolegomenon' (2004) 121 SALJ 278.

79 My first published article builds on Canadian multiculturalism scholarship in thinking about South Africa's equality jurisprudence. Richard Stacey, '"We the People": The Relationship between the South African Constitution and the ANC's

my intellectual efforts to the pursuit and defence of the very same values that shaped my early thinking about the law. In that light, I cannot stomach the idea that the Charter can be read as contemplating the abandonment of the rule of law or the values it serves to protect. I believe that Weinrib, an architect of the jurisprudence that has shaped me, feels the same.

Transformation Policies' (2003) 30 Politikon 133. The professor who first introduced me to legal theory at the University of the Witwatersrand was a Canadian philosopher, Brian Penrose.

Contributors

Jean-Christophe Bédard-Rubin Assistant Professor, Faculty of Law, University of Toronto, Toronto, Ontario, Canada. Email: jc.bedardrubin@utoronto.ca.

Peter Benson Professor of Law and Donald R. Crawshaw Professor of Private Law, University of Toronto, Toronto, Ontario, Canada. Email: p.benson@utoronto.ca.

Jutta Brunnée Dean, University Professor, and James Marshall Tory Dean's Chair, Faculty of Law, University of Toronto, Toronto, Ontario, Canada. Email: jutta.brunnee@utoronto.ca.

Brenda Cossman Professor, Faculty of Law, University of Toronto, Toronto, Ontario, Canada. Email: b.cossman@utoronto.ca.

Christopher Essert Professor, Faculty of Law, University of Toronto, Toronto, Ontario, Canada. Email: chris.essert@utoronto.ca.

Angela Fernandez Professor, Faculty of Law and Department of History, University of Toronto, Toronto, Ontario, Canada. Email: angela.fernandez@utoronto.ca.

Edward M Iacobucci TSE Chair in Capital Markets, Faculty of Law, University of Toronto, Toronto, Ontario, Canada. Email: edward.iacobucci@utoronto.ca.

Jim Phillips Professor, Faculty of Law and Department of History, University of Toronto, Toronto, Ontario, Canada. Email: j.phillips@utoronto.ca.

Mariana Mota Prado Professor, Faculty of Law, University of Toronto, Toronto, Ontario, Canada. Email: mariana.prado@utoronto.ca.

Arthur Ripstein University Professor, Faculty of Law and Department of Philosophy, University of Toronto, Toronto, Ontario, Canada. Email: arthur.ripstein@utoronto.ca.

Kent Roach Faculty of Law, University of Toronto, Toronto, Ontario, Canada. Email: kent.roach@utoronto.ca.

Martha Shaffer Professor, Faculty of Law, University of Toronto, Toronto, Ontario, Canada. Email: m.shaffer@utoronto.ca.

Richard Stacey Associate Professor, Faculty of Law, University of Toronto, Toronto, Ontario, Canada. Email: richard.stacey@utoronto.ca.

Hamish Stewart Professor, Faculty of Law, University of Toronto, Toronto, Ontario, Canada. Email: hamish.stewart@utoronto.ca.

Anna Su Associate Professor, Faculty of Law, University of Toronto, Toronto, Ontario, Canada. Email: anna.su@utoronto.ca

Malcolm Thorburn Professor of Law and Chair in Law and Innovation, Faculty of Law, University of Toronto, Toronto, Ontario, Canada. Email: malcolm.thorburn@utoronto.ca.

Biographies of Subjects

Alan Brudner was a professor at the Faculty of Law from 1984 to 2012. He served as editor of the *University of Toronto Law Journal* from 2000 to 2007. In 2011, he was elected a Fellow of the Royal Society of Canada. He is a graduate of the University of Toronto (BA (Hon), 1966; MA, 1968; PhD, 1976; LLB, 1983).

Rebecca Cook was a professor at the Faculty of Law from 1987 to 2012. She founded the International Human Rights Program at the Faculty of Law in 1987 and is the Co-Director of the International Reproductive and Sexual Health Law Program. She is an Ethical and Legal Issues in Reproductive Health co-editor of the *International Journal of Gynecology and Obstetrics* and serves on the advisory editorial board of the Human Rights Quarterly. She is a member of the Order of Canada and a Fellow of the Royal Society of Canada. She is a graduate of Barnard College (BA, 1970), Tufts University (MA, 1972), Harvard University (MPA, 1973), Georgetown University (JD, 1982), and Columbia University (LLM, 1988; JSD, 1994).

Martin Friedland joined the Faculty of Law in 1965 and served as Dean from 1972 to 1979. He was appointed to the rank of University Professor in 1985. In 1990, he was appointed an Officer of the Order of Canada; in 2003, he was promoted to Companion of the Order of Canada. He is a graduate of the University of Toronto (BComm, 1955; LLB, 1958) and Cambridge University (PhD, 1967; LLD, 1997). He also holds two honorary doctor of laws degrees, awarded by the University of Toronto in 2001 and York University in 2003.

Alan Mewett was a professor at the Faculty of Law from 1968 to 2001. He served as editor of the *Criminal Law Quarterly* for over thirty years. In his honour, the University of Toronto's Alan Mewett Award is granted to members of the Faculty of Law for excellence in teaching. He was a graduate of Birmingham University (LLB, 1952), Oxford University (BCL), and the University of Michigan (LLM; SJD).

Denise Réaume was a professor at the Faculty of Law from 1982 to 2021. She served as Associate Dean (Graduate Studies) from 1990 to 1995. She is a past editor of the *Canadian Journal of Women and the Law* and was a faculty supervisor at the *Journal of Law and Equality*. She is a graduate of Queen's University (BA, 1977; LLB, 1980) and Oxford University (BCL, 1982).

R.C.B. Risk was a member of the Faculty of Law from 1962 to 1998. He was a graduate of the University of Toronto (BA, LLB, 1959) and Harvard University (LLM, 1962).

Carol Rogerson was a professor at the Faculty of Law from 1983 to 2021. She served as Associate Dean of the Faculty of Law from 1991 to 1993. In 2015, she was awarded the University of Toronto's Carolyn Tuohy Prize for Impact on Public Policy for her work as co-author of the Spousal Support Advisory Guidelines for the Canadian Department of Justice. She is a graduate of the University of Alberta (BA, 1974), the University of Toronto (MA, 1977; LLB, 1982), and Harvard University (LLM, 1983).

Robert Sharpe joined the Faculty of Law in 1976 and served as Dean from 1990 to 1995. He was appointed as a judge of the Ontario Court of Justice (General Division) in 1995; in 1999, he was elevated to the Court of Appeal for Ontario. He is a Fellow of the Royal Society of Canada, and, in 2023, he was appointed an Officer of the Order of Canada. He is a graduate of the University of Western Ontario (BA, 1966), the University of Toronto (LLB, 1970), and Oxford University (DPhil, 1974). He holds honorary degrees from the Law Society of Ontario and the University of Windsor.

Katherine Swinton was a professor at the Faculty of Law from 1979 to 1995. She was appointed to the Ontario Court of Justice (General Division) in 1997. She has served as an adviser to federal and provincial governments on issues of constitutional law and federalism. She is a graduate of the University of Alberta (BA (Hon), 1971), Osgoode Hall Law School (LLB, 1975), and Yale University (LLM, 1977).

Michael Trebilcock was a professor at the Faculty of Law from 1972 to 2021. He was appointed to the rank of University Professor in 1990. He is a Fellow of the Royal Society of Canada (1987), recipient of the Ontario Attorney General's Mundell Medal (2007), and an International Honorary Member of the American Academy of Arts and Sciences (2002). In 2010, he received the Ontario Premier's Discovery Award for the Social Sciences. He is a graduate of the University of Canterbury (LLB, 1962) and the University of Adelaide (LLM, 1965).

Stephen Waddams was a professor at the Faculty of Law from 1968 to 2023. He was appointed to the rank of University Professor in 2005. He was a Fellow of the Royal Society of Canada and recipient of the David W. Mundell Medal for contributions to law and letters. He was a graduate of the University of Toronto (BA, 1963; LLB, 1967), the University of Michigan (LLM, 1968; SJD, 1972), and Cambridge University (MA, 1969; PhD, 1994).

Ernest Weinrib was a professor at the Faculty of Law from 1972 to 2021. He was appointed to the rank of University Professor in 1999. In 2009, the Canada Council for the Arts awarded him the Killam Prize, Canada's highest honour for academic achievement. He is a Fellow of the Royal Society of Canada and an International Honorary Member of the American Academy of Arts and Sciences. He is a graduate of the University of Toronto (BA, 1965; JD, 1972) and Harvard University (PhD, 1968).

Lorraine Weinrib was a professor at the Faculty of Law from 1988 to 2021. Previously, she worked as a Crown Law Officer for the Ministry of the Attorney General of Ontario, holding the position of Deputy Director of Constitutional Law and Policy at the time of her departure. She is a graduate of York University (BA, 1970), the University of Toronto (LLB, 1973), and Yale University (LLM, 1985).

John Willis was a founding member of the Faculty of Law, serving as Professor from 1949 to 1952 and again from 1959 to 1972. He earned his BA from Oxford University in 1929, with a 'double first' in classics and jurisprudence, then studied at Harvard Law School from 1930 to 1932 on a Commonwealth Fund (Harkness) Fellowship. During his last six years at the University of Toronto, he served concurrently as a part-time member of the Ontario Securities Commission.

Cecil 'Caesar' Augustus Wright was the first Dean of the 'modern' Faculty of Law at the University of Toronto, serving from 1949 to 1967. He earned a BA from the University of Western Ontario in 1923, an LLM from Osgoode Hall Law School in 1926, and a JSD from Harvard University in 1927.